Teaching Israel

The Mandel-Brandeis Series in Jewish Education

SHARON FEIMAN-NEMSER, JONATHAN KRASNER, *and* JON A. LEVISOHN, *Editors*

The Mandel-Brandeis Series in Jewish Education, established by the Jack, Joseph, and Morton Mandel Center for Studies in Jewish Education, publishes scholarly monographs and edited volumes of compelling research on Jewish educational settings and processes. The series is made possible through the Mandel Foundation.

For a complete list of books that are available in the series, visit https://brandeisuniversitypress.com/series/jewish-education/.

SIVAN ZAKAI and MATT REINGOLD, eds.
Teaching Israel: Studies of Pedagogy from the Field

ZIVA R. HASSENFELD
The Second Conversation: Interpretive Authority in the Bible Classroom

JOSEPH REIMER
Making Shabbat: Celebrating and Learning at American Jewish Summer Camps

ALEX POMSON and JACK WERTHEIMER
Inside Jewish Day Schools: Leadership, Learning, and Community

Teaching Israel
Studies of Pedagogy from the Field

Edited by Sivan Zakai and Matt Reingold

BRANDEIS UNIVERSITY PRESS
Waltham, Massachusetts

Brandeis University Press
© 2024 by Brandeis University Press
All rights reserved
Manufactured in the United States of America
Typeset in Meno by Richard Lipton

For permission to reproduce any of the material in this book, contact Brandeis University Press, 415 South Street, Waltham MA 02453, or visit brandeisuniversitypress.com

LIBRARY OF CONGRESS CATALOGING-IN-PUBLISHING DATA
Names: Zakai, Sivan, editor. | Reingold, Matt, editor.

Title: Teaching Israel : studies of pedagogy from the field / Edited by Sivan Zakai and Matt Reingold.

Description: Waltham, Massachusetts : Brandeis University Press, 2024 | Series: The Mandel-Brandeis series in Jewish education | Includes index. | Summary: "This book resituates teaching—the questions, dilemmas, and decision-making that teachers face—as central to both Israel Studies and Israel education. It illuminates how teachers from differing pedagogical orientations and who teach in a range of educational settings learn, understand, do, and ultimately improve the work of teaching Israel." — Provided by publisher.

Identifiers: LCCN 2023047346 (print) | LCCN 2023047347 (ebook) | ISBN 9781684581177 (paperback) | ISBN 9781684581160 (cloth) | ISBN 9781684581184 (ebook)

Subjects: LCSH: Jews—Education. | Israel—Study and teaching. | Culturally relevant pedagogy. | Teachers—Training of. | Jewish religious education—Philosophy. | Jews—Attitudes toward Israel.

Classification: LCC LC719.T43 2024 (print) | LCC LC719 (ebook) | DDC 371.829/924—dc23/eng/20231127

LC record available at https://lccn.loc.gov/2023047346
LC ebook record available at https://lccn.loc.gov/2023047347

5 4 3 2 1

*For our parents,
our first teachers*

Contents

Acknowledgments   xi

Introduction · SIVAN ZAKAI   1

Part I · The Reflective Teacher

1 Teaching About Israel as a Modern State of Migration: Learning With Diverse, Inner-City, Nontraditional College Students in New York City
ROBIN A. HARPER   35

2 Navigating Complexities: Teaching Israel Studies in the Professional Military Education Context
AMIN TARZI   61

3 Voices on the Page and in the Room: A Pedagogy of Jewish Text Study in Israel Education
JOSHUA LADON   83

Part II · Using Student Voices to Examine Teacher Choices

4 Complex Texts and Complex Identities: Helping Students Navigate Personally and Emotionally Resonant Topics About Israeli Society
MATT REINGOLD, ALEXA JACOBY, and BENJAMIN DAY   107

5 Into the Intimate Discourse: Rachel Korazim as an Exemplary Israel Educator
DIANE TICKTON SCHUSTER   129

6 Knowledge, Connection, and Stance:
   Toward a More Enduring Israel Engagement
   JONATHAN GOLDEN and YONI KADDEN   151

Part III · Navigating the Teaching of Politics and the Politics of Teaching

7 Cultivating Critical Inquiry About Israel:
   Teaching Israel in Our Time
   BETHAMIE HOROWITZ   179

8 Activism and Identity: Teaching (About) BDS
   in the Israeli–Palestinian Relations Classroom
   MIRA SUCHAROV   205

9 Barriers to Entry: Exploring Educator Reticence
   for Engaging With the Israeli–Palestinian Conflict
   KEREN E. FRAIMAN   229

Part IV · When Teachers Learn

10 "What Are We Doing?": The Pedagogical Questions of
   Jewish Early Childhood Educators and Teacher Educators
   SIVAN ZAKAI and LAUREN APPLEBAUM   257

11 Teaching Who They Are: Understanding Teachers'
   Connections With Israel and How Those Enter
   Into the Classroom
   LAURA NOVAK WINER   283

12 Nurturing Jewish Consciousness: Utilizing Values
   at Synagogue Supplementary Schools to Teach Israel
   EZRA KOPELOWITZ and ABBY PITKOWSKY   309

13 A Kite on a String and a Box That Opens: The Challenges of Transformative Professional Learning for Israel Educators
LAUREN APPLEBAUM 333

Conclusion · MATT REINGOLD 355

Contributors 381
Index 385

Acknowledgments

We believe that teaching is critically important and demandingly difficult. We are so grateful for the many people who have helped us investigate some of the profound questions and dilemmas that sit at the heart of this work.

We would like to thank the editors of the Mandel-Brandeis Series in Jewish Education, who supported this project from the moment we proposed it. Sharon Feiman-Nemser has long been both mentor and guide in thinking about deep questions of teaching and teacher learning. Jonathan Krasner always reads with a careful eye for detail and an impressive memory of vast literatures, offering support and suggestions with a gentle touch. Jon Levisohn's thoughtful questions helped us think through the often-blurry boundaries between scholarship of teaching and teaching as a practice. As a trio, they are a formidable force, and we're so glad to have that force pushing us in the right direction.

Long before we signed a contract with Brandeis University Press, we knew that this was the place where we wanted our book to find a home. We feel so fortunate to have had the opportunity to work with Sylvia Fuks Fried, Sue Ramin, Anthony Lipscomb, Benjamin Woollard, and Hannah Krasikov. Together, they have made it possible for us to transform a collection of ideas into this book.

All academic books undergo external review, and we are so grateful that this book was reviewed by Lisa Grant and Alex Pomson, both of whom we have long admired. Their own scholarship shaped our thinking about the core questions of *Teaching Israel* long before we set out to create this book, and their specific feedback about an earlier draft of the manuscript has substantively shaped this final product.

Each of the authors in this book—Abby, Alexa, Amin, Benjamin, Bethamie, Diane, Ezra, Jonathan, Joshua, Keren, Laura, Lauren, Mira, Robin, and Yoni—have responded with great thought and care to each of the many rounds of revisions we have requested and have done so while balancing the complicated demands of professional and personal obligations in the midst of an ongoing pandemic. Each of you has taught us to think about teaching in new ways, and we are so grateful for your contributions to this work.

The labor of so many others has also contributed to this book, but we want to call special attention to three. Jenny Small was our coordinator extraordinaire throughout the process of copyediting. Samantha Shinder helped us compile and format the manuscript, oftentimes knowing the formatting instructions better than we did. Jessica Freeman compiled the index.

To collaborate on a book across coasts and countries is no small feat, and it would not have been possible without support on each of our "home fronts." Sivan's colleagues at the Hebrew Union College-Jewish Institute of Religion (HUC-JIR) in Los Angeles and Matt's colleagues at TanenbaumCHAT in Toronto have been a source of support and companionship. Special HUC-JIR shoutouts to Miriam Heller Stern, Laura Novak Winer, and Lauren Applebaum, who together help create a culture that honors and investigates complex questions of teaching and learning; to Sarah Benor and Leah Hochman, who helped think through how this book fits into a larger professional trajectory; and to Lynn Flanzbaum, who patiently helped us navigate some complicated budgeting issues. At TanenbaumCHAT, Eli Mandel, Renee Cohen, Lyla Farbstein, and Rachel Urowitz have all played important roles in helping support a culture of exploration where history—even when it is messy—can be taught.

Sivan would also like to thank her family and her *ke'ilu* family (you know who you are!) for your ongoing support and love. Igor, nothing happens without your steady presence. Eytan, Ilan, and Liam, the moral of this story is to find yourself great teachers and learn from them!

Matt would like to thank his family for their ongoing support, curiosity, and understanding always and especially during the preparation of this manuscript. He hopes that his children—Sloan, Nora, Micah, and Boaz—find themselves in Israel-education classrooms like many of the ones described in this volume. Lastly, Matt wants to thank Chani. In addition to being the best partner, if not for her suggestion of a Matt-Sivan collaboration, *Teaching Israel* would never have been produced. For that, we are both so very grateful.

Of course, no book on teaching could exist without our own teachers.

It was our teachers who taught us how to write, how to think, and how to ask the kinds of questions that make writing and thinking worthwhile in the first place. You inspired us to become teachers ourselves, and even if we did not always understand it at the time, we know now how very difficult and how very important your work has always been.

The very first teachers we ever had were our parents. We have dedicated this book to them with love.

Postscript

On October 7, 2023, as this book was going to print, Hamas committed heinous attacks on southern Israeli communities. This violence caused seismic shifts not only in and around Israel but also for those who teach about Israel from everywhere on the globe. In the aftermath of the terror attacks—and in response to Hamas's violence; Israel's unfolding military, political, and diplomatic response; and the troubling rise of both antisemitism and anti-Israel sentiments around the world—teachers have had to rapidly adjust both their pedagogical approaches and their course content.

This volume was completed and typeset before these events, and their *contexts* predate the horrors of October 7, 2023 and its aftermath. As we have argued throughout this book, context surely matters for educational decision-making. Yet, the central *questions* that lie at the heart of this book—How can teachers who teach about Israel investigate and learn from their own teaching practice? How can students help teachers better understand this work and its challenges? What choices and tradeoffs must teachers make in an increasingly polarized political climate? What kinds of professional support and ongoing learning opportunities do teachers need to be able to engage in the difficult work of teaching about Israel?—are more relevant than ever as professors of Israel studies and Israel educators in Jewish schools and synagogues must reorient to new conditions. It is not yet clear how teachers in different educational milieu will reframe their own teaching practices and/or reframe Israel in response to these events. What is clear is the enduring power of education, and the work of teachers in particular, to guide people through a rapidly changing world.

Teaching Israel

Introduction
SIVAN ZAKAI

Sophie, Asaf, and Lilly all live in the United States and teach about Israel, but at first glance they appear to have little else in common.[1] Sophie is a middle school social studies teacher at a nondenominational Jewish day school. Asaf directs the religious school at a Conservative synagogue that serves students from preschool to high school. Lilly is a professor of education who teaches university graduate students and teachers, including Sophie and Asaf, who enroll in continuing education courses.

The three teachers' differences extend much deeper than their job titles and the types of institutions in which they teach. Not only do Sophie, Asaf, and Lilly have different disciplinary backgrounds—in history, theater, and education, respectively—but they also have radically different orientations to both pedagogy and politics. Sophie, a self-proclaimed "leftist American Jew," describes herself as having a "critical relationship with Israel that still [contains] an emotional attachment," and she views her work teaching about Israel as part of a larger disciplinary commitment to teaching about a complicated past. Asaf, an Israeli-born educator whose politics lean right of center, views his teaching about Israel as "a spiritual calling," and he situates his work as an attempt to "teach about Israel's strengths and the good that Israel does, especially since Israel is often a political target nowadays." Lilly reveals little about her own politics in the classroom, a deliberate choice that reflects her commitment to helping her students "reflect on who *they* want to be as teachers, so they can gain clarity about their own approaches to the messy work of teaching Israel."

Although they all teach about Israel in their classrooms, the trio have different pedagogical goals, teach students of different ages and backgrounds, and situate themselves differently in relation to students and subject matter. Therefore, when Sophie and Asaf meet in one of Lilly's continuing education courses, it surprises all three of them that Sophie and

Asaf quickly gravitate towards one another as "critical friends," colleagues who come together to support and challenge each other's work (Costa & Kallick, 1993; Storey & Richard, 2013). Lilly designs her class around highly structured protocols that are intended to help her adult students investigate and learn from their own professional challenges (McDonald et al., 2015). When Sophie brings to the class a "conversation with a colleague that went badly"—her co-teacher had told a group of parents that the school would teach their children "all of the positive things about Israel" when Sophie herself had been trying to convey to parents that "we can teach them complicated things from day one"—it is Asaf who helps. He encourages her to think about how the teachers at her school might collaborate to create a larger educational vision for their institution. And when Asaf shares his own challenging moment—a class discussion in which his student "used the word 'occupation,'" a word that he believed to be "biased" and "highly problematic"—it is to Sophie he turns for guidance. She challenges him to rethink his pedagogical stance from "conveyer of truth" to what he begins to call "a guide that helps [students] navigate through multiple ideas and points of view." As Lilly facilitates these conversations, she likens the professional relationship among the three of them to a high-powered microscope that "forces all of us to see what's often hidden to the eye: our own assumptions, our flaws, and our strengths as teachers."

In fact, although the contexts in which they teach and their approaches to teaching Israel are quite different, Sophie, Asaf, and Lilly ask many of the same questions about their own pedagogical practice: In the face of limited time with my students, what's most important to teach about Israel? How should I navigate the wide spectrum of political beliefs about Israel that exist among my students? How, if at all, ought my own relationship to Israel and my own political leanings factor into my teaching given that my voice carries power in the classroom? What can I learn from other educators in the field who are grappling with similar questions?

Despite differences in their students and contexts, all three believe that a better understanding of how *others* teach about Israel can help them refine their own pedagogical practice. These teachers know that teaching is a complex task that relies not only on subject matter knowledge but also on a deep understanding of both general pedagogy and the particular form of pedagogy, called pedagogical content knowledge, that allows teachers to teach specific content (Shulman, 1986). And all three recognize that their work involves navigating multiple and often competing aims for teaching (e.g., Ball, 1993) as they are called upon to meet the intellectual, moral, spiritual, and emotional needs of students (Kessler, 2000; Noddings, 2005; Simon, 2001), the expectations of their institutions and departments (Talbert & McLaughlin, 1992, 1994), and the political and social aims of society (Labaree, 1997).

This is a book about teachers and teaching, and it spotlights teachers like Sophie, Asaf, and Lilly, who teach about Israel to diverse student populations in different educational contexts. Teaching Israel—not teaching *in* Israel, but rather teaching in which Israel is the subject matter to be taught and learned—offers a particularly rich case for studying the questions, dilemmas, and decision-making processes that lie at the heart of teaching. Teaching and learning about Israel span a wide range of disciplines (including history, political science, literature, art, religion, and more), and as such it draws from and contributes to an array of discipline-specific teaching ideas and practices. Israel is taught and learned in a wide variety of disparate educational settings—in Jewish schools and synagogues, on university campuses and in pre-college gap years, in the training of clergy and military professionals, as part of adult education, and elsewhere. Israel is also a highly politicized topic, functioning as a "hot button issue" in both higher education (e.g., Wright et al., 2019; Zimmerman, 2016) and within the North American Jewish community (Kurtzer et al., 2019; Waxman, 2016). It ignites the passions of people with a broad range of religious, ethnic, and political affiliations and, as such, is a subject "strewn with emotional land mines" (Sokatch, 2021, p. 6). Because of each of these features—its interdisciplinary, cross-institutional, and highly political nature—teaching Israel sits at the intersection of the past and present, cognitive and affective, real and symbolic, personal and collective, sacred and profane, educational and ideological. Thus, teaching Israel requires teachers at all levels and in all contexts to make complicated choices about pedagogy and politics, curriculum and community. This book offers a scholarly investigation into some of those complicated choices by teachers working in a wide range of settings who teach learners of different ages and backgrounds.

Although teaching sits at the heart of most educational endeavors, the study of teaching has long been overlooked in the contexts where Israel is most commonly taught in North America: in university seminars and lecture halls as part of the academic field of Israel studies, and in Jewish educational institutions as part of the educational enterprise commonly called Israel education (Attias, 2019; Horowitz, 2012). Despite the recent proliferation of Israel studies courses taught in higher education (Minkin & Chertok, 2020), and despite the fact that Israel education has long been understood as a central component of Jewish education (Chazan, 1979; Grant & Kopelowitz, 2012), there is little scholarship that focuses on the complexities of teaching about Israel.

This book is an attempt to resituate teaching—and the questions, dilemmas, and decision-making processes that teachers face as they teach—as central to the work of both Israel studies and Israel education. In this introduction, I set forth how this volume frames "teaching," "Israel," and the work of "teaching Israel." In doing so, I present this collection of essays not as an attempt to name best practices *for* teaching Israel, but instead as a series of investigations into the practices *of* teaching Israel to learners from early childhood through adult education, and in diverse settings ranging from Jewish schools to university classrooms to the U.S. military. By spotlighting the work of teachers with differing pedagogical orientations and who teach in a range of educational settings, this volume illuminates how teachers understand, do, learn about, and ultimately improve the work of teaching Israel.

Teaching

Teaching, and especially good teaching, is a complex task. Teachers teach students, making choices about how to meet the needs of learners with multiple interests and backgrounds and differing knowledge and experiences (e.g., Banks et al., 2005). Teachers teach content, determining how to represent and sequence subject matter knowledge and skills (e.g., Grossman et al., 2005; Lampert, 1990). Teachers teach within contexts, navigating both the institutions in which they teach and the larger societies in which those institutions exist (e.g., Ho et al., 2017; McLaughlin & Talbert, 1993). As teachers shape and are shaped by myriad interactions—among students, between students and teacher, with colleagues, in relationship to content, and within institutional and societal contexts (Cohen et al., 2003)—they often function as "broker[s] of contradictory interests" (Lampert, 1985, p. 178), managing dilemmas that arise from attempting to uphold competing priorities (e.g., Ball, 1993; Cohen, 2011; Cuban, 1992).

In this volume, we view the complexities inherent in teaching as central to the work of education. We take a broad view of what "counts" as teaching and thus who may be considered a teacher. Teaching may certainly occur within the walls of a classroom (Intrator, 2005), but it may also happen on a tour bus (Kelner, 2010) or online (Young, 2006), in a seminary (Siew, 2006) or in the military (Kennedy et al., 2002). Teachers may have the job title "teacher," but they may also have other roles that obscure the fact that they nonetheless make pedagogical and curricular decisions that impact learning: camp counselor (Sales & Saxe, 2002; Saxe, 2004), museum docent (Burnham & Kai-Kee, 2011), tour guide (Katz, 1985), rabbi (Schein, 1988). Teachers may teach the very youngest of children (e.g., Rodríguez-Carrillo et al., 2020) or they may teach adults (e.g., Wlodkowski & Ginsberg, 2017), and some teachers teach others who are themselves teachers (Darling-Hammond, 2000). Our broad view of teaching also incorporates the work that teachers do even when they are not face-to-face with their students: planning (Cornish et al., 2018), assessing and understanding student work (Brookhart & Oakley, 2021), and reflecting on their own practice in order to learn from it (Zeichner & Liston, 2013). This understanding of teaching encompasses a range of contexts, actions, and relationships, positioning teaching not as a single act but as a complex and situated practice. It views teachers as practitioners of a skilled profession (Shulman, 1998) that requires specific ways of thinking, knowing, and acting in their work (Feiman-Nemser, 2008).

The essays that constitute this volume rest on two assumptions about the work of teaching: that teaching is inexorably tied to learning and that teaching is worthy of scholarly study.

1. Teaching Is Inexorably Linked With Learning

Teaching is, at its core, about facilitating learning. In the words of the philosopher of education Israel Scheffler (1965), "Teaching may be characterized as an activity aimed at achievement of learning, and practiced in such manner as to respect the student's intellectual integrity and capacity for independent judgment" (p. 131). Or, as the philosopher of education Paul H. Hirst (1971) explains, "There is no such thing as teaching without the intention to bring about learning.... The characterization and raison d'être of teaching rests on that of learning" (p. 9). Teaching, in this view, occurs whenever a person makes purposeful (even if imperfect) decisions aimed at facilitating the learning of other people who also have agency over their own learning.

Yet teaching is also tied to learning because it relies on the continual learning process of the teacher. As the educational-policy scholar Linda Darling-Hammond (2008) explains, "The professional teacher is one who learns from teaching, rather than one who has finished learning how to teach" (p. 95). Teachers themselves are learners (e.g., Shulman & Sherin, 2004) who learn both as they enter the profession (Feiman-Nemser, 2003) and as they develop professional knowledge and skills over time (Borko, 2004; Darling-Hammond & Richardson, 2009). Teachers may learn as part of pre-service preparation and practice (Feiman-Nemser, 2012) and/or as a result of in-service professional development, collaborative or self-directed study of their own practice, coaching, and/or mentoring (Drago-Severson, 2004). Adopting this wide lens towards teacher learning sees teaching not as an innate or static trait, but rather as a craft that can be learned and honed over time.

In this volume, we recognize the learning of both students and teachers as an inherent part of the process of teaching. Some of the essays in this volume focus explicitly on what teachers and their students learn from one another. Others highlight the learning of teachers at various points in their professional trajectories. Others still place teacher decision-making processes in the foreground but nonetheless continue to frame student learning as an essential backdrop to the work of teaching.

2. Teaching Is Worthy of Scholarly Investigation

We view teaching as worthy of study both because of its profound implications for the practical work of education and because, as a complex and often ambiguous task, it has intrinsic worth as a site of scholarly investigation and interrogation. By focusing on teaching, this book is at once an attempt to influence a scholarly conversation and a field of practice.

Empirical studies of teaching have long shaped both the practices and conceptions of teaching. Yet while there are subject-specific literatures about the practices and dilemmas of teaching in disciplines ranging from mathematics (e.g., Ball, 1993; Chazan, 2000; Lampert, 2001) to history (e.g., Stearns et al., 2000; VanSledright, 2002), empirical scholarship on teaching the interdisciplinary subject of Israel is only beginning to emerge. The paucity of a robust literature on subject-specific teaching exists across the diverse settings in which Israel is taught.

For example, in the context of Israel studies in the academy, developing new knowledge about Israeli history, culture, and politics has outpaced scholarship on teaching that knowledge. Despite both the growing number and increasing breadth and depth of Israel studies courses taught in institutions of higher learning (Koren et al., 2013; Weinreb, 2022), and despite concerted efforts to offer professional-learning opportunities for professors of Israel studies (e.g., Koren & Fleisch, 2014; Minkin & Chertok, 2020), scholarship on *teaching* Israel studies remains underdeveloped. As Annette Koren and Shira Fishman (2015) explain, many scholars of Israel studies "are interested in content, but they are less interested in pedagogy. Many assume they know how to teach" (p. 25), and thus they do not investigate or strive to learn from or contribute to scholarly discourse about the practice of teaching. Even when scholars of Israel studies *do* investigate questions of pedagogy, they are often met with skepticism, asked by their colleagues, "To what field was this [scholarship] contributing?" (Weinreb, 2022, p. 6).

Devaluing research on pedagogy is certainly a challenge that transcends Israel studies. Work that is often called "scholarship of teaching" (e.g., Boyer, 1990; Ochoa, 2011) or "pedagogical scholarship" (Weimer, 2006) has been uneven across fields, as many institutions of higher education reward the production of disciplinary knowledge over the production of knowledge of teaching in decisions that relate to promotion and tenure (Chalmers, 2011). This larger trend has played out in Israel studies with a robust scholarly conversation focused on teaching *in* Israel (e.g., Orit, 2003; Tadmor-Shimony & Raichel, 2013) and a dearth of research investigating the teaching *of* Israel. For while there have been important scholarly conversations about specific pedagogical approaches and challenges of teaching the Arab–Israeli conflict in particular (e.g., Harris, 2019), there have not yet been sustained investigations into teaching the broader range of subjects and disciplines that constitute Israel studies.

Another primary context in which Israel is taught is in Israel education, a subfield of Jewish education. Questions of teaching are more explicitly visible in Israel education than they are in Israel studies. Some teachers have conducted self-studies of their own practice (e.g., Reingold 2017, 2018), and scholars have highlighted both teacher stances towards their work (e.g., Pomson et al., 2014) and teachers' roles in curricular (Katz, 2015) and pedagogical (Reingold, 2021a, 2021b) decision-making. Yet studies of teaching are the exception rather than the rule in Israel education, where the preponderance of scholarship has focused on two primary areas: philosophy of Israel education and empirical research about Jewish learners.

The predominant discourse in Israel education has long focused on philosophical principles for teaching about Israel (e.g., Alexander, 2015; Chazan, 2016; Sinclair, 2013). Scholars have engaged in robust debates about the questions "Why teach about Israel in the context of Jewish education?" (e.g., Chazan, 2004; Davis & Alexander, 2023; Hassenfeld, 2023; Zakai, 2014) and "What are the purposes of Israel education?" (e.g., Grant et al., 2012; Isaacs, 2011; Pomson, 2023). This philosophical discourse, while valuable for highlighting a range of possible goals for teaching about Israel, has not illuminated the work *of* teaching (Ball & Forzani, 2009), and therefore windows into teachers and their pedagogical decision-making processes have remained closed.

In more recent years, scholarship in Israel education has also begun to illuminate a spectrum of experiences and beliefs of young Diaspora Jews as they learn about Israel. The emerging portrait has captured how Jewish learners in early childhood (e.g., Applebaum et al., 2021), primary school (e.g., Zakai, 2022), secondary school (e.g., Hassenfeld, 2018), and young adulthood (e.g., Saxe & Chazan, 2008; Saxe et al., 2009) make sense of Israel and its place in Diaspora Jewish life. This work has been crucial for illuminating student understanding even as it has often glossed over the role of teaching in facilitating learning.

When taken together, the two primary conversations among scholars of Israel education—philosophical debates about the desired purposes of Israel education and empirical investigations into the experiences of young

Jewish learners—have put a spotlight on educational outcomes. Scholars have debated the question "What *ought* students understand, feel, and believe?" and investigated the question "What *do* students understand, feel, and believe?" Not yet illuminated are the types of pedagogical choices that allow for, or hinder, these outcomes.

Shifting away from trends in both Israel studies and Israel education, this volume situates questions of teaching at its core. Some chapters are teacher self-studies in which teachers investigate—at times solo and at times in collaboration with their students—their own practice. Other chapters are scholarly investigations of teachers, broadly defined, and their work. Although these chapters raise important theoretical and philosophical questions about teaching, all are rooted in empirical inquiry. As a collection, the chapters highlight teaching as worthy of study both because it is an often-overlooked area of scholarship and because it is a means to improve teaching and learning in practice.

Israel in Teaching

Just as we take a broad view of what constitutes teaching, so too do we have a broad understanding of what constitutes Israel. On its surface, that may appear counterintuitive. After all, Israel is a concrete, physical place. Yet what may at first glance appear to be a single entity is, in reality, a multiplicity of Israels past and present, real and symbolic, tangible and ephemeral (Avni et al., 2012).

As a subject matter to be learned and taught, Israel may fall within any number of disciplinary homes, including history (e.g., Shapira, 2012), geography (e.g., Gradus et al., 2006), political science (e.g., Bialer, 2020), law (Sandberg, 2022), visual and performing arts (e.g., Harris, 2017; Reingold, 2022), religious studies (e.g., Ariel, 2017; Ellenson, 2017; Stillman, 2017), environmental studies (Tal, 2002), literature (e.g., Grumberg, 2012), and more. As a modern nation-state, Israel is home to a range of communities with varying cultural, political, and religious practices (Rubin, 2012), each of which may be highlighted and/or downplayed in the selection and framing of learning materials. As a place of spiritual meaning, Israel is—at once—a Jewish state and a holy site for multiple religious communities (Troen & Fish, 2017). As a physical place, Israel has borders that have shifted over time and that remain a source of political contention today (Cohen, 2020). As the site of an ongoing intractable conflict (Bar-Tal, 2013), Israel/Palestine has contested status both within international law (Kontorovich, 2013) and educational discourse (Gur-Ze'ev, 2000). Teachers who teach about Israel have to contend with a broad range of options not only about how to curate learning materials and learning experiences, but also about how to define and frame what Israel *is* and why it ought to be a subject of study.

In this volume, we take no unified stance about which of these many "Israels" (Avni et al., 2012) ought to be taught and how, and this is because we view both teaching and learning as situated practices that are rooted in particular contexts and relationships (Lave & Wenger, 1991; Rogoff, 1990). Discerning readers will find in the pages of this volume the voices of teachers whose answers to the questions "Which Israel should be taught?" and "Why should Israel be taught?" are diametrically opposed, and who nonetheless are tied together by a deep commitment to understanding the craft of teaching Israel.

Despite the range of both teaching practices and ways of framing Israel spotlighted in this book, readers will find common threads that run throughout its pages. As discussed previously, the essays in this volume share two common stances towards teaching—situating teaching as inexorably tied to the learning processes of students and teachers alike, and framing teaching as a subject worthy of scholarly investigation. They also draw upon two common stances toward Israel: situating Israel as a subject matter to be taught and learned, and framing teaching Israel as an act that is both educational and political. Yet, while the two stances towards teaching unify the authors in this volume and the teachers whose work they study, the two stances towards Israel function simultaneously as unifiers and as dividers. Thus, while the teachers whose work is investigated in this book are united by Israel as the common subject matter that they teach, they are also divided by how they position Israel as a subject matter in their work. Similarly, the teachers and the scholars who study their teaching in this volume all recognize that teaching Israel is implicated by politics even as they are divided by the particular political stances they take in their work.

1. Israel as a Subject Matter Unites and Divides

Subject matter stands as one of the commonplaces of education (Schwab, 1973). Explaining the notion of commonplaces (McKeon, 1954; Schwab, 1978), the educational philosopher Isa Aron (2009) writes,

> Think of a map, which is a simplified representation of the overwhelmingly complex reality of the Earth. Elementary school students, sailors, hikers, and geographers all utilize maps, but each has a different set of interests and each requires a map that presents the necessary information, without causing undue confusion. Thus we have globes for basic understanding, flat maps for navigation, topographical maps for hikers, atlases for in-depth study, and so on. What all these maps have in common is that they feature *common places*—countries, cities, rivers, and so on. Of course, the relationship between the various common places might be represented differently on different maps, and particular places might not appear on particular maps—a factor that is, in itself, revealing. (p. 3)

Educational commonplaces—including but not limited to teacher, student, and subject matter—may, like the common points on different types of maps, appear differently in different contexts or at different moments in time (Aron, 2009). Yet, while what constitutes a "teacher" may be radically different in a university classroom, a professional apprenticeship, and a summer camp, the work of a teacher in carefully crafting an environment aimed at generating learning remains a constant across contexts. So too may the particular subject matter differ in various educational contexts and with different teachers who shape and are shaped by them, even as in any educational context there is subject matter to be taught and learned.

The teachers whose work is spotlighted in this volume all position Israel as a primary subject matter in their teaching; at the same time, the ways that they understand this subject matter reflects two primary—yet different—schools of thought about Israel as subject matter. The first school of thought casts Israeli history, literature, geography, politics, art, and more as subject matter. In this view, Israel is a particular—and often a particularly fruitful—case of a disciplinary or interdisciplinary approach to teaching and learning. For example, history teachers may use Israel as a case for studying the past. Political science professors may employ Israel as a case for investigating issues of politics and power. Arts educators may turn to Israeli music, theater, or film to explore medium and meaning. Teachers of religion may delve into Israel as a site for considering the sacred and the profane in multiple religious traditions. This approach views any one of the many "Israels" as rich subject matter, and it privileges cognitive understanding of Israel as a complex society.

The second school of thought, common among Jewish educators, suggests that the subject matter of teaching Israel is not any of these discipline-specific or interdisciplinary bodies of knowledge. "The subject of Israel education," argues the educational philosopher Barry Chazan (2016), "is not Israel but the fostering of a personal relationship with Israel" (p. 16). Many educators in Jewish educational contexts view the very purpose of Israel education as "forg[ing] a relationship between the individual person and Israel, so that it becomes part of how a person thinks about him/herself as a Jew" (Horowitz, 2012, p. 3). This approach places "human bodies and not bodies of knowledge" (Chazan, 2016, p. 18) at the heart of the educational enterprise, and it privileges the affective over the cognitive.

In this volume, these two schools of thought function not as a binary but as the endpoints of a broad spectrum. Some of the teachers in these pages clearly fall within a particular disciplinary home and frame Israel as a case for teaching and learning within that discipline. Some of the teachers whose work is investigated in this volume view not Israel, but the learner's relationship to Israel, as the primary subject matter that they teach. Yet, other teachers whose stories are in this book may, in different moments and in different ways, raise up and/or mute Israel and the learner's relationship to Israel, making shifting choices about how to navigate cognition and emotion, connection and understanding. Thus, while particular teachers and scholars of teaching whose work constitutes this book may fall at a particular point along this spectrum, the volume as a whole rests on a broad understanding of what constitutes the subject matter of teaching Israel. At the book's core is both a unified understanding that meaningful learning happens when teachers and students work in relationship to one another and to rich content (Hawkins, 1974; Raider-Roth & Holzer, 2009) and a spectrum of beliefs about what constitutes the content of teaching Israel.

2. Teaching Israel as a Political Endeavor Unites and Divides

Teaching is inherently political work (Freire, 1968/2018). The choices that teachers make about what and how to teach can reinforce and/or reshape the values of a society, and as such, teachers have the power to influence not only the hearts, minds, and values of their learners but also what counts as in the interest of the common good. As the critical-pedagogy theorist Henry A. Giroux (2010) explains, "The way we educate our youth is related to the future that we hope for" (p. 337), and thus teaching choices can reflect the world as it is and/or move towards the world as it might someday be.

Although this volume understands subject matter as a core component of teaching practice, it also recognizes that teaching is never about subject matter alone. As the multicultural- and bilingual-education expert Sonia Nieto (2006) explains, teaching is "also about who is heard, listened to, and read, who gets to count, and who can paint the picture. It's about who moves ahead and who gets left behind. In this sense, teaching is political work" (p. 9). Choices about which voices matters in the curation of content, which voices matter in decisions about pedagogy, and which voices matter in the unfolding of learning are all decisions about power and community and thus ultimately about politics.

If all teaching is political, then teaching Israel is especially so. This is because in addition to the issues of politics that shape *all* teaching—the extent to which teaching ought to reflect, reinforce, reenvision, and/or recreate key structures and issues in society—Israel itself is a political subject matter. Those who teach Israel must grapple with the political nature of Israel on multiple distinct but interrelated levels.

On one level, teachers must contend with the politics *in* Israel. On this plane, Israel is political because it is, like all societies, a place in which people must negotiate how to live together, and in which debates about policy shape both the work of the government and the work of education (Hess & McAvoy, 2014). More so, Israel is a politically polarized society (Gidron et al., 2022; Harel et al., 2020). Israelis are deeply divided about a range of issues, including the balance of power between the executive and judiciary arms of government (Rubin et al., 2023) and the relationship between religion and state (Ben Porat & Filc, 2022). The divided electorate has radically different visions for what the democratic and/or Jewish character of the state ought to be (Yadgar, 2020). When a nation is deeply polarized, as Israeli society is today, it creates not only political challenges, but also *pedagogical* challenges as teachers make decisions about when and how to address politically contentious issues in the classroom (McAvoy & Hess, 2013; Pollak et al., 2018).

On another level, teachers who teach about Israel in North America must also navigate the politics *of* Israel in their own communities. On this plane, Israel is political because it has become a partisan issue in an increasingly polarized North American political landscape (Gilboa, 2020, 2021). As Americans become more and more hostile towards their political opponents (Abramowitz, 2022), American public opinion about Israel has become increasingly partisan (Cavari & Freedman, 2020). In this tense political climate, Israel has come to occupy a "uniquely charged place in the American mind" (Mead, 2022, p. 9). As a result, teachers must make pedagogical choices not only about how to frame political issues that matter to the Israeli electorate, but also about whether and how to address questions about Israel's role in the North American political landscape.

Those who teach about Israel in Jewish educational institutions must also contend with the politics of Jewish life *vis-à-vis* Israel. Within the Jewish communities of North America, Israel has become "so deeply ideologically rooted and so divisive" (Gordis, 2019, p. 18) that it is "fast becoming a source of division rather than unity" (Waxman, 2016). As Kelman and Baron (2019) explain, "Israel has become such a fraught issue that [Jewish] communities, organizations, congregations, and schools (to say nothing of families) regularly avoid the issue rather than risk what they fear might be a significant disagreement" (p. 497). As a result, Israel has become a wedge issue in Jewish education (Gringras, 2023; Zakai, 2023), and Jewish educators have to juggle not only the politics in Israel and the politics of Israel in North America, but also the Israel politics of Jewish communal life.

Teachers do and should make a variety of decisions about how, and even whether, to explicitly address these different levels of politics. This is in part because of the importance of "situated pedagogic practice" (Hennessy, 2006), in which teaching choices reflect the particular context in which the teaching is embedded. An elementary school teacher and a college professor, for example, cannot frame political matters in the same way both because of the differing developmental capacities of their respective students and because of the differing political climates in elementary and higher education. Yet teachers' differing choices also reflect differing pedagogical *orientations* towards the politics of education. Thus, two university professors in the same department, or two Jewish day school educators, might make different choices from one another about whether and how to give explicit attention to the politics in Israel, the politics of Israel in North America, and the Jewish communal politics vis-à-vis Israel.

The notion that teaching Israel is inherently political work runs throughout the chapters in this volume even as the teachers whose work is spotlighted make very different decisions about both the forms of teaching and the form of Israel they would like to see in the world. Some chapters in this volume spotlight the work of teachers who teach about politics in Israel, framing for students the governmental structure and key political issues that animate Israeli society. Some chapters highlight the work of teachers who teach about the politics of Israel, spotlighting the ways that Israel has become a political lightning rod on North American university campuses and/or within the global Jewish community. Others still focus on teaching about other disciplines—literature, history, religion—that may nonetheless illuminate political issues surrounding how society does or should function. Thus, the political nature of teaching Israel, like Israel as subject matter, simultaneously unites and divides the chapters in this volume.

Teachers reasonably disagree about a range of questions central to the teaching of politics and the politics of teaching. How central and/or peripheral ought particular political issues be in choices about curriculum and pedagogy (Hess, 2009)? To what extent ought teaching highlight issues that are timely and/or timeless, focusing on what is enduring and/or what is current about Israeli society, culture, and politics? At what moments, and in what contexts, ought teachers reveal and/or conceal their own partisan stances and the values that animate their teaching choices (Hess & McAvoy, 2014)? How, and to what extent, should teachers aim to help their students understand the world as it is and/or reconstruct it as it ought to be (Zakai, 2019)? The authors in this volume take no unified stance on these questions but are nonetheless keenly aware that any particular teacher's ways of thinking about these questions has profound implications for the processes of teaching and learning. Thus, while this volume as a whole takes no particular position on specific political issues in Israel, the politics of Israel in North America, Jewish communal politics vis-à-vis Israel, or the politics of teaching, it calls attention to the fact that *any* way of framing core educational questions about teaching Israel necessarily implicates matters of politics.

Teaching Israel

Building on beliefs about teaching as a complex practice worthy of scholarly investigation, and an understanding of Israel as a multidisciplinary subject matter with shifting, and often political, geographic and conceptual borders, this volume focuses on a range of pedagogical practices and orientations that teachers in different contexts use to teach about Israel. In doing so, this volume differs from prior scholarly conversations about Israel in multiple ways.

First, we bring together investigations of teaching in which Israel is the common subject matter in a range of educational institutions with teachers who take different stances towards both their subject matter and its purpose in a larger process of education. Readers will find in the pages of this volume studies of teachers and teaching in a variety of different contexts: early childhood education, K–12 education, post-secondary education, higher education, military education, adult education, and teacher education. This is a deliberate attempt to shift a conversation that is typically bifurcated between Israel studies—the academic scholarship and teaching about Israel that occurs on ethnically and religiously diverse university campuses—and Israel education—the attempts within Jewish educational institutions to build a connection to Israel as part of a larger sense of contemporary Jewish life (Horowitz, 2012). This volume seeks to shift the discourse in both of these fields by locating *all* scholarly investigations into teaching Israel as part of a single conversation. Thus, we view this book neither as a book about Israel studies nor as a book about Israel education, though particular contributing authors may position their work in one of these fields or the other. Instead, this is a book about *teaching* and the pedagogical choices that teachers make when Israel, in all its many forms, is the subject matter.

The very title of this volume, *Teaching Israel*, differs from previous ways that this term has been used in scholarly conversations about Jewish education. As Jews in North America have situated Israel as an ongoing (Krasner, 2005, 2006) and increasingly central (Grant & Kopelowitz, 2012; Zakai, 2022) aspect of Jewish Diaspora education, they have used evolving language to describe how and why Jews outside of the Jewish state ought to learn about it. In the early to mid-1900s, before Israel was an independent country, Jewish schooling often focused on "teaching *eretz Yisrael* [the land of Israel]," a term used to connote that Jewish learners ought to internalize connections to the physical site of the origins of the Jewish people (Chazan, 2015, pp. 87–88). In his linguistic analysis of Jewish curricula and textbooks, Barry Chazan (2015) demonstrates how this term morphed into "teaching about Palestine" during the period of the British Mandate and then "teaching about Israel" after the establishment of the state. These terms were used to focus learners' attention to "the heroic effort to build a new Jewish country" and to direct teachers towards pedagogies that "encompassed both the transmission of facts and ideas and the development of positive attitudes" (p. 87). As Israel developed, so too did the terms that North American Jews used in their educational institutions, as "teaching about Israel" gave way to "teaching Israel," a subtle linguistic shift that signified an educational turn towards resituating Israel as the meeting point of land, state, people, and religious values and towards promoting traditional classroom-based pedagogies that were content driven. Only at the turn of the 21st century did the now-prevalent language of "Israel education" arise. As Chazan explains,

> This new phraseology reflected the concern to broaden the enterprise in two senses. First, it advocated the expansion of the venue of Israel from a school-based framework to a multivenued arena encompassing youth groups, camps, retreats, and travel to Israel. Second, it affirmed a shift in priorities from teaching as an activity defined by schooling to a broader spectrum of pedagogic activities rooted in contemporary theories of learning, identity, and experiential education. (pp. 88–89)

The moniker "Israel education" has supplanted "teaching Israel" in both scholarship and practice. Thus, while there are robust debates within the field about whether Israel education ought to focus on the cognitive and/

or the affective (Horowitz, 2012; Koren et al., 2015), the personal and/or the collective (Chazan, 2016; Sinclair, 2013), the historical and/or the contemporary (Gringras, 2020; Stein, 2020), the term "Israel education" has clearly become the dominant way to describe a broad range of orientations and practices in contemporary Jewish education.

Upon first glance, it may appear that by calling our volume *Teaching Israel*, we are stepping backwards into a Jewish educational past that located Israel at the center of collective Jewish life and assumed that a classroom was a traditional space with four walls and a person titled "teacher" at the front of the room. Instead, it is our intention to repurpose an old term and imbue it with new meaning, situating "teaching Israel" in its rightful place as the corollary practice to "learning Israel," both of which are essential to the work of Israel studies and Israel education alike. Building upon recent trends in Israel education, we acknowledge that Israel can be taught and learned in a wide range of institutional settings, and we take a broad view of the types of pedagogical practices that might constitute its work. Our primary goal is to shift conversations in both Israel education and Israel studies towards scholarly investigations into teaching and the types of decisions, trade-offs, and educational values that animate teachers' thoughts and actions.

In this move towards investigating teaching, we attempt to stimulate further conversations about the broader practices of education in which teaching and learning coexist, each influencing and influenced by the other. As discussed previously, we view teaching and learning as inexorably tied, so this focus on teaching is not intended to erase or even to call attention away from important scholarly conversations about learning. It is, rather, an attempt to broaden a conversation often focused on learning outcomes alone to one that recognizes that teaching and learning occur in tandem and that the scholarly discourse on teaching Israel has to-date lagged behind the important scholarly conversations about learning Israel.

A final shift that we are attempting to make in this volume is to expand the pool of authorial voices who contribute to conversations about teaching Israel. In the broader field of education, there is often a bifurcation between scholars and practitioners, each operating in their own siloed spaces even as the two are bound together by a shared interest in meaningful teaching and learning. In this volume, we bring together the voices of scholars who study teachers, teachers who study their own teaching practice, and students who study the teaching of their teachers. We view those who teach as capable of investigating teaching and those who study teaching as teachers in their own right. We understand students as offering essential voices on teaching, and we view teachers as learners along with their students. Therefore, we have curated a collection of essays deliberately designed to blur the often rigid boundaries between scholarly and practice-oriented conversations about teaching.

Understanding This Volume

Like other scholarship that takes seriously the study of teaching, the purpose of this volume is not to present a case for "what works" in teaching Israel, but rather to investigate the work of teaching and the questions and problems that arise from doing this work (Lampert, 2001). Each of the sections in this book are structured around a particular set of questions or issues related to the teaching of Israel.

Part 1, "The Reflective Teacher," highlights teachers who investigate their own teaching in order to better understand and improve it. The chapters in this section examine the teaching of Israel in radically different contexts—as part of university Israel studies, professional military education, and Jewish education—but they are united by a common methodology: the teacher self-study. "Self-study," explains the scholar of teacher education John Loughran (2008), "is a field that opens up the complex world of teaching and learning about teaching in ways that can only be done by those who are participants in the work" (p. 1179). Although teacher self-study encompasses a broad range of methods, its through-line is a commitment to reflecting on practice in order to rethink and potentially reshape meaningful teaching and learning (Hamilton & Pinnegar, 1998).

In this section, thoughtful educators reflect on their own pedagogical choices and ways that those choices shape and are shaped by particular beliefs about students and subject matter. In Chapter 1, the political scientist Robin A. Harper investigates the classroom in which she teaches about Israel to first-generation working-class college students from ethnically, racially, and religiously diverse communities. Drawing upon a rich set of artifacts of practice (Ball & Cohen, 1999) ranging from student work to her own teaching journal, Harper explores her own attempts to make pedagogical choices that simultaneously honor the diversity of her classroom and build a deeper understanding of modern Israel. Chapter 2 spotlights Amin Tarzi's work as director of Middle East studies at the Marine Corps University, where he teaches about Israel in the context of professional military education. Reflecting on his own journey as a student and teacher of Israel studies, Tarzi illuminates how he helps students understand—and distinguish between—their professional interests in Israel because of its military and security implications and their often passionate personal beliefs about Israel. In Chapter 3, the Jewish educator and researcher Joshua Ladon investigates a particular pedagogical tool he commonly uses in his own teaching of Jewish learners: the source sheet. By examining both the historical evolution of the source sheet and his own orientation towards its use in teaching, Ladon raises profound questions about the relationships among Israel, Zionism, Judaism, and pedagogy. The chapters in this section are situated in different educational settings yet grounded in a shared commitment to lifting up "the voices of teachers, the questions and problems they pose, [and] the frameworks they use to interpret and improve practice" (Lytle & Cochran-Smith, 1990, p. 83). In each of these chapters, thoughtful teachers reflect on their own teaching choices and on the vocation they share.

The chapters in Part 2, "Using Student Voices to Examine Teacher Choices," honor the voices of students as central to the work of teaching. "When we open up opportunities for [students] to express themselves," explains the reading and literacy expert David Booth (2013), "we help them develop a sense of self-efficacy, that they, alongside their parents and teachers, can be effective agents of their own learning and growth" (p. 9). When teachers listen carefully to students, student voices can also function as a powerful tool for improving teaching (DeFur & Korinek, 2010). In other words, making space for students to share their own experiences—including the ways that they encounter and understand the work of their teachers—matters both for students' agency in learning and for teachers' evolving practice.

In this section, students and teachers collaborate to illuminate the kinds of choices that teachers currently make and might make in the future. In Chapter 4, the high school Jewish history teacher Matt Reingold and his students Alexa Jacoby and Benjamin Day co-investigate Reingold's choices about how to frame difficult conversations in the Jewish history classroom. Jacoby and Day both recall moments in Reingold's classroom when they learned information about Israeli policies that unsettled their previous beliefs and understanding, reflecting together with their teacher about the pedagogical choices that allowed for their intellectual and emotional growth. In Chapter 5, Diane Tickton Schuster develops a detailed portrait of her teacher Rachel Korazim. Writing as both an expert in Jewish adult education and as a student in Korazim's Israeli literature class, Schuster illuminates her teacher's pedagogical approach to bringing Diaspora Jewish adult learners "into the intimate discourse" of Israelis. Chapter 6 spotlights the work of the veteran high school Israel educators Jonathan Golden and Yoni Kadden, who turn to recent alumni of their school in order to better understand a new framework for teaching Israel that they have developed. Toggling back and forth between the reflections of their former students and their own evolving work, Golden and Kadden consider what it takes to help students develop knowledge about, connections to, and stances on key issues in Israeli society. By deliberately lifting up the voices of students, each of the chapters in Part 2 situate teaching not as a hierarchy in which teachers attempt to inculcate their knowledge into students, but instead as a collaborative process that requires the contributions of teachers and students alike.

In Part 3, "Navigating the Teaching of Politics and the Politics of Teaching," scholars and practitioners examine explicitly political questions that arise when teaching about Israel in classrooms and university lecture halls. Although teaching is inherently political work (e.g., Nieto, 2006), only some classrooms are what Diana Hess and Paula McAvoy (2014) call "political classrooms," classrooms in which students and teachers deliberately consider how people ought to live together in society. Teaching in these classrooms requires particular kinds of pedagogical decision-making that position contested issues as both worthy of learning and possible to discuss in educational settings (Noddings & Brooks, 2017; Zimmerman & Robertson, 2017).

Each of the chapters in Part 3 investigates the relationship between teaching and politics, highlighting cases of political issues that teachers must navigate when deciding how to teach about contentious issues relating to Israel. In Chapter 7, the sociopsychologist Bethamie Horowitz studies Kivunim, a post-secondary gap year program in Israel, as a way of illuminating pedagogies that promote critical engagement with Israel. Horowitz reveals how Kivunim educators make deliberate choices about how they represent Israel and its relationship to both Arab and Jewish communities as part of a "pedagogy of inquiry." The political scientist Mira Sucharov tackles the highly contested BDS (boycott, divestment, and sanctions) movement in Chapter 8 by exploring the pedagogical conundrums that arise in relation to political activism on campus. Using her own classroom as a laboratory, Sucharov examines both the educational and the political messages that she conveys when she and her students consider the implications of academic and cultural boycott. In Chapter 9, the international relations expert Keren E. Fraiman illuminates the work of Jewish educators who express both deep commitment to, and serious reservations about, teaching the Israeli–Palestinian conflict. By uncovering the barriers that educators face in attempting to teach about the history and politics of Israeli–Palestinian relations, Fraiman illuminates how conflict education is, at once, a core and a highly contested practice in contemporary Jewish education.

The book's final section, "When Teachers Learn," situates professional educators as both teachers and learners (Feiman-Nemser, 2012). Building on an understanding of teaching as a complex practice that is learned over time (Cochran-Smith, 2012), the chapters in this section investigate how teachers learn to teach, reteach, and rethink their teaching about Israel. These chapters all build upon a belief that "effective teaching is both complex and counter-intuitive—but it can be taught" (Ball & Forzani, 2010, p. 40), and they explicitly highlight implications for professional development and ongoing teacher learning.

The chapters in Part 4 examine contexts in which teachers—and those who teach teachers—learn about and from practice. In Chapter 10, the teacher-learning expert Lauren Applebaum and I study the work of both early childhood educators learning about Israel education and our own work teaching these educators in professional-learning seminars. We investigate the questions that the early childhood educators ask about their pedagogical practices and the questions that they raise about our own work as teacher-educators. In Chapter 11, the scholar of Jewish education

Laura Novak Winer explores how teachers in synagogue supplementary schools consider their own connections to and understandings of Israel. In doing so, Winer uncovers how teachers' beliefs and experiences impact the decisions they make about what and how to teach, and she maps a range of orientations that teachers have towards Israel and towards teaching Israel. Chapter 12 spotlights the Qushiyot Fellowship, a professional-development program for synagogue educators seeking to improve the teaching and learning of Israel in their institutions. In this chapter, the sociologist Ezra Kopelowitz and the veteran Jewish educator Abby Pitkowsky illuminate how synagogue educators learn to articulate and plan towards their goals of helping young Jewish learners develop a sense of personal connection to Israel within a larger collective context. Finally, in Chapter 13, Lauren Applebaum probes the thinking of Jewish day school teachers engaged in ongoing professional learning about Israel education. She demonstrates how and why teachers change—or don't change—their beliefs and practices about teaching Israel. When taken as a whole, the chapters in this section respond to calls for a more robust scholarly conversation about the capacities of educators who teach about Israel and the training and professional development that might support their work (Sinclair et al., 2013).

In each of these sections, and in the book's concluding chapter, which weaves together the theoretical and practical implications of this volume, are stories of teachers who work with students, with one another, and with their own teachers to better understand the practices of teaching Israel. Throughout this volume, we situate teaching Israel as a relational practice in which teachers, students, and particular content relating to Israel all interact and, in doing so, have the possibility of transforming one another. We locate teaching Israel as a contextual practice, rooted in particular educational milieus which are, themselves, positioned in larger cultural, religious, and political contexts. We frame teaching Israel as a professional practice that requires the ongoing exercise of professional judgment and continual professional learning. As a whole, this volume offers a window into the complex work of teachers who teach who they are (Palmer, 1998/2017), meet students where they are (e.g., Sponenberg, 2012), and together engage in "fruitful deliberations" about what Israel is (Troen & Fish, 2017, p. 2).

NOTES

1. The names used in this opening story are pseudonyms, but the experiences and reflections on teaching are real. All quotations come from interview data I gathered as part of an IRB-reviewed study of educators who teach about Israel in a variety of educational contexts.

REFERENCES

Abramowitz, A. I. (2022). The polarized American electorate: The rise of partisan-ideological consistency and its consequences. *Political Science Quarterly, 137*(4), 645–674. https://doi.org/10.1002/polq.13388

Alexander, H. A. (2015). Mature Zionism: Education and the scholarly study of Israel. *Journal of Jewish Education, 81*(2), 136–161. https://doi.org/10.1080/15244113.2015.1035979

Applebaum, L., Hartman, A., & Zakai, S. (2021). A little bit more far than Mexico: How 3- and 4-year-old Jewish children understand Israel. *Journal of Jewish Education, 87*(1), 4–34. https://doi.org/10.1080/15244113.2020.1834890

Ariel, Y. (2017). Contemporary Christianity and Israel. In S. I. Troen & R. Fish (Eds.), *Essential Israel: Essays for the 21st century* (pp. 280–310). Indiana University Press.

Aron, I. (2009). *Reading Daniel Pekarsky's vision at work with students at the Rhea Hirsch School of Education, HUC-JIR*. Unpublished manuscript. The Jack, Joseph, and Morton Mandel Foundation.

Attias, S. (2019). Intersections between Israel Studies and Israel Education. In C. Schapkow & K. Hodl (Eds.), *Jewish studies and Israel studies in the twenty-first century: Intersections and prospects* (pp. 157–172). Lexington Books.

Avni, S., Kattan, S., & Zakai, S. (2012). *Purposes and practices of Israel/Hebrew education: Towards a joint agenda for applied research*. The Consortium for Applied Studies in Jewish Education.

Ball, D. L. (1993). With an eye on the mathematical horizon: Dilemmas of teaching elementary school mathematics. *The Elementary School Journal, 93*(4), 373–397. https://doi.org/10.1086/461730

Ball, D. L., & Cohen, D. K. (1999). Developing practice, developing practitioners: Toward a practice-based theory of professional education. In L. Darling-Hammond & G. Sykes (Eds.), *Teaching as the learning profession: Handbook of policy and practice* (pp. 3–22). Jossey-Bass.

Ball, D. L., & Forzani, F. M. (2009). The work of teaching and the challenge for teacher education. *Journal of Teacher Education, 60*(5), 497–511. https://doi.org/10.1177/0022487109348479

Ball, D. L., & Forzani, F. M. (2010). Teaching skillful teaching. *Educational Leadership, 68*(4), 40–45.

Banks, J., Cochran-Smith, M., Moll, L., Richert, A., Zeichner, K., LePage, P., Darling-Hammond, L., and Duffy, H., with McDonald, M. (2005). Teaching diverse learners. In L. Darling-Hammond & J. Bransford (Eds.), *Preparing teachers for a changing world: What teachers should learn and be able to do* (pp. 232–274). Jossey-Bass.

Bar-Tal, D. (2013). *Intractable conflicts: Socio-psychological foundations and dynamics*. Cambridge University Press.

Ben Porat, G., & Filc, D. (2022). Remember to be Jewish: Religious populism in Israel. *Politics and Religion*, *15*(1), 61–84. https://doi.org/10.1017/S1755048320000681

Bialer, U. (2020). *Israeli foreign policy: A people shall not dwell alone*. Indiana University Press.

Booth, D. (2013). *I've got something to say: How student voices inform our teaching*. Pembroke Publishers Limited.

Borko, H. (2004). Professional development and teacher learning: Mapping the terrain. *Educational Researcher*, *33*(8), 3–15. https://doi.org/10.3102/0013189X033008003

Boyer, E. (1990). *Scholarship reconsidered: Priorities of the professoriate*. The Carnegie Foundation.

Brookhart, S. M., & Oakley, A. (2021). *How to look at student work to uncover student thinking*. ASCD.

Burnham, R., & Kai-Kee, E. (2011). *Teaching in the art museum: Interpretation as experience*. Getty Publications.

Cavari, A., & Freedman, G. (2020). *American public opinion toward Israel: From consensus to divide*. Routledge.

Chalmers, D. (2011). Progress and challenges to the recognition and reward of the scholarship of teaching in higher education. *Higher Education Research & Development*, *30*(1), 25–38. https://doi.org/10.1080/07294360.2011.536970

Chazan, B. (1979). Israel in American Jewish schools revisited. *Journal of Jewish Education*, *47*(2), 7–17. https://doi.org/10.1080/0021642790470203

Chazan, B. (2004). Schechter's lament: Israel and Jewish education once again. *Agenda: Jewish Education*, *18*, 4–5.

Chazan, B. (2015). A linguistic analysis of the role of Israel in American Jewish schooling. *Journal of Jewish Education*, *81*(1), 85–92. https://doi.org/10.1080/15244113.2015.1007016

Chazan, B. (2016). *A philosophy of Israel education: A relational approach*. Palgrave Macmillan.

Chazan, D. (2000). *Beyond formulas in mathematics and teaching: Dynamics of the high school algebra classroom*. Teachers College Press.

Cochran-Smith, M. (2012). A tale of two teachers: Learning to teach over time. *Kappa Delta Pi Record*, *48*(3), 108–122. https://doi.org/10.1080/00228958.2012.707501

Cohen, D. K. (2011). *Teaching and its predicaments*. Harvard University Press.

Cohen, D. K., Raudenbush, S. W., & Ball, D. L. (2003). Resources, instruction, and research. *Educational Evaluation and Policy Analysis*, *25*(2), 119–142. https://doi.org/10.3102/01623737025002119

Cohen, S. B. (2020). *The geopolitics of Israel's border question*. Routledge.

Cornish, L., Bannister-Tyrrell, M., Charteris, J., Jenkins, K., & Jones, M. A. (2018). Planning for teaching. In J. Allen & S. White (Eds.), *Learning to teach in a new era* (pp. 198–242). Cambridge University Press.

Costa, A. L., & Kallick, B. (1993). Through the lens of a critical friend. *Educational Leadership*, *51*(2), 49–51.

Cuban, L. (1992). Managing dilemmas while building professional communities. *Educational Researcher*, *21*(1), 4–11. https://doi.org/10.3102/0013189X021001004

Darling-Hammond, L. (2000). How teacher education matters. *Journal of Teacher Education*, *51*(3), 166–173. https://doi.org/10.1177/0022487100051003002

Darling-Hammond, L. (2008). Teacher learning that supports student learning. In B. Z. Presseisen (Ed.), *Teaching for intelligence* (2nd ed., pp. 91–100). Corwin.

Darling-Hammond, L., & Richardson, N. (2009). Research review/teacher learning: What matters. *Educational Leadership*, *66*(5), 46–53.

Davis, B., and Alexander, H. (2023). Israel education: A philosophical analysis. *Journal of Jewish Education*, *89*(1), 6–33. https://doi.org/10.1080/15244113.2023.2169213

DeFur, S. H., & Korinek, L. (2010). Listening to student voices. *The Clearing House: A Journal of Educational Strategies, Issues and Ideas*, *83*(1), 15–19. https://doi.org/10.1080/00098650903267677

Drago-Severson, E. (2004). *Helping teachers learn: Principal leadership for adult growth and development*. Corwin Press.

Ellenson, D. (2017). "Jewishness" in Israel: Israel as a Jewish state. In S. I. Troen & R. Fish (Eds.), *Essential Israel: Essays for the 21st century* (pp. 262–279). Indiana University Press.

Feiman-Nemser, S. (2003). What new teachers need to learn. *Educational leadership*, *60*(8), 25–29.

Feiman-Nemser, S. (2008). Teacher learning: How do teachers learn to teach? In M. Cochran-Smith, S. Feiman-Nemser, D. J. McIntyre, & K. E. Demers (Eds.), *Handbook of research on teacher education: Enduring questions in changing contexts* (pp. 697–705). Routledge. https://doi.org/10.4324/9780203938690

Feiman-Nemser, S. (2012). *Teachers as learners*. Harvard Education Press.

Freire, P. (2018). *Pedagogy of the oppressed* (M. B. Ramos, Trans.). Bloomsbury Publishing. (Original work published 1968)

Gidron, N., Sheffer, L., & Mor, G. (2022). The Israel polarization panel dataset, 2019–2021. *Electoral Studies*, *80*, Article 102512. https://doi.org/10.1016/j.electstud.2022.102512

Gilboa, E. (2020). *The American public and Israel in the twenty-first century*. Begin-Sadat Center for Strategic Studies.

Gilboa, E. (2021). What do Americans think of Israel? Long-term trends and socio-demographic shifts. *Currents: Briefs on Contemporary Israel*, *3*.

Giroux, H. A. (2010). Paulo Freire and the crisis of the political. *Power and Education*, *2*(3), 335–340. https://doi.org/10.2304/power.2010.2.3.335

Gordis, D. (2019). *We stand divided: The rift between American Jews and Israel*. Ecco/Harper Collins.

Gradus, Y., Krakover, S., & Razin, E. (2006). *The industrial geography of Israel*. Routledge.

Grant, L., & Kopelowitz, E. (2012). *Israel education matters: A 21st century paradigm for Jewish education*. Center for Jewish Peoplehood Education.

Grant, L. D., Marom, D., & Werchow, Y. (2012). *Israel education for what? An investigation of the purposes and possible outcomes of Israel education*. Consortium for Applied Studies in Jewish Education. http://www.bjpa.org/Publications/details.cfm?PublicationID=20971

Gringras, R. (2020). Israel in real life: The four Hatikvah questions. In J. Ariel (Ed.), *Israel education: The next edge* (pp. 75–81). Makom/Jewish Agency for Israel.

Gringras, R. (2023). Israel education: Agreeing to disagree. *Journal of Jewish Education*, *89*(1), 82–89. https://doi.org/10.1080/15244113.2023.2169498

Grossman, P., Schoenfeld, A., & Lee, C. (2005). Teaching subject matter. In L. Darling-

Hammond & J. Bransford (Eds.), *Preparing teachers for a changing world: What teachers should learn and be able to do* (pp. 201–231). Jossey-Bass.

Grumberg, K. (2012). *Place and ideology in contemporary Hebrew literature*. Syracuse University Press.

Gur-Ze'ev, I. (Ed.). (2000). *Conflicting philosophies of education in Israel/Palestine*. Springer Science+Business Media Dordrecht.

Hamilton, M. L., & Pinnegar, S. (1998). Reconceptualizing teaching practice. In M. L. Hamilton, S. Pinnegar, T. Russell, J. Loughran, & V. LaBoskey (Eds.), *Reconceptualizing teaching practice: Self-study in teacher education* (pp. 1–4). Psychology Press.

Harel, T. O., Maoz, I., & Halperin, E. (2020). A conflict within a conflict: Intragroup ideological polarization and intergroup intractable conflict. *Current Opinion in Behavioral Sciences, 34*, 52–57. https://doi.org/10.1016/j.cobeha.2019.11.013

Harris, R. S. (2017). *Warriors, witches, whores: Women in Israeli cinema*. Wayne State University Press.

Harris, R. S. (Ed.). (2019). *Teaching the Arab-Israeli conflict*. Wayne State University Press.

Hassenfeld, J. (2018). Landscapes of collective belonging: Jewish Americans narrate the history of Israel after an organized tour. *Journal of Jewish Education, 84*(2), 131–160. https://doi.org/10.1080/15244113.2018.1449482

Hassenfeld, J. (2023). What's love got to do with it: Reevaluating attachment as the goal of Israel education. *Journal of Jewish Education, 89*(1), 75–81. https://doi.org/10.1080/15244113.2023.2169514

Hawkins, D. (1974). *The informed vision*. Agathon Press, Inc.

Hennessy, S. (2006). Integrating technology into teaching and learning of school science: A situated perspective on pedagogical issues in research. *Studies in Science Education, 42*(1), 1–48. https://doi.org/10.1080/03057260608560219

Hess, D. E. (2009). *Controversy in the classroom: The democratic power of discussion*. Routledge.

Hess, D. E., & McAvoy, P. (2014). *The political classroom: Evidence and ethics in democratic education*. Routledge.

Hirst, P. H. (1971). What is teaching? *Journal of Curriculum Studies, 3*(1), 5–18. https://doi.org/10.1080/0022027710030102

Ho, L., McAvoy, P., Hess, D., & Gibbs, B. (2017). Teaching and learning about controversial issues and topics in the social studies. In M. M. Manfra & C. M. Bolick (Eds.), *The Wiley handbook of social studies research* (pp. 319–335). John Wiley and Sons.

Horowitz, B. (2012). *Defining Israel education*. The iCenter.

Intrator, S. M. (2005). *Tuned in and fired up: How teaching can inspire real learning in the classroom*. Yale University Press.

Isaacs, A. (2011). Israel education: Purposes and practices. In H. Miller, L. Grant, & A. Pomson (Eds.), *International handbook of Jewish education* (pp. 479–496). Springer, Dordrecht.

Katz, M. (2015). Harnessing teacher potential as Israel education curriculum developers. *Journal of Jewish Education, 81*(2), 162–188. https://doi.org/10.1080/15244113.2015.1034046

Katz, S. (1985). The Israeli teacher-guide: The emergence and perpetuation of a role. *Annals of Tourism Research, 12*(1), 49–72. https://doi.org/10.1016/0160-7383(85)90039-8

Kelman, A. Y., & Baron, I. Z. (2019). Framing conflict: Why American congregations cannot not talk about Israel. *Contemporary Jewry, 39*(3-4), 497-522. https://doi.org/10.1007/s12397-019-09305-2

Kelner, S. (2010). *Tours that bind: Diaspora, pilgrimage, and Israeli birthright tourism.* New York University Press.

Kennedy, G., Kennedy, G. C., & Neilson, K. (Eds.). (2002). *Military education: Past, present, and future.* Greenwood Publishing Group.

Kessler, R. (2000). *The soul of education: Helping students find connection, compassion, and character at school.* ASCD.

Kontorovich, E. (2013). Israel/Palestine—the ICC's uncharted territory. *Journal of International Criminal Justice, 11*(5), 979-999. https://doi.org/10.1093/jicj/mqt070

Koren, A., Aronson, J. K., & Saxe, L. (2013). Teaching Israel at American universities: Growth, placement, and future prospects. *Israel Studies, 18*(3), 158-178. https://doi.org/10.2979/israelstudies.18.3.158

Koren, A., & Fishman, S. (2015). *The summer institute for Israel studies: 2015.* Maurice and Marilyn Cohen Center for Modern Jewish Studies at Brandeis University.

Koren, A., Fishman, S., Aronson, J. K., & Saxe, L. (2015). *The Israel literacy measurement project: 2015 report.* Cohen Center for Modern Jewish Studies.

Koren, A., & Fleisch, E. (2014). *The summer institute for Israel studies: The first decade and looking ahead.* Maurice and Marilyn Cohen Center for Modern Jewish Studies at Brandeis University.

Krasner, J. (2005). Jewish education and American Jewish education, part II. *Journal of Jewish Education, 71*(3), 279-317. https://doi.org/10.1080/00216240500341906

Krasner, J. (2006). Jewish education and American Jewish education, part III. *Journal of Jewish Education, 72*(1), 29-76. https://doi.org/10.1080/00216240600581591

Kurtzer, Y., Adland, N., Baird, J., & Tucker, G. (2019). *Courageous leadership: The challenges facing Jewish leadership in a partisan age.* Shalom Hartman Institute.

Labaree, D. F. (1997). Public goods, private goods: The American struggle over educational goals. *American Educational Research Journal, 34*(1), 39-81. https://doi.org/10.3102/00028312034001039

Lampert, M. (1985). How do teachers manage to teach? Perspectives on problems in practice. *Harvard Educational Review, 55*(2), 178-195. https://doi.org/10.17763/haer.55.2.56142234616x4352

Lampert, M. (1990). When the problem is not the question and the solution is not the answer: Mathematical knowing and teaching. *American Educational Research Journal, 27*(1), 29-63. https://doi.org/10.3102/00028312027001029

Lampert, M. (2001). *Teaching problems and the problems of teaching.* Yale University Press.

Lave, J., & Wenger, E. (1991). *Situated learning: Legitimate peripheral participation.* Cambridge University Press.

Loughran, J. (2008). Toward a better understanding of teaching and learning about teaching. In M. Cochran-Smith, S. Feiman-Nemser, D. J. McIntyre, & K. E. Demers (Eds.), *Handbook of research on teacher education: Enduring questions in changing contexts* (pp. 1177-1182). Routledge.

Lytle, S. L., & Cochran-Smith, M. (1990). Learning from teacher research: A working typology. *Teachers College Record, 92*(1), 83-103. https://doi.org/10.1177/016146819009200104

McAvoy, P., & Hess, D. (2013). Classroom deliberation in an era of political polarization. *Curriculum Inquiry*, *43*(1), 14–47.

McDonald, J. P., Mohr, N., Dichter, A., & McDonald, E. C. (2015). *The power of protocols: An educator's guide to better practice, third edition*. New York: Teachers College Press.

McKeon, R. (1954). *Thought, action, and passion*. University of Chicago Press.

McLaughlin, M. W., & Talbert, J. E. (1993). Understanding teaching in context. In D. K. Cohen (Ed.), *Teaching for understanding: Challenges for policy and practice* (pp. 167–206). Jossey-Bass.

Mead, W. R. (2022). *The arc of a covenant: The United States, Israel, and the fate of the Jewish People*. Alfred A. Knopf.

Minkin, R., & Chertok, F. (2020). *The summer institute for Israel studies: 2019 annual survey*. Maurice and Marilyn Cohen Center for Modern Jewish Studies.

Nieto, S. (2006). *Teaching as political work: Learning from courageous and caring teachers*. Child Development Institute, Sarah Lawrence College. http://ns3.slc.edu/media/cdi/pdf/Occasional%20Papers/CDI_Occasional_Paper_2006_Nieto.pdf

Noddings, N. (2005). What does it mean to educate the whole child? *Educational leadership*, *63*(1), 1–11.

Noddings, N., & Brooks, L. (2017). *Teaching controversial issues: The case for critical thinking and moral commitment in the classroom*. Teachers College Press.

Ochoa, A. (2011). The scholarship of teaching: Yesterday, today, and tomorrow. *The Journal of the Professoriate*, *6*(1), 100–116.

Orit, I. (2003). Teaching civics in a divided society: The case of Israel. *International Studies in Sociology of Education*, *13*(3), 219–242. https://doi.org/10.1080/09620210300200111

Palmer, P. (2017). *The courage to teach: Exploring the inner landscape of a teacher's life*. John Wiley & Sons. (Original work published 1998)

Pollak, I., Segal, A., Lefstein, A., & Meshulam, A. (2018). Teaching controversial issues in a fragile democracy: Defusing deliberation in Israeli primary classrooms. *Journal of Curriculum Studies*, *50*(3), 387–409. https://doi.org/10.1080/00220272.2017.1397757

Pomson, A. (2023). Israel education. Clarifying the job to be done. *Journal of Jewish Education*, *89*(1), 34–38. https://doi.org/10.1080/15244113.2023.2169504

Pomson, A., Wertheimer, J., & Wolf, H. H. (2014). *Hearts and minds: Israel in North American Jewish day schools*. Avi Chai.

Raider-Roth, M., & Holzer, E. (2009). Learning to be present: How hevruta learning can activate teachers' relationships to self, other and text. *Journal of Jewish Education*, *75*(3), 216–239. https://doi.org/10.1080/15244110903079045

Reingold, M. (2017). Not the Israel of my elementary school: An exploration of Jewish-Canadian secondary students' attempts to process morally complex Israeli narratives. *The Social Studies*, *108*(3), 87–98. https://doi.org/10.1080/00377996.2017.1324392

Reingold, M. (2018). Broadening perspectives on immigrant experiences: Secondary students study the absorption difficulties faced by Mizrachi immigrants in Israel. *Journal of Jewish Education*, *84*(3), 312–329. https://doi.org/10.1080/15244113.2018.1478531

Reingold, M. (2021a). Changing students' perceptions by humanizing Dati Israelis through comics. *Religious Education*, *116*(3), 278–295. https://doi.org/10.1080/00344087.2021.1917848

Reingold, M. (2021b). Confronting BDS in the classroom: Jewish high school students build community by watching BDS demonstrations on university campuses. *Canadian Jewish Studies/Études juives canadiennes, 31*, 69–88. https://doi.org/10.25071/1916-0925.40210

Reingold, M. (2022). *Reenvisioning Israel through political cartoons: Visual discourses during the 2018-2021 electoral crisis*. Lexington.

Rodríguez-Carrillo, J., Mérida-Serrano, R., & González-Alfaya, M. E. (2020). "A teacher's hug can make you feel better": listening to US children's voices on high-quality early childhood teaching. *European Early Childhood Education Research Journal, 28*(4), 504–518. https://doi.org/10.1080/1350293X.2020.1783925

Rogoff, B. (1990). *Apprenticeship in thinking: Cognitive development in social context*. Oxford University Press.

Rubin, B. (2012). *Israel: An introduction*. Yale University Press.

Rubin, S., Berger, M., & Taylor, A. (2023, March 27). What to know about Israel's protests and judicial overhaul. *The Washington Post*. https://www.washingtonpost.com/world/2023/03/27/israel-protests-judicial-reform/

Sales, A. L., & Saxe, L. (2002). *Limud by the lake: Fulfilling the educational potential of Jewish summer camps*. Avi Chai.

Sandberg, H. (2022). *Land law and policy in Israel: A prism of identity*. Indiana University Press.

Saxe, L. (2004). *"How goodly are thy tents": Summer camps as Jewish socializing experiences*. University Press of New England.

Saxe, L., & Chazan, B. (2008). *Ten days of Birthright Israel: A journey in young adult identity*. University Press of New England.

Saxe, L., Phillips, B., Sasson, T., Hecht, S., Shain, M., Wright, G., & Kadushin, C. (2009). *Generation Birthright Israel: The impact of an Israel experience on Jewish identity and choices*. Brandeis University, Maurice and Marilyn Cohen Center for Modern Jewish Studies.

Scheffler, I. (1965). Philosophical models of teaching. *Harvard Educational Review, 35*(2), 131–143. https://doi.org/10.17763/haer.35.2.1662lq64330ml253

Schein, J. (1988). Rabbi as teacher: The process of formulating educational goals for Jewish leadership. *Jewish Education, 56*(2), 15–17. https://doi.org/10.1080/0021642880560203

Schwab, J. J. (1973). The practical 3: Translation into curriculum. *The School Review, 81*(4), 501–522. https://doi.org/10.1086/443100

Schwab, J. J. (1978). The practical: Arts of eclectic. In I. Westbury & N. Wilkof (Eds.), *Science, curriculum, and liberal education* (pp. 322–361). University of Chicago Press.

Shapira, A. (2012). *Israel: A history*. University Press of New England.

Shulman, L. S. (1986). Those who understand: Knowledge growth in teaching. *Educational Researcher, 15*(2), 4–14. https://doi.org/10.3102/0013189X015002004

Shulman, L. S. (1998). Theory, practice, and the education of professionals. *The Elementary School Journal, 98*(5), 511–526. https://doi.org/10.1086/461912

Shulman, L. S., & Sherin, M. G. (2004). Fostering communities of teachers as learners: Disciplinary perspectives. *Journal of Curriculum Studies, 36*(2), 135–140. https://doi.org/10.1080/0022027032000135049

Siew, Y. M. (2006). Fostering community and a culture of learning in seminary classrooms: A personal journey. *Christian Education Journal*, *3*(1), 79–91. https://doi.org/10.1177/073989130600300106

Simon, K. G. (2001). *Moral questions in the classroom*. Yale University Press.

Sinclair, A. (2013). *Loving the real Israel: An educational agenda for liberal Zionism*. Ben Yehuda Press.

Sinclair, A., Solmsen, B., & Goldwater, C. (2013). *The Israel educator: An inquiry into the preparation and capacities of effective Israel educators*. The Consortium for Applied Studies in Jewish Education. http://www.israel.org/sites/default/files/docs/the-israel-educator.pdf

Sokatch, D. (2021). *Can we talk about Israel?: A guide for the curious, confused, and conflicted*. Bloomsbury Publishing.

Sponenberg, A. K. (2012). Introduction: Meeting students where they are. *Pedagogy*, *12*(3), 541–543.

Stearns, P. N., Seixas, P., & Wineburg, S. (Eds.). (2000). *Knowing, teaching, and learning history: National and international perspectives*. NYU Press.

Stein, K. (2020). Proven success in Israel education: Context, sources, and perspective. In J. Ariel (Ed.), *Israel education: The next edge* (pp. 89–94). Makom/Jewish Agency for Israel.

Stillman, N. (2017). Perceptions and understandings of Israel within Islam. In S.I. Troen & R. Fish (Eds.), *Essential Israel: Essays for the 21st century* (pp. 311–326). Indiana University Press.

Storey, V. A., & Richard, B. M. (2013). Critical friends groups: Moving beyond mentoring. In V. A. Storey (Ed.), *Redesigning professional education doctorates*. Palgrave Macmillan. https://doi.org/10.1057/9781137358295_2

Tadmor-Shimony, T., & Raichel, N. (2013). The Hebrew teachers as creators of the Zionist community in (the land of) Israel. *Israel Studies Review*, *28*(1), 120–141. https://doi.org/10.3167/isr.2013.280108

Tal, A. (2002). Pollution in a promised land. In *Pollution in a Promised Land*. University of California Press.

Talbert, J. E., & McLaughlin, M. W. (1992). *Understanding teaching in context*. Center for Research on the Context of Secondary School Teaching.

Talbert, J. E., & McLaughlin, M. W. (1994). Teacher professionalism in local school contexts. *American Journal of Education*, *102*(2), 123–153. https://doi.org/10.1086/444062

Troen, S. I., & Fish, R. (2017). An invitation to Israel literacy. In S. I. Troen & R. Fish (Eds.), *Essential Israel: Essays for the 21st century* (pp. 1–11). Indiana University Press.

VanSledright, B. (2002). *In search of America's past: Learning to read history in elementary school*. Teachers College Press.

Waxman, D. (2016). *Trouble in the tribe: The American Jewish conflict over Israel*. Princeton University Press

Weimer, M. (2006). *Enhancing scholarly work on teaching and learning*. Jossey-Bass.

Weinreb, A. R. (2022). *Teaching Israel studies: Global, virtual, and ethnographic approaches to active learning*. Palgrave.

Wlodkowski, R. J., & Ginsberg, M. B. (2017). *Enhancing adult motivation to learn: A comprehensive guide for teaching all adults*. John Wiley & Sons.

Wright, G., Hecht, S., Shain, M., Saxe, L., & Howland, S. (2019). *Politics on the quad: Students report on division and disagreement at five US universities*. Brandeis University, Maurice and Marilyn Cohen Center for Modern Jewish Studies.

Yadgar, Y. (2020). *Israel's Jewish identity crisis: State and politics in the Middle East* (Vol. 11). Cambridge University Press.

Young, S. (2006). Student views of effective online teaching in higher education. *The American Journal of Distance Education*, *20*(2), 65–77. https://doi.org/10.1207/s15389286ajde2002_2

Zakai, S. (2014). "My heart is in the East and I am in the West": Enduring questions of Israel education in North America. *Journal of Jewish Education*, *80*(3), 287–318. https://doi.org/10.1080/15244113.2014.937192

Zakai, S. (2019). "Bad things happened": How children of the digital age make sense of violent current events. *The Social Studies*, *110*(2), 67–85. https://doi.org/10.1080/00377996.2018.1517113

Zakai, S. (2022). *My second favorite country: How American Jewish children think about Israel*. NYU Press.

Zakai, S. (2023). The philosophies of Israel education. *Journal of Jewish Education*, *89*(1), 1–5. https://doi.org/10.1080/15244113.2023.2174738

Zeichner, K. M., & Liston, D. P. (2013). *Reflective teaching: An introduction*. Routledge.

Zimmerman, J. (2016). *Campus politics: What everyone needs to know*. Oxford University Press.

Zimmerman, J., & Robertson, E. (2017). *The case for contention*. University of Chicago Press.

PART I
The Reflective Teacher

1
Teaching About Israel as a Modern State of Migration
Learning With Diverse, Inner-City, Nontraditional College Students in New York City

ROBIN A. HARPER

Sitting on the bus from Jerusalem to Tel Aviv, I plan my syllabus for a section on Israel. The bus is air-conditioned but steamy because of people bouncing off each other as the bus lurches in afternoon traffic: Orthodox men with their black-and-white clothes and side-curled hair argue in Yiddish. A solider with a long, blond ponytail giggles with another soldier of Ethiopian origin, guns on their laps, planning their night of drinking and dancing. A few school children rap obscene lyrics in English. A Filipina woman, lap laden with plastic bags, returns to work from her day off. Bored, barely dressed teenagers fixate on their phones. Beehive-hatted Orthodox women's lips quiver while reading prayer books. Outside, Palestinian Israelis queue for buses to Arab towns. Approaching Tel Aviv Central Station, napping Sudanese refugees perch on top of bus shelters as swarthy Jewish shopkeepers beckon passersby to their fruit, furniture, or clothing shops. As I look around, I think: How could I possibly explain this place to my students?

There are many ways to teach about Israel as a modern state of (im)-migration. Israel can be framed in terms of evolving peoplehood, colonialism (mandate period) and post-colonialism,[1] establishing a common language and common culture, managing unfixed administrative/political borders with informal internal borders, conflicts between peoples over shared territorial space, accommodating waves of kaleidoscopes of Olim/(im)migrants/refugees,[2] intra-ethnic (Ashkenazi/Mizrahi/religious/secular)[3] and inter-ethnic (Jewish–Arab) strife, citizen/nation splits, temporary labor migration, or unanticipated large-scale (non-Jewish) irregular migration. Instructors must provide theoretical and historical context. But Israel in many ways defies standard categories—Israel is exceptional as the world's only Jewish state, its history of Hebrew language revival, its creation, and its mass absorption of refugees and immigrants (and exclusion of other refugees), and yet, in many fundamental ways, the Israeli state is just like all other states attempting to meet the needs of its citizens and residents. Should the instructor emphasize uniqueness or similarity or comparative analysis? How ought the instructor challenge preconceived or nonexistent or negative conceptions of Israel?

In this chapter, I deconstruct, illustrate, and explain my own pedagogic decision-making for student-centered teaching about Israel as a modern state of migration with nontraditional students (i.e., urban, ethnic/racial minority, first-generation, working-class, predominantly Muslim or Christian, often older college students). My thoughts are based on my experiences teaching about Israel at York College, a four-year college with a vibrant, diverse, nontraditional student body in the City University of New York system. I set forth a series of pedagogic principles that I have developed for my teaching, using illustrative examples from my class to demonstrate how I enact those principles in my teaching practice. I argue that teaching first-generation, working-class students from diverse backgrounds requires careful attention to the composition of the class and students' prior knowledge and framing the subject matter in a way that is culturally responsive. I mine my own teaching diary and classroom experiences to demonstrate how particular types of pedagogic choices—those that focus on assessing and extending student knowledge by explicitly highlighting the diverse narratives of both students and subject matter—invite students to consider new orientations and understandings of modern Israel. These ideas may be helpful for teaching all students but may be especially so for nontraditional students, as they invite students with disparate backgrounds and levels of preparation into the conversation. As they reimagine Israel and share perspectives, I, too, gain new prisms for perceiving Israel and immigrant incorporation.

My students often have little to no exposure to Israel or, when they do, it is often negative. I may be their first teacher to broach internal Jewish conflict and Israeli–Palestinian issues in an academic environment. Israel is a subject of study in most tertiary learning institutions. Yet, how do we teach effectively when there is a dearth of scholarly literature about teaching Israel to nontraditional students? There are some general-audience pieces reporting experiential learning in Israel to create alliances.[4] In some ways, my students are just like other students: Some are prepared, and others need additional support. Some material will be hard to comprehend. They will need to learn how to learn, not just learn about Israel. To teach them, I draw on best practices from the scholarship of teaching and learning for college students in general as illustrated by the educational researchers included in Susan Ambrose et al.'s (2010) *How Learning Works: Seven Research-Based Principles for Smart Teaching* and Ken Bain's (2004) *What the Best College Teachers Do* and literature focusing on learning needs for teaching nontraditional, minority, diverse college students.

Teaching so students learn is a process and not an outcome. Through interaction and experience, we teach not just learning what to learn (fact-cramming content), but how to learn. These practices increase the likelihood for improved performance and future learning (Ambrose et al., 2010). Real learning changes our knowledge base and also beliefs, behaviors, and attitudes, which can impact other parts of our lives. Learning is thus not something we do to our students but something students do themselves. As Ambrose et al. (2010) argue, "Learning is the direct result of how students interpret and respond to their experiences—conscious and unconscious, past and present" (p. 3). Learning is something that we teachers do *with* our students. Dialogic engagement with students sharpens our teaching as it improves their learning: We learn how to present topics by observing how our students think and reimagine our pedagogy, and they, in turn, learn how to learn better, engaging with new and challenging material.

Classroom Context

To help the reader imagine my classroom, I could cite York College's institutional research boasting students from 80 countries speaking 70 languages; 45% are foreign-born. A quarter are between 25 and 44 years old. Racially, they are 37% Black or African American, 27% Hispanic or Latino, 23% Asian, 6% white, and 7% others (two or more races, Native American, Hawaiians, and others). But these facts often occlude more than they illuminate. My students have been white Africans, Black Germans, Chinese Jamaicans, Indo-Caribbean Trinidadians, and Latinx with surnames like Schmidt and Kobayashi. "African American" means native-born whose families have been in the United States for generations; African-descended immigrants from the Caribbean, Latin America, or elsewhere; international students; and new African immigrants. Many have multiple race or national-origin parents. Muslim students may be American-born African Americans, Middle Easterners, Bosnians, Kosovans, Turks, or Filipinos. Many wear hijab (modest Muslim attire). Jewish students are typically Jews of color (native-born or adopted) or minorities (like Central Asian Bukharin). I am not infrequently the only native-born American person in the classroom. Like 64% of New York City, most belong to immigrant families. They work full-time (holding multiple jobs!) often while caring for children or family. Their economic class is equally diverse: welfare recipients or healthcare workers or retail workers or owners of apartment buildings abroad. My classes benefit from this rich tapestry that makes New York City unique and creates opportunities and challenges to teach students from a kaleidoscope of backgrounds with equally disparate preparation for college. Teaching Israel adds another layer of complexity.

In the next sections, I outline pedagogic principles when teaching about Israel. I cite best practices from the scholarship of teaching and learning, highlighting nontraditional students: situating the course, organizing knowledge, shaping the course by assessing what students know, spurring learning by harnessing conflict.

Teaching the (Partially?) Unknown

Although Israel is daily news, it is virtually acontextual for most of my students. Their familiarity with Israel may be limited to Bible stories or Israel as an aggressor in human rights abuses with Palestinians. As my students learn, their engagement with Israel might evolve into what Reingold (2018) describes for his students as learning "morally complex narratives" (p. 313). They may (rarely!) have visited as Christian pilgrims. Overall, they have no cognizance of Hebrew, history of Judaism, modern Israel, or the conflict-imbued siloed Israeliness described by Kimmerling (2005). This should not be surprising. Given the incendiary nature of political discourse about Israel and fear of introducing religion and politics into the classroom, teachers avoid Israel as a case for comparative government. Since there is no overt campus presence of Hillel or Chabad or anything Jewish, and benign indifference or entrenched antipathy in their neighborhoods, most Israel discourse comes from niche media, music lyrics, and community groups that link America-based racism to the Palestinian plight and assert pro-Palestinian stances about Israel (both factual and hyperbolic).

Teaching my students about the tantalizing array of political and social puzzles in Israel is like and unlike teaching traditional students. The standard concerns in Israel studies—lack of knowledge and preparation—are found in my classroom. Like the students surveyed in the 2015 study at Brandeis University's Cohen Center for Modern Jewish Studies (Koren et al., 2015), my students have knowledge gaps and cannot place facts in context or situate geography or religiosity in Israel. What's different is the goal for my teaching. Unlike teacher-activists who endeavor to make Israel meaningful to their students for the sake of Jewish survival or to enrich Jewish identity (Horowitz, 2012; Winer, 2019) or those who frame learning about Israel as a form of Jewish education (Zakai, 2014), my teaching is firmly rooted in political science, not activism. One of my mentors, the late Israel political scientist Asher Arian, explained about Israel: "It's a state, like any state. It's just a case." My research and teaching engage Israel as a case of migration policy and immigrant incorporation to compare to other states' experience. I state this goal explicitly here to normalize teaching about Israel. We don't expect or demand that people who teach about, say, Zambia or Guyana to have an ulterior (e.g., evangelizing, apologizing, or lambasting) motive; we assess their work on its merits. Teaching Israel need not be different.

Like my students, I came to Israel as an outsider. I learned about Israel from peripheral insiders as an American Field Service exchange student placed with a Yemenite Jewish family. In the 1930s the family's elders fled to Israel, anticipating acceptance in the Jewish homeland, and instead for generations met with discrimination and exclusion from other Jews.[5] Their bittersweet experiences piqued my curiosity about life on the periphery and became part of my professional research agenda studying citizenship borders of inclusion and exclusion. My Israel research explores temporary labor migrants in the Israeli national narrative. In the classroom, I incorporate Israel through multiple perspectives in the required and elective political science classes I teach.

Pedagogic Plans

Teaching students to be good learners requires establishing good learning practices. I want to show my students how to engage with primary sources, learn context by listening to different voices, perform critical analysis, and always remember the purpose of the learning quest (Ambrose et al., 2010). To introduce Israel to students with little to no exposure and use their diversity (in background and thought) to our advantage, I begin with poetry since it requires no prior knowledge and allows me to invite the students into my pedagogic plan. I assess their prior knowledge and use the data to guide discussion and context. Using provocative multimedia materials—film, cartoons, political advertisements, and so on—to elicit a spectrum of thought, we practice having civil, contentious discussions. Hands-on critical mapmaking empowers them. We discuss policy successes and failings and cui bono questions. Admittedly, sometimes I fail, and then, I must invent new approaches to achieve our learning objectives.

To immerse my students in (unknown) Israeli life and illustrate the political in everyday life, including problematic narratives, I show photos and play audio and video recordings depicting electioneering and commercials, soldiers visiting historic sites, open-air markets, supermarkets, schools, bag searches at mall entries, ubiquitous technology use, Shabbat sirens, the separation wall, border-crossing, farms, tony neighborhoods, asylum seekers sleeping on bus shelters, and Tel Aviv beaches. I take images, embed them in context, and model critical thinking. We read Yehuda Amichai's poem "Tourists" (1980/2013), which laments how tourists visit ruins, pay respects at Yad Vashem (Holocaust museum), and have fun yet are oblivious to contemporary Israel before their eyes. I use this poem to remind my students that we too are tourists, observing, remembering, and enjoying learning, but we are not studying institutions of power in Israel for their own sake but because they are created by and affect real people. Amichai (1980/2013) writes:

> I said to myself: redemption will come only if their guide tells them, "You see that arch from the Roman period? It's not important: but next to it, left and down a bit, there sits a man who's bought fruit and vegetables for his family." (pp. 137–138)

Like Amichai's guide, our institutional analysis requires thinking about institutional creation and its impact on Israelis and considering how institutions should work, where they fail, how the institutional rules affect outcomes, and more. "Neutral" practices of governance may have disparate effects on Jewish, Palestinian, and the spectrum of other non-Jewish citizens and residents of Israel. Nontraditional students often lament texts ignoring minority presence. By making explicit that laws, practices, and institutions affect groups in different (and sometimes unanticipated) ways, my students see their experiences mirrored elsewhere and gain new ways of framing issues and seeking solutions.

Assess What Students Know and Work From There

In considering what the best college teachers do, Ken Bain (2004) asks, "What should my students be able to do intellectually, physically or emotionally as a result of their leaning?" "How can I best help and encourage them to develop those abilities and the habits of the heart and mind to use them?" (p. 49). Like many before him (Tyler, 1949; Wiggins & McTighe, 1998), Bain suggests everything follows from the learning objectives: asking what I want students to know by semester's end and then working backwards. For a course on migration in Israel, I want them to understand how states and societies are inclusive and exclusive, contextual issues giving rise to political and social conflicts, and connections between disparate groups in Israel and its neighbors. They should know how to make evidenced-based arguments. I imagine how to develop those competences and map them onto a 15-week semester.

To estimate students' knowledge, I use a survey (see Appendix) derived from the Israel Literacy Measurement Project (Koren et al., 2015). Usually, students laugh when completing the survey, which—despite its superficiality—reveals knowledge gaps. Sometimes, students hold firm convictions, so the thrust of the class is developing arguments and counterarguments by exposing, examining, and critiquing evidence. Students may misperceive Israel because they misunderstand evidence or because Israel is unknown. In the latter case, my teaching is no different than when presenting any other low-emotion topic, like rentier states or parliamentary democracy. I have to tantalize them with interesting texts. Students must trust that the professor knows what to teach and that the material is important for their education. When students don't know, instructors must lead. When students do know, instructors must push them to the next level. More problematic is teaching students with firm, unsupported positions. Ambrose et al. (2010) suggest that inaccurate or flawed prior knowledge is the most difficult to dislodge because it "predispos[es] students to ignore, discount, or resist evidence that conflicts with what they believe to be true" (p. 24). In my classroom, some students may fervently assert that Israel has a religious ultraorthodox demographic majority or is politically unified in supporting expansionist, militaristic greater Israel. The challenge remains getting them to trust me so they consider contradictory information.

One powerful tool to engage students with any degree of familiarity with Israel is student-created maps. Mapping Israel teaches observation, situating context, topography, and the administrative reach of the state. It etches material into the students' minds. Most critically, students generate their own view, as "(a) map is a scientific abstraction of reality. A map merely represents something which already exists objectively 'there'" (Anderson, 1983, p. 173). For students who know little about Israel, their maps likely summarize and reflect reference books. However, for those attempting to express ideas about Israel, like my more advanced students, the relationship is reversed. The map anticipates "spatial reality, not vice versa," as Anderson (1983) explained about 19th-century cartographic representations that made their own reality to control space (p.173). "(The) map was a model for, rather than a model of, what it purported to represent," and further the map had become "a real instrument to concretize projections on the earth's surface" (Anderson, 1983, p. 174). There is an element of power in drawing, including and excluding, and shaping imaginations of space and place for student-cartographers and viewers.

Students are given a blank sheet of paper and a week to draw a map of Israel. On purpose, I leave decisions about what to include or omit and where to get information, situate borders, sites, and so on to the students' discretion. The more choice, the more opportunity to create conversations about contention and agreement. For maximum value, maps must be hand drawn. These are the directions:

All students are responsible for drawing a map of Israel. It must be hand drawn, reflecting the political borders of the state. You should include built spaces and any important topographic items like waterways, mountains, deserts, etc. Mark items that you believe are important for representing Israel.

I couple this exercise with excerpts or full articles by Yair Wallach (2011) or Christine Leuenberger and Izhak Schnell (2010) about the politics of mapmaking about Israel.

On sharing day, we sit in a circle as students present their maps. We discuss the images and decisions for borders, capital, major cities, and so on. I ask them to note how the maps differ. Some include occupied territory and some don't. Some mark Jerusalem or West Jerusalem as the capital, some write Al-Quds, still others Tel Aviv. Some know why they made their choices; others state they "just copied it," and we discuss why different sources might name different cities as the capital. This allows teaching critical information consumption and production in the service of the politics of naming, citing, remembering, and forgetting. Our readings interrogate the politics of the representation of Israel in maps—contested areas, morphing lines, the timing of this particular iteration, how the lines appeared at different moments, and more. I ask probing questions to identify how topography might shape experience.

Mapmaking projects teach Israel through *legibility* and *imageability*. Mapmaking is a tangible and concrete activity that forces students to lay bare their assumptions and reveal knowing and not knowing. In Lynch's (1960) mapmaking work, local residents were asked to sketch their neighborhoods, intending to make their mental maps explicit. These maps conveyed *legibility*, or "the ease with which... [city] parts can be recognized and can be organized into coherent patterns," and *imageability*, or "that quality in a physical object which gives it a high probability of evoking a strong image in any given observer" (p. 9).

My students' maps sharpen perception through geographic legibility (based on Bar-Gal, 1979). Every stroke situates Israel in their minds and makes it tangible. Decisions about what to render and what to ignore provoke critical cartography, illustrating that maps are neither value-free nor politically neutral. Mapmaking creates, internalizes, reflects, and perpetuates power relations, normally in favor of the dominant group. Especially in states with contested borders, drawing maps provokes critical thinking, exploring and exposing visual rhetoric carved into the map. Students learn that states manipulate borders to meet their needs, and these politics get written into borders and the perceptions of borders (Anderson, 1991; Bar-Gal, 1979; Leuenberger & Schnell, 2010; Shachar, 2020). Further, borders and other markers exist (in memory and practice) long after they have been dismantled and are denied (in memory and practice), even when they are physically present (Green, 2018).

Mapmaking exercises empower students to name and claim sites, territory, and power relations. Students must defend choices they may have deemed inconsequential and appreciate how decisions reflect real political choices. Sometimes, students are apprehensive with their maps, unsure why they selected or named an item, and must work to defend their maps. It can be awkward making assertions when other classmates disagree or are indifferent. As the instructor, my job here is to help the students engage in a conversation. For those who simply copied, I can ask them to look at the other maps and ask other students about their choices, or I ask where they got their information and ask them to use their cell phones to look up alternative sites. The assigned readings discuss the spectrum of choices and maps over time so we can return to the readings to deepen understanding. For traditionally disempowered students, it's challenging to assert the imagination and "power" to move a capital or a border. This exercise can be uneasy for some and for others empowering, revealing that anyone with a politically winning narrative can reshape space.

At semester's end, I assign a second revision: "Knowing what you know now, what would you change?" Again, it is a heady power to render reality on paper. We reconvene, taking our places in the circle. Students show "before" and "after" maps. Sometimes, maps remain unchanged. (Solidified conviction? Laziness? Pleased with initial orientations? I don't know.) Students' maps may adopt new perspectives, highlighting elements absent in the first map and eliminating other items. Sometimes names change or points of interest emerge. Decisions to use a Hebrew or an Arabic or an English name imbues meaning, as does drawing the separation wall or including (or excluding) occupied territories or changing the capital city. Similarly, situating markets or tourist sites or military outposts or communal farms (kibbutzim) also carries meaning. Using critical cartography, I ask the students to explain and defend their choices. The exercise provides a vocabulary for teaching and learning about Israel and a structure to discuss Israel long after they have left this classroom. This exercise pushes students to become self-directed learners—the most effective way to engrain practices for lifelong learners (Ambrose et al., 2010)—applying skills and reflecting what they want to express or repress about Israel.

Making Use of Diversity, Cultural Competences, and Conflict

The delightful advantage of teaching in diverse classrooms is that students bring different perspectives on issues and readings. This is not to say that it is not challenging; it is! Teaching a classroom of diverse, nontraditional students requires cultural competence—integrated attitudes, knowledge, and skills to teach diverse cultures, groups, and communities—and flexibility. Some students link their personal identity and collective racial or ethnic destiny with the Palestinian cause. Expected conflicts emerge over the morality of the origins and expansion of Israel or devolve into lobs about Israeli militarism and connecting it to racial conflict in the United States. It's sometimes hard to keep the class on topic. Conflicts can be helpful in teaching, though, helping students learn debate parameters, multiple perspectives, and honing arguments (Bain, 2004). It is critical that instructors establish a firm plan and keep the learning objectives in mind: We are not having a conversation about "stuff," but using readings and discussion to achieve learning objectives. Different perspectives are not impediments but alternate pathways to the learning objectives! Free discussion of ideas can lead the conversation astray, so I intervene with probing questions and ask others to comment to get us back on track. I use an online discussion board and post multiple opposing-viewpoint articles about the topic that "led us astray."

One way to approach culturally competent teaching and learning is to show the "multiple Israels" (Marom, 2012), to anchor on what students already know, to meet them where they are, and to expose what intrigues them intellectually. Marom's (2012) Israel course revolved around seven different Israels that connect across time: biblical Israel, rabbinic Israel, Christian and Anglo-Christian Israel, Islamic Israel, Zionist Israel, Palestinian Israel, American Jewish Zion. Although this might work for a group somewhat or very familiar with Jewish Israel, it ignores other perspectives on Israel that could be helpful. Marom (2012) notes that his students brought two more Israels to his attention: African American and messianic Israel. From my own work, I would add immigration-land Israel, and, outside my parochial interest, there is also high-tech Israel, LGBTQ+ Israel, military-industrial Israel. This relationship model displays the state and society in three dimensions—looking at historic, ideologic, religious, ethnic, international relations, and other perspectives—and it reveals the multifaceted state and society over time and space. This mode of teaching permits students to jump in at any point they are comfortable and makes connections with the instructor helping the students to compare and explore elements of sameness, difference, and change by viewing Israel from different perspectives. Our richly multicultural classrooms are perfectly situated to engage diversity for its best aspect: the ability to draw on disparate perspectives to make sense of political and social puzzles.

Students find greater motivation and perform better academically when instructional methods complement student-learning characteristics (Gentry & Ellison, 1981). The education professor James Vasquez (1990) asserts,

"Teachers who boast that they 'treat all students the same' are not showing their democratic disposition, but rather that they are not yet prepared to teach in the pluralistic classrooms of American schools" (p. 300). My students are not monolithically "minority" but an absolute spectrum of diversity, each requiring a panoply of cultural competences to learn about Israel. To be effective, I need to know my students. I learn their names and connect lectures by recalling something that Charles or Aisha said the previous week.[6] My teaching must incorporate culturally diverse perspectives and encourage opinion sharing and challenges to me, their classmates, and our readings. I must develop their trust by being student-centered inside and outside the classroom and through availability, mentoring, or "othermothering" (Guiffrida, 2005). In upper-level, smaller classes, it is easier than in large lectures. I anticipate opposition over facts or interpretations and fixed positions and prepare counters. But where to start?

Share What Excites You and Provide Context to Build Comprehension

Teaching migration requires contextual knowledge to grasp the push-and-pull factors that provoke migration; movement, settlement, and interactions with others; intractable violence; historical moments; state policies and reactions; and so on. Israel presents some enigmatic issues as both a new modern state and a historically ancient state, with waves of mass Jewish migration and interspersed other kinds of migration, inclusion and exclusion, and, throughout, conflict over migration, neighbors and territory. These complexities and contradictions have always intrigued me because I found it exciting to see how modern migration regimes emerge by tracing how a relatively new state like Israel made policy decisions, how people engaged with those policies, and then how the interaction gave birth to new policies and problems.

Ken Bain (2004) suggests in *What the Best College Teachers Do* that deep learning happens when instructors frame learning experiences as big questions and problems. Effective instructors reflect on what drew them to study a certain discipline, consider what issues intrigue contemporary students, and make explicit connections between the two. The instructor needs to show how the course material matters and connects it to pressing problems.

The first step was determining how to situate our conversations about the state's founding and concomitant migration. But where to begin: Religion? The history of antisemitism, the Holocaust, and Zionism? Colonialism, settlement, terrorism against Palestinians? I must address inaccurate prior knowledge that can impede students' learning (Ambrose et al., 2010). In the following section, I draw from my teaching diary,[7] anticipating and reflecting on teaching a section about Israel.[8]

I couldn't sleep the night before the lesson about Israel. With so much antisemitism and anti-Israel sentiment in colleges across the nation, what will my class be like? Will there be backlash? Will my class end up on social media? I wonder if my students know the story of the covenant?[9] By practice, I never mention religion in class, but how can I explain competing claims to territory if they don't know this fundamental narrative? I must present religious, historic, ideologic, and legal claims. The person I am most concerned about is Lamin, an intelligent, reserved, devout Muslim from west Africa. I open the lesson recounting the covenant with Abraham. There's a lot of head-shaking and big-eyes. Lamin is the first to speak, "Professor, Abraham is Ishmael's father. So, the land goes to the children of Ishmael." I tell him that the Jews tell the story differently and that in the Jewish version Hagar is the handmaiden, not the wife of Abraham. So, the land goes to his first child with his wife, Sarah. "No way! Hagar was his wife!" (I am viscerally stung by every "no way." This lesson is hard.) Lamin sits incredulously shaking his head, "Really? The Jews believe that?" Michael, a Caribbean-American student whose mother traveled to Israel with her church, announces, "It's in the Old Testament!" The rest of the students look at me blankly... I talk about the origins of Zionism in Europe as part of a discussion about nationalism in the 19th and 20th centuries. None had ever thought of Zionism as "just another 'ism,'" another 19th century political ideology. I say a few words about colonialism and the mandate period. No reaction from anyone. I mention that Israeli settlement can be understood as late-arriving colonialism. Still no reaction. This is new information... I come to the Holocaust. Looking at their faces, I realize some of my students have never seen pictures of the Shoah.[10] The students look in horror at the pictures.

I feared this lesson would be difficult because of strongly held beliefs. That was true, but it was also hard because they had no knowledge on which to build. This had serious implications for our lesson. I had not anticipated their lack of knowledge about the Holocaust and their shock. I needed to be more empathic and prepare them appropriately. After all, the rationale for the establishment of the state of Israel would make no sense without knowing about historical antisemitism and the Holocaust. Was this lack of knowledge a general student problem or only students like mine? Fifty-six percent of American college students polled by the Conference on Jewish Material Claims Against Germany in the U.S. Millennial Holocaust Knowledge and Awareness Survey (2020) were unaware of Auschwitz.[11] My students were like many other U.S. college students, lacking historical context and exposure.

> *The lecture continued about refugees sneaking into mandate Palestine, seeking international recognition, and the struggle over rights to land. I explained modes of land acquisition—ceding, buying, conquest, expulsion, etc. At some point, I must have said something like "There were no Palestinians yet." Lamin pounced: "Are you denying there were no people there?" "Of course, there were people living on that land since forever! At the end of the Arab-Israeli war (1948–1949), ushering in the modern State of Israel, 700,000 Arabs became refugees, unable to return to their homes." Lamin said, "Then how can you say there were no Palestinians!" [More buzzing in the class. I love that my students feel comfortable challenging me and their classmates but it can be unnerving sometimes; this was one of them.] I said to him again that there were no "Palestinians" in the current sense. There were also no "Israelis." Lamin's face contorted, perplexed. I explained: Becoming Palestinian was a not a primordial fact, but required the development of the idea of being Palestinian. Being Israeli was no different. There were no Israelis until there was an Israel and a collective sense of belonging. They became "Israelis" with a unique culture larger than Jewish religious practices as they developed politics, language, economy, ways of thinking, etc.[12] Becoming Palestinian in the modern sense took time to cultivate. The May 1964 First Arab Palestine Congress established the Palestine Liberation Organization. Its call for Palestinians to unite to demand Palestine as their homeland generated a solidified idea of Palestinianism. In so doing, they claimed the right*

> to peoplehood. In international law, only peoples have claims to land, not collectives of individuals. The Palestinians needed to become a people before they could claim rights as a people. Lamin smiled. "Ok. I get it, Professor. That makes sense." He understood I was holding Israelis and Palestinians to the same standard; each needed to create a people in order to be one.

This journal entry reveals the importance of providing multiple narratives, allowing space for students to ask questions and to contest ideas, using prior knowledge to build ideas, taking students seriously, and being honest in our presentation. Migration stories are fraught, reflecting the ruptures that occur with leaving, arriving, settling, engaging, in-betweenness, longing, belonging, attachment, and exclusion. As the instructor, even with assessments, it's not easy to know how much information students need to make sense of the narratives around migration. Without some contextual foundation in religion, antisemitism, the Holocaust, Zionist ideology, relations with the Palestinians and Israel's neighbors and the international community—topics often beyond the usual scope of migration studies—it would be very hard for students to grasp how Israel's refugee resettlement/absorption policies emerged and Israel's conflicts as a modern migration state. I was afraid to confront my students about the origins of the state of Israel, mostly because it is, candidly, uncomfortable to talk about religion and antisemitism in the classroom. The not discussing religion aspect reflects a desire to be perceived as "modern" and "scientific" and a very American practice of keeping private beliefs outside of public discourse.

My students are passionately engaged in questions of racism, but other social injustices—sexism, antisemitism, homophobia, caste issues, income inequality, and so on—do not always have the same resonance. I had not anticipated their lack of exposure to the Holocaust. There must be a first time to view these gruesome images. (Why in my class?!) As instructors, we must be prepared for students' shock and plan time and discussion. Mentioning antisemitism opens the door to potential conflict. My students may be deniers or underestimate contemporary antisemitism or be unaware of the historic and contemporary antisemitism that provokes Jewish migration to Israel and elsewhere. Teaching contentious concepts requires courage, especially when the facts are politically or socially unpopular. It can be an unpleasant experience. However, for students to learn, candor is the most important quality, and that requires being honest brokers when presenting Israel as a way to develop trust.

Being Honest Brokers and Engaging Prior Knowledge

As a long-time instructor, the demographic changes in the student body are obvious in my classroom. When I began teaching, students were older, sandwich generation students, arriving from work in their uniforms. They read texts differently than my contemporary students, often because they had lived some of the "history" I teach now. There was no fact-checking in class—partly because there was no Google! They challenged instructors on meaning and interpretation. My students today are younger, more technologically savvy, and bombarded with information of varying degrees of truth. They are suspicious of official perspectives and those that run contrary to their established positions. Developing trust and convincing students of the validity of narratives is often a critical challenge. This means knowing and presenting multiple perspectives and critiques.

I am not alone in this estimation. Across the political spectrum, experts assert the importance of truth in teaching millennial and Gen Z students.[13] The author of U.S. Senate Special Committee on Aging reports on workforce management, Ann Arnof Fishman (2016), asserted, "Critical to understanding this generation is knowing how they respond to *honesty*. Quite simply, they *demand* it" (emphasis in the original; p. 255). In the contentious Israel Project's Global Language Dictionary (communications strategies to convince people to support Israel's policies), the communications strategist Frank Luntz (2009) speaks specifically about teaching about Israel and explains that if professors want to reach millennial and Gen Z students when they teach about Israel, they need to "get real" and tell the whole story—good, bad, embarrassing, iconic, and so on. Contemporary students will reject anything that appears one-sided. Strong students will reject the whole message if their trusted teachers impart a positively curated story. Telling the whole truth and teaching students to critically evaluate information and narratives can be complicated and painful. Engaging with morally complex narratives is hard, but through confrontation, students can develop stronger and more sophisticated relationships to the subject matter, in this case, Israel (Reingold, 2018).

In my class, I use film to introduce a complex narrative in an accessible way. Through *James' Journey to Jerusalem* (Alexandrowicz, 2003), a poignant, bittersweet film about a Christian pilgrim turned temporary labor migrant in Israel, we travel together to a place completely different and absolutely the same as home. James is a religious tourist, but police assume he is an illegal border crosser and imprison him. Awaiting deportation, James prays for intervention. A "miracle" happens: James is released to an unscrupulous manpower recruiter who forces James to join a migrant crew performing dirty, dull, and dangerous work or face deportation. James works in Israelis' homes, observing relationships between and among Israelis and foreigners. An elderly man befriends James, teaching him a theme of Israeli culture: Don't become a sucker. James follows this advice and makes his time more lucrative by subcontracting work to other migrants and working side jobs. James laments how everyone cheats each other: Israelis cheat migrants, migrant churches feign support while mercilessly extracting migrants' savings, migrants subcontract thus cheating other migrants, families abandon the elderly, and Israelis cheat each other. Immigration police capture James for deportation. Still, James longs to complete his pilgrimage to Jerusalem. The audience is left puzzling what is still "holy" in the holy land and yet... believers still believe.

James's tale is not an unusual migration story in any country where wanted and unwanted migrants seek work. It lays bare the precarity experienced by labor migrants who leave their homes to work abroad ostensibly for a delimited time: facing discrimination and othering, desperate to earn money, longing for home, and questioning whether their journey was worth the cost. James's "pilgrimage" is perhaps exceptional. However, migration often carries an almost religious aura.

My immigrant students (or their families) know this migration narrative intimately: James's journey is their journey too. For some, they, their parents, or family friends work as domestics, nannies, or gardeners. They understand the precarity and loneliness of immigrant life. They commiserate with being cheated by the receiving society and co-ethnics. They fear failing. We talk about how James's migration story is both typical and exceptional. I am embarrassed by the Israelis portrayed in the film, as I would be observing anyone's unscrupulous behavior. I admit to myself that there is a risk in having this conversation: I know some students will leave the class thinking only of Israeli misdeeds and confirm any latent beliefs of Israel as a site of unethical behavior. To return to my earlier analogy, whether teaching about Zambia or Guyana or Israel, with limited views of foreign places, it's critical but complicated to present a fair perspective so students can decide for themselves. I have to trust that my earlier lessons about Israel presented a multifaceted image: a state and society where things function well and also don't, where people are included and excluded, where the economy works well and also fails. By showing them a film offering a complex view of Israel, we can discuss hard truths, and then they might trust me on other issues too.

Engage Students by Building on Prior Knowledge

Except for classes on the sociology of religion or anthropology or religion as a political force, religion is normally outside social science curricula. Our academic tradition treats science and religion as fundamentally different: Social science is built on facts and proof, and religion, as part of the humanities, on faith and reason.[14] In teaching, we keep religion separate because of religion's propensity to exclude (especially when endeavoring to open the university to ethnically and religiously pluralistic student bodies), assertions about the incompatibility of science and religion, lack of competence about religion(s), and so on. Ironically, avoiding religious discourse may preclude tools to learn about Israel. Unlike many traditional students who eschew religion, many of my students, raised in the Black church or other religious traditions, are comfortable with religious discourse and expression. Black Americans are considered the most religious segment of the U.S. population (Pew Forum, 2014). Some Muslim students may be accustomed to public religious expression, as they often wear traditional and modest garb and pray publicly. (Our college allots a corridor for prayer and offers a Wudu room for ablutions in anticipation of prayer.)[15] Immigrants (especially first generation) often look to religious practice and communities to navigate the emotional dislocation experienced through immigration (Sall, 2021). In her study on Black African immigrants in NYC schools, Sall (2021) reveals that religion is part of students' daily lives and shapes understanding of racial and ethnic boundaries. Professors can use religious knowledge to explain concepts, building from this prior knowledge to provide an anchor for student learning (Ambrose et al., 2010; Bain, 2004).

Talking about Israel, the home of the three Abrahamic religions (and their various sects) and an important site for other religions,[16] as well as the site of conflicts and chasms between the religious and secular, requires at least a basic familiarity with religious traditions. Even if Israeli current affairs are unknown, my students may be intimate with Jerusalem from religious practice. Jerusalem is not foreign to them; it is the site where Jesus walked or Mohammad ascended. "Knowing" Jerusalem facilitates a conversation. It's a beginning. They can tell me about these places and then move from the ancient and religious/mythic to the contemporary, or from their religious practice to religious conflicts in contemporary Israel. This connects to what Marom (2012) calls "multiple Israels" and is what allows students to connect to Israel across time and space and to understand the development of Israel. Attachment to religious imaginations can be both useful and fraught. Positively, the instructor can use familiarity to build a connection of how religions order daily life or celebrate events or what have you to grasp, for example, Israel's lack of separation of church and state (a concept that is extremely arduous for American students to comprehend, especially when the "church" is not Christian!). For instance, if we discuss the ways the state carves space for various groups to establish rules for their own members, students comprehend that each religion—not the civil state—legally establishes its own rules for marriage and divorce and the ways that might be problematic.[17] Negatively, for many with no knowledge of modern Israel, their children's Bible Israel picture clashes with their mind-image of ubiquitous soldiers meandering around Israel. They struggle in making sense of this cognitive dissonance and with accepting Israel as a normal place with bus stops, jails, shopping malls, schools, bars, and so on. For those without a religious connection or knowledge of modern Israel, the place remains foreign. I must use images, texts, film, music, and more to render it real, a task that is not different from the difficulty teaching any completely unknown concept or place.

From my classroom experience, a diverse Israel composed of the "ingathering of the exiles" and their families from across the globe, Palestinian Israelis, temporary labor migrants, and African asylum seekers is quizzical. Middle Eastern or African-origin Muslims with some knowledge of the region are intrigued by faces of Israeli Jews from North Africa and Asia (Mizrahi) and Ethiopia, expecting Israelis to be fairer skinned and monolithic. The only image that never surprises them is the ubiquitous Israeli soldier, an image hammered in the media and their political discourse.

Conclusion

How can we teach urban, ethnic/racial minority, first-generation, working-class, predominantly Muslim or Christian or nones, often older, mostly non-Jewish college students about Israel? This is what I hope this chapter adds to the conversation. Teaching about Israel has been a core concern of Jewish educators for decades. Its purpose remains contentious and its goals unclear (Grant et al., 2013). This fraught lack of clarity matches the feelings Jewish students have about Israel (Zakai, 2011). Teaching about Israel often renders it into advocacy training to defend Israel from detractors and denies the existence of conflicting plural opinions about Israel (Grant et al., 2013). These efforts focus on anticipating detractors rather than creating space for the learners to wrestle with their thoughts about Israel (Grant et al., 2013).

Further, teaching Israel has generally been considered a "Jewish endeavor." An Israel scholar once quizzically asked me: "If they're not Jewish why would they take your class about Israel?" My answer is that we study immigration in France and Germany, why not Israel? Israel provides a fascinating case of settlement and return, refugees/asylum seekers, absorption and exclusion, border policies and citizenship, temporary labor migration, and ethnonational citizenship. In Israel in 2018, 23% of the Jewish majority was foreign born, 32% was second generation (Israelis born to immigrant parents), and 47% was third generation (Israelis born to Israeli-born parents; Raijman, 2020). Israel is among the world's top sites for temporary labor migration and remittances. Simultaneously, as the Pew Research Center (Davis & Fry, 2019) determined, students attending college are more ethnically and racially diverse than ever before. There are more students on campus who are unlikely to have any relationship to Israel, and if they do, it's often negative. Some students, native-born and immigrant alike, have adopted Israel-critical discourses or Palestinian calls for statehood as tied to their own racial/ethnic justice pleas. If we teach honestly and coherently about Israel, they will have facts, a spectrum of interpretations, and the ability to engage in analytical inquiry to form their own arguments buttressed by good evidence. In this way, we can provide a meaningful education about Israel for all of our students.

Appendix

Name _____

Survey of knowledge about Israel

1. Circle Israel on the map below: (map is not included in this volume but is provided to students in class)

2. What form of government does Israel have? _____

3. When was the State of Israel founded? _____

4. How many people live in Israel? _____

5. What kinds of people live in Israel? _____
_____

6. When you think of Israel, what comes to mind? _____
_____

7. What issues are important in Israeli politics? _____
_____

8. What kinds of conflicts are there in Israeli society? _____
_____

9. What role does religion play in Israel? _____
_____

10. Have you or a family member/friend ever visited Israel? _____

ACKNOWLEDGMENTS

I would like to thank my students for being willing to take a chance on learning new things. I would like to thank Professors Antonia Layard, Irving Leonard Markovitz, Michael Sharpe; the anonymous reviewers; and the editors of this book, Matt Reingold and Sivan Zakai, for their comments on previous drafts. Any remaining errors are, of course, mine.

NOTES

1. From 1918–1948, the British controlled Palestine as a result of a League of Nations mandate.

2. Jews immigrating to Israel are understood to be "Olim," or those returning to Israel.

3. Ashkenazi Jews trace familial roots from Europe, whereas Mizrahi Jews trace familial roots from the Middle East and North Africa.

4. See Hennerson (2021); Fullwood (2018).

5. My student-exchange host sister critically chronicled the family's journey from Yemen to Israel (Tsabari, 2019).

6. All students mentioned in this paper are referred to by pseudonym.

7. My teaching diaries are notes, diagrams, and reflections about successful and failing lessons. These scribbles and involved fieldnotes ameliorate my pedagogy.

8. Italics are the fieldnotes. Normal text is my reflections after the fact. The language has been edited for clarity.

9. The biblical agreement between God and Abraham establishing monotheism in exchange for promising a great nation.

10. Hebrew term for the Holocaust.

11. A 50-state survey on Holocaust knowledge among millennials and Gen Z.

12. I am not arguing for or against any group's historical claim to Israel-Palestine or suggesting that there was no unbroken presence of Jews or Arabs in Israel-Palestine. Rather, the development of constituent stories of peoplehood which include coherent narratives (Smith, 2003) shape identity, political action, and render claims for rights in the modern nation-state system.

13. Millennials were born 1980–1996. Gen Z was born 1997–2012.

14. Clearly, different religious traditions have competing ideas about questioning, faith, good works, etc.

15. Wudu is a traditional Muslim ritual cleansing in preparation for prayer.

16. The Bahá'í World Center is located in Haifa. Samaritans and other nonofficially recognized religions also call Israel home.

17. For more information, see Schultz (2023).

REFERENCES

Ambrose, S. A., Bridges, M. W., DiPietro, M., Lovett, M. C., & Norman, M. K. (2010). *How learning works: Seven research-based principles for smart teaching*. Jossey-Bass, A Wiley Imprint.

Amichai, Y. (2013). *The selected poetry of Yehuda Amichai*. University of California Press. (Original work published 1980)

Alexandrowicz, R., Shibe, S. M., Dau, S., & Elias, A. (2004). *James' Journey to Jerusalem*. Zeitgeist Films.

Anderson, B. (1983). *Imagined communities: Reflections on the origin and spread of nationalism* (2nd ed.). Verso books. https://hdl.handle.net/2027/heb.01609

Bain, K. (2004). *What the best college teachers do*. Harvard University Press. https://doi.org/10.5465/amle.2008.32712626

Bar-Gal, Y. (1979). Perception of borders in a changing territory: The case of Israel. *Journal of Geography*, 78(7), 273–276. https://doi.org/10.1080/00221347908980631

Claims Conference. (2020). *First-ever 50-state survey on holocaust knowledge of American millennials and Gen z reveals shocking results*. U.S. Millennial Holocaust Knowledge and Awareness Survey, Claims Conference. https://www.claimscon.org/millennial-study/

Davis, L., & Fry, R. (2019, July 31). College faculty have become more racially and ethnically diverse, but remain far less so than students. *Pew Research Center*. https://www.pewresearch.org/fact-tank/2019/07/31/us-college-faculty-student-diversity/

Fishman, A. A. (2016). How generational differences will impact America's aging workforce: Strategies for dealing with aging millennials, Generation X, and baby boomers. *Strategic HR Review* 15(6), 250–257. https://doi.org/10.1108/SHR-08-2016-0068

Fullwood, A. (2018, August 7). *The relationship between African-American students and Israel*. The FAMUAN. http://www.thefamuanonline.com/2018/08/07/the-relationship-between-african-american-students-and-israel

Gentry, R., & Ellison, V. G. (1981, February). *Instructional strategies that challenge Black college students in the area of exceptional child education* [Paper presentation]. The Council for Exceptional Children Conference on The Exceptional Black Child, New Orleans, LA, United States.

Grant, L. D., Marom, D., & Werchow, Y. (2013). *Israel education for what? An investigation of the purposes and possible outcomes of Israel education*. Israel Education Research Briefs for the Consortium for Applied Studies in Jewish Education. https://www.bjpa.org/search-results/publication/20971

Green, S. F. (2018). Lines, traces, and tidemarks: Further reflections on forms of border. in O. Demetriou & R. Dimova (Eds.), *The political materialities of borders: New theoretical Directions: Vol. 2. Rethinking Borders* (pp. 67–83). University of Manchester.

Guiffrida, D. (2005). Othermothering as a framework for understanding African American students' definitions of student-centered faculty. *The Journal of Higher Education*, 76(6), 701–723. https://doi.org/10.1353/jhe.2005.0041

Hennerson, E. T. (2021, March 4). Black college students visit Israel in alliance to fight anti-Semitism, bias. *Tennessee Tribune*. https://tntribune.com/black-college-students-visit-israel-in-alliance-to-fight-anti-semitism-bias

Horowitz, B. (2012). *Defining Israel education*. The iCenter for Israel Education. https://

theicenter.org/wp-content/uploads/2021/03/Defining-Israel-Education-January-2012.pdf

Kimmerling, B. (2005). *The Invention and decline of Israeliness: State, society, and the Military*. University of California Press.

Koren, A., Fishman, S., Aronson, J. K., & Saxe, L. (2015). *The Israel literacy measurement project: 2015 Report*. Brandeis University Cohen Center for Modern Jewish Studies. https://bir.brandeis.edu/bitstream/handle/10192/31191/IsraelLiteracyMeasurement1.pdf

Leuenberger, C., & Schnell, I. (2010). The politics of maps: Constructing national territories in Israel. *Social Studies of Science, 40*(6), 803–842. https://doi.org/10.1177/0306312710370377

Luntz, F. (2009). *Global language dictionary*. The Israel Project. https://www.transcend.org/tms/wp-content/uploads/2014/07/sf-israel-projects-2009-global-language-dictionary.pdf

Lynch, K. (1960). *The Image of the City*. MIT Press.

Marom, D. (2012). *Israel and the liberal arts: Notes from a teaching experiment*. Jewish Virtual Library. https://www.jewishvirtuallibrary.org/jsource/isdf/IsraelLiberalArts_Marom.pdf

Pew Forum. (2014). *U.S. religious landscape study* [Infographic]. Pew Research Center. https://www.pewforum.org/religious-landscape-study/importance-of-religion-in-ones-life/among/racial-and-ethnic-composition/black/

Raijman, R. (2020, June 5). A warm welcome for some: Israel embraces immigration of Jewish diaspora, sharply restricts labor migrants and asylum seekers. *Migration Policy Institute*. https://www.migrationpolicy.org/article/israel-law-of-return-asylum-labor-migration

Reingold, M. (2018). Broadening perspectives on immigrant experiences: Secondary students study the absorption difficulties faced by Mizrachi immigrants in Israel. *Journal of Jewish Education, 84*(3), 312–329. https://doi.org/10.1080/15244113.2018.1478531

Sall, D. (2021). Love thy neighbour? Religion and ethnoracial boundaries among second-generation West African youth. *Ethnic and Racial Studies*. https://doi.org/10.1080/01419870.2021.2001026

Schultz, R. G. (2023). *Civil marriage in Israel*. My Jewish Learning. https://www.myjewishlearning.com/article/civil-marriage-in-israel

Shachar, A. (2020). *The shifting border: Legal cartographies of migration and mobility*. Manchester University Press.

Smith, R. M. (2003). *Stories of peoplehood: The politics and morals of political membership*. Cambridge University Press. https://doi.org/10.1017/CBO9780511490347

Tsabari, A. (2019). *The art of leaving: A memoir*. Random House.

Tyler, R. W. (1949). *Basic principles of curriculum and instruction*. The University of Chicago Press.

Vasquez, J. A. (1990). Teaching to the distinctive traits of minority students. *The Clearing House: A Journal of Educational Strategies, Issues and Ideas, 63*(7), 299–304. https://doi.org/10.1080/00098655.1990.10114113

Wallach, Y. (2011). Trapped in mirror-images: The rhetoric of maps in Israel/Palestine. *Political Geography, 30*(7), 358–369. https://doi.org/10.1016/j.polgeo.2011.07.004

Wiggins, G., & McTighe, J. (1998). *Understanding by design*. ASCD.

Winer, L. N. (2019). *Teaching who they are: American-born supplementary school teachers connections with Israel* [Doctoral dissertation, The Jewish Theological Seminary of America]. ProQuest Dissertations Publishing. https://www.proquest.com/openview/4f7df7d2d80492079b57d2d0133852d4/1?pq-origsite=gscholar&cbl=18750&diss=y

Zakai, S. (2011). Values in tension: Israel education at a US Jewish day school. *Journal of Jewish Education, 77*(3), 239–265. https://doi.org/10.1080/15244113.2011.603070

Zakai, S. (2014). "My heart is in the East and I am in the West": Enduring questions of Israel education in North America. *Journal of Jewish Education, 80*(3), 287–318. https://doi.org/10.1080/15244113.2014.937192

2
Navigating Complexities
Teaching Israel Studies in the Professional Military Education Context

AMIN TARZI

Audi alteram partem.

Foundational in law, philosophy, and international relations, the principle "hear the other side" is a personal and professional mantra of mine. It has shaped how I approach my practice as a teacher, parent, diplomat, and human being. Students often hear me extolling its wisdom, and it led me to teach classes on Israel in the professional military education (PME) environment. My students are professional warfighters, which brings a unique perspective to the study of Israel. They are also individuals, who have their own ideas about how Israel factors into their personal and professional lives. This chapter is a personal reflection on the reasons why I began teaching a course exclusively on Israel where none had existed (nor was there a requirement to offer such a course), the approaches I take in the class, and how this course has evolved in the last five academic years. Throughout, I will be reflecting on my own journey of becoming Israel literate, mainly to illustrate the interrelationship among the instructor, the subject, and the students. Unlike established teachers of Israel studies, my personal and pedagogical approaches to the subject have not been shaped by the dramatic shifts in how Israel and the study thereof generally are regarded on mainstream U.S. campuses (Divine, 2019, p. 38). I was not intimately involved in Israel studies, nor had I any personal connections with the story of Israel. Additionally, I am in a practitioner institution with exceptionally defined curricula aligned to operational imperatives. While most chapters in this volume focus exclusively on classroom practice, and I do discuss that, I preface my chapter with the work that I did to grow interest in and then prepare myself for the varied responses to the course content. My journey in gaining course acceptance and expanding my understanding may be helpful for professors seeking to bring controversial or impassioned topics to their institutions and students.[1] Lastly, I will share how this course has challenged and changed my own pedagogical development beyond Israel studies. Prior to discussing the why and how of teaching about Israel at U.S. Marine Corps University (MCU) in Quantico, Virginia, it is necessary to contextualize the PME institutions in the United States as well as place the status of Israel studies therein.

PME and Israel Studies

The 2018 U.S. National Defense Strategy tasked PME institutions with placing more emphasis on intellectual leadership and military professionalism in the art and science of warfighting and deepening students' knowledge of history. They were to change the focus of the PME continuum from mandatory credit to lethality and ingenuity. In short, the message of this overarching strategy, which guides all of the U.S. military education, was to move away from mundane courses to action-oriented concepts that assist in the intellectual development of thinking warfighters who are capable of taking independent action when communications in combat situations are degraded or lost. One crucial goal of PME is to build trust among and interoperability with U.S. joint forces as well as allied and partner forces (U.S. Department of Defense, 2018, p. 8). Guided by national and departmental guidance, each service adds their particular lens to PME instruction. For the U.S. Marine Corps, that comes in the form of the *Commandant's Planning Guidance*, a document that each commandant issues at the beginning of their tenure at the helm of the force. The current guidance issued in July 2019 by the 38th commandant of the Marine Corps, General David H. Berger, requires that PME be changed from "an industrial age model, to an information age model." In other words, Marine Corps PME moves away from the "lecture, memorize fact, regurgitate facts on command"

(Berger, 2019, p. 13) model, or knowledge-acquisition model, towards the concept of learning as a process, not a product (Tarzi, 2018, p. 9), or of how to think (Training and Education Command, 2020, p. 6). The *Planning Guidance* requires Marine PME institutions to focus on approaches that are student centered and that use problem-posing methodologies to enable the students to "think critically" (Berger, 2019, p. 16).

MCU was formed in 1989 to provide unity of effort in the PME continuum of the U.S. Marine Corps. The university's goal is to advance the legacy of Marine Corps warfighting excellence through a forward-thinking military academic institution.[2] To achieve this end, the university develops and delivers PME and training through resident and distance learning programs. Three colleges—Marine Corps War College (MCWAR), School of Advanced Warfighting (SAW), and Command and Staff College (CSC)—within MCU's officer PME programs award master's degrees in resident programs. There are distance and blended-degree awarding programs within CSC as well. Curriculum within the university's colleges is primarily based on core thematic blocks or sections. For example, at CSC, some of the major core themes include profession of arms, strategy and operational art, organizational culture, diplomacy, and information politics. Additionally, there are more specific blocks dealing with Russia, China, and the Asia-Pacific campaigns of World War II that all students have to study. In January, CSC offers students the opportunity to explore topics of interest to faculty not covered by the existing program of study, and CSC students must select two classes from over 40 offerings for 20 class hours each spread over the month. The subjects for the elective classes are at the discretion of the proposing faculty, and there is a prerequisite minimum number of registrations for the class to be offered. Several months prior to the electives block, MCU presents the students a catalog of the offerings, and there is an elective open house where instructors discuss their course offerings to interested students.[3]

From 2007, when I arrived at MCU, until 2018, there was no Israel-specific course offered in MCU curricular blocks or as an elective. A short unscientific survey of the PME continuum across U.S. service schools indicated that there were very few course offerings that centered on or dealt directly with the State of Israel.[4] In Air University, located on Maxwell Air Force Base, Alabama, there is a course on the Arab–Israeli conflict, designed to help students develop an appreciation for the complexity of the conflict as well as the ongoing impact on regional and American security. There is also a seminar designed around Israel at the National War College, located on Fort Lesley J. McNair, Washington, DC, entitled "Israel and the United States in an Age of Great Power Competition" and offered as part of the school's core courses in National Security Strategy Research and Practicum and Applications in National Security Strategy.[5] Among the four-year military academies, the survey found that only the U.S. Naval Academy (USNA) in Annapolis, Maryland, offered a course entitled Palestinian–Israeli Conflict, whose description states that "the conflict between Arabs and Jews over Palestine is one of the most important factors shaping Middle East politics." The course "identifies key actors and motivations in the conflict as well as the conflict's intractability."[6] This course was an outlier among PME institutions. The USNA had an endowed distinguished visiting scholar in Israel studies from 2016 to 2018, a role filled by Dr. Shayna Weiss, who has written about her experience teaching this class in *Teaching the Arab-Israeli Conflict* (Weiss, 2019). The endowed chair was not renewed after 2018.

The Journey to Teaching Israel at MCU

I have been serving as the director of Middle East Studies at MCU since its inception in 2007 and was hired primarily to focus on Iran. While fascinated by, and respecting the history of, Israel, and having many great friends in that country, I am not Jewish, nor have I any religious or ethnic connections to the story of Israel. Why would I, then, in a very structured teaching environment, decide to offer as my only class outside of the required academic programs an elective on Israel covering the history of Zionism and birth of Israel, its society, security challenges, political system, international relations—including the special and changing bonds between Israel and the United States—and the Palestinian question? Responding to this question requires a cursory overview of my own journey as a student of Israel studies.

My interest began while studying political science and history at Queens College, City University of New York, in the 1980s. This trend continued throughout my master and doctoral studies at the Department of Near Eastern Languages and Literature at New York University (NYU).⁷ In both institutions I took courses ranging from the history of Jews in ancient Egypt, to Judaism, to the modern Middle East. While a student at NYU, I also worked as the political advisor to the Permanent Mission of the Kingdom of Saudi Arabia to the United Nations during a period that began months before the signing of the 1993 Oslo Accords and ended two months after the assassination of the late Israeli prime minister Yitzhak Rabin in 1995. The duality of academic learning about international relations and practical application thereof became part of my personal education and career journey and has continued to shape my approach to teaching as well as my research responsibilities at MCU.

My academic-practitioner career continued in the first academic job I held at the Center for Nonproliferation Studies (CNS) at the Monterey Institute for International Studies in California.⁸ Without going into much detail, my selection at CNS to lead the Middle East section of the Proliferation Research and Assessment Program was partly related to political administrative issues indirectly related to Israel. My main area of research at CNS was nuclear proliferation involving the Middle East region, with Iraq, Iran, and Libya being the countries of emphasis. In addition to research, I taught graduate courses on Middle East security issues with specific attention paid to nonproliferation. My first trips to Israel occurred in 2000 while I was working at CNS in an effort to expand research on regional proliferation concerns and find research centers with which to partner.

Becoming educated in Israel studies, for me, had an almost exclusive military and security dimension. My first forays into the country were in the think tank world and, through those contacts, with officials in the Israeli defense establishment. My main focus was nuclear and missile threats to Israel and others in and around the Middle East region. Connections made in Israel allowed me to host former senior Israeli strategists and diplomats at CNS.

One of my earliest experiences teaching about Israel occurred in an informal setting in Monterey. A number of students had organized a simulated debate on the Israeli-Palestinian question and could not find a debater among their peers prepared, or perhaps willing, to represent Israel. One of my students approached me with the offer to represent Israel due to my trips to that country and my familiarity with the Israelis whom I had invited to the campus. I accepted the challenge and worked to represent the Israeli position dispassionately and accurately. I based my position on official Israeli documents on the beginnings of the Second or Al Aqsa Intifada in September–October 2000, including graphic photographs. At the end of a heated debate, my Palestinian challenger, originally from another Arab state, lightheartedly said that he was glad I was not on Israel's actual team of diplomats. However, a number of other attendees were overtly upset by my adoptive posture defending Israel's justifications for its counterterrorism measures in the West Bank and Gaza. The debate was my first direct experience with the contestations, parallelism of narratives, and anger that, in many occasions, preclude a composed study of Israel.

When I was hired at MCU, the Middle East Studies Center was envisioned as an open-source PME research and teaching center and resource on Iran for MCU and U.S. naval fleet commanders. In the ensuing 15 years, the Middle East Studies Center has expanded to align with Marine Corps needs and requirements, serving as the center of expertise for the Marine Corps on the greater Middle East and its maritime domains, to include parts of South and Central Asia and the Eastern Mediterranean and Black Sea as well as Northern and Eastern Africa regions.

Israel, specifically, was not part of the initial job description; however, studying Iran geopolitically naturally encompasses Israel as does any general course on the Middle East. It was my intention to explore the feasibility of expanding the scope of the Middle East Studies Center at MCU to not only include spaces and issues that had immediacy to Marine Corps operational environments but also design curricula to help our students to critically contextualize the historical events that have led to current realities and encourage them to analyze future potentialities based on their interpretations. One of my first short courses for MCWAR's Diplomacy and Statecraft block centered on the Middle East security settings beginning with the end of the Second World War. To situate the learning—or, in military parlance, conduct the first phase of the intelligence preparation of the battlespace (define the environment)—I mentioned, among other things, how Middle East political identities since 1945 have been shaped by the birth of the State of Israel. This short course generated interest in Israel amongst the students. As discussed previously, this topic has traditionally not been a major subject of discussion within U.S. PME programs.

In the early 2010s, MCWAR had a short course entitled The Arab-Israeli-Palestinian Conflict, which formed part of the Diplomacy and Statecraft core curriculum. I agreed to teach this course and, thus, began my first formal teaching directly centered on Israel. I designed the course with an overview of Israel's strategic outlook, then provided a review of the Palestinian question and an analysis of the Iranian threat through their proxies among the Palestinians. The class ended with a discussion of American-Israeli relations. The short course's learning objectives were to promote critical thinking by having students examine the role played by the United States to initiate and sustain the peace process among Israel, the Palestinians, and Arab states; evaluate the status of Palestinian-Israeli engagement and conflict; explore what a final settlement of this conflict could look like and how this settlement might be achieved realistically; analyze the origin and historical background of the conflict from both perspectives; and finally, assess the impact of the conflict on the international system at large and the Middle East region in particular. The class focused on the centrality of identity in the Israeli-Palestinian conflict, which I contrasted with the United States experience, where generally identity in war has been downplayed. I found that Robert I. Rotberg's (2006) double helix analogy to be the most fitting, accessible metaphor to explain the Palestinian-Israeli conflict as two sides "locked together in struggle, tightly entangled, and enveloped by a historical cocoon of growing complexity, fundamental disagreement, and overriding misperception of motives" (p. 2). And from the outset of my lectures, I leveraged Michael Walzer's (2015) work to argue that both Zionism and later Palestinian-liberation movements, while at heart secular discourses, were constructed on argumentation based on Judaism and Islam—and less so Christianity—which ensured representation of the religious-identity dimension of this conflict (pp. 34-67). Additionally, the role of the United States in this conflict, among other strategic and domestic dimensions, added another layer of complexity.[9]

After a few semesters of teaching this course, through dialogue with students and course feedback, it became apparent students wanted more. Their genuine interest in learning more about Israel was not limited to a strict security/threat assessment frame or narrowly focused on the

Palestinian issue. One of the persistent sentiments expressed in student evaluations of this short course was the desire for deeper study. One student even expressed feeling "short changed" by the time allotted to the class on Israel. The three overarching themes found in student questions and comments were on United States–Israel relations, personal religious convictions as a determinant of their thinking on Israel, and inquisitiveness about Israeli democracy and political institutions.

One of my challenges was that a small number of my students dismissed the complexity of the Israeli–Palestinian conflict, basing their evaluations or preferences on preconceptions of the righteousness of one side's arguments and grounding them in religiosity that lacked critical analysis. A civilian student in one of my classes declared that dealing with Israel had nothing to do with worldly affairs, adding that according to the Bible, anyone who blessed Israel would be blessed and those cursing it would be damned.[10]

While such perspectives were a very small minority, they reminded me that, as educators, we must tackle the difficult and the controversial, and we must do it dispassionately and from a position of deep understanding of the varied perspectives at play to be able to enliven self-growth in our students. I found it necessary to further educate myself about such beliefs to facilitate a more fruitful and nuanced discussion for all of the students. Obviously, just knowing that the statement was a reference to the promise made by God to Abraham in Genesis 12:3 was insufficient for having a meaningful educational experience (Spector, 2009, pp. 23–24). Further, I recognized that understanding the emotional ties that a significant segment of the American population has to Israel and their direct correlation to the overall strategic relationship between the two countries and beyond was critical. I came to realize that I needed to head back to the classroom myself so that I could present a more engaging class that would allow discovery and debate on these challenging topics. A fortuitous encounter at the Middle East Studies Association annual meeting in 2016 provided an avenue. I visited a gathering hosted by the Association of Israel Studies where, among others, I met Professor S. Ilan Troen and discussed with him my desire to learn more about Israel holistically, while explaining my time and linguistic limitations. With his gentle deportment, Professor Troen mentioned and encouraged me to apply for the Schusterman Center's

Summer Institute for Israel Studies.[11] The following year, I soaked in the knowledge offered to me during the two weeks at Brandeis University and the subsequent tour of Israel. The program requirement to draft a syllabus for a class on Israel positioned me well to offer an elective on Israel, which I have taught at the CSC since 2018.

Additionally, I found a lesson learned from my days as political advisor to the Saudi UN mission informed my decision to offer this elective and guide student learning through the topic of Israel studies. Working with the Saudis, I learned firsthand that dealing with Israel was different from dealing with other states. While in the post-Oslo atmosphere of openness, several Arab states began to recognize Israel as a reality that could not be ignored. Direct dealings with Israelis were still a political taboo. A memorable incident highlighted this tension for me when an Israeli diplomat at the United Nations asked, through a third party, if I would have lunch with him. My superiors acquiesced to my request to meet the Israeli diplomat at a local restaurant. I had to agree to not make any commitments and just listen to the Israeli side. For me, the lunch meeting, which may not have had any measurable impact on the overall Arab–Israeli relations, was a watershed moment of hopefulness for future possibilities for better understanding and acceptance and also a realization that much work remained to be done for normalization of relations between these neighboring states. Moreover, looking back to my lunch meeting, and several other casual meetings, I see that I was an intermediary rather than a Saudi diplomat—an outsider trying to listen and learn as dispassionately as possible about both narratives and informing both sides of the other's positions. I felt it was critical that students develop this habit of mind or practice.

These myriad factors culminated in my decision to offer the elective and seek opportunities to teach about Israel in my other classes. In my classes on Israel at MCU, I rely on my role as an informed and nonjudgmental outsider, relaying the contested story and realities of Israel to my students. My goal is not to alter their perspectives or convictions about that country or what to think about it. Rather I seek to grow their abilities in perspective taking, listening, and analyzing objectively complex, layered situations, places, and people. Through the lens of Israel, I hope they learn these skills and apply them in their future military endeavors. The following are some of my strategies for inspiring this learning.

A Case for Hearing the Other Side

In 2018, when I first offered my elective course, entitled The State of Israel in Context, I had more students sign up than the 12 allowed in one seminar. This did not surprise me because of the overwhelming interest expressed by prospective students during the open house. In the end, CSC leadership and I decided to allow a few more students in. During the electives open house, I placed an Israeli national flag behind my nameplate so as to indicate that my course was focused specifically on that state. In addition to U.S. military and civilian students, five officers from foreign states, two of which at the time did not recognize the State of Israel, were also enrolled in the course. One international student approached me privately to tell me that his country recognized Palestine and not Israel and that he was very interested in learning about Israel. With the student's genuine desire to learn, despite the official stance of his country, I encouraged him to register. I approached my rationale to the individual student on the basis of the overall goals of education for a military professional. Unlike training, which is predicated on learning through practical applications, PME is intellectual development that includes the understanding of opposing views and arguments. I assured the prospective student that the elective was designed as a historical and intellectual journey to challenge the presumptions of all sides and that the discussion would be respectful and open to alternate views. Indeed, I reasoned with the student that not only would he learn from the class, but that our collective learning experience would be enhanced by his presence and participation in the seminar. After a second meeting in my office, the student registered for the elective, and his contributions throughout the class were professional and added to our overall understanding of the complexities Israel presents.

Moving Through, Not Beyond, Emotions to Deeper Understanding

While my students have a professional immediacy to their learning, they also bring their personal journeys to class. To acknowledge the professional space, I frame my elective through a practical lens, rather than a purely academic one. My students lack the luxury of time for purely academic pursuits in this environment. Considering the comments and questions from my MCWAR experiences, however, I thought it would be beneficial and important for the professional military learners to delve deeper beyond personally held beliefs and vague notions to understand root causes of the conflict that the modern State of Israel has faced. Military practitioners need to learn to dispassionately approach emotionally charged situations, provide thoughtful, informed analysis, and then, of course, decisively act. They need to ensure their personal positions do not cloud their professional judgements when making operational decisions.

My intention is to have students discuss and debate the complex nature of Israel's history, society, and politics in a protected space as an exemplar for future practice when the space may be contested. In my introduction to the course, I acknowledge that the study of Israel, perhaps more than any other state, in the United States evokes passions linked to each learner's personal beliefs. So, it is a good exercise! Such beliefs are based on particular understandings of historical, religious, or geographical narratives. Oftentimes, I argue, these narratives negate any counterarguments. For example, the basic political preference of whether an individual student supports the two-state solution or not often is revelatory of these underlying narratives and can lead to passionate debate. At MCU, we like to say we use the Socratic method of teaching to foster dialogue between the teacher and students and deepen learning; however, the reality often continues to be "lecture, memorize facts, regurgitate facts on command" (Berger, 2019, p. 16). I chose to return to the classical sense of the method to challenge rigid thinking, deepen understanding, and broaden perspective. I use the visual depiction of a DNA double-helix diagram to illustrate the proximity and oneness of the two narratives, yet also their perpetual separation. I position readings and class materials intentionally to present opposing or contradictory positions. Through posing questions to students, I facilitate debate and discussion, offering students the opportunity to get uncomfortable with their preconceived ideas and move to greater understanding.

Switching It Up to Spur Discussion

To stimulate thought at the beginning of the elective seminar, I offer the students different terms used for the same geographical locations, events, or groups of people, for example, using different maps which label the same territory as the West Bank, Judea and Samaria, Palestine, or not just as part of Israel. In my lectures and discussions, I often use the West Bank. However, when discussing specific political perspectives, I offer the alternative terminology without providing further clarifications. For this particular case, most of my students tend to utilize the less-contested "West Bank" designation; however, some have preferred using "Judea and Samaria" or just "Israel." I do this to challenge preconceived notions and ingrained understandings and to remove blinders and blind acceptance of labels. Such choices have led to constructive discussions. I use this technique frequently because, as military professionals, they need to consider how their words and the labels they use shape interaction dynamics.[12]

Not Exceptionalizing Israel

The military profession involves encounters with any and all states. I chose my course framing intentionally to position Israel as one of many states these students may encounter or need to factor into strategic calculations in their careers. I treat Israel like any other state, one with its own peculiar history and stories. Oftentimes, the subject of Israel is taboo, perceived only as an intractable conflict, considered too controversial or difficult, or seen as exceptional, different among states. I seek to destigmatize and normalize the study of Israel. In our class, we study Israel as we would other states, based on an assessment of theoretical, historical, and factual documents from various viewpoints with the interjection of critique and analysis. We study Israel's founding documents, read political critiques, delve into its political structure, watch documentaries, and hear from practitioners and academicians presenting different facets of Israeli society. It sounds ordinary, but not if we pause and think about how Israel is typically handled and considered in curricula. Through this, students are able to experience Israel more comprehensively and understand it and its peoples more fully and, I assert, more fairly.

Using the Study of Israel to Promote Creative Problem-Solving

Military practitioners have to decisively act in ambiguous and confusing situations. The problems they face and are expected to solve require innovation and novel approaches, oftentimes during moments of intense physical, psychological, and emotional strain. In PME, it is important to present these practitioners with opportunities to try to solve or seek solutions to seemingly intractable problems, to look differently or more expansively at a known situation, and to collaborate and critique ideas with their colleagues. The study of Israel and the parallel narratives of the Israelis and Palestinians (or Jews and Arabs) provide a rich context for such learning. The narratives of the two main peoples living in the State of Israel and in the West Bank and Gaza compete with and contradict each other. This palette of competing colors affords students an array of choices and opportunities to design and display their ideas and solutions to the complex challenges Israel presents. To promote this, as I mentioned earlier, I challenge students during class through open-ended questioning and debate facilitation. Students are required to actively participate in classroom discussions, work together to develop solutions to the complex challenges facing Israel and its region, and then judge their viability through debate. As professional warfighters, my students have a vested interest in conflict understanding and resolution. I use these exchanges to challenge and expand their thinking about the reasons for conflict and possible solutions.

Handling Confounding Identities With an Open Door

Who I am, or rather, who others assume I am can be an obstacle for some. My last name leads people to all sorts of assumptions about my ethnic origin (they are usually wrong), my religion (they are usually wrong), and my position on any number of world events (they are usually wrong). When it comes to Israel, yep, they are usually wrong. I am not naive. I was a student of international relations with a focus on Middle East studies in the 1980s, when poststructuralism and the works of Michel Foucault and Edward Said dominated the debates about the relationship between power and knowledge. I am keenly aware of my own identity, or more accurately stated, those assigned to me or perceived by others based on my name, country of origin, status as a political asylee, and what they perceived to be my religious sensitivities, if not convictions. In my view, the complexity of an instructor's identity is an asset, bringing additional perspective and nuance to the table, which has contributed to my own success in helping students move through their emotions on personally and professionally charged topics.

This awareness informed how I designed the elective. I wanted to ensure that the class led to a better and deeper understanding of Israel for my students rather than becoming a forum for religious contentions or a debate on my identity and motivations for choosing to teach a class on Israel. Some students have found it odd that I teach about Israel—despite the fact that the country is located in the geographical area of responsibility of the center I lead. To quell these suspicions and reorient students on the course intent, I begin the class with a brief discussion on the origins of the course—my personal as well as students' interest in and curiosity about the country being the main driving force. I usually do not reveal my preferences, for example, on the issue of the future arrangement of the Palestinian question. Rather, I strive for them to discuss and discover their own thinking on the subject, especially at the beginning.

In our classrooms, while discussions on the subjects covered are very open, the relationship of the teacher to students, in most cases, is governed by the military structure. My students refer to me as "Sir" and, in most cases, do not delve into personal questions of why I care about Israel. However, this professional distance diminishes as the course progresses and our conversations become more relaxed and personal. I have an open-door policy for office hours, in-person or through usage of electronic communication systems, which my students use regularly. Questions run the gamut, for example, about my religious background, my stance on the decision to move the U.S. embassy to Jerusalem, or whether the Haredim (ultra-Orthodox Jews) should be serving in the Israel Defense Forces (IDF).[13] In response to these examples, I talk openly with them about my personal and professional stances and use such questions as learning tools, centering the discussion on student inquiries and diving deeper into the larger theoretical, political, and historical discussions. Oftentimes, with the study of Israel, one feels you have to take sides and that to see value or anything positive in the other side is tantamount to treason. Through this exchange, students experience how to be a professional while maintaining personal identity and position and learn how one can study controversial and complex topics without losing or compromising oneself.

Use of Reflection

When I first designed the course, the writing requirement was the typical analytical paper on a student-selected topic related to the seminar discussions based on primary and secondary sources. While I still maintain that requirement, as I do find it a useful exercise for students, I have, since January 2021, included a two-to-three-page reflective essay. I began to sense that many of the students desired to include their personal reflections on the topic, to convey their personal response to the materials, and to privately (between me and them) explore their discomfort, mixed feelings, or excitement about the materials or learning journey. Thus, I included a reflection paper, which I have them write after the first four class sessions to stimulate their thinking. The essay is designed to represent the individual student's views on, response to, and understanding of the topic or reading, not a summary thereof. The reflective essay challenges them to investigate and interrogate their own inner valuations, not only in reflecting mentally, but also in having to write them down for another person to read and respond to. The papers have been incredibly impressive and indicative of the passions and viewpoints of the individual writers, which otherwise would not have surfaced in a research paper. Students were afforded the opportunity to discuss their essays with me prior to, and after, their submission. The feedback from the students on the reflective-essay requirement has been very positive, so I have maintained it as part of the elective. In the coming course iterations, I may borrow an idea from Ashley Passmore (2019) at Texas A&M and position the essay earlier to capture student beliefs and thoughts on Israel and then have them revisit their work at the end of the class as an exercise in self-evaluation (p. 52). Instructor feedback is useful. It can affirm our efforts or provide opportunities for improvement. Self-evaluation makes us pause and consider. This introspection is helpful in gaining insights into our own learning journey and self-development. As professionals, our students are stewards of their own learning; they are charged with continually gaining knowledge and insight. At PME institutions, we seek to provide them the skills to do that. Self-reflection and evaluation are key to a fulfilling and rewarding life-long learning journey.

Broadening Perspectives

Perspective taking is a critical skill for all of us, and especially military practitioners, and one that is in need of refreshment and refinement. Throughout my personal and professional journey, the idea of *audi alteram partem* (hear the other side) has guided me, and I believe it is critical for learners to contemplate beyond themselves and their understandings to be considered learned.

I intentionally seek diverse and, at times, opposing viewpoints to present topics to challenge students, to make them check themselves, and to get them to a point of intellectual confusion and frustration that can then lead to deeper understanding. I use, of course, readings, both primary and secondary sources and from varied perspectives. I select guest speakers to present different voices to the students. Being situated in the Washington, DC area and having good contacts have allowed me to enhance student learning by inviting guest lecturers to add perspective and address particular interests of students. I have been fortunate to have the support of former Assistant Commandant of the U.S. Marine Corps (ACMC) General Robert Magnus, who has graciously taught a segment of my class. Before retiring in 2008, as ACMC, General Magnus served for three years as the second-in-command of the Marine Corps, making him the highest-ranking officer with a Jewish background in that branch of the U.S. military. In addition to General Magnus, guests have included a retired IDF general officer, an active duty IDF colonel serving at the Israeli Embassy in Washington, and an active-duty U.S. colonel who is also a rabbi. These guests offer students unique perspectives about Jewishness and the Israeli and U.S. military establishments. They also lend a different level of legitimacy due to their particular insider status that I as an outsider cannot. That said, my outsider status affords me the emotional distance to the subject that allows students to evolve in their understanding through debate and discussion. My positions are based on study, not on deeply held convictions, freeing me from potential conflict or offense that others may experience. These guest speakers offer students opportunities to hear different external voices and internalize them as they see fit.

In addition to guest speakers and readings, I use the documentary on the *Altalena* Affair directed by Ilana Tsur (1994). The film is a case in point as to how intentional material selection leads to greater learning. I selected this specifically because of the relevance of its subject to my student body. The film is the context. The perspectives are those held within and among the students. For the students, there is an innate tension between their professional and personal identities as they consider the *Altalena* Affair through various lenses, including laws of war, effects of international realpolitik on tenuous local events, theory of monopoly over use of violence by central state authorities, and leadership roles in crisis, among other issues. As they watch the film and then discuss it, the students have a space to work through these tensions, ones they will encounter in their professional careers. They need to prepare for the discomfort such tensions can cause and have the tools and mental scripts available to work through them and still perform their role.

Keeping a Professional Frame

My students' professional status is an important factor to keep in mind. They are not students of Israel, nor do they necessarily have a deep love for or personal connection to the country. They do, however, have a professional interest that may be accompanied by personal interest or curiosity. When my students come to class, they bring with them life experiences and responsibilities very different from mainstream college students. This shapes how I approach them and the subjects we discuss, always keeping in mind the operational imperative. Not being immersed in ongoing debates on transformative education theories and suppositions to posit a scientific analysis on my teaching philosophies, I do believe that, for my students, I strive to ensure they are prepared for the fog and friction of war and for the complexities of the international security environment they will encounter. The objective of our education is not only to be transformed through the Greek maxim of "know thyself" (Achesen & Dirkx, 2021, p. 296), but also to be informed by Sun Tzu's dictum of "knowing thy enemies." My course, while hopefully being transformative in providing the students opportunities for self-improvement, is designed to instill in our warfighters and partners critical thinking skills, the abilities to consider varied perspectives and to listen attentively and respectfully, and the confidence in their analytical skills to act decisively and effectively when required without being directed.

So, Why Israel?

I chose the topic of Israel, one, because of personal interest and, two, because it provides an exceptionally useful, interesting palette that inspires students to learn and grow due to Israel's complexity and its prominence in national-security debates and contexts. I have thought, why not teach about Country X? And it is because with Israel I can get my military students quickly (we only have four weeks) to where the following student (Institutional Research, Assessment, and Planning, 2018) ended up:

> Absolutely, this elective was the most enjoyable and enriching period of instruction I received at CSC, thus far. I say that from a perspective that the CSC curriculum was both beneficial and effective as a whole to date. Dr. Tarzi's course does a great job of demonstrating the importance of challenging ingrained biases within a subject matter that elicits strong emotional opinions from all sides. It touched on critical thinking, the importance of information operations and narratives on affecting national politics and world opinion, an examination of state craft and security strategies, political maneuvering, the effects of interstate proxy conflicts and politics.

I believe it is the combination of teaching methods, individual instructor qualities, and content area that makes this possible. It is why I advocate for inclusion of Israel studies, when feasible, throughout the curriculum.

Concluding Thoughts

Through my experience of bringing Israel studies to MCU, I have improved as an educator. First, I recognized within myself a need to deepen my own understanding before teaching others, especially in light of the passions tied to the subject. Thus, I became a student again. This awareness and my willingness to accept my own deficiencies compelled me to improve myself, which exposed me to amazing resources, innovative ideas, and seasoned educators on the subject. Second, this class made me pause and reflect, unlike most others where the subjects are less contested, which challenged me to grow in technique and seek different methods and resources. I reflected on my life as a diplomat, negotiator, and military professional to bring lessons, life experiences, and practices to working with my students and shaping how I approached this subject. Through this class, I discovered the usefulness of the art of reflection as an intentional practice for students. This was the first time I had used it. I now include it in my other courses as well.

My journey continues. I am under no illusion that I have finished my journey as a student of Israel. This lifetime will not afford me enough time to master the subject, especially since I began much later than most. At MCU, the short classes on Israel at MCU's MCWAR and CSC as well as the elective at the latter have established Israel studies within one PME institution. While it has been my aim to continue to expand and enhance my own Israel literacy, with the very obvious limitation of not knowing the Hebrew language, I am always aware of the sensitivities surrounding teaching and discussing an issue that traverses U.S. foreign and domestic policies as well as individual students' beliefs and convictions. However, when students write that in the seminar I have managed to "come across as impartial on issues that generally are quite divisive" (Institutional Research, Assessment, and Planning, 2019) or that they "didn't think it was possible" to present a "topic so complex and emotional" from "multiple points of view and in a neutral manner" (Middle East Studies, MCU, 2019), I believe as an educator I succeeded. Most of the students have informed me that their class and our discussions have caused them to think more critically about a subject they had chosen to study and one about which they held many preconceptions based on personal backgrounds, assumptions, and faith.

At MCU, we have dedicated curricular space to Israel studies, framed through the lens of professional military education, to inspire critical thinking, overcome bias, speak dispassionately and listen respectfully about an impassioned topic, hone analytical skills, and deepen understanding about a very complex state with significant impact on the strategic environment in which our students operate. Collectively, we have started to lay the foundations of a small but increasingly serious Israel studies program in a corner of the U.S. PME system.

ACKNOWLEDGMENTS

The opinions and conclusions expressed herein are those of the individual author and do not necessarily represent the views of either the United States Marine Corps University or any other U.S. governmental agency. The author would like to express gratitude to Major General William F. Mullen (USMC retired), who read drafts of this paper and provided valuable insights on professional military education. I am indebted to Erika A. Tarzi, my spouse and someone whose work I have used in this piece, for her continued support of my academic endeavors.

NOTES

1. While there are points where I do draw upon my own biography, for the most part, I have chosen to not write this chapter as an auto-ethnography of my own pedagogy. Admittedly, this type of writing is common practice in education research. My decision to deviate from this approach is guided by a belief that by framing this chapter around myself, readers may erroneously conclude that the success of the course I am writing about is exclusively tied to my role as the educator and that what I am describing cannot be replicated at their institutions. By authoring this chapter, my intention is to convince educators who teach at sites where Israel studies is not routinely taught that including courses about Israel can provide meaningful educational experiences for learners no matter the religious, ethnic, or political background of the teacher.

2. For more on MCU, see: https://www.usmcu.edu/About-MCU/Strategic-Plan/.

3. Since the COVID-19 pandemic, the open house has been replaced with a virtual meet and greet session.

4. I appreciate the research support provided by Cadet Bridget A. Hughes (Virginia Military Institute, 2022), who interned at MCU in Summer 2021, and by First Lieutenant Jacob Marshall (USMC), assistant operations officer at the Brute Krulak Center for Innovation & Future Warfare.

5. I am very thankful to Professor and Colonel Adam Oler, Chair, Department of Security Studies, National War College, for discussing his course on Israel and providing me with a copy of his syllabus.

6. Email correspondence with MCU summer intern Cadet Hughes, July 26, 2021.

7. The department changed its name while I was a student there to Middle Eastern Studies, and after my graduation, it rebranded as Middle Eastern and Islamic Studies.
8. After my departure, CNS changed its name to James Martin Center for Nonproliferation Studies, and Middlebury College acquired the Monterey Institute.
9. For more on this, see Levite & Shimshoni, 2018.
10. The MCU student body encompasses members of all U.S. military branches, officers from a number of foreign countries, and civilian U.S. government officials representing various agencies. For an example of MCU resident demographics for academic year 2020–2021, see Slide 7 in the Command Brief, https://www.usmcu.edu/About-MCU/Command-Brief/.
11. I am indebted to Professor Troen for his encouragement and onward support of my efforts to become more "literate about Israel." I also want to thank everyone at the Schusterman Center for Israel Studies, including Professor Emeritus David Ellenson and Professor Rachel Fish, who served as the center's executive director at the time.
12. In classes where I talk about the Arab Gulf states, all U.S. allies, I ask my students to consider the name of the body of water near the Gulf States and the significance of the naming convention they use (the Persian Gulf, Arabian Gulf, or simply the Gulf). Many had not considered the tension between the label we use in the U.S.—Persian Gulf—and the U.S. political position. It helps my students to be more deliberate and mindful in cultural exchange.
13. The vast majority of Haredim do not serve in the IDF. This is based on a 1948 understanding that, while they study the Torah, they are exempt from compulsory military service. For more, see Bick, 2010; Cohen & Susser, 2009; Røislien, 2012.

REFERENCES

Acheson, K., & Dirkx, J. M. (2021). Editors' introduction to the special issue of the *Journal of Transformative Education* on assessing transformative learning. *Journal of Transformative Education, 19*(4), 295–305. https://doi.org/10.1177/15413446211045158

Berger, D. H. (2019). *Commandant's planning guidance*. United States Marine Corps. https://www.marines.mil/Portals/1/Publications/Commandant's%20Planning%20Guidance_2019.pdf?ver=2019-07-17-090732-937

Bick, E. (2010). The Tal Law: A missed opportunity for "bridging social capital" in Israel. *Journal of Church and State, 52*(2), 298–322. http://www.jstor.org/stable/23921868

Cohan, A., & Susser, B. (2009). Service in the IDF and the boundaries of Israeli's Jewish collective. In A. Sagi & O. Hachtomy (Eds.), *The multicultural challenge in Israel* (pp. 180–199). Academic Studies Press.

Divine, D. R. (2019). Teaching students how to think, not what to think, about Middle East conflict. In R. S. Harris (Ed.), *Teaching the Arab-Israeli conflict* (pp. 58–62). Wayne State University Press.

Institutional Research, Assessment, and Planning. (2018). *CSC electives survey AY 18: The State of Israel in context, 1948–2018*. Marine Corps University.

Institutional Research, Assessment, and Planning. (2019). *CSC electives survey AY 19: The State of Israel in context*. Marine Corps University.

Levite, A. E., & Shimshoni, J. (2018). The strategic challenge of society-centric warfare. *Survival, 60*(6), 91–118. https://doi.org/10.1080/00396338.2018.1542806

Middle East Studies, Marine Corps University. (2019). MES elective on Israel garners student support. *MES Insights, 10*(2), 4. United States Marine Corps. https://www.usmcu.edu/Portals/218/MES_insights_v10_i2_lo.pdf?ver=tNi4M7dXNwW88_nVQ_erlg%3d%3d

Passmore, A. (2019). Teaching conflict as a critical thinking (dis)course. In R. S. Harris (Ed.), *Teaching the Arab-Israeli conflict* (pp. 51–57). Wayne State University Press.

Røislien, H. E. (2012). Religion and military conscription: The case of the Israel Defense Forces (IDF). *Armed Forces & Society, 39*(2), 213–232. https://www.jstor.org/stable/48609178

Rotberg, R. I. (2006). Building legitimacy through narrative. In R. I. Rotberg (Ed.), *Israeli and Palestinian narrative of conflict: History's double helix*. Indiana University Press.

Spector, S. (2009). *Evangelicals and Israel: The story of American Christian Zionism*. Oxford University Press.

Tarzi, E. (2018). *An applied report—Educating marines: Reorienting professional military education on the target*. Center for Advanced Operational Culture Learning. https://www.usmcu.edu/Portals/218/CAOCL/Educating%20Marines_PMEPEL%20Report%20041019%20Updated.pdf

Training and Education Command (2020). *Vision and strategy for 21st century learning*. United States Marine Corps. https://www.tecom.marines.mil/Portals/90/3284_TECOM%20Vision%20&%20Strategy_v%2013_1.pdf

Tsur, I. (Director). (1994). *Altalena* [Film]. Jewish Film Institute.

U.S. Department of Defense. (2018). *2018 U.S. national defense strategy*. United States Department of Defense.

Walzer, M. (2015). *The paradox of liberation: Secular revolutions and religious counterrevolutions*. Yale University Press.

Weiss, S. (2019). Teaching the 1948 War in the U.S. Naval Academy. In R. S. Harris (Ed.), *Teaching the Arab-Israeli conflict* (pp. 127–132). Wayne State University Press.

3
Voices on the Page and in the Room
A Pedagogy of Jewish Text Study in Israel Education

JOSHUA LADON

While teaching at a Jewish high school, I was tasked with creating a yearlong Israel elective for 11th and 12th graders. I turned to the Shalom Hartman Institute's iEngage curriculum and built a class rooted in the Jewish textual tradition that dealt with conceptions of Jewish power and responsibility, Judaism and democracy, just wars and morality.[1] Mid-semester, a frustrated student piped up and asked a prescient question: "Why are we looking at all these Jewish texts?—I thought this class was about Israel!"

Indeed, the one question I've been asked more than any other over the course of my teaching career is why I use so many Jewish texts when teaching about Israel. As my own professional journey has turned to working with Jewish educators and other communal professionals in partnership with other Jewish organizations (spanning Hillels, Jewish Community Centers (JCCs), synagogues, and day schools), this question about Israel education's relationship to Jewish education still rings in my ears. A classic example occurred in 2021 as I was preparing to teach a cohort of early career Jewish campus-engagement professionals who focus on recruiting students for immersive Israel experiences. I was asked by the program director who organized the group "to teach something Jewish and not Israel focused" and to send the source sheet I created in advance of the class for review.

The request to prioritize an *Israel*-related topic to the exclusion of one that is Jewish in nature (or the reverse: a Jewish topic that is separate from Israel) exemplifies the pedagogical challenge at the heart of this chapter, a challenge I encounter daily in my work with faculty of the Shalom Hartman Institute, a center where Jewish texts and topics are taught to adults and teenagers living in North America and in Israel. This pedagogical challenge is born out of a vision for Israel education that is neither ubiquitous nor shared. Unlike more common approaches to Israel education that focus on building knowledge about the modern state of Israel in service of fostering connection, my approach situates teaching about Israel as the outgrowth of deep Jewish questions and is ultimately about enculturating people into an unfolding, millennia old, Jewish civic conversation, which is manifest in traditional and modern Jewish texts.

The ongoing tension that I see between Jewish and Israel education manifests across the field of Israel education but is especially acute in the phenomenon of source sheets and their use. Source sheets are self-designed curricular artifacts embedded with different textual quotations which teachers refer to, read out loud, and instruct with during classes. While using textual instructional tools is not new, source sheets have only recently emerged in the past couple of decades, and their popularity has transformed the activity of teaching Jewish texts (Lockspeiser & Foer, 2012; Sheskin & Liben, 2015; Silow-Carrol, 2017). As an educator committed to an approach to teaching Israel rooted in a rich Jewish textual tradition, I regularly face profound pedagogical questions situated in the relationship between "Israel" and "Jewish." In the example on the previous page, the director and I had already discussed using Jewish holidays as a framework for engaging big Jewish ideas that relate to the cohort's work with students on campus. I was slated to teach in advance of Tu b'Shvat, the Jewish new year of the trees—a holiday whose observance was virtually unknown outside of small segments of the Jewish population until Zionists renewed its observance during the 20th century. In my mind I debated including a reflection on Tu b'Shvat by the Israeli poet Uri Zvi Greenberg on the source sheet. Reflecting on my nervousness about sharing such a document, I realized that there were deeper issues at play than just whether or not to include Greenberg. My source sheet for the class was no different from the source sheets I always make, consisting of several Jewish sources—some ancient, some modern—with no indication of how I will use the texts found on it. While some passages might have an explicit link to the topic at hand, others might appear only tenuously related at best. But that only points to the bigger issue: What could someone possibly learn about my class and how I intended to use such texts just by looking at my source sheet? What would seeing a source written about Israel by an Israeli on the page suggest to them about my pedagogical choices? For that matter, what did the director even mean by his request to "teach something Jewish but not Israel focused"? Behind these questions lie unarticulated assumptions about the purpose of Israel education, the activities of Israel education, and the role of textuality in stirring national sentiment.

The two-pronged nature of requests like these—about content and its medium—reflects a particular set of misconceptions regarding pedagogy in general and about the divide between Jewish and Israel education in particular. Addressing these misconceptions—as I do in my professional practice and in this chapter—offers a unique opportunity to speak to what constitutes a viable integrated vision of both in the 21st century. The typical division of Jewish and Israel education rests on a particular conception of the Zionist project which sees Israel as a political entity tasked with ensuring the safety of the Jewish body politic, but a closer look at the history of Israel education reveals one with deep roots in the textual tradition of studying the great works of Hebrew and Jewish culture. At the same time, the request to review source sheets containing such texts in order to "vet" their message rests on a view that education is a causal practice of inputs and outputs in which one can finely tune a system of interventions in service of predetermined outcomes. A 21st-century vision of Israel and Jewish pedagogy that I set forth in this chapter draws Jews into conversation with one another and the tradition in a way that takes seriously challenges of contemporary Israel and seeds possibilities for an unknowable Jewish future. Properly understood, source sheets constitute not an end but the beginning of such a conversation, a foundation upon which voices from the tradition and voices in the room wrestle together with the contemporary Jewish condition. Through these means, Israel education can be an activity of Jewish civic practice, in which participants are acculturated into a set of values, ideas, and affects.

Cultural Zionism and the Recovery of the Textual Tradition

In order to explicate my educational vision and the pedagogical practices that help me enact it, I begin by drawing a connection between current questions in Israel education and the earliest voices in cultural Zionism. It is by engaging with the writings of these Zionist thinkers that I, and in turn my students, gain greater clarity about the relationships between "Israel" and "Jewish." Admittedly, articulating the relationship between Israel and Jewish education is no easy matter. Their ambiguous relationship is part of the broader confusion over the conceptions and goals of the field of Israel education (Attias, 2015; Horowitz, 2012; Isaacs, 2011; Zakai, 2014). Coming to grips with this issue begins by recognizing a shift in the language used in the field at the turn of the century. As Horowitz (2012) notes, Israel education emerged in the early 2000s as a response to several phenomena, including concerns over Jewish continuity, the Second Intifada, and the shifting ideological perspectives of the majority of American Jews. Prior to this emergence, the aim of Israel-based education was "Zionist" in its outlook and specifically geared at reconstituting Judaism in the form of migration to Israel (*aliyah*). By moving from the language of "Zionist" to "Israel" education, the field aspired to enhance the diasporic Jewish connection to the State of Israel without sending the message that immigration was the successful outcome of Zionist education. But this shift also exacerbated existing questions about the nature of the field's relationship to Jewish education. What does it mean to educate towards Jewish national awareness for those who will live outside of Israel? What does a vibrant Hebrew culture look like for non-Hebrew-speaking Jews? For American Jews, what does it mean to feel connected to Israel, and how does that manifest in the practice of American Jewish life? While these questions seem firmly rooted in the contemporary moment, I want to suggest that they have a historical lineage in the writings and educational initiatives of cultural Zionism.

Before I trace that lineage, I want to offer a clearer picture of the more recent history of this cultural Zionism. One noteworthy sketch of this history and the ways Israel has been understood as a Jewish educational project tied to the study of Jewish texts can be found in Dr. Ruth Calderon's inaugural speech as a member of the Israeli Knesset in February of 2013 (Calderon, 2013). The founder of Alma, a secular *beit midrash* (house of study), Calderon began her address by describing her own upbringing in a classic "New Zionist" home informed by the idea of a "new" kind of Jew: the Israeli. As the child of Sefardi and Ashkenazi parents who raised her in a secular-traditional-religious home, her early existence was built around the new vision of Israeliness. As she acknowledged, "I was educated like everyone else my age—public education in the spirit of 'from Tanach to Palmach' [from the Bible to Zionist Israeli history]. I was not acquainted with the Mishna, the Talmud, Kabbala or Hasidism" (par. 4). These are genres of Jewish literature written in the intervening 2500 years between the close of the Biblical canon and the rise of Zionism. It is not a surprise that these genres of Jewish "religious" literature were absent from Calderon's educational and cultural experience, as the denigration of anything diasporic in origin was central to the early secular Zionist project, including diasporic traditions, iconography, and especially literature (Schweid, 1984; Shapira, 2004). Calderon herself is at pains not to blame anyone for the absence of rabbinic literature in her childhood. Rather, she sees its absence as collateral damage in the face of more pressing and material needs: "we gave it away, with our own hands, when it seemed that another task was more important and urgent: building a state, raising an army, developing agriculture and industry" (Calderon, 2013, par. 7).

Yet while Calderon acknowledges the advantages of the "new Hebrew" for the nascent nation-state of Israel and how the "Zionist" educational philosophy she and her peers received "realized the dream" of the country's founding generation, she nevertheless laments the loss of those texts in the curriculum and the "void" left behind by their absence. For her that void was only filled when she discovered the Talmud, inspiring in her a lifetime of study and eventually becoming the focus of her doctorate.

Calderon uses her biography as leadup to her main point—the reclamation of the Jewish textual tradition as a means for a healthy, vibrant Israeli culture. Just as some early Zionists looked to the Bible to create their vision of the new Jew, Calderon sees the study of an expanded curriculum of Jewish literature beyond the Bible as one that leads directly to a rejuvenated form of Israel education:

I am convinced that studying the great works of Hebrew and Jewish culture are crucial to construct a new Hebrew culture for Israel. It is impossible to stride toward the future without knowing where we came from and who we are, without knowing, intimately and in every particular, the sublime as well as the outrageous and the ridiculous. The Torah is not the property of one movement or another. It is a gift that every one of us received, and we have all been granted the opportunity to meditate upon it as we create the realities of our lives (par. 7).

It is here that Calderon offers the central insight that I draw upon in my own approach to teaching. She sees study of the Talmud and "the Tradition" more broadly as a project which can inform all types of Jews, not because it leads to a particular religious orientation but because it gives voice and depth to lived Jewish reality. It is a meeting place and an inheritance for all Jews—the kind of inheritance that can find its way into source sheets. In building upon Calderon's framing of the crucial role of textual tradition, I am not advocating a classical vision of cultural Zionism instead of more recent pushes towards Israel education. Rather, I want to frame cultural Zionism as a helpful analogue for thinking about a pedagogy of Israel education which uses textual (and other) resources as a way of building a 21st-century Jewish civic ethic.

The Textual Tradition in Early Zionism

By tying a flourishing Israel to the study of Jewish texts, Calderon articulates the ways culture is both an educational and political project. But the vision of Israel education she proposed was not a new idea, but a revival of early cultural-Zionist voices from the past, like the essayist Ahad Ha'am (1856–1927) and the poet Hayim Nachman Bialik (1873–1934), both of whom advocated a Zionism "in which the boundaries between Judaism and nationalism were fluid and ambiguous" (Rubin, 2004, p. 250). Almost a century earlier, Ahad Ha'am and Bialik focused on creating curricular materials that could arouse nationalist feelings among the Jews. In pre-state Israel and the decades that followed independence, the production of textual resources used to facilitate that educational project was seen as central for building the national culture of the state (Bartal, 1997; Tsahor, 2018; Urban, 2009). Ahad Ha'am in particular saw education as the core method for developing a lasting Zionism that renewed Jewish culture (Rubin, 2004; Zipperstein, 2012). In his proposal for an encyclopedia known as the *Otsar Hayahadut Belashon Ivrit* (*A Treasury of Judaism in the Hebrew Language*), Ahad Ha'am wrote, "If there's any hope in getting young people to love Judaism these days, they must know its value and know all of the good hidden within it in a way that this knowledge, in and of itself, will create national sentiment within them" (*"all devar otsar,"* p. 211, as quoted in Rubin, 2004, p. 255). To love Judaism required access to Jewish texts—the very same texts that could evoke nationalist sentiments.

Though never realized, the idea of a compendium of Jewish texts that could stir up these feelings would come to play a deeply influential role in the development of other Jewish anthologies, most famously Bialik's project of *kinnus* (cultural ingathering) and its crown jewel, the *Sefer ha-Aggadah*, which he compiled with Y. H. Rawnitzki (Fishbane, 1993; Kiel, 1997; Rubin, 2008). Bialik and Rawnitzki's collection aimed to seed the fledgling Hebrew culture with the literary tools to construct a new Hebrew future. Unlike his mentor's *Otsar Hayahadut* project, which was imagined as an encyclopedia filled with articles about classical Judaism, Bialik strived to produce an "unmediated" encounter with the Divine through a compendium of classical Hebrew sources. *Sefer ha-Aggadah* is a selection of texts ranging across Biblical and rabbinic sources, organized first in a chronology of the Jewish people and then thematically according to Jewish value-concepts which aspire towards an international humanist culture (Sebba-Elran, 2013). The liberties he and Rawnitzki took in their renderings aimed to reframe the tradition not as a staid and dusty collection but as a source for Jewish vibrancy. *Aggadah* (folklore) served as Bialik's vision for a lived Jewish experience, inverting the traditional view that *halakha* (law) is the ultimate manifestation of Jewish existence. In his well-known essay, "*Halakhah* and *Aggadah*," he writes that *aggadah* "deals with what ought to be; to read it is to learn what have been the desires, the preoccupations, the ideals of the Jewish people" (Bialik, 1916/2000, p. 74). For Bialik, *aggadah* brings forth the *halakha*.

Why this excursion into the early history of cultural Zionism? Because this is also the early history of source sheets—a key pedagogical tool for contemporary teaching practice. Of course, matters were much different

125 years ago. It's not just the technological advantages I can avail myself of through the miracle of the cut and paste function on my word processor—it's the very availability of such texts being just a click away on the internet. The situation was vastly different over a century ago. The dramatic entrance into Europe wrought by emancipation in the 19th century created a population wherein some members lacked familiarity with traditional Jewish texts (Bartal, 1997; Rubin, 2004). Moreover, the specific quotations which spoke to Jewish national sentiments were not easily available but required the patience and familiarity of an expert to find them within the rich Jewish textual tradition. Widespread access to Jewish texts simply did not exist when Ahad Ha'am and Bialik developed their projects, and many Jews living in pre-state Palestine did not have a collection of Jewish books they could call their own or libraries with robust collections (Sever, 1975). In fact, in the 1940s when the famous Israeli Bible scholar Nehama Leibowitz (1905-1997) began the practice of creating her own curricular materials and teaching with *gilyonot* (mimeographed worksheets) produced for weekly *parshat hashavua* (the Torah reading of the week) classes, she often had to go to the national library herself and meticulously copy a quotation by hand before typing it up (Abramowitz, 2003; Unterman, 2009). Today the hurdles are lower for producing source sheets, but their pedagogical power remains.

In short, the creation of curricular materials, anthologies, and encyclopedias was seen as a central strategy for both evoking nationalist sentiment *and* instilling Zionism with a sense of Jewish meaning and purpose. Pre-state and early state Zionism saw the flourishing of presses and educational projects dedicated to developing literary materials for cultural transmission, which aimed at constructing a new national culture that simultaneously emerged organically from the Jewish tradition while also breaking from it in seeding Zionist sentiments (Schweid, 1984; Schweid et al., 2008; Tsahor, 2018). As Bartal (1997) observes, this textual dance created a challenge, for these new Jews were not interested in rejecting their heritage full stop and yet were "not supposed to continue using Jewish text in the way they traditionally had"—in keeping with the Zionist agenda of sidelining diasporic textual traditions—"nor reading all the texts that had been in use in traditional Jewish society"—the Jewish "religious" literature that was excised from the curriculum Calderon and her peers were taught (p. 78).

Instead, the Zionist project offered a new educational model, hoping that the "new Jew" "would read the traditional texts in a new way and find in them what their ancestors had not found" (Bartal, 1997, p. 78).

Bartal's observation reveals a deep truth about pedagogy, one that informs the second part of my argument about the potential for Israel education to be a "big tent" where Jews of all stripes can engage one another and the tradition in order to wrestle together with the contemporary Jewish condition. The creation of these early anthologies reflected explicit educational goals by their editors, who assumed that reading these texts would "naturally" evoke nationalist sentiments. Implicit in this view is a pedagogical model that assumes texts transparently convey the intentions of their authors or compilers. And yet despite the emphasis on text production in early Zionism, mere *reproduction* of the tradition was not enough to ensure its continued survival when the nascent state of Israel needed a certain kind of Jew. Anthologies could enable Jewish study, but these had to be mediated by the adoption of a Zionist hermeneutic that could continue the tradition while enlivening Jewish text in new ways. The new Zionism did just that, albeit in ways quite at odds with the aims of cultural Zionism—promoting a particular conception of what it meant to be Jewish (Israeli) at the cost of jettisoning the methods and aims of the earlier tradition.

The pedagogical lesson to be drawn is simply this: Because text is static, it appears like a vessel for information transfer. This is the illusion that captured the minds of the cultural Zionists. But in truth one can only share texts—or source sheets—not the meaning the curator and the student find in them. Indeed, the request to vet source sheets in advance of their use as a pedagogical tool partakes of the very same assumptions regarding the unmediated transmission of knowledge from the text alone, when in fact the truth is just the opposite: Texts and source sheets alike require something more than just being read. They require interpretation.

The Strange Bedfellows of Knowledge Transmission

Before I talk about the specific issues involved in what's misguided about the request to provide source sheets for vetting, I want to pause to consider the broader implications of this notion of texts offering an unmediated transmission of knowledge. This idea of transferable information is rooted in Western notions of cognition and the primacy of text in organizing human behavior (Wogan, 2001) and has been seen as the formative explanation for the rise of nationalism itself. In his much-celebrated book *Imagined Communities: Reflections on the Origin and Spread of Nationalism*, Anderson (1983) offers a compelling argument that print capitalism enabled nationalism to come into being because novels and newspapers "provided the technical means for 'representing' the *kind* of imagined community that is the nation" (p. 25). The mass distribution of literature and the creation of the "solitary reader" allowed humans to see themselves bound up with others who shared their language and narratives. Ahad Ha'am and Bialik's activity in proposing and creating compendiums of Hebrew texts designed to evoke nationalist sentiments should be viewed in just such a light.

In this view, the act of reading is equated with cognitively imbibing and embracing an entire worldview. This belief of Anderson's in the fixed, universal, and cognitive quality of print, first articulated by scholars like Ong, Goody, and Olson, has been heavily criticized by Wogan (2001). He and other scholars like Keller-Cohen (1993) note the ubiquitous use of the term "literacy" (as in culinary literacy, cultural literacy, and even car literacy) as one way the misguided conflation of the printed word with cognition has spread. As Keller-Cohen (1993) explains, "The image of learning through print is evoked to characterize what is acquired, as though the prototypical case of learning was through literacy" (p. 295).

Of course, literacy is a close companion to education, and as we have seen, the project of nation building is always accompanied by a vision of education. The assumed link between print and cognition therefore serves as fuel for a myriad of concerns over the power of the printed work in education (Apple, 1992; Apple & Christian-Smith, 2017; Tyson-Bernstein, 1988). Yet it's remarkable to note that the same belief/concern/outrage over the power of the written word to "brainwash" the minds of young readers is just as much at work in liberal critiques as it is in conservative attacks.

On the left, these concerns are framed through the notion of a "hidden curriculum" (Giroux & Penna, 1979; Martin, 1976)—the unstated and unofficial norms and beliefs which are not explicitly part of any lesson but are taught nonetheless—and the way it expresses norms that propagate systems of economic, racial, or other forms of discriminatory power. The concept has become especially important as increasing attention is given to the ways in which sexist, racist, ableist, and other forms of marginalization are propagated through education (even if the stated educational goals might reflect the opposite intention). Because of print's fixed nature, literature, textbooks, and other similar cultural artifacts are often a target for progressive reformers (Giroux & Penna, 1979; Sleeter & Grant, 2017; Tyson-Bernstein, 1988). Undergirding these attacks is the belief that reading certain texts leads in an unmediated fashion to thinking the wrong thoughts.

Concern over curriculum and its power to influence also emerges from more conservative voices. On the right, the emphasis on what should be taught and what books should be found in classrooms has come from critics decrying the dissolution of literacy and lack of a shared American cultural heritage (Hirsch, 1988; Stern, 2003), as well as by Christian Evangelicals (Boyer, 1996) concerned with a progressive agenda. Like their progressive brethren, the unstated assumption in conservative attacks is a belief that reading texts functions as a kind of divine intervention, implanting values directly into the mind of the reader. What's essential to note is that while they may differ in their political orientations, those raising concerns over curricular materials both embrace a kind of "hermeneutic naivety" (Tomlinson, 1993, p. 34, as cited in Kirsch, 2007) while simultaneously dismissing or diminishing the agency of the reader.

Pedagogy and the Interpretation of Source Sheets

Both sides of this debate emphasize the power of curriculum. Yet those of us who have taught know that cognition is not automatic, and the classroom is far more dynamic than anyone can predict. Missing in the discussion over the textual transmission of knowledge is what happens to curriculum in the hands of an educator—the interpretive nature of pedagogy. The Israeli educator Miriam Ben-Peretz (1975) points the way towards a more pragmatic and nuanced model for understanding the relationship between curriculum and teaching. While not denying that curriculum is designed with an end in mind, Ben-Peretz explains how curriculum serves as the fertile soil in which unanticipated and unintended insights can sprout—what she calls "curriculum potential." Perhaps a student points out something in a text that the teacher has never noticed before or a text leads the class to alight on a new metaphor to describe something they have experienced in common. Perhaps an event in someone's life, their community, or even in the news influences how the text under consideration comes alive for them. Curriculum potential recognizes that educational materials, though designed with specific intentions in mind, should be understood as tools which have a wealth of interpretive possibilities within them. Instead of thinking of texts as rigid in their intended uses and outcomes, Ben-Peretz (1975) instead draws attention to how "flexible [they are] in the face of a variety of instructional situations" as well as how they "lend themselves to the imaginative use by teachers" (p. 158).

Concerns over the "hidden curriculum" on the left and the dissolution of literacy on the right reflect a negative assessment of the implicit and unintended outcomes of an educational experience. But it also remarkably diminishes the role of the teacher in the process of learning. When a direct link between reading and cognition is assumed, the role of the teacher fades to the background while the student is seen as a vessel to be filled with knowledge. The activity of interpretation is all but ignored, and the project of education is understood as a mere technical process of transfer. It is no surprise to discover that in the proliferation of curricula available to educators are many that come with a line-by-line script for teachers to follow. Contrast that model to the "curriculum potential" vision of Ben-Peretz, where learning emerges from the quality of the curricular material as well as the awareness and pedagogical moves of the pedagogue. As she wisely explains, "Teachers have to be actively and intentionally involved in uncovering multiple uses of curriculum materials in their setting" (Ben-Peretz, 1990, p. 51).

In settings where an educator receives an existing curriculum, such as in a public school math class, the pedagogical questions that emerge quite naturally focus on how a teacher can use an inherited curriculum. But because of the increased access to textual (and other) resources available on the internet, in Jewish educational settings (especially those focused on adults and emerging adults), practitioners regularly build their own instructional materials. Indeed, in comparison to the era spanning Ahad Ha'am to Nehama Leibowitz, educators working today have a treasure trove of texts at their fingertips, which not only offers educators the ability to customize their materials but hides the critical fact that curricular choices implicitly involve pedagogical decisions. And nowhere is this phenomenon more "evident" than in source sheets.

The source sheet is an intentionally designed curricular tool, made possible by digital access to the Jewish textual tradition in both the original and in translation. As source sheets have become a more common tool for teaching, spurred by the growth of online searchable digital archives of the Jewish textual tradition, teachers can now customize their own curricular materials for each educational encounter. Whereas access to the Jewish textual tradition was long mediated by publishers and knowledge of Jewish languages, today, we have the broadest access ever to the Jewish textual tradition in both the original and in translation. Educators' ability to manipulate and customize their own curricular materials raises questions around how we design these instructional tools in service of educational practice and instructional episodes. Brown (2011) argues, "Understanding how teachers use curriculum resources to craft instruction requires being explicit about the representations curriculum materials use to communicate concepts and actions, being attentive to the ways in which teachers perceive and interpret these representations, and understanding how these representations can constrain and afford teacher practice" (p. 18). Developing an understanding of the "teacher–tool relationship" cultivates a sensitivity to how instructional materials portray Judaism and Jewish ideas, how we, as educators, interpret these depictions of Judaism, and how these tools mediate and shape our educational practices.

As someone who uses source sheets, it is undeniably true that my thinking and my teaching are shaped by my capacities to find digitized sources and arrange them on the page. But that woefully under-describes the enormous range of pedagogical decisions I make in creating and using these source sheets. They are properly understood as a tool which simultaneously constrains and enables my action. Teaching with a source sheet is what Wertsch (1998) calls "mediated action." The various sources which appear on the pages of source sheets do not make clear how I will use these sources in a class, what I might say about them, or the questions I might ask of students. Source sheets are the result of a host of practitioner decisions which are not visible to others. Only enacted in the classroom does the full curricular potential of a source sheet come to light.

And it is precisely at this juncture where the request to review a source sheet goes awry. Asking to review a source sheet reveals deep and misguided assumptions about cognition and the meaning embedded in those texts. It is analogous to how people treat PowerPoint presentations. PowerPoints are both events—presentations aided visually by a digital document—as well as the document itself (Knoblauch, 2013). When understood as a presentation, the document is a tool for a complex set of interactions between humans supported and mediated by computers. It allows for an exploration of ideas and the generation of knowledge. Because the PowerPoint document remains as an artifact of that event, the information encoded in the document becomes decontextualized and transferable, allowing one to send the PowerPoint to someone else. But lost in that transfer is what the PowerPoint meant—something that could only be grasped through the interaction between audience, text, and presenter.

Source sheets are the analog equivalent of a PowerPoint. They are designed to facilitate an educational encounter, and the information embedded in them only emerges in the "action, interaction, and performance" of a class, which "bestows meanings and thus situationally creates knowledge not inscribed or encoded in the documents" (Knoblauch, 2013, p. 20). When transferred to another, their meaning—available only when enacted in the classroom—becomes untethered and inscrutable. Reviewing another's source sheet is receiving a musical score that has lyrics and chords but is stripped of any references to tempo, pitch, meter, melody, or even instruments. Any attempt to reconstitute (in the case of the PowerPoint) or anticipate (in the case of the source sheet) what the music sounds or will sound like is a fruitless exercise.

Instrumentalization and the Aims of Education

The transferable nature of the source sheet offers the fantasy that the information embedded within it translates through cognition into knowledge. When someone asks me for my source sheet in advance of a class, they only see the texts embedded in it and not the range of pedagogical moves I may employ around and within these texts. Asking to review the curricular artifact emphasizes an importance of text over the voice of the practitioner and the other students in the room. What I want to suggest in its place is how a renewed emphasis on pedagogy offers a way out of this conundrum and moreover offers a philosophical alternative to the belief that education should serve fixed and predetermined ideological outcomes—putting in its place a view that centers discussion and debate concerning the tradition as the ultimate goal.

As seen in the history of textual tradition recounted earlier, the desire to force particular educational outcomes can lead not just to the instrumentalization of content, but what is worse, the instrumentalization of the student—especially when the goals are aimed at "noble" aims like societal repair and cultural transformation. This was precisely the critique levelled at Ahad Ha'am and cultural Zionism by the Yiddish linguist Nokhum Shtif:

> The point of departure for the Hebraists is not the child himself, but rather national goals.... One never asks if the child wants to study Hebrew or is capable of doing so. You Hebraists don't bother with this question at all because to you the child is not an end but a means. This echoes the viewpoint of our ancestors, for whom the Jew existed only for the sake of something else, whether preserving the people or strengthening the religion. (Cited in Rubin, 2004, p. 256)

Shtif's critique of Ahad Ha'am could easily be levelled at 21st-century diasporic Israel education, which often (though not exclusively) emphasizes identification with contemporary Israel as its end goal (Attias, 2015; Horowitz, 2012; Isaacs, 2011; Zakai, 2014). Identification with a national entity is not inherently problematic; however, unchecked, this can lead to educational practices that border on indoctrination. The problem isn't with transferable textual curricular artifacts per se; as I have argued previously, they do not have an inherent pedagogical outlook embedded in them. It's rather the ends to which they are put—ends that too often ignore the participants in the room. Changing the texts that appear on the page won't address this concern any more than changing them will necessarily lead to students supporting state Zionism or the ends of Israel education. Where the discussion needs to move is in how source sheets are used, and therefore into an exploration of the broader goals of pedagogy.

Instrumentalization in education is not unique to Israel education but a facet of our contemporary moment, which Biesta (2013, 2017) sees emerging as a result of what he calls the "learnification" of education. Although the turn to "learning" emerged from certain positive educational transformations (including the rise of student-centered learning, critiques of authoritarian teaching models, and an increased diversity of materials via digital media), he draws attention to two important unintended consequences of this "new language of learning" (2013, p. 63). The first is how learning is framed solely as a process, devoid of content, direction, and purpose, and the second is how learning is an individual process focused on inputs and outcomes for an individual. As a result, the language of learning masks the role relationships play in education (between students and teachers, students and content, students and the world, among a group of students...) and obscures "crucial dimensions of educational processes and practices—that is, aspects of content, purpose, and relationships" (Biesta, 2013, p. 64). This masking gives rise to a view of education as a series of causal inputs and outputs that lead to learning outcomes. In contrast, when we approach education as a set of experiences and encounters with voices on the page and in the room, that is, directed but not manipulative, our conception of education broadens. Israel education using source sheets becomes a collective knowledge-building activity and an apprenticeship in active Jewish citizenship. While apprenticeship can be conceived of as a hierarchical relationship focused on skill development for economic output, I am drawing upon apprenticeship as a way of expressing a mode that, in its wholistic approach, enables the "transformative possibilities of being and becoming complex, full cultural-historical participants in the world" (Lave & Wenger, 1991, p. 32).

What I would like to offer as an alternative to an instrumentalized pedagogy is a reorientation that uses source sheets to facilitate an interpretive dialogic encounter among students, teachers, and texts (Cohen et al., 2003). One manifestation of this outlook can be found in the work of Biesta (2013), who views good teaching as a balanced triangulation between content, purpose, and relationships. This approach towards teaching moves beyond the dualism of thinking about education as either requiring a production model rooted in causal functions of inputs and outputs or based on an antiauthoritarian rejection of curriculum mentality that places individual well-being above any other virtue. In its place is a vision of education that as a real-world event contains risks because the outcome is undetermined and not guaranteed—an approach that embraces "the coming into the world of free subjects, not in the production of docile objects" (Biesta, 2013, p. 140).

This is a pedagogy that tempers the instrumental impulse, where goals and purposes meet with the material world, other people, and ideas that both confine and enlarge the worlds of students. Simon (1992) observes that "educational practice is a power relationship that participates in both enabling and constraining what is understood as knowledge and truth. When we teach, we are always implicated in the construction of a horizon of possibility for ourselves, our students, and our communities" (p. 56). Such a pedagogy creates a horizon for an alternative approach for what Israel education could be—one centered on bringing Jews into conversation with one another and the tradition.

Holzer and Kent's (2013) work on *havruta*, the activity of study in pairs or small groups, is one iteration of this type of work, which looks at a process, *havruta*, and imbues it with a purpose (social-emotional growth, relational ways of being, attuned interpretive skills). *Havruta* does not automatically lead to better interpretations, stronger relationships, or emotional growth; rather, through directed and intentional design, Holzer and Kent argue, it can lead to powerful educational experiences. This is one pedagogical tool that takes these concerns seriously. I am proposing a related suggestion that teachers develop practices for intentionally designed instructional material (source sheets) in service of constructing dialogical educational episodes, which may employ *havruta* and may employ other similar moves.

When I produce a source sheet, I simultaneously consider how these texts represent the ideas I hope to illuminate *and* how I might construct an encounter with these texts and the others in the room. It is not enough to simply present sources as though they are citations in an essay. The source sheet is designed in service of the educational event with the "intent of provoking experience that will simultaneously organize and disorganize a variety of understandings of our natural and social world" (Simon, 1992, p. 56). There is no denying that through these pedagogical practices, even as I introduce new ideas and texts to my students, I also frame particular perspectives and encounters. There is no escaping the fact that pedagogy establishes some rubric of normative value. The question is how open is the horizon of possibility one wants to construct.

Conclusion: Jewish/Israel Education for the 21st Century

While cultural Zionism has long understood its educational goals as focused on arousing nationalist sentiment through the project of Jewish textual production, there are radical differences between today's Jewish world and the one Ahad Ha'am and Bialik faced. On the one hand, today's Jews have an incredible plethora of programs that offer free or discounted travel to Israel. They can watch Israeli television programs on Netflix, and a host of Israeli advocacy groups offer a continuous array of programming in person and online for anyone who wants to engage with Israel and lobby on its behalf. Much of today's Israel education is aimed at offering unmediated access to Israel, its inhabitants, and its popular culture in service of affiliation and support—the kind of access that would have been unimaginable to Ahad Ha'am and Bialik.

On the other hand, the construction of the Jewish state is no longer an imagined project, nor are Jews a weak and powerless people in search of state power and protection. Over the last 100 years, Judaism has seen the emergence of new and exciting ways of being Jewish in both the State of Israel as well as the Diaspora, especially as Jews in the United States have flourished. Jewish power in Israel and the United States is robust, as seen in the ongoing occupation of land conquered in the 1967 six-day war and ongoing support for the State of Israel by both Democratic and Republican administrations. The ostensible purpose of state Zionism has been more than met. What then should be the ends of Israel education?

The current milieu is ripe for a pedagogical approach that offers an encounter in the analog world beyond hot takes and memes, in which the possibilities of the Jewish peoplehood and Jewish nationalism are explored through serious investigation and discussion. At its core, questions of Jewish sovereignty, responsibility, and virtue as they manifest in the realpolitik of Jewish existence should be debated and argued. On this approach the source sheet should be understood as one of an array of tools for facilitating these kinds of discussions when coupled with a non-instrumentalist pedagogy. It should be intentionally populated with the broad range of Jewish (and even at times non-Jewish) voices which speak to whatever issue at hand an educator is engaging. These textual voices should be held as contributions to a conversation that also takes students' voices seriously. The classroom, boardroom, living room, camp dining room, campus bar, or wherever Jews are sitting together and studying should offer an experience of the Jewish tradition's multivocality. It is the role of the educator to draw participants into the ever-evolving tradition and invite them to prod, pushback, listen, and ponder.

Perhaps unsurprisingly, we can find inspiration for this vision in the tradition itself—in Bialik's project of public communal conversation known as *oneg shabbat* (delight in the sabbath; Helman, 2013; Millgram, 2018). Though the new Jews of Tel Aviv saw little interest in spending the sabbath in synagogue, Bialik infused the public square with a sense of Jewishness by actively engaging them in public conversations that were contemporary versions of the rebbe's *tisch* (gathering around a rabbi's table). These public discussions of literature, philosophy, and politics were infused with references to classical Jewish texts and modern Hebrew poetry and concluded with both traditional/liturgical and modern Hebrew songs.

This approach broadens the scope of what Israel education is ultimately about. It resists the impulse to separate Jewish education and Israel education, the instrumentalization of education for national aims, and the shrinking of Jewish communal discourse. By emphasizing the role of pedagogy, such an approach sees source sheets as an opportunity to encounter the Jewish textual tradition and Jewish people in a way that is alive and present, moving Israel education from a set of goals rooted in inputs and outputs to an ongoing activity that examines the promise and possibilities of the Jewish people.

NOTES

1. The Shalom Hartman Institute is a center for applied Jewish thought and education in Israel and North America. Its iEngage project, which includes five different curricula, has been taught in Hillels, JCCs, camps, and over 500 synagogues in North America.

REFERENCES

Abramowitz, L. (2003). *Tales of Nehama: Impressions of the life and teaching of Nehama Leibowitz*. Gefen Publishing House Ltd.

Anderson, B. (1983). *Imagined communities: Reflections on the origin and spread of nationalism* (2nd ed.). Verso books.

Apple, M. W. (1992). The text and cultural politics. *Educational Researcher, 21*(7), 4–19. https://doi.org/10.2307/1176356

Apple, M., & Christian-Smith, L. (2017). *The politics of the textbook*. Routledge. https://doi.org/10.4324/9781315021089

Attias, S. (2015). What's in a name? In pursuit of Israel education. *Journal of Jewish Education, 81*(2), 101–135. https://doi.org/10.1080/15244113.2015.1028314

Bartal, I. (1997). The ingathering of traditions: Zionism's anthology projects. *Prooftexts, 17*(1), 77–93. https://www.jstor.org/stable/20689470

Ben-Peretz, M. (1975). The concept of curriculum potential. *Curriculum Theory Network, 5*(2), 151–159. https://doi.org/10.2307/1179278

Ben-Peretz, M. (1990). *The teacher-curriculum encounter: Freeing teachers from the tyranny of texts*. State University of New York Press. https://doi.org/10.1177/027046769201200273

Bialik, H. N. (2000). *Revealment and concealment: Five essays* (L. Simon, Trans.). Ibis Editions. (Original work published 1916)

Biesta, G. (2017). Lead learner or head teacher? Exploring connections between curriculum, leadership and evaluation in an "age of measurement." In *Bridging educational leadership, curriculum theory and didaktik* (pp. 181–198). Springer, Cham. https://doi.org/10.1007/978-3-319-58650-2_3

Biesta, G. J. J. (2013). *Beautiful risk of education*. Routledge, Taylor & Francis Group.

Boyer, P. (1996). In search of the fourth "R": The treatment of religion in American history textbooks and survey courses. *The History Teacher, 29*(2), 195–216. https://doi.org/10.2307/494740

Brown, M. W. (2011). The teacher-tool relationship: Theorizing the design and use of curricular materials. In J. T. Remillard, B. A. Herbel-Eisenmann, & G. M. Lloyd (Eds.), *Mathematics teachers at work: Connecting curriculum materials and classroom instruction* (pp. 17–36). Taylor & Francis.

Calderon, R. (2013, February 13). *The heritage of all Israel* (E. Fischer, Trans.). The New York Jewish Week. https://www.jta.org/2013/02/14/ny/the-heritage-of-all-israel

Cohen, D. K., Raudenbush, S. W., & Ball, D. L. (2003). Resources, Instruction, and Research. *Educational Evaluation and Policy Analysis, 25*(2), 119–142. https://doi.org/10.3102/01623737025002119

Fishbane, M. (1993). The Aggadah: Fragments of delight. *Prooftexts, 13*(2), 181–190. https://www.jstor.org/stable/20689364

Giroux, H. A., & Penna, A. N. (1979). Social education in the classroom: The dynamics of the hidden curriculum. *Theory & Research in Social Education, 7*(1), 21–42. https://doi.org/10.1080/00933104.1979.10506048

Helman, A. (2013). Was there anything particularly Jewish about "the first Hebrew city"? In B. Kirshenblatt-Gimblett & J. Karp (Eds.), *The art of being Jewish in modern times* (pp. 116–127). University of Pennsylvania Press. https://doi.org/10.9783/9780812208863.116

Hirsch, E. D. (1988). *Cultural literacy: What every American needs to know*. Vintage.

Holzer, E., & Kent, O. (2013). *A philosophy of havruta*. Academic Studies Press.
Horowitz, B. (2012). *Defining Israel education*. The iCenter for Israel Education.
Isaacs, A. (2011). Israel education: Purposes and practices. In H. Miller, L. D. Grant, & A. Pomson (Eds.), *The international handbook of Jewish education* (pp. 479–496). Springer.
Keller-Cohen, D. (1993). Rethinking literacy: Comparing colonial and contemporary America. *Anthropology & Education Quarterly*, 24(4), 288–307. https://doi.org/10.1525/aeq.1993.24.4.04x0061i
Kiel, M. W. (1997). Sefer ha'aggadah: Creating a classic anthology for the people and by the people. *Prooftexts*, 17(2), 177–197. https://www.jstor.org/stable/20689479
Kirsch, T. (2007). Ways of reading as religious power in print globalization. *American Ethnologist*, 34(3), 509–520. https://doi.org/10.1525/ae.2007.34.3.509
Knoblauch, H. (2013). *PowerPoint, communication, and the knowledge society*. Cambridge University Press.
Lave, J., & Wenger, E. (1991). *Situated learning: Legitimate peripheral participation*. Cambridge University Press.
Lockspeiser, B., & Foer, J. (2012). Opening the source of Jewish literary wisdom. *Contact: The Journal of the Steinhardt Foundation for Jewish Life*, 15(1), 15.
Martin, J. R. (1976). What should we do with a hidden curriculum when we find one? *Curriculum Inquiry*, 6(2), 135–151. https://doi.org/10.2307/1179759
Millgram, A. E. (2018). *The Sabbath anthology*. The Jewish Publication Society.
Rubin, A. (2004). Jewish nationalism and the encyclopaedic imagination. *Journal of Modern Studies*, 3(3), 247–267. https://doi.org/10.1080/1472588042000292349
Rubin, A. (2008). "Like a necklace of black pearls whose string has snapped": Bialik's "aron ha-sefarim" and the sacralization of Zionism. *Prooftexts: A Journal of Jewish Literary History*, 28(2), 157–196. https://doi.org/10.2979/pft.2008.28.2.157
Schweid, E. (1984). The rejection of the diaspora in Zionist thought: Two approaches. *Studies in Zionism*, 5(1), 43–70. https://doi.org/10.1080/13531048408575854
Schweid, E., Hadary, A., & Levin, L. (2008). *Idea of modern Jewish culture: Reference library of Jewish intellectual history*. Academic Studies Press.
Sebba-Elran, T. (2013). From *Sefer ha'aggadah* to the Jewish bookcase: Dynamics of a cultural change. *Jewish Studies Quarterly*, 20(3), 272. https://doi.org/10.1628/0944570 13X13745056601568
Sever, S. (1975). Reading patterns and libraries in Israel. *Journal of Library and Information Science*, 1(2), 1–24. https://www.proquest.com/scholarly-journals/reading-patterns-libraries-israel/docview/2001103465/se-2
Shapira, A. (2004). The Bible and Israeli identity. *AJS Review*, 28(1), 11–41. https://doi.org/10.1017/S0364009404000030
Sheskin, I. M., & Liben, M. (2015). The people of the nook: Jewish use of the Internet. In S. D. Brunn (Ed.), *The Changing World Religion Map* (pp. 3831–3856). Springer.
Silow-Carrol, A. (2017, October 3). This Torah study tool is everywhere—But you may have never heard of it. *Jewish Telegraphic Agency*. https://www.jta.org/2017/10/03/lifestyle/this-torah-study-tool-is-everywhere-but-you-may-have-never-heard-of-it
Simon, R. I. (1992). *Teaching against the grain: Texts for a pedagogy of possibility*. Bergin & Garvey.
Sleeter, C. E., & Grant, C. A. (2017). Race, class, gender, and disability in current text-

books. In M. Apple & L. Christian-Smith (Eds.), *The politics of the textbook* (pp. 78–110). Routledge.

Stern, S. (2003). *Breaking free: Public school lessons and the imperative of school choice*. Encounter Books.

Tsahor, D. (2018). "A compass to our culture": A history of Haentsiklopedia Haivrit, 1944–1980. *Israel Studies*, 23(1), 106–128. https://doi.org/10.2979/israelstudies.23.1.06

Tyson-Bernstein, H. (1988). *A conspiracy of good intentions: America's textbook fiasco*. Council for Basic Education.

Unterman, Y. (2009). *Nehama Leibowitz: Teacher and Bible scholar*. Urim Publications.

Urban, M. (2009). *Aesthetics of renewal*. University of Chicago Press.

Wertsch, J. V. (1998). *Mind as action*. Oxford University Press.

Wogan, P. (2001). Imagined communities reconsidered: Is print-capitalism what we think it is? *Anthropological Theory*, 1(4), 403–418. https://doi.org/10.1177/14634990122228809

Zakai, S. (2014). "My heart is in the East and I am in the West": Enduring questions of Israel education in North America. *Journal of Jewish Education*, 80(3), 287–318. https://doi.org/10.1080/15244113.2014.937192

Zipperstein, S. J. (2012). *Ahad Ha'am elusive prophet: Ahad Ha'am and the origins of Zionism*. Halban.

PART II

Using Student Voices to Examine Teacher Choices

4
Complex Texts and Complex Identities
Helping Students Navigate Personally and Emotionally Resonant Topics About Israeli Society

MATT REINGOLD, ALEXA JACOBY,
and BENJAMIN DAY

This chapter is built around narratives about how two students and one teacher navigated the challenges of teaching and learning complex topics in Israeli society. The stories that shape the chapter revolve around moments of crisis, where students are deeply challenged by Israeli policies and practices, and how their teacher helped them better understand themselves and their relationships with Israel. Our chapter is coauthored by Matt Reingold, a high school educator, and two of his former high school students, Benjamin Day (class of 2019) and Alexa Jacoby (class of 2021). Both Day and Jacoby were veteran Jewish day school students, with each attending Jewish elementary and secondary schools for 14 years, and yet, when they studied contemporary Israeli society alongside Reingold, each would come to learn that the Israel they had been previously taught was an incomplete Israel. For Day, this would involve realizing that because of his mother's conversion to Judaism by a Reform rabbinical court, he was not permitted full inclusion as a citizen in Israeli society should he choose to immigrate to the country. Conversely, for Jacoby, internal conflict ensued between her left-wing values and her love of Israel when she learned that religious policies in the country excluded people who she believed were Jewish, but the state did not believe likewise. Guiding them through these complex encounters was Reingold, a teacher with 15 years of experience and the codeveloper of the course on Israeli society.

Like the mentor-teacher and mentee-teacher dynamic described in Sidney Trubowitz and Maureen Picard Robins' (2003) *The Good Teacher Mentor*, we also value the unique perspectives and insights that each of us can offer for understanding classroom phenomena because we arrived in the classroom with differing roles, responsibilities, agencies, perspectives, and personal and professional experiences. Prior to collaborating, we did not know what the others thought and experienced in our shared classrooms, and therefore our respective takeaways from the lessons were incomplete and partial; working together afforded us a more expansive and holistic understanding of an educational experience.[1] In this chapter, we have collaborated to explore how one teacher (Reingold) worked with two students (Day and Jacoby) who experienced personal disappointment and confusion with Israel as a result of learning about the country's immigration policies.

While Day's and Jacoby's stories are unique to each author based on their personal experiences in Reingold's class, in the almost 10 years that Reingold has been teaching an elective course on contemporary Israeli society, he has come to see them as part of a wider pattern of student experiences. As his students come to more deeply understand the degrees of complexity in Israeli society due to the interconnectedness of different religious, national, and ethnic groups, he has observed that some begin to realize that these complexities challenge their own understandings of and relationships with Israel. Invariably, these new discoveries result in some type of statement—either said aloud in front of the whole class or in private directly to him—that Israel is not what they had thought it was. Both Day and Jacoby felt this in the classroom too. This chapter is built on a premise that analyzing a classroom occurrence from the perspectives of different stakeholders—in our case students and teacher—provides opportunities for gaining new insights into teaching. By piecing together the narratives from three distinct voices, we aim to shed light on what pedagogical moves an educator made and how these choices helped his students traverse complex moral and personal terrain.

The topic of how learning about complexities in Israeli society can lead to emotional reactions from students is one that is of interest to Israel education researchers (Hassenfeld, 2016; Reingold, 2017; Sinclair et al., 2010). This is because many classroom educators are deeply concerned with strengthening the relationship that students have with Israel (Zakai, 2014). Learning that there is evidence of violence perpetrated by pre-state soldiers against Palestinians in 1948 or that immigrants throughout Israel's history have struggled integrating into Israeli society is upsetting for students, and the greater the degree of personal connection to the topic, perhaps the greater the likelihood that the relationship might rupture because of new knowledge. These studies focus on the student experience and how students navigate their relationship with Israel; they demonstrate that despite learning upsetting content, students eventually return to homeostasis in their orientation towards Israel, with many even feeling more deeply connected to the country because they can now better understand it. Our chapter is similarly interested in the student experience, but our focus lies in trying to reflectively understand what Reingold, as the teacher, did to help Day and Jacoby, the students, work through learning new and upsetting aspects of Israeli society which challenged aspects of their own identities as Jews and Canadians. Their understandings of the texts that were studied in class and the implications of these understandings led to them—and in Day's case quite literally—calling out in the lesson and asking about their respective Jewish identities.

While intimately tied to classroom learning, we believe that both Day's and Jacoby's classroom observations fell outside the scope of the preplanned lesson. Ronald Beghetto (2013) has called these instances "micromoments," a term he uses to describe classroom exchanges where "the planned curriculum meets the lived curriculum" (p. 134). These micromoments "provide opportunities for teachers (and students) to explore, learn, and experience something new, unscripted, and unplanned" (Beghetto, 2013, p. 134). Beghetto (2009) argues that teachers ought to embrace micromoments because it is in them that hidden creative insights can emerge and result in meaningful and transformative educational experiences. In our case, the micromoments of Day's and Jacoby's learning led to new understandings of Israeli society and new understandings of their relationships with the country and with Judaism. It also led to new pedagogical understandings for Reingold as the educator in the classroom.

Israel educators often care deeply about presenting a truthful portrait of a complex society while also being sensitive towards the emotional relationship that exists between student and subject matter (Isaacs, 2011; Zakai, 2014). Therefore micromoments should be of great relevance to them. And yet, suggest both Katherine Simon (2001) and Beghetto (2009), teachers in all disciplines often dismiss students' interjections instead of finding ways to entertain them during the lesson. Dismissals happen for several reasons: Teachers worry about exploring less-familiar topics, teachers are concerned about whether the interruption is really a distraction from the curriculum, and teachers can even feel discomfort with the potential risks associated with pursuing new lines of inquiry in the classroom. The unintended consequence of dismissing the micromoment is that it leads students to be less willing to take intellectual risks because the rejection reinforces adopting normative and safer classroom behaviors (Beghetto, 2013). Conversely, creating an environment that embraces the micromoment establishes a space that is safe enough for students to take intellectual and emotional risks and to experience growth in these two domains (Beghetto, 2013). It also leads students to becoming more engaged in their learning and the wider world (Simon, 2001). As will be seen, both Jacoby's and Day's classroom experiences involved specific micromoments wherein Jacoby and Day each steered the learning in a new direction; their reflections highlight the ways that Reingold navigated their micromoments to facilitate meaningful educational experiences for teacher and student alike.

The Educational Milieu

TanenbaumCHAT is a coeducational Jewish high school in Toronto where Reingold has been teaching since September 2008. While there, he codeveloped a Grade 12 elective about contemporary Israeli society, and he has been teaching the course for eight years. Day was a student in Reingold's class in 2018–2019, and Jacoby was a student of his in 2020–2021. Both students were active members in the classroom community, participating regularly in conversations and asking thoughtful questions.

The pedagogical approach that guides Reingold's practice is influenced by Hanan A. Alexander's (2015) concept of the pedagogy of difference. This approach is built on the assumption that "students learn how to discover problems in their own received narratives or in the narratives they have chosen by viewing them from alternative perspectives" (p. 157), and students are therefore purposefully and explicitly encouraged to critically assess their own assumptions about Israel by reading, watching, and listening to primary and secondary sources that present Israel in contrasting ways.

One of the course's first texts is the Law of Return, an original Israeli law that grants citizenship to Jews worldwide (Israel First Knesset, 2008). The text is taught alongside a legal case about Brother Daniel, a Holocaust survivor who was denied citizenship in Israel after choosing to convert from Judaism to Christianity to save his life during World War II and his subsequent decision to reaffirm his Christianity after the war's end (Israel Supreme Court, 2008). Students read the Supreme Court's decision wherein the justices opined that, despite Brother Daniel's many merits, which included saving Jewish lives and being born Jewish, a practicing Christian clergyman is not a Jew, and he is therefore ineligible for citizenship under the Law of Return. Instead, the court ruled that the law is intended specifically for Jews who self-identify as Jews.

The two texts—The Law of Return and the Supreme Court's ruling on Brother Daniel's citizenship—are included in the curriculum because they raise important questions about Israel's identity as a Jewish state and what criteria should be used when determining eligibility for citizenship in the country. The texts were also considered in light of the impact of the Supreme Court's ruling on Israeli society. Reingold taught that when the justices decided to prevent Brother Daniel from immigrating, their response had a far-reaching impact. This is because their position—that immigration should be available for any practicing Jew—allowed immigration from people who self-identify as Jewish based upon a broad set of criteria that was inclusive of global Jewry's religious diversity. However, not all these criteria are recognized as legitimate markers of Jewishness by Israel's religious courts, which adhere to more stringent and narrow criteria. For example, conversion to Reform and Conservative Judaism is recognized as legitimate by the Israeli Supreme Court and therefore their converts are eligible for citizenship; simultaneously, these same converts are not recognized as Jewish by the Israeli religious courts because the religious justices do not recognize the religious legitimacy of Reform or Conservative conversions.

As a result of the religious and secular courts' positions, a dichotomy emerged wherein some Jews were deemed eligible for citizenship, which falls under the purview of the Supreme Court, but denied recognition as Jews by the state's religious courts, which govern issues like marriage and divorce. These immigrants are simultaneously recognized in Israel as both Jewish *and* not Jewish. Individuals who find themselves in this situation are legally permitted to immigrate to the country and receive citizenship but are unable to avail themselves of any of the services provided by the religious courts. Most notably, these services include marriage and divorce; and therefore, due to the absence of civil marriage in Israel, individuals in this unenviable position are unable to legally wed in the country.

Being Personally Affected by Israeli Religious Policies: Day's Classroom Experiences

Prior to taking Dr. Reingold's Grade 12 course Israeli Society, I had a strong, passionate relationship with Israel. I had the privilege to visit the country three times and had learned about its history for over 13 years. I was brought up in a Conservative Jewish home. My parents taught me the importance of religious values, traditions, and customs and instilled in me a deep-rooted passion for Israel and Zionism. Most importantly, I attended Jewish day school starting at four years old, and as soon as I was old enough, our family took a 14-day trip to Israel. I attended a Zionist Jewish elementary school from kindergarten through Grade 8, and it was here where I believe my passion for Judaism and Israel was rooted.

From Grades 9 through 12, I had the privilege of attending Tanenbaum-CHAT. There, I learned about the importance of Jewish national independence with Israel, the rightful home of the Jewish people. It was in Grade 11 when the curriculum was steered towards the Arab–Israeli conflict. I was able to learn the nation's complex history and about the longstanding war over the land. This class, alongside the opportunity to participate in the March of the Living during April of 2018, instilled my love for Israel and, more importantly, a belief in the rightfulness of the Jewish state.

However, even with all my education and experience, I had never had an opportunity to discover the internal issues and complexities of Israel. I was thrilled to take the course Israeli Society in Grade 12 since, unlike other Jewish history classes I had taken, the course focused primarily on the modern-day complexities of the State of Israel. I can confidently say that the course was one of the most fascinating classes I took in high school. The content and teacher encouraged students to investigate Israel with a critical lens by encouraging students to ask controversial questions and discuss difficult topics. The classroom served as a safe environment for intellectual sociopolitical discussion, something I had never experienced before in an academic setting. I was able to learn about the nation's modern-day strengths and flaws, as well as its internal turmoil between church and state, or more specifically, the Supreme Court and the Rabbinate. Unbeknownst to me, the course would alter my perspective on the State of Israel and enable me to question and rediscover what it means to be Jewish.

I remember that a long discussion ensued about the repercussions and consequences of the Brother Daniel case. Dr. Reingold discussed how there are cases where only the Supreme Court would classify someone as Jewish, whereas the Rabbinate would not, or vice-versa. In hindsight, I would have benefitted from Dr. Reingold providing situations where the definition of "Jewish" was ambiguous when it came to right of return. I feel as though this might have allowed me to get a firmer grasp on the internal complexities between the Rabbinate and the government within Israel. What happened instead was a student asking what would happen if someone converted to Judaism and then tried to get Israeli citizenship. Dr. Reingold explained that in this situation, the only case where both parties, the Supreme Court and the Rabbinate, would qualify said person as Jewish would be if the non-Jew underwent an Orthodox conversion.

Without thinking twice, I raised my hand to ask a question. I explained how when my father, a born Jew, married my mother, born Christian, she underwent a Reform conversion. I asked what this meant for my Jewish identity and what would happen if I were to immigrate to Israel. Dr. Reingold explained that, unfortunately, because my mother did not convert through an Orthodox process, she was not Jewish in the eyes of the Rabbinate.

I was stunned into silence.

In Orthodox Jewish law, you are only considered Jewish through your mother's side. Since the Rabbinate did not classify my mother as Jewish, I learned that the Rabbinate of Israel did not classify me as Jewish either. This meant that if I ever wanted to make *aliyah* (immigrate), I would be granted citizenship *only* by the Supreme Court, not from the Rabbinate. In the Rabbinate's eyes, I was not a Jew, meaning I was not entitled to Israeli citizenship. Further, since there is no such thing as a civil marriage in Israel, I learned that I cannot get married in Israel since I am not classified as Jewish. This meant that activities with a religious connection in Israel, such as getting married, would only be recognized and authorized by the state, not by the Rabbinate.

After hearing this news, I remember the entire class went dead silent. However, while I certainly understood my situation, I was yet to comprehend its deeper implications. Unbeknownst to me, this would soon be a pivotal turning point for my religious identification, and more importantly, for my perspective on the sociopolitical and religious complexities of modern Israeli society.

After class, Dr. Reingold came up to me to comfort me and said something along the lines of "I'm sure this is a very difficult thing to wrap your head around, and I want to help if there's anything you want to talk about." I remember just laughing about it naively because I had not yet understood the magnitude of this revelation. At that point, the Rabbinate's opinion on my status as a Jew had minimal impact on me, and I was yet to process how it could alter my judgment of Israel.

About a week later, our class had an assignment that asked us to reflect on the content discussed in the politics unit. Evidently, I had some important points to discuss. Only once I began to put my thoughts on paper did I realize how much the divide between church and state impacted my self-identification as Jewish. The final paragraphs of my assignment are shown in the following excerpt and display the emotional and religious distress I experienced:

> My mother was born in New Zealand and practiced Christianity. After meeting my father, who was born Jewish, she performed a Reform conversion. Therefore, because my mother converted to Judaism in a non-Orthodox process, the Rabbinate states that I am not Jewish. This

was an incredibly painful realization. Being raised as Jew by attending Jewish day school my entire life, separating meat and milk dishes, eating kosher foods, celebrating Jewish holidays, attending synagogue, or having Shabbat dinner every Friday night for 17 years feels different now because, according to the Rabbinate, I simply am not Jewish. I cannot even get married in Israel without undergoing an Orthodox conversion.

Thus, the case of Brother Daniel not only had an impact on Israeli politics and Israeli society, but it also had a profound impact on Jews in the Diaspora and their religious identification. I, therefore, find the case to be truly compelling because I, myself, am a Diaspora Jew. Not only have I begun to question the functionality of the state of Israel, but I have begun to question my identity as a member of the Jewish people.

In a way, I felt betrayed by Israel. I believed that the religion and community I had devoted so much of my time and mental space to was essentially alienating me from the larger demographic of "Jews," and according to the Rabbinate, I was never entitled to view Israel as my second homeland. I began to question what it meant to be Jewish altogether and how the Haredi, Conservative, and Reform communities of the religion can function symbiotically within Israel without a standardized definition of what it means to be Jewish. Only then did I begin to comprehend the internal turmoil between the church and state, and in turn, the vast complexities engraved into modern Israeli society.

Considering the impact that the revelation had on my Jewish identity, I was reluctant to discuss the issue in-depth for personal reasons. I believe that Dr. Reingold did an excellent job helping me cope and navigate the troubling situation by approaching me after class as well as consistently checking in on me in the following weeks at school.

However, what I now realize is that Dr. Reingold's support started far before my revelation. Rather, Dr. Reingold put effort towards creating a supportive, inclusive, and interactive classroom experience, something I certainly took for granted while taking his class. I found that Israeli Society, that is, the course, needed an educated, respected, and knowledgeable educator to lead and teach it since the content digs deep into controversial political, social, religious, and legal matters associated with Israel and motivates students to ask difficult questions. In my opinion,

Dr. Reingold actively worked to create an educational environment that embraced micromoments and encouraged students to question Israeli society on a secular and religious level, as well as question Judaic culture and law overall. More importantly, he knew the value of finding personal meaning in class content and encouraged students to share their personal thoughts and experiences if they felt comfortable. To develop and sustain this environment, we would regularly have informal group discussions and reflection periods. Through doing so, Dr. Reingold developed a thought-provoking and healthy class dynamic. I clearly felt so comfortable with my peers that I felt no hesitation to raise my hand and ask an extremely personal question regarding the Law of Return and Brother Daniel.

After I asked about what it meant for my status as a Jew in Israel, Dr. Reingold made sure to display emotional intelligence by recognizing that it was a really difficult situation, especially since it happened in front of all of my peers. By checking in with me in the days after, I felt as though it wasn't just my teacher looking out for one of his students, but it was someone being there for another person who was experiencing a harsh realization.

Dr. Reingold served as a vital resource in helping me navigate my situation. He helped me realize an important distinction between Israel and Judaism overall. I learned that even though the Israeli Rabbinate does not consider me Jewish, it does not invalidate my personal identification as Jewish, and most importantly, the value I find in my religious beliefs and practices. Moreover, Dr. Reingold, and the Israeli Society course overall, helped me view Israel through an analytical lens to identify flaws in Israeli society, all while still maintaining the passion and love of Israel I always had. I learned that my relationship with Israeli society did not have to be strictly binary, in that I either loved it or rejected it. Rather, I realized that I could still be a passionate Zionist and Jew without loving everything that Israel and Judaism believe in and represent.

Learning the Good and the Bad Sides of Israel's History: Jacoby's Classroom Experiences

Growing up, my Israel story was never my own. My middle school was a Zionist Hebrew school, and while I adored it there, it had its issues when it came to teaching Israel to children. I was not given the tools or the space to form my own opinion of Israel, because the narrative laid out before me was oversimplified, overwhelmingly positive, and somewhat misleading. For instance, while we learned the basic overview of wars fought by Israel, we often looked at them from a very one-sided lens. We would focus on Israel's positive actions during times of war, their rationale behind participating in these wars, and their victories. This is not entirely shocking because one of the school's core values was to instill a deep love of Israel in its students, but when I look back, this approach appears somewhat problematic. The course material was very selective, and while I supposedly learned about the "good" and "bad" sides of Israel's history, we did not discuss any issues that were too "sensitive" due to the young age of the students. As a result, I never took the time to formulate my own opinion about Israel. I had a strong love and connection to the country, and as far as I was concerned, I already knew everything I had to know.

In September of 2020, I began to take a course entitled Israeli Society. It was here that I finally began to receive a more in-depth and nuanced Israel education, and I spent over two months learning about Israel's history, people, religious disputes, and, naturally, society. This is also when I was introduced to the story of Brother Daniel and the Law of Return. This story showed me some of the prominent issues within Israeli society, especially those concerning immigration and citizenship.

After hearing about Brother Daniel's impact on the Law of Return, the Rabbinate's power, and the repercussions being felt today, I was very angry. It was extremely challenging to learn about the discrimination that was occurring within the country, but also within the Jewish community. I couldn't believe that after years of being expelled and rejected from our homes that we, the Jewish people, would turn around and do the same thing to other Jews. This was especially upsetting and confusing for me because I had been taught my whole life that Israel was supposed to be a haven for all Jewish people. If that is truly what Israel is supposed to be, then why are only some Jews recognized as Jewish and permitted to take part in important practices, while others are not? Why are we causing conflict within our community by drawing a line in the sand and evaluating the "Jewishness" of our Jewish siblings? I was very passionate about these issues after they were brought to my attention, and I felt as if I had more questions than answers.

This one text had single-handedly changed the way that I thought about

Israel. I was very bothered by what I learned about Israel's immigration policies because it seems to go against what the country originally stood for based on its Declaration of Independence, which we also studied at length. More specifically, the Israeli Declaration of Independence states that not only will the State of Israel "be open for Jewish immigration" but that "it will foster the development of the country for the benefit of all its inhabits" and "it will ensure complete equality of social and political rights to all its inhabitants irrespective of religion, race or sex" (*Declaration of Independence*, 1948).

Although the word "Jewish" is not defined, the emphasis on developing the country to benefit "all" of its inhabitants and ensuring that "all" of them are granted equal rights is significant. Additionally, this excerpt clearly states that religion would not play a role in deciding who is able to do what within Israel, which does not appear to be the case today seeing as the Rabbinate continues to favor Orthodox Jews over other Jews. Furthermore, this text also strengthened my feelings of anger and frustration toward the Rabbinate, and it gave me a deeper understanding of how much power the Rabbinate holds in Israeli society.

I was always puzzled by the fact that one small group of Jews had the authority to make decisions that affected every single Jew in the country, especially if their decisions typically seemed to favor Orthodox Jews. I wondered how it was fair that one group of more traditional and religious Jews gets to determine who can and can't get married, especially since they are going to exclude people that don't fit their criteria of what they think a Jew is. Moreover, I was also upset that Jews within Israel were treated differently based on factors that I did not consider to be significant, for example, whether your mother was considered Jewish or whether or not you followed the customs of Orthodox Judaism. In my mind, and perhaps in my naivete, I assumed that all Jewish people would fall under the umbrella term of "Jew" regardless of where they came from, who their family was, and the type of Judaism they practiced. The differentiation between halachic Jews and non-halachic Jews made no sense to me and seemed rather arbitrary.

During this emotionally charged time, I turned to my Israel educator, Dr. Reingold, for support. Based on my experience as a student, to create an effective learning environment, a strong Israel educator is defined by the successful fulfillment of three criteria. First, they must create a learning environment where students feel comfortable sharing their opinions. Second, they must present information in an unbiased way, without sugarcoating any of Israel's past or present decisions, to promote honesty within the class. Finally, they must demonstrate the ability to empathize with their students, as the subjects being taught can be controversial, upsetting, and even infuriating. It is my opinion that Dr. Reingold successfully fulfilled these criteria, which ultimately led to my success in his class.

Despite my previous lack of an opinion on issues within Israeli society, I have always been a strongly opinionated person. In Dr. Reingold's class, I was able to freely articulate my opinion thanks to the way the material was taught. I felt this way because of the discussion questions that Dr. Reingold always gave us at the end of every lesson. After particularly challenging lessons, giving opportunities to reflect as a group or as individuals was a very effective strategy for taking the pulse of the classroom and its learners. Dr. Reingold did this by putting us into groups to answer his questions, which always sparked discussion. This made me feel like my opinion was valued and helped me share it with others because instead of discouraging controversial discussion, Dr. Reingold promoted it. The topics we were covering were not easy, like the implications of Brother Daniel's story, and yet we were always invited to share our thoughts. Even though I was a high school student, I never felt like my opinion was worth less than Dr. Reingold's; when he came to visit my group, I always felt like he was really listening to what I was saying. By allowing us to have discussions with one another, and then later engaging in those discussions with us in an encouraging and supportive way, Dr. Reingold allowed me to became more comfortable sharing my opinion.

In addition, Dr. Reingold was always honest with us about Israel and never sugarcoated anything to make Israel seem different than what it is. For example, when discussing controversies within the Israeli government, he would never shy away from telling us the truth about these issues. Although he always managed to remain impartial, he was unafraid of sharing the reality of the system of government that Israel has in place. We openly discussed the coalition system, including the complex and often fragile nature of these agreements. Dr. Reingold talked about the political implications of certain coalitions and how some representatives used each other to get the positions that they wanted in government. There are times, however, where I do think Dr. Reingold could have shared even more of the reactions of different communities in Israel to the issues we covered in class. I would have appreciated learning about how different groups, such as Jewish communities of varying religious-observance levels and non-Jewish communities, felt about the events we were learning. While we did cover this in class to some degree, I felt that we could have gone into more detail when examining the opinions and reactions of different groups across the country. Despite this, Dr. Reingold's honesty when it came to the course material made me feel more comfortable being honest in return. I never feared that my honest responses to the issues we discussed would be scrutinized by Dr. Reingold or my peers, because he had established a class culture based on honesty. If Dr. Reingold could be honest, then his students could be as well.

I believe that it is the responsibility of educators, especially those tasked with teaching Israel, to present an unbiased collection of facts to their students. Dr. Reingold's teaching methods and presentation of the facts allowed me to formulate my own opinion in my own time. When talking about a new issue, he would ensure that his students saw every side before finalizing their opinions. For instance, when talking about issues that concerned Jews of varying political beliefs and/or levels of religious devotion, he would always present the topic from multiple perspectives. This was best demonstrated through the work we did for our final summative assignment. Dr. Reingold divided us into groups of five, and each member of the group was assigned an Israeli political party to represent. My group's topic was the increase of domestic violence within Israel during the COVID-19 pandemic, and our assignment was to come up with a plan to mitigate this issue. This meant that all group members had to research their party, and how their party would respond, before joining forces and compromising with the other "parties" to find a solution. This activity forced us to research and learn about different opinions on complicated topics, like how to balance Jewish and democratic values with regards to Sabbath observance or how to tackle unemployment in marginalized population sectors. These research projects allowed us to form our own opinions in the process.

Finally, one of Dr. Reingold's strengths was his ability to establish his classroom as a safe space for his students. He would take time at the beginning of every class to remind us that we were all experiencing this together and that if we needed to leave the class at any time, we could. He also explained that all questions were welcome, and that he would not judge us for expressing our anger or disbelief. The Israel educator was never condescending and always regarded us as equals. Feeling safe enough to ask questions without being embarrassed, and to express outrage without being punished, helped me navigate my conflicting feelings and emotions at the time. He was also aware that some of the lessons taught could potentially be upsetting for his students, and his empathy during these times was greatly appreciated in navigating the complexities. In my opinion, what ultimately makes a strong Israel educator is the ability to strike a balance between telling the truth and providing support for the emotions that come with the truth. Having both a teacher and a close confidant, a presenter of harsh truths and an emotional support system, allowed me to better navigate my frustrations.

If my middle school self saw me today, she would be surprised to see how opinionated I am when it comes to Israeli society. She would probably laugh at me, but I wouldn't take it too personally. Ultimately, I know that if she had been given the same tools, support, and resources that I have been so lucky to have, she would feel the same way I do today. Providing said tools and setting up a support system for students is what makes an effective Israel educator; in other words, being considered a "good teacher" is only the beginning. The Israel educators that students will remember are not necessarily the easiest markers or the best at teaching; they are the ones who go the extra mile to make their students feel comfortable. Their students look forward to spending many hours a week with them because they know that their class is going to be worthwhile. They are the ones who make an effort to treat their students as equals, who are willing to engage in intellectual conversations, who make their classes engaging, and who are willing to support their students during emotionally challenging times.

A Teacher's View: Reingold's Classroom Experiences

As the educator in a high school classroom, I find it at times difficult to ascertain the degree to which students are interested in a specific text or topic. This is not the case with teaching the Law of Return and the case of

Brother Daniel; having taught them together over 20 times, they never fail to elicit strong reactions from students. When preparing to teach the texts each year, I remind myself that the texts challenge students to think about Israel in new ways which might cause discomfort or even disappointment. I therefore anticipate encountering students like Jacoby, who are staunchly Zionist but whose orientation is left leaning and secular. Variations on Jacoby's experiences of finding the learning disruptive because it challenges preconceived assumptions of Israel are evidenced on an almost yearly basis from some students. As an educator, I am deeply aware that Jacoby's feelings reflect legitimate pressure points in students' relationships with Israel and that if not effectively managed, this can not only detract students from being willing to express themselves in the classroom but also push them away from Israel. Unlike other texts that I teach which can be done by rote, prior to teaching these topics, I purposefully remind myself that they are new for most of the learners and challenging for many of the learners, and therefore I need to be more acutely aware of the emotional tenor in the classroom.

Unlike Jacoby's experiences, which do happen to varying degrees on a yearly basis, I had been teaching about Brother Daniel for many years before any students shared that the case had practical implications for their own Jewish status in Israel. This does not, of course, mean that no one else was in a similar situation to Day. Rather, he was the first to state so publicly and bring himself into the learning. I vividly remember when Day asked his question and the silence that took over the classroom. I always knew that there might be students with personal connections to the topic in the classroom, but this was not something that I had planned for or thought about how to engage with in a lesson.

I concur with Day's descriptions of what transpired; I responded to him in front of the class and then suspended the lesson to discuss with him in private. My rationale for doing so reflects the many concerns that immediately manifested. First and foremost was a concern for Day. No longer were the Israeli laws abstract texts; they were documents that explicitly excluded a member of my classroom from full inclusion in Israeli society, and ensuring his emotional wellbeing was paramount. Secondly, I felt an obligation to tell the truth. I concur with the many other scholars who have written about the importance of teaching difficult history (e.g., Gross &

Terra, 2018; Zakai, 2020), and despite my own discomfort in Day's unique case, the reality of the situation was that he had correctly analyzed the texts considering his family's Jewish story, and to mitigate or minimize the reality would only lead to future confusion for all learners.

My guiding principles with both Jacoby and Day are grounded in a dual commitment to emotional sensitivity and truth. As a high school Israel educator, I cannot (nor do I want to) just tell truths about Israel with no consideration for the emotional impact of these truths on the learners; additionally, I don't want to make their emotional journeys so smooth that I have mitigated all conflict by presenting them with simplified narratives. These dual concerns justify my decision to embrace the micromoments that Day and Jacoby introduced and to provide space for follow-up questions and discussion with both the larger class and with them as individuals. While I did worry that I might not do a good enough job in allaying their respective disappointments, I feared that to shut the conversation down would be a far worse option because it would fail to create a space for Day to have his narrative validated or for Jacoby to experience an evolution in her understanding of the nature of Israeli society.

Analysis

There is a growing body of literature that analyzes the moves that educators make in their classrooms when teaching content that learners find emotionally difficult, and we see our chapter as contributing to this conversation. Derald Wing Sue et al.'s (2009) study of learner perceptions of racially based classroom dialogues is particularly informative for identifying the key role played by educators as facilitators or inhibitors of meaningful classroom dialogue. The authors reported the following strategies to be particularly beneficial: "legitimizing the discussion on race, validating feelings of the participants in class, willingness to accept a different racial reality from students of color, comfort in addressing race and racism, and using a direct approach in managing the discussion" (p. 188). Additionally, their findings revealed that difficult conversations were not neutral exchanges; when conducted effectively, "difficult dialogues proved a valuable learning experience" (p. 188). The researchers conclude that the educator's knowledge, openness, and ability to facilitate dialogue play a significant role in shaping the classroom experience because they also model for other learners how to engage in important yet challenging conversations.

Jacoby's and Day's analyses of their classroom experiences document a pedagogy that promotes a critical thinking that embraces complex learning. Their observations reflect Magdalena H. Gross's (2014) study of how contemporary Polish youth reckoned with Poland's historical mistreatment of Jews during the Holocaust. Gross contends that the history educator must create an environment that allows students to experience simultaneous truths—Poles were victims *and* perpetrators—because only then can learners "deconstruct myths to open constructive dialogue" (p. 460). Gross's conclusions are informative for our purposes because despite having very different classroom experiences, Day and Jacoby were each challenged to grapple with an Israel that was significantly more complex than they had previously thought.

Day's and Jacoby's reflections also offer new lines of inquiry for understanding what the effective Israel educator does during classroom learning. First and foremost, Jacoby's descriptions of Reingold's pedagogy involve clear examples of dissonance, but in her recollection, it served the purpose of allowing her to form her own opinions about Israel. The purposeful juxtaposition of competing and contrasting narratives facilitated an experience of dissonance that necessitated arriving at her own understanding of Israel, and this new understanding could reflect one of the texts that were taught, a synthesis of multiple texts, or an entirely different perspective.

Both Jacoby and Day wrote about the experience of being in a classroom where learners were seen as partners in the educative process and not as receptacles for learning. We candidly acknowledged being encouraged to draw upon our prior knowledge of Israel—gained from prior schooling, trips to Israel, family conversations, and media exposure—and bringing those experiences into the classroom as texts that become part of the classroom. Our reflections about the value of being treated as active participants in meaning making has parallels with the work of the Brazilian philosopher and educator Paulo Freire (2018). At the center of Freire's work was a rejection of what he termed the "banking model of education," a system that positions the educator as the content expert and the learner as a passive recipient. Freire opposed this approach to teaching for its affirmation of a power imbalance between the parties and for its failure to account for what students can bring of themselves into the classroom that can shape the nature of the experience for themselves, their classmates, and their teachers. Day's unintended interruption of Reingold's lesson is an excellent example of how students can dictate the flow of the lesson, but both he and Jacoby identify Reingold's willingness to cede authority in the classroom to the students' own contributions as what allowed the meaningful conversations to occur in the first place. What the two observed was more than just Reingold demonstrating respect towards students; they observed a pedagogical orientation to the place of the learner as a partner in the educative process, in which each meaningfully contributes to learning and teaching. One component of this partnership, noted Jacoby, was Reingold's willingness to be honest about Israel's limitations, even when the truths might be painful, like Day realized.[2]

Our reflections also highlight the importance of emotional sensitivity during lessons where the learning is complex and students are apt to be upset with aspects of the content. Both Jacoby and Day remarked that not only was Reingold aware of which topics in the syllabus might lead to strong emotional reactions, but he was prepared to check in with the learners throughout to gauge the temperature in the room and the emotional impact of deeply personal learning. Jacoby identified Reingold's patience in allowing her to process the implications of loaded content and in not moving on to new material too quickly before she was ready. In Day's case, he recognized that Reingold understood the significance of the classroom revelation even before Day himself did, with Reingold finding time to discuss Day's new understanding of his Jewish status on multiple occasions.[3]

Conclusion

Our chapter is not designed to definitively explain "what exemplary Israel educators do" in their pedagogy. Instead, we have chosen to focus on a case study of a single educator and two former students' analyses of the pedagogical decisions and moves that he makes. We believe our approach allows for a more detailed consideration of specific classroom instances and how the educator creates a space where students engage in the complex learning that is Israel education. The micromoments of classroom learning, those minute times outside of the proscribed curriculum, are the times when educators signify to students their acceptance or rejection of extracurricular interruption. While perhaps short in duration, as demonstrated in all three of our reflections, micromoments have the potential to become significant, transformative, and memorable moments in the long-term shaping of a student's or educator's thinking about Israel. Day's and Jacoby's experiences, which took place in two different years, show similarities in Reingold's approach to helping students navigate morally complex topics, providing evidence that these moves are part of a philosophy of teaching Israel. This is a philosophy that values students' emotional reactions, emphasizes truth telling, and positions the learner's prior experiences and reactions to new content and ideas at the heart of Israel education, with the educator serving as a facilitator of dialogue and deeper engagement with Israel in all its complexity.

NOTES

1. The following steps were taken to mitigate against the possibility that Day's and Jacoby's writings were informed by their positive relationships with Reingold or by a shared desire to craft a particular narrative: 1) Their sections were written independently of each other; 2) at the time of their writing, neither were current students of Reingold and both had already graduated from the school; 3) their sections were screened for explicit bias by Sivan Zakai.

2. Jacoby's interest in learning truths, even when painful, supports an earlier finding of Reingold's (2017) that showed that students preferred to learn about Israel's complexity rather than single-sided narratives that glossed over moral complexity in Israeli history and contemporary society.

3. Reingold adds that he also conferred with Day's parents. This was not done because Reingold regretted having taught the material or for having been the one to inform Day about his contested Jewish status in Israel; rather, it emerged out of a desire to best support the learner who (at that time) was a minor and to ensure that he was also being supported by his parents in this new revelation.

REFERENCES

Alexander, H. A. (2015). Mature Zionism: Education and the scholarly study of Israel. *Journal of Jewish Education*, *81*(2), 136–161. https://doi.org/10.1080/15244113.2015.1035979

Beghetto, R. A. (2009). In search of the unexpected: Finding creativity in the micromoments of the classroom. *Psychology of Aesthetics, Creativity, and the Arts*, *3*(1), 2–5. https://doi.org/10.1037/a0014831

Beghetto, R.A. (2013). Expect the unexpected: Teaching for creativity in the micromoments. In M. B. Gregerson, J. C. Kaufman, & H. T. Snyder (Eds.), *Teaching creatively and teaching creativity* (pp. 133–148). Springer. https://doi.org/10.1007/978-1-4614-5185-3_10

Declaration of Independence. (1948). The Knesset. Retrieved December 18, 2021, from https://knesset.gov.il/en/about/pages/declaration.aspx

Freire, P. (2018). *Pedagogy of the oppressed*. Bloomsbury Academic.

Gross, M. H. (2014). Struggling to deal with the difficult past: Polish students confront the Holocaust. *Journal of Curriculum Studies, 46*(4), 441–463. https://doi.org/10.1080/00220272.2014.923513

Gross, M. H., and Terra, L. (2018). What makes difficult history difficult? *The Phi Delta Kappan, 99*(8), 51–56. https://www.jstor.org/stable/26552405

Hassenfeld, J. (2016). Negotiating critical analysis and collective belonging: Jewish American students write the history of Israel. *Contemporary Jewry, 36*(1), 55–84. https://doi.org/10.1007/s12397-016-9157-6

Isaacs, A. (2011). Israel education: Purposes and practices. In H. Miller, L. D. Grant, & A. Pomson (Eds.), *International handbook of Jewish education* (pp. 479–496). Springer Netherlands.

Israel First Knesset. (2008). The law of return. In I. Rabinovich & J. Reinharz (Eds.), *Israel in the Middle East: Documents and readings on society, politics, and foreign relations, pre-1948 to the present* (pp. 102–103). Brandeis University Press.

Israel Supreme Court. (2008). Jewish religion and Israeli nationality: The Brother Daniel case. In I. Rabinovich & J. Reinharz (Eds.), *Israel in the Middle East: Documents and readings on society, politics, and foreign Relations, pre-1948 to the present* (pp. 172–174). Brandeis University Press.

Reingold, M. (2017). Not the Israel of my elementary school: An exploration of Jewish-Canadian secondary students' attempts to process morally complex Israeli narratives. *The Social Studies, 108*(3), 87–98. https://doi.org/10.1080/00377996.2017.1324392

Simon, K. G. (2001). *Moral questions in the classroom: How to get kids to think deeply about real life and their schoolwork*. Yale University Press.

Sinclair, A., Backenroth, O., and Bell-Klinger, R. (2010). Breaking myths, building identity: Practitioner-researcher reflections on running an Israel seminar for Jewish education graduate students. *International Journal of Jewish Education Research*, 49–74. https://www.bjpa.org/search-results/publication/20980

Sue, D. W., Lin, A. I., Torino, G. C., Capodilupo, C. M., & Rivera, D. P. (2009). Racial microaggressions and difficult dialogues on race in the classroom. *Cultural Diversity and Ethnic Minority Psychology, 15*(2), 183–190. https://psycnet.apa.org/doi/10.1037/a0014191

Trubowitz, S., & Picard Robins, M. (2003). *The good teacher mentor: Setting the standard for support and success*. Teachers College Press.

Zakai, S. (2014). "My heart is in the East and I am in the West": Enduring questions of Israel education in North America. *Journal of Jewish Education, 80*(3), 287–318. https://doi.org/10.1080/15244113.2014.937192

Zakai, S. (2020). When past and present collide: Dilemmas in teaching the history of the Israeli-Palestinian conflict. In M. H. Gross and L. Terra (Eds.), *Teaching and learning the difficult past: Comparative perspectives* (pp. 104–118). Routledge.

5
Into the Intimate Discourse
Rachel Korazim as an Exemplary Israel Educator

DIANE TICKTON SCHUSTER

Three months into the COVID-19 pandemic, a friend in London sends me an email about the arrival of her first grandchild and says how bereft she is not to be able to visit the baby and her parents in Liverpool. Almost as an afterthought she notes:

> BTW here is one of my Zoom courses that might interest you—I am sending a link to recorded sessions about Israeli poetry by Rachel Korazim, but you can find her on Facebook or her website (she has about 250 people for each lecture and probably as many as half from the States, so maybe you've heard about her). Check out https://www.korazim.com/lectures/categories/the-great-hebrew-poets.

I recognize Rachel Korazim's name—I have just seen it in the listing of online summer classes offered by the Hartman Institute to its immense Diaspora audience—but we have never met. I trust my friend's judgment: She is a vibrant lifelong learner who has been immersing herself in Jewish study programs for years. And since I am intrigued by the mention of such a large attendance at Korazim's lectures, I am predisposed to be impressed when I tune in to her Hartman class on gender in Israeli poetry and song. What I am not prepared for is the adrenaline rush I experience when I observe Korazim presenting her material. There is something in her delivery that feels particularly compelling, and I sense an excitement I have rarely felt in the dozens of Jewish education classes I've taken or observed over the years. Intrigued, I review the source sheets from the class and try to reconstruct how Korazim has engaged learners: what she says and what she does that feels so distinctive. It's hard to pin down, but as someone who has spent decades writing about adult Jewish learning, I realize that Korazim's approach appears to embody many of the best adult educator practices described in my analysis of Rabbi David Nelson and other top-notch adult Jewish educators in *Jewish Lives, Jewish Learning* (2003) and summarized in more recent work by such scholars as Sivan Zakai (2014) and Barry Chazan (2016) in their descriptions of skills used most effectively by Israel educators. As a researcher interested in adult Jewish learning and Israel education, I conclude that I need to observe this teacher more closely to identify key elements of her pedagogy and assess possible implications for Israel educators who work with adult students.

In my dual roles as Korazim's student and as an expert in contemporary Jewish adult education (Schuster, 2022), I have a front-row seat observing the pedagogical choices she makes. I am particularly interested in how Korazim encourages Diaspora Jewish learners to Zoom into her teaching space and gain access both to her as an educator and to elements of Israeli society with which they may not be familiar. Korazim herself describes her pedagogy in terms of "the intimate Israeli discourse"—terminology that is novel in scholarship about Israel education.

Research Agenda

After I attend several of Korazim's Hartman classes, I ask if I might interview her with a view toward developing a research project about her and her learners. We engage in a series of Zoom conversations in which I probe for details about her background, teaching philosophy, experiences with educating adults, responses to life during the pandemic, and the like. In these discussions I learn that the bulk of Rachel Korazim's work is directed to Jews in the Diaspora and that she is deeply invested in helping non-Israeli adults to understand Israel in nuanced, complex ways. When she mentions that she is about to host a limited-attendance book club (made up primarily of North Americans) about the work of the Israeli author Emuna Elon, I suggest that this group might become the basis for research about Israel education. With Korazim's cooperation, I reach out to the 40 people who have signed on for the book club that is about to begin. The account that follows is of Rachel Korazim and her learners, as informed by my own role as a participant-observer in the five-session book group that took place in August–September 2020.[1]

Methodology

In August 2020 I joined Rachel Korazim's five-session "Monday Book Club" as a participant-observer with the intent to gather data that could be developed into a portrait of an Israel educator who engages Diaspora learners through study of Israeli literature. Portraiture is a method of social science inquiry pioneered by Sara Lawrence-Lightfoot in which the researcher forms a familiar relationship with the person being studied in order to capture the "richness, complexity and dimensionality of human experience" (Lawrence-Lightfoot & Davis, 1997, p. 3). The portrait emerges as the subject and portraitist interact over time, with the picture enriched by dialogue and other information that may become available while they engage. By design, portraiture is a mixture of science and art, combining "systematic, empirical description with aesthetic expression" (Lawrence-Lightfoot & Davis, 1997, p. 3). The result is a thick narrative description that enables the reader to "see" the teacher in action—a result that is particularly useful in Israel education, a field that lacks systematic documentation about how outstanding teachers practice their craft. In its focus on the "convergence of narrative and analysis," portraiture zeroes in on a single case within which the reader will find "resonant universal themes" that can be generalized to larger practice (Lawrence-Lightfoot & Davis, 1997, p. 14).

My analysis of Korazim's approach as an Israel educator is situated in the tradition of grounded theory research (Strauss & Corbin, 1994), in which the researcher draws on her findings to explore further ideas about what she has observed. In addition to systematic coding of my notes about the group sessions, I reviewed transcripts of my seven 90-minute interviews with Korazim and tallied demographic data obtained in an online questionnaire from 30 of the 40 book club members.[2]

Rachel Korazim

A PowerPoint slide that Rachel Korazim sometimes shares when introducing herself to online audiences includes a 1946 photo of a group of Holocaust survivors standing on the deck of the ship *Max Nordau* as they await arrival in Palestine. "I am in the picture too," explains Korazim, "but you can't yet see me. The woman on the lower deck with the white scarf is my mother, pregnant with me." Korazim is open about her age, currently 74, and forthright about the fact that 1) her birth occurred shortly before the founding of the State of Israel, and 2) her world view was very much shaped by her Hungarian mother, a Holocaust survivor. Details of Korazim's life story are inextricably woven into her teaching: how she grew up in Haifa, studied literature as an undergraduate, served in the IDF, and later created an educational program for soldiers from disadvantaged backgrounds—her first foray into adult education. When she was recruited in the early 1980s to become a *shlichah*—an emissary of the Jewish Agency for Israel—to Canada, she was, in her own words, "A typical Israeli who literally knew nothing about Jewish life outside of Israel." She describes her three years in Montreal as a watershed experience in which she came to understand how differently from Israelis the Jews in the Diaspora perceive an array of core issues: Jewish identity, Jewish peoplehood, the legacy of the Holocaust, and the history of the State of Israel. She cites a significant lesson she learned at that time from historian Ruth Wisse about the different paradigms that have long differentiated views of Israel, paradigms that may require us to reframe our understanding of Israel. Korazim offered this summary of Wisse's position:

> From time immemorial, we have had two paradigms. There is the very, very ancient paradigm of "On the rivers of Babylon, we sat and wept because we remembered Zion." So we were miserable in Diaspora, we were in exile, Jerusalem was great. We are longing. We are weeping: Oy.
>
> Then fast forward, 1500 years and you are in Spain of the Middle Ages. And there is Yehuda HaLevy, and he is in Cordova and Cordova is amazing. And he writes, "I am in the West and my heart is in the East" and "How can I rejoice here in Cordova when Jerusalem is in

ruins?" This is the second paradigm: I have a great life in Diaspora, while Jerusalem is miserable.

These are the two paradigms.... And now, in our reality, we live a totally different construct. Jerusalem is not in ruins and Jews in the Diaspora do not suffer, meaning we have two successful Jewish commonwealths: the State of Israel and the North American Jewish community. But we have no idea how to handle that. We don't have the [right] paradigm.

During her time in Canada, Korazim set out to discern elements of these paradigmatic differences by listening carefully to different constituencies in the Montreal Jewish community. She speaks about how she learned for the first time about North American Jewish organizational and communal structures. She describes as well, how, under the influence of Canadian Holocaust educators (especially those associated with the Precious Legacy docent program), she found herself developing a different understanding of the Shoah, one that focused on more than just the "fighting heroes' narrative" she had learned growing up in Israel. She offered to share her library of recent Israeli books with members of the Montreal Israeli immigrant community and then was asked by other Montrealers to share those books with them as well. As she prepared handmade translations of these books, Korazim realized that her non-Hebrew-speaking Canadian audience had little familiarity with what shaped Israeli writers' storytelling; nor did they really have much first-hand experience with the "real" Israel. Her understanding of Diaspora Jews' need for a new kind of "Israel education" was consolidated as a result of a formative conversation with one of the women she had begun to teach:

> I started sharing what was new in Israeli literature, and then a woman comes up to me and says, "Rachel, you have no idea what this is doing to us." And I look at her: what is this woman so excited about? This is the stuff I've [taught] most of my life.
>
> She says to me, "No, Rachel, you don't get it. Do you know how we Montreal Jews get to know about Israel? There are three venues:
>
> There's [the voice] from the pulpit 'cause from that particular *parsha* [weekly Torah portion], you know, your *Lech lecha* [literally "go forth,"

the name of a Torah portion], that the rabbi will address. It can be very insightful, but what can I tell you: not very contemporary.

Then there is the Israel from fundraising. And you know what that looks like: the more miserable they make it look, the better it is for fundraising.

And there is the Israel [that is distorted by] the media."

But then she says, "Reading this with you, it is as if you have invited us into your own living room and let us *listen to the Israeli intimate discourse*, the kind of stuff you Israelis tell each other when we Diaspora Jews are not listening."

Bringing Diaspora Jews Into the Israeli Intimate Discourse

For more than 30 years, Rachel Korazim has "taught Israel," designing curricula that help Diaspora Jews gain insight into the kinds of complex issues that Israelis wrestle with as individuals and as a community. Moreover, her capacities conform with what Zakai (2014) lists as ideal criteria for success—criteria rarely found in a single Israel educator. Korazim is "fluent in both Hebrew and English and equally fluid in the cultural cues that accompany these languages." She understands Diaspora Judaism and the educational contexts in differing Jewish communities, has deep subject matter understanding (in this case Israeli literature), as well as "knowledge of Israeli history and geography, Zionist history and philosophy, and Israeli cultural and religious customs." She is "well-versed in contemporary Israeli and Middle Eastern politics" and is "equipped to teach not only about complexity in Israel, but also about the complex role that it plays in the life of [Diaspora] Judaism" (Zakai, 2014, p. 301).

The portrait of Korazim's teaching that follows reveals elements of these capacities that mark Korazim's exceptional ability to help Diaspora Jews "get inside" the intimate Israeli discourse. Her approach actively embraces a commitment to the "complexity hypothesis" that argues that Israel education should "no longer deal only with simplistic understandings of Israel [and] must relate to questions of personal meaning and identity" (Sinclair et al., 2013). In addition, her pedagogy mirrors what the literature on teaching adults describes as the "quintessential educational process": to help learners acquire a "a critically alert cast of mind—one that is skeptical of claims to final truths or ultimate solutions to problems, is open to alternatives, and acknowledges the contextuality of knowledge" (Brookfield, 1990, pp. 21–22). Korazim's book club members are mature Jewish adults who bring considerable sophistication and life experience to their learning; their participation in what has been advertised as an interactive small-group learning opportunity suggests that they are open to dialogue, debate, and opportunities for personal reflection. All have either visited Israel or lived there for some period of time, so they come to the group with ideas and opinions shaped by previous encounters.

An Israel Educator in Action

August 17, 2020.[3] The first session of the Monday Summer Book Club is scheduled to begin at 11 a.m. in my West Coast location, 2 p.m. on the East Coast, and 9 p.m. in Rachel Korazim's hometown of Tel Aviv. We will be studying the work of Emuna Elon, an Israeli author whose work is not widely known in the Diaspora. Over a five-week period, the book club will read two selections: a short story called "The Maidservant's Son"[4] and a novel, *House on Endless Waters*.[5]

A welcome-to-the-book-club email has provided a time schedule; I log onto the Zoom link 10 minutes early and am startled to discover that a conversation is already well under way. Korazim is greeting people, asking for volunteers to serve as a Zoom "muter" and oral readers, giving out the link to her website, and counting down the minutes: "We have two minutes to go. Is there anyone who is a first-timer? Where are you from? Welcome. Okay: one minute to go." By 11 a.m., the participant count has inched up to more than 35 and within minutes the full roster of 40 has tuned in.

Speaking from her home office, Korazim formally welcomes the group and mentions that although she doesn't personally know some of us, she goes way back with "Nira from Toronto" and "Zsusa from Budapest." She reminds us that she is leading two book groups this month (the Sunday Club, already in session for two weeks, and now the Monday Club), with both reading Emuna Elon's short story (which she has sent as an email attachment), so in case we miss anything we are welcome to access recordings on her website.[6]

Shifting from the group's Zoom gallery view to screen share, she displays a photo of Emuna Elon and images of her book covers in both Hebrew and English. Korazim provides a quick summary of Elon's story, reminding us that the protagonist, Sarit, is a Jewish woman in the West Bank settlement community of Beit El who hires Intisar, a Muslim woman from the neighboring refugee camp of Jezoun, to serve as her house cleaner; after several years in which the two women negotiate the inequities in their employer–employee relationship, Intisar comes to Sarit to beg her to hide her son Adnan, a young man whose Jezoun neighbors suspect is an Israeli collaborator.

Korazim then says that a conversation two weeks ago in the Sunday Book Club has had an impact on her thinking about something she wants us to confront in our group's discussion: how we see and talk about settlers. She explains:

> When the group met, somebody said, "I wouldn't believe, Rachel, that a settler would be so sensitive to the point of view of Palestinians." And that [comment] got me thinking how oftentimes we are positioned in our own corners and have preconceived ideas about anybody that we perceive as the other side.

Korazim goes on to say that even though she has never met Emuna Elon—and that indeed Elon's late husband, Rabbi Benny Elon, was a leader in the settler movement and espoused political views quite different from Korazim's own—she believes it is important for the book club members to examine their "preconceived ideas" about people who are "other." She imagines that most of the book-group participants have little direct experience with settlers or with Palestinians whose families and homes were displaced by settler housing developments. With this in mind, she has used her Facebook network to get contact information for Elon and already has invited her to meet with both book clubs during our final session. With the author's visit on the horizon, she urges us to begin thinking about questions we will want to ask Elon. Moving beyond this announcement, Korazim speaks in a reflective mode about the decisions she makes as a teacher who both recognizes the diversity of the learners in her audience and strives to create an even playing field for conversation about complex, politically charged issues:

I'm using the time [now] to share with you a personal dilemma that is always there when I prepare my classes—and much more so on an occasion like this—because we are going to throw around notions like settlers, like settlements, like Judea and Samaria, like occupied territories, like liberated territories, etc. And Israelis like myself, and maybe a few other people, will assume that everybody knows what we're talking about. And then again, among the 40 of us today, there might be a few people who do not. So, I think we all deserve a certain introduction. And some of you who are into it may find this a little bit boring and a little bit of "Come on, I knew that," but please bear with me for a few minutes.

In the ensuing quarter hour, Korazim provides a capsule view of the history of the settlement movement, pointing out that the politics around land rights have undergone many changes since the founding of the state. She supplements her remarks with photos from the 1970s of left-wing Israeli leaders (such as Yitzhak Rabin and Shimon Peres) who actually paved the way for developments in the West Bank, noting that some years later these same leaders became vociferous opponents to the settlements whose construction they had previously advocated.

Korazim displays PowerPoint slides of the temporary tents and trailers that early settlement newcomers lived in and then a picture of the kind of red-roofed "Swiss cottage" houses that Emuna Elon described in her depiction of the changing Beit El landscape. She explains how the locations of some settlement communities are associated with kibbutzim that were destroyed in Israel's War of Independence and how their locations were advertised as being easily accessed from Tel Aviv and other Israeli locales. As she moves into talking about "The Maidservant's Son," she shows a map of Israel, mentioning the connection between details in the story and its author:

> Emuna Elon comes from Beit El. So I wanted you to look at the map with things that you can recognize so you can go very easily with me from Tel Aviv, and then you go a little bit to the right, which is east, and you will be hitting Modi'in. So, you know, that airport where you have just landed is nearby. And if you continue to the right, you see that the red dot is Beit El and Jerusalem is below.

Continuing in a bit of "virtual tour guide" mode, Korazim shares a photo of how Beit El looks today. She understands that we, her learners, need to be reminded of what it actually looks like, a town with "shopping malls and supermarkets and banks and high schools and yeshivas." As she presents a series of carefully prepared images of Beit El, she points out that the settlements are not as far distant as many of us might imagine:

> So what am I telling you? In some people's minds, the settlements are like behind the dark mountains, far away. And what I need for you to see on the map is that they are actually closer to Tel Aviv than Jerusalem is. The distances, the size of the country, oftentimes make us think of a place, because of our ideology, as a far-away distance: "I would never go there." But as a matter of fact, geographically, they are very close to places that you visit and you go to practically daily, or every other day.

Shifting gears, Korazim situates the issues of land rights and occupation in the complex political climate of the 1967 Six Day War, saying: "A word about ideology. And this is important to me." She then presents on the screen an image of a June 1967 column in *Maariv* (at that time a right-of-center newspaper) by Natan Alterman in which the left-wing journalist cited Israel's historical presence in the land as a justification for erasure of the "border between the State of Israel and the land of Israel." She walks us through the article and uses an onscreen highlighter to point out where Alterman scoffed at the idea that Israel had occupied the territories (claiming instead that the Arabs "occupied us"). She concludes by saying that as much as she has long identified with Alterman's left-leaning outlook, the statements in the 1967 article reveal the omnipresent fluidity in Israeli views about land ownership:

> Alterman said in one of the last things he wrote that whoever will want *ever* to return any of these lands will have to write a new Bible: *yitztarech lichtov Tanakh chadash*. He was totally committed to that cause. I need for you to be aware of that because, again, it is not just a right and left thing.

Korazim delivers this last message with intensity as she again reminds the group that shifts in ideology are part of the larger reality of Israeli life: that there is more to consider than just "a right and left thing."

The clock is ticking and Korazim explains one of today's goals was to provide a context for thinking about the settlements that had been in existence for 20 years by the time Emuna Elon wrote "The Maidservant's Son." She draws our attention to the title of the story and says that when there's a reference to a maid it implies that there is also someone employing that person; she then makes explicit that it is not hard to make the leap to seeing Sarit symbolically as the biblical Sara, Intisar as Hagar, and Adnan as Ishmael: "Even before the story begins the Jewish reader will make these connections," she says. She then draws out group members' perceptions of the relationship between the female characters, a relationship fraught with power imbalances and awkward shifts in dominance as Intisar assumes a position of authority in her employer's home. After the book club participants debate back and forth whether it is Sarit or Intisar who is "invading" the other's territory, Korazim makes a summative statement, posing a final question for our next meeting:

> I think what we managed to see is... Intisar and Sarit as the sort of symbolic Hagar and Sarah [and] also as very real two women in the Israeli/Palestinian locale....
>
> What I would like for us to discuss next week is to speak a little bit more about biblical metaphors in contemporary Israeli literature so that we put the story in a larger context. Because this practice—this way of writing, of telling a totally contemporary story by heavily rooting it in the biblical elements that we recognize so easily—this is not something that Emuna Elon has invented. It is a solid part of Israeli writing.
>
> And [when] we conclude the story about Sarit, Intisar, and Adnan, the son, [we will be asking:] Do the modern Sarah, Hagar, and Ishmael have a chance in contemporary Israel?

It is 10:15 p.m. in Israel, the time the book club is scheduled to conclude, but rather than exiting the Zoom screen, Korazim announces that she is available to continue talking:

> Ladies and Gentlemen: Our official time is up, but as those of you who know me will tell all the others, *I'm not going anywhere* [emphasis in her delivery]. I'm staying here as long as you want to talk to me or to each other about it. And please feel free [to leave]. I will say thank you and until we meet again, to everybody who needs to leave—I totally understand—but I welcome everybody who would like to stay to continue the conversation.

Although a few people log off, most of the participants stay for the informal discussion. Over the next 40 minutes, group members trade thoughts back and forth, returning again and again to their perceptions of power dynamics between Sarit and Intisar, the ambivalence many women feel about asserting their authority, and how many of us, like Sarit, remain naive about the political complexities of Israel.

It is not ancillary but a central piece of Korazim's pedagogy that she remains accessible to students even after the formal period of her class has ended. This is the way that Korazim enacts what the adult-learning expert Stephen Brookfield (2006) calls "personhood," a stance that allows learners to see "their teachers are flesh and blood human beings with lives and identities outside the classroom" (p. 77). It is an additional form of intimacy that she offers: access not only to the discourse of Israeli literature and society, but also to her whole self and to her personal—less bounded—teaching space.

Analyzing Korazim's Approach

My initial analysis of Rachel Korazim's pedagogy is informed by the literature on adult learning in general and adult Jewish learning in particular.[7] However, when I place Korazim's teaching and her students' reactions in the context of Barry Chazan's (2016) theory of "relational Israel education," I discover a particularly relevant framework for unpacking what makes this educator's practice so distinctive. Chazan identifies three "skill sets" an Israel educator should prioritize in order to encourage the learner's ongoing engagement with the complexities of Israel: relationship building, facilitating discussion, and culture building.[8] Beyond these skill sets, Chazan suggests, is a larger sensibility about what distinguishes the finest

Israel educators: the kind of requisite "courage" that has been described by the educational philosopher Parker Palmer (1998).

1. Relationship Building

Chazan characterizes this skill as the educator's ability to function as a *connector* between the student and the idea of Israel. One of Rachel Korazim's key strengths as an Israel educator is her ability to bring Diaspora Jews into the intimate Israeli discourse—to help her students engage in discussion about the kinds of complex issues that contemporary Israelis routinely deal with. Her decision to launch the book club series with a story about Israeli settlers in Beit El pushes the book club members to begin to confront the complexities of such "hot button issues" as settlements, land rights, loyalty, and other aspects of the Israeli–Arab divide. In Korazim's introduction to the group's first meeting, she describes Elon's political history with the Israeli right and then says that it is unlikely most of the book club members have had direct experience with settlers or with Palestinians. From the beginning, she challenges group members to think about their assumptions about Israel and about people they might consider "other." She puts the learners on notice: The discussion will lead to critical reflection about "them" and "us." Moreover, Korazim explains that, having listened to comments by members of the Sunday book club, she has reached out to Emuna Elon, inviting her to meet with both groups to talk candidly about complex cultural issues. She urges the Monday group members to begin forming questions they want to ask the author. By shifting the focus onto the group's relationship with the book's author, this Israel educator displays a willingness to step back from the spotlight and not be the only voice in the room.

Most of all, when Korazim introduces images of the left-wing Israeli leaders from the 1970s who encouraged settlement on the West Bank, she sets the stage for helping the learners connect to the idea that Israel's political climate is always in flux. In this sense, one of Korazim's pedagogical moves is to disrupt old tropes (in this case the left–right divide) by asking the learners to hold onto a fluid (rather than fixed) mindset when thinking about the country's history and political debates. She uses the Natan Alterman column to illustrate how ideologies can shift when a geopolitical climate is volatile. The first session of the book club is marked by Korazim's set induction about the importance of the learners holding a relationship with Israel that is framed by more than one narrative about the country and its story.

2. Facilitation of Discussion About Texts That Show Different Israel Narratives

Korazim's talent for selecting the right texts—what Chazan (2016) labels "texts that talk" (p. 22)—and then her skill at prompting meaningful conversation about them demonstrates her mastery as an Israel educator. She not only brings sophisticated understanding of the material, but she also shows the students how to access deeper meanings and consider diverse points of view. To provide context and to scaffold content, Korazim spends at least half of the 75 minutes of the book group's formal "meeting time" giving mini-lectures. But intermittently she closes the screen share, brings the group back to gallery view, and invites a group member to read aloud a short portion of "The Maidservant's Son." She then asks for comments and questions about the particular segment that has been read, showing the learners how to engage in "close reading" of the content. In this instance the content is about the relationship between the protagonist, Sarit, and her Arab housecleaner, Intisar. Korazim points out the biblical symbolism—the characters metaphorically representing Sarah and Hagar—and mentions that she knows that, in the United States, Kathryn Stockett's novel, *The Help*, has addressed the same theme of interaction between women from different ethnic and socioeconomic groups. In this way, Korazim "sets up" the conversation that follows, which spills over into the spontaneous after-class discussion. Throughout the conversation, the learners make associations between the Jewish Israeli narrative and their own (and their mothers') experiences with domestic help.

3. Culture Building

Rachel Korazim's use of Israeli literature as a vehicle for teaching Israel exemplifies a point Barry Chazan (2016) makes about the importance of incorporating a cultural, even an aesthetic, understanding of Israeli life into Israel education:

> The pedagogy of culture building includes understanding and structuring of physical space, use of music and art, [Israeli] literature, travel to Israel posters, and regalia of Israel. This skill set is rooted in general cultural sensibility and sensitivity which, while having specific Israeli content, has elements of the mindsets and perspectives of a Steven Spielberg, Zubin Mehta, and Cirque du Soleil. (p. 44)

In the book club session, Korazim interlaces the reading of Elon's text about life in the settlement community of Beit El with comments about the nature of life in the settlement areas. She shows PowerPoint slides of images of Beit El prior to the building of the settlement (temporary tents and trailers) and then pictures of the "red-roofed Swiss cottages" that Emuna Elon describes in "The Maidservant's Son." She also presents maps to demonstrate how close Beit El is to Tel Aviv and Ben Gurion airport and contemporary pictures of life in the now-bustling West Bank community. And toward the end of the session, she points out the textual roots that underlie Israeli literature, emphasizing that no matter how secular Israeli writers might be, they bring biblical themes into their stories. Although Korazim's "delivery" may not be as theatrical as those of "Spielberg, Mehta, and Cirque du Soleil," she brings creativity, vitality, and a strong aesthetic sensibility to her presentation of visual materials. Moreover, she shows the Diaspora learners how Israeli literature can provide an important window into the issues Israelis grapple with in everyday life.

4. *Courage*

Beyond the aforementioned skill sets, Chazan asserts, there is something at a qualitatively different level that distinguishes the pedagogy of outstanding teachers. Citing the work of Parker Palmer, he explains: "It is about something much deeper which is at the core. It is about the relationship within or the landscape of the teacher's inner soul" (Chazan, 2016, p. 44). He further notes that the mark of a truly relational Israel educator is the person's ability—indeed her *courage*—to "teach from within...from that spot where mind and heart come together to shape a total human being" (Chazan, 2016, p. 45). Chazan reminds us that "courageous" teachers are those willing to reveal both their *identity* (the self that has been shaped by their background, culture, positive and negative life experiences, etc.) and their *integrity* (what they discern as integral to their selfhood, what they choose to assert as their core values). He sees Israel education as the perfect setting for educators who are courageous enough to "model commitment, thinking, feeling, doubt, questioning, joy, sadness, certainty, and epistemological modesty" (Chazan, 2016, p. 45). Indeed, he writes, "A subject as beloved, complicated, engaging, and confusing as Israel deserves a Parker Palmer teacher" (Chazan, 2016, p. 45).

To analyze in depth how Rachel Korazim brings "the landscape of her inner soul" to her teaching is beyond the scope of this brief written account. Nonetheless, within the description of the first session of the book club are some indicators of how Korazim's "identity and integrity" are manifested. First, the account reveals the *expansive spirit* that Korazim extends through her ongoing messages of welcome. From her warm greetings in her home office 10 minutes before the hour, to her graciousness in familiarizing newcomers with her programs, to her message that she has reached out to Emuna Elon, to her invitation to stay on after the meeting, Korazim is consistently hospitable. In addition, when she shares that she has been thinking about how some book group members have never had first-hand experience with settlers and would benefit from examining their preconceived ideas about people who are "other," she exhibits her commitment to helping learners expand their ways of knowing.

Further, in her reflective statements about her decisions as a teacher—such as her thoughts about how best to accommodate learner diversity; her recognition that, as an Israeli, she might make wrong assumptions about what matters to the learners; her assertion about the value of providing an introductory overview to assure that everyone has the basics for entering the conversation—we encounter Rachel Korazim's true courage as an Israel educator. Implicit in her reflections is Korazim's deep resolve to speak her truth while making it safe for others to voice what may be alternative perspectives. This message is amplified later when she says, "A word about ideology...this is important to me," and goes on to say that, even though she tends to be left-leaning in her personal outlook, the important thing is that we all recognize that, in Israel, politics are not "just a right and left thing" and that over time anyone's views might change.

Finally, it is in the discussion that takes place after the book club session is due to conclude—when it is already after 10:15 p.m. in Israel—that Korazim gets out from behind her PowerPoint and spontaneously brings her whole self to her learners. And, curiously, this "self" is someone who models how important it is to make space for others. Rather than continue at center stage, Korazim opens the mic for the learners to voice their insights, questions, and concerns. In an interview, I asked Korazim about this aspect of her pedagogy, and she enthused:

> I love that time. It gives me feedback and allows me to be lighter, less structured.... It is a totally free ambiance. I made a commitment that I'm not leaving until everybody who wanted to say anything will say their word, and therefore I can let people speak and I don't have to stop them.

An important result of these post-group conversations is that they help build a sense of community among the learners: Jewish adults from far-flung locations who develop ties with one another as they collectively create their own discourse about Israel. Korazim's understanding of the group members' need to connect with one another—and not with just her—is a manifestation of this teacher's courage to bring both her expansiveness *and* her ability to pull back to her practice.

Teaching as an Act of Intimacy

Some months after the conclusion of the Monday Book Club, I tune in to one of Rachel Korazim's twice-weekly online poetry classes. There she is, again: welcoming learners, guiding discussion, carefully laying out alternative perspectives about Israel, using literature as a vehicle for explaining Israeli tropes and sensibilities. And, as has happened in our earlier encounters, I find myself enlivened in her presence, alert to the energy and dynamism she brings to teaching Israel. As I watch her on the screen, I realize that Korazim too is watching me and all the other students across

Zoom's gallery view. Her instructional comments, carefully constructed PowerPoint slides, heartfelt invitations for student reflections, and occasional instant polls about our preferences, all show that she is continually striving to see what we, her learners, need. Even though she is staying "on task" by covering the day's content, she is also quietly adapting her responses to match the group's mood and interests.

And then I realize that embedded in this reciprocal relationship is an *intimacy* that cannot be ignored. Aha! There again is the word Korazim herself mentioned when recounting what she heard in Montreal decades ago: that she is inviting Diaspora Jews to "listen in" to the kinds of discussions Israelis intimately have with one another. Indeed, here we are in *Korazim's* Tel Aviv apartment, not only seeing family photos in the background and occasionally hearing comments from her husband in the next room, but also hearing firsthand about her life during the pandemic.[9]

In this regard, Korazim—an Israeli—is cultivating a close-in conversation with us and showing us how she and those around her are continually grappling with the complexities of Israel and Israeli life. Her commentaries and visual materials and literary references are drawn from her Israeli milieu, and she is helping us to incorporate this content into how we think about a context different from our own. At the same time, she is incorporating us into that complicated context, helping us to process whatever concerns we might bring to the encounter. Her commitment to intimacy on so many levels—inviting students into her home office, allowing them to see her real personhood, enabling them to access the kinds of discussions Israelis have with one another, and courageously acknowledging how challenging it sometimes is for her to work across divides (both in the room and in a diverse world)—affirms the standards of teaching excellence delineated by Zakai (2014) and Chazan (2016).[10]

However, Korazim's approach suggests yet a further dimension of excellence that should and can be factored into how Israel educators conceptualize their roles and responsibilities. Korazim's commitment to "intimate discourse" reveals that this teacher genuinely sees herself as participating in an *ongoing* dialogue with her learners. Again and again, she sends a message of availability and accessibility. She consistently conveys a spirit of reciprocity as she attentively listens, probes learners' ideas, shares reactions, and welcomes opportunities to cocreate knowledge. By communicating that she expects her learners to "engage complexity" by listening to voices of "the other," she establishes the importance of maintaining a safe environment in which a multiplicity of opinions can be considered.

In this sense, Korazim's talent goes beyond what earlier scholars have proposed as crucial elements of pedagogy in Israel education. For most Diaspora Jews, the opportunity to have a sustained connection with an Israeli—especially an Israeli as intellectually engaged and uninhibitedly forthright as Korazim—is atypical. Clearly this Israel educator derives great pleasure from the sociability of these interactions, but what stands out to me is her deep awareness of—and respect for—how much her learners *want* to be involved in open, critical, and intimate discourse that enables them to understand Israel and Israeli life in meaningful ways.

The novelist Brad Meltzer (2011) writes: "There's nothing more intimate in life than simply being understood. And understanding someone else" (p. 85). Rachel Korazim's distinctive gift as an Israel educator is her capacity to make her learners feel understood while helping them more fully understand the Israel she teaches. Her example sets a new bar for those who follow in her footsteps.

NOTES

1. For the sake of brevity and focus, this paper centers on only the first sessions of the book club, although data were collected about all five meetings.

2. The survey results revealed that the group was predominantly female (two men), ages mid-50s to early 80s; 87% had advanced degrees (including six doctorates); more than half had served in a professional capacity in the Jewish community (rabbis, educators, librarians, etc.). Members were Conservative (8), Reform (6), Orthodox (5), Cultural (3), Secular (2), Other (6). They were not currently active in synagogue life, but all but three survey respondents indicated that they recently had attended at least two Jewish gatherings online (e.g., Passover seder, Jewish meditation class). All had participated in other adult Jewish learning programs. As a group, they represent what Grant and Schuster (2011) called "the committed core": well-informed Jewish adults who consistently participate in adult Jewish learning programs to enrich their understanding of Judaism and themselves as Jews.

3. A video recording of the session may be found at: https://www.dropbox.com/s/qj1zj9qql4qe6os/Maidservant%27s%20Son%20I%20%28B%29%20-%20Book%20Clubs%20-%20Aug%2017th%202020.mp4?dl=0

4. Korazim mentions that "The Maidservant's Son" has not been published in English; the translation she sent us via email is one she has worked on herself. The issue of

translation from Hebrew to English will come up throughout the book group sessions. Frequently Korazim will comment on how much is "lost in translation" and will use each opportunity to teasingly admonish the learners that this is why we should all learn Hebrew.

5. At the time the book club started, Elon's novel had not yet been named as a finalist for the *2020 National Jewish Book Award*. That news some months later significantly increased her popularity among the larger community of Jewish book clubs.

6. https://www.korazim.com/

7. For a broad overview about adult learning, see Merriam & Baumgartner, 2020. For a comprehensive discussion of the learning needs and priorities of adult Jewish learners, see Schuster, 2003; Schuster & Grant, 2005; and Schuster & Grant, 2008.

8. A fourth skill set is "an approach to rituals [which show] the pervasive Israeli presence in these areas of Jewish life" (Chazan, 2016, p. 44). Although I observed Korazim demonstrating this skill in later sessions of the book club, it was not evident in the first meeting of the group.

9. This kind of close-in exposure occurred with particular force on May 11, 2021, when, five minutes into her poetry class, we heard Korazim's husband Yossi telling her she must stop teaching and head with him into their "safe room" because the threat of mortar attacks from Gaza had become immediate. As the Zoom screen suddenly darkened for the 200+ learners from around the globe, the reality of the complexities of Israel became more familiar than ever.

10. Although Zakai opined that the ideal she described was likely too "herculean" for any one individual to achieve (p. 301), Korazim's approach provides evidence that that kind of teaching is possible.

REFERENCES

Brookfield, S. (1990). *The skillful teacher*. Jossey-Bass.
Chazan, B. (2016). *A philosophy of Israel education*. Palgrave.
Lawrence-Lightfoot S., & Davis, J. H. (1997). *The art and science of portraiture*. Jossey-Bass.
Meltzer, B. (2011). *The inner circle*. Grand Central Publishing.
Merriam, S. B., & Baumgartner, L. M. (2020). *Adult learning: A comprehensive guide* (4th ed.). Jossey-Bass.
Palmer, P. (1998). *The courage to teach: Exploring the inner landscape of a teacher's life*. Jossey-Bass.
Schuster, D. T. (2003). *Jewish lives, Jewish learning: Adult Jewish learning in theory and practice*. Behrman House.
Schuster, D. T. (2022). *Portraits of adult Jewish learning: Making meaning at many tables*. Wipf and Stock.
Schuster, D. T., & Grant, L. (2005). Adult Jewish learning: What do we know? What do we need to know? *Journal of Jewish Education, 7*(2), 179–200. https://doi.org/10.1080/00216240500179090

Schuster, D. T., & Grant L. (2008). What we know about adult Jewish learning. In R. Goodman, P. Flexner, & L. Bloomberg (Eds.), *What we now know about Jewish education* (pp. 161–172). Torah Aura.

Sinclair, A., Solmsen, B., & Goldwater, C. (2013). *The Israel educator: An inquiry into the preparation and capacities of effective Israel educators*. The Consortium for Applied Studies in Jewish Education. https://www.casje.org/resources/israel-education-brief-israel-educator

Strauss, A., & Corbin, J. (1994). Grounded theory methodology: An overview. In N. Denzin & Y. Lincoln (Eds.), *Handbook of qualitative research* (pp. 273–284). Sage.

Zakai, S. (2014). "My heart is in the East and I am in the West": Enduring questions of Israel education in North America. *Journal of Jewish Education*, *80*(3), 287–318. https://doi.org/10.1080/15244113.2014.937192

6

Knowledge, Connection, and Stance

Toward a More Enduring Israel Engagement

JONATHAN GOLDEN and YONI KADDEN

American-born Rachel graduated Gann Academy, a pluralistic Jewish high school, and shortly thereafter enlisted in the Israeli Army.[1] Rachel's enlistment was surprising to many—including to us as her teachers. She was one of Gann Academy's most outspoken proponents on racial justice and other progressive causes often associated with organizations critical of the State of Israel. Furthermore, Rachel remembered:

> I used to hate going to temple, I used to hate Shabbat dinner, and I actually hated every single thing about it.... I used to tell [my parents] I don't like Israel, I don't like being Jewish, I don't want to have a Bat Mitzvah, I don't want to learn Hebrew... [and] I don't want anything to do with it.

Rachel was not a student who would have proudly told people that she'd be signing up for the Israeli army after graduation. But there she found herself, in the spring of 2021, wearing the uniform of an army then embroiled in a war with Hamas in Gaza.

It was a deeply challenging moment for Rachel, and she responded to that challenge in the way she best knew how: by asking her unit commanders to consider Palestinian perspectives in the conflict. She drew on and quoted from sources she read in her 12th-grade Israeli–Palestinian Conflict class that placed Israeli and Palestinian narratives side-by-side. She was now embracing texts that she had once found "boring" and had predicted "wouldn't be useful for me later in life."

Yet there was Rachel asking her commander what he thought about the conflict. She reflected on that moment:

> You're supposed to have... a distance with your commander and I think I kind of broke that which is not really allowed but I was really curious.... [He] lives in Jerusalem [and] I wanted to know... "Is your family safe and what is your opinion?"... It's something I'm curious about and something I want to learn about and so I blurted it out and he didn't seem to mind. I just felt like if I knew a lot about the topic... I could talk about it and so I asked.

As a student, she was decidedly progressive and did not find nuanced presentations of the Israeli–Palestinian conflict useful. Yet, this recent Gann graduate is now deeply connected to the State of Israel and is ready to take informed stances by challenging her army compatriots and commanders to consider the positions of the other side.

In many ways, Rachel is an exemplary graduate of Gann's Israel education program. In some ways she might seem like an obvious success story; what day school wouldn't proudly tout its *Tzahal* (Israel Defense Forces) alumni as a clear Israel education victory? But we view Rachel as a Gann success story less because of her enlistment in the Israeli army and more because of what she's done while in it. A successfully educated Gann graduate will have acquired a level of knowledge about Israel, will feel connections to Israel, and will be prepared to take—and be practiced in taking—stances on Israel. Rachel has used the knowledge she acquired about Israel to take stances all the while more deeply connecting her to the Jewish state and its people.

In 2016, Gann Academy redesigned its Israel education goals and implemented them in its Israel education program. We, the coauthors of this article, were members of the redesign team of the Israel education goals. Through the lens of a teacher self-study, this article will explore the new paradigm of Israel education we helped develop at Gann and investigate the pedagogy needed to implement this paradigm.

In short, we argue that a critical element of Israel education has been missing in many Jewish educational settings. While many teachers focus on students acquiring knowledge about—and developing connections to—Israel, we contend that a critical component to cultivating a connection to Israel is teaching students how to take stances on an array of Israel-related topics (and then providing the opportunities for them to do so). This chapter presents the reflections of a small sample of recent Gann graduates about their Israel education and our own reflections about what we have learned by teaching and studying them. In doing so, it illuminates how we have developed and learned about our own educational paradigm and how other teachers can learn from our investigation of our work.

Origins of the Gann Israel Education Paradigm in the Context of the Field of Israel Education

Gann Academy, a pluralistic Jewish high school of 320 students in Waltham, Massachusetts, teaches students about Israel over four years through experiential education, a six-week experience in Israel, and learning in Hebrew, Jewish Studies, and Israel courses. For example, students are taught about Israeli society and culture in their Hebrew class. In 10th grade World History, students learn about the development of the modern state of Israel in a four-week unit at the end of the course. They engage in informal educational programming, including Yom Ha'atzma'ut (Israeli Independence Day) celebrations and Yom Hazikaron (Memorial Day) commemorations. The most critical component of their education is a six-week trip at the end of their sophomore year. In 2016, a core group of Jewish studies and history educators (including the authors of this chapter) gathered to redesign how students would learn about Israel over their four years at the school. Those conversations and the final product were deeply influenced by the existing literature on Israel education.

Connection

When designing the Israel educational goals at Gann, educators were surprised to not find comprehensive models at other institutions. One clear Israel education objective we desired, and which is commonly found in the scholarly literature about Israel education, is "affect," namely, how to connect students to Israel. This sense of connection, assumed to be in the realm of love and care, is often balanced by exposure to challenges in Israel in a "'commitment and critique' paradigm" (Perlman, 2008) that calls for "hugging and wrestling" with Israel (Gringras, 2006) or for teaching a "mature" love of Israel (Alexander, 2015). No matter the paradigm, Zakai (2014) observes that "the sentiment is the same: good Israel education should inculcate in students a feeling of connection to Israel *while at the same time* exposing students to multiple facets of Israel, good and bad" (pp. 306–307). However, the nature of the challenge is captured in the catch-all term "complexity," which is sometimes vague and not easily defined.

Connection would thus be one of the three key Israel education goals of Gann's program. Connection signifies the affective goals of the program in which students build connections to Israel through its people. The school aspires for students to have a "deep and lasting connection to Israel" by cultivating "lasting relationships with Israelis" (see Appendix for Gann's Israel Education Outcome Goals). This concept of relationship building informs the design of the school's Israel travel experience, which privileges side-by-side travel with Israeli students from our sister high school Ironi Hey in Haifa.

While the school could measure connection quantitatively by the number of connections or friendships that students form, the focus is instead on storytelling. Ideally, a student would be able to tell stories about the connection between the Jewish people and Israel and find inspiration in those stories. This outcome goal demonstrates a belief that connection to Israel involves connection with the entire Jewish people. It is our hope that from these stories, students can cultivate personal meaning from an ongoing relationship with Israel because a deep sense of connection can foster strong emotional responses to events in Israel's past and present. Depending on the types of connection and the event, the responses could be ones of joy, pride, disappointment, sadness, or anger. The ultimate goal is for students to feel deep investment in a relationship with Israel and to believe that the future of Israel matters.

Knowledge

The team then wondered to what degree "knowledge" about Israel is a critical component of Israel education. Might a strong connection with or without knowledge be a satisfactory result of Israel education at Gann Academy?

Israel "knowledge" education at Gann asks students to articulate their knowledge in a variety of areas, including history, religion, culture, and Hebrew language (see Appendix). Acquisition of particular knowledge is not the goal, as Gann draws on the "inventory" model of knowledge (Zakai, 2019). Students should use whatever knowledge they have acquired in real-life situations, ask and answer authentic questions, and be able to explain a diversity of perspectives. In other words, the acquisition of knowledge is action oriented and deeply connected to the third pillar of a Gann Israel education: stance.

The Move to Student Stance

The team once again turned back to the literature to determine whether or not "taking stances" on Israel might be an essential element of a successful Israel education. The focus of Israel education has shifted from Jewish continuity and cultural literacy to a search for personal meaning (Chazan, 2016, pp. 2, 8). Hassenfeld's (2016) research into how students told the story of Israel concluded that "students managed to synthesize multiple narratives together while still using a Jewish perspective to frame their account demonstrating that students can be historically sophisticated without abandoning a commitment to their heritage" (p. 55). To avoid a "preoccupation with Israel and neglect of the student," sophisticated Israel education means taking a Kohlbergian approach to moral questions that focus on stakeholder choice in any particular case (Chazan, 2016, pp. 7, 25). In reviewing the scholarly literature on the efficacy of teaching debate, Shen (n.d.) notes that effective debate generally incorporates the elements of idea development, classification of opinions through reason, and perspective taking. Shen points to studies that show that debate "facilitates engagement" as "students take up more responsibility for comprehension of the subject matter and invest more serious study effort." Shen goes on to argue that debating "improves learning outcomes" and "students' appreciation of complexity of the subject matter."

Gann educators believe that stance is the synthesis of a student's connection and knowledge. Since each student will acquire their own set of connections and knowledge, stances will differ from student to student. We aim for students to take stances on big questions about Israel that may be provisional and which may evolve and change over time. With practice, students will be able to articulate a stance that may navigate internal dilemmas with both confidence and humility. In other words, students can be both decisive about their point of view at that moment and be open to the possibility that they may not yet have a definitive stance on any given question.

Defining the Parameters of Connection and Stance

As the educational team started to think through some of the hypothetical questions likely to emerge in actual classroom settings, the team found itself needing to think through and resolve some thorny questions. In a lengthy discussion regarding what "connection" to Israel might look like, the educator team found common ground in the premise that the wellbeing of the over six million Jews living in the State of Israel was something all Gann students should care about. It would not be an acceptable outcome for a Gann student to say, "I don't care what happens to the Jews who live in Israel today." What happens to the Jewish State happens to the Jewish people who live there. Students would thus need to find a connection to the State of Israel.

To develop student connections to Israel, the Israel education team set a curriculum requiring students to take stances on an array of questions about Israel. One source of inspiration of our committee was Gann Academy's mission:

> The mission of Gann Academy is to educate, to inspire, and to empower intellectually confident, passionately engaged, ethically responsible Jews who, through critical thinking and the contribution of their unique voices, will create a vibrant Jewish future and build a better world where human dignity will flourish.

The opening verbs "educate, inspire, and empower" align with "knowledge, connection, stance." This trifurcated paradigm centers everything we do and is driven by its purposes, which include Israel advocacy but are not limited to it either. Our mission is to develop academic self-assuredness and committed civic participation, all grounded in a commitment to ethical and moral rigor. The purpose of this educational mission is the vibrancy of the Jewish future and the flourishing of human dignity. Simply put, we believe that the best way to ensure the flourishing of the Jewish people and human dignity entails asking students to learn about Israel, feel connected to Israel, and take stances on Israel.

In evaluating how and when to ask students to take stances, the educators concluded that certain values were not up for debate, particularly the mission-driven belief in human dignity. In our history classes, Gann teaches students to periodize and engage in historical thinking. Students make arguments as to when the Israeli–Palestinian conflict began, where critical turning-point moments occurred, and whether particular events represented change or continuity over time. These choices make a big difference in how the story of the conflict is told. Marking the start of the story in 1881, when the first wave of Zionist settlement began (Morris, 1999), for example, is very different than beginning the story in 1898, when the term "Palestinian" was used for the first time (Beška & Foster, 2021). Thinking about historical choices like turning points help students to honor and recognize the different worldviews that one can bring to a story.

What Does a Stance-Oriented Class Look Like at Gann Academy? The Hebron-Lesson-Plan Case Study

There are two underlying philosophies that guide the lesson planning of stance-oriented Israeli history at Gann Academy. The first principle is that the students must be able and willing to do the intellectual work. The second principle is that students must trust that their teachers do not have an underlying agenda that they come away with particular beliefs or that they will be expected to parrot a particular set of conclusions. One sample lesson plan will illustrate how these guiding philosophies take concrete shape.

The overarching goal of the lesson is that students understand how the settler movement in the West Bank began, will grapple with the set of complicated questions that informed the government's decision to allow the 1968 settlers of Hebron to stay (Gorenberg, 2006), and will interrogate, sharpen, and articulate their beliefs about the West Bank settler movement. It bears noting that the decision to home in on the 1968 settlement of Hebron evolved from a lesson in which students examined the transcript of a cabinet debate in the days immediately after 1967's Six Day War (Morris, 1999). Ministers weighed their options on the future of the land taken from Jordan during the war, and the range of opinions in June 1967 mirrors the range of opinions still debated today. While the source is a useful one, the lesson plan itself initially remained in the abstract, with little intellectual work for the students to do. At that moment in history, the government had yet to make a choice, and there was no complex decision for students to unpack. After struggling to engage students in deeper thought around the question of the future of the West Bank, the Gann Israel education team chose a moment in which the government was forced to make a complex and hard-to-understand decision. The hotly contested choice to allow Moshe Levinger and his followers to remain in Hebron after they had promised that they would leave (Gorenberg, 2006) turns out to have been just that historical moment.

After telling the students the dramatic story of how the band of settlers found their way into a Hebron hotel for Passover (Gorenberg, 2006), the teachers set up the equally dramatic story of the choice faced by Eshkol, Dayan, and their team when the settlers refused to leave. Students are asked to make an initial prediction of what the government would do. After learning about the students' predictions, the actual outcome is revealed and the discussion moves to try to explain why the settlers promised to leave but didn't and why the government permitted the settlers to remain. The actions of both defy easy explanation, making the exercise that much more interesting.

After unpacking the moment with the distance of an historian, the teachers lead students to the much more fraught space of stance taking. What might two Israelis in 1968 have said about the cabinet decision to let Levinger and his followers stay (Gorenberg, 2006)? When team-taught, the two teachers might model a debate on the topic. Alternatively, teachers might ask students to model that debate. At that point, students offer what they think of the settlers' decision and the government's decision. Students may be asked to evaluate the decisions from the perspective of 1968 or today.

Trust is key to the success of this lesson, namely, the belief by students that their teachers are not seeking some set of desired political or intellectual outcomes. Students must believe that their teachers care about *how* they arrive at their deeply held beliefs, not *what* those deeply held beliefs ought to be. Teachers will push students when they feel that students haven't analyzed the evidence sharply enough. On fairly drawn conclusions, teachers allow students to go where their interpretations of the evidence lead them. Of equal importance, teachers see students as partners in the learning and aim to be transparent and overtly reflective with each move in the lesson. When the teachers express a personal stance, they will name that for the students. When teachers don't know something, they openly admit it and invite students into the discovery process. Gann teachers model open stances and reward thoughtful questions as much as carefully arrived-at conclusions.

Student Learnings and Reflections on Stance

Given the Gann approach to the concept of stance, we gathered data to discover what kind of stances Gann graduates might be taking once out in the "real world." We collected evidence from fourteen students who graduated from Gann in either 2019 or 2020, the first cohorts to learn about Israel through our new trifurcated educational approach. Nine of the alumni graduated in 2019 and five graduated in 2020. These were 14 of 141 total possible respondents, roughly 10%. Alumni data came from a written survey, follow-up interviews over Zoom, and email exchanges after the initial interviews.

We reached out via email to all of the students who graduated Gann Academy in the years 2019 and 2020 with a request that they complete a survey and an invitation to schedule an interview with us over Zoom. Eight of the 14 respondents elected to have a conversation in addition to completing the survey. We interviewed eight students, five self-identifying males and three self-identifying females. Although this small sample size may not be representative of the entirety of our school's alumni, it does serve as a helpful mirror into the power, limits, and next steps for our three-part approach to Israel education. Walter R. Borg and Meredith D. Gall (cited in Slekar, 2005) argue,

> A study that probes deeply into the characteristics of a small sample often provides more knowledge than a study that attacks the same problem by collecting only shallow information on a large sample. So it is not only possible to use a small sample, but sometimes it is preferable. (p. 81)

Thus, like other scholars who situate their research on Israel education in the context of Jewish day schools (e.g., Hassenfeld, 2018; Katz, 2015; Reingold, 2017; Zakai, 2011), we use this small number of alumni to illuminate larger issues and questions about our school's teaching practices.

Our research questions were primarily designed to elicit responses related to the three core pillars of our educational philosophy: knowledge, connection, and stance. Our investigation into our alumni focused on these questions:

1. Did the students/alumni take stances on Israel while at Gann? In the years since being at Gann?
2. Did the students manifest connections to the state of Israel while at Gann? (Or to the people or land of Israel?) In the years since being at Gann?
3. Did the students demonstrate knowledge about Israel while at Gann Academy? In the years since being at Gann Academy?
4. What perceptions do they have about how (and what) Gann taught them about Israel?

The interviews were recorded, transcribed, and coded in order to guide our analysis. We coded self-assessments by looking for positively or negatively valanced descriptors, such as "I felt like I could hold my own in that debate" or "I didn't know enough to engage with that person." While our educational goals around knowledge are more objective (and we tracked that in our analysis as well), we also believe that feeling that one possesses knowledge increases the likelihood of stance taking, which can ultimately lead to connection building.

To determine whether students objectively possessed significant knowledge about Israel, we noted examples of specific facts that they referenced either directly to us or reported referencing on other occasions. Examples of demonstrations of knowledge included "I told her that the British promised the Jews a home in Palestine" or "Eurovision has been an important platform for Israeli musical artists to showcase their talent to the world."

To measure if a student felt connected to Israel, we looked for affective language that described either a positive or negative emotion. Whether a student noted feeling "love" or "allegiance" to Israel or "anger" or "disappointment," we determined that the student felt "connected" to Israel. We argue that feeling connected to someone or something doesn't necessarily entail positive feelings.

Finally, we evaluated a student's stance taking by analyzing whether, and in what contexts, students reported or described articulating a position on any issue related to Israel. The setting of that voicing may be in a class, on social media, in the quad, or in a dorm room, and the topic may be around the Israeli–Palestinian conflict, Israeli culture, politics, or what have you. So long as a student noted that she had weighed in on something related to Israel, we counted it as "stance taking."

Stance Taking at Gann

Most alumni with whom we spoke identified how taking stances on Israel helped develop their connections to Israel and acquire knowledge about Israel. They viewed stance taking as the linchpin to developing high rates of connection and knowledge on Israel. Brian remembers teachers establishing spaces that allowed students to take their own stances.

> All the education I received at Gann was crucial and helped me form an opinion. [Teachers] never... came down and said... "you need to

support Israel and you need to think these things about settlements or whatever"; it was just presenting the facts and then we could sort it out on our own.

Interestingly, Brian doesn't remember teachers "[telling] us to debate about Israel but rather that it was just kind of the by-product" of a Gann education. Stance taking emerges at Gann, Brian says, out of the "strong opinions that are formed and how comfortable people are sharing their opinions in the smaller class environment."

Unlike Brian, Reza remembers being explicitly asked to take stances in Gann's Israeli–Palestinian Conflict (IPC) class. He credits the course for helping him take stances with more sophistication.

> One of the main things that I learned from IPC is that you really can't [draw conclusions from] one fact. There's always context, always more information, and you're not necessarily going to know all of that... but it's important to first acknowledge that one fact isn't the whole story.

Menachem agreed with Reza and Brian that stance taking is central to a Gann Academy education. That said, he doesn't believe that Gann teachers encouraged students to apply those skills to Israel.

> I would want to make sure that students are... able to apply the same critical thinking skills that we learn in other parts of education to issues on Israel... I don't think that Gann always... encourage[d] us to think critically [about Israel].

Menachem's concerns about critical thinking and Israel were surprising to us, but they reify the notion that student and teacher experiences do not always correlate. More importantly, as the only student to make this observation, his comments raise questions for us about to what extent this sentiment was felt more broadly amongst the wider student population. This is important to us as educators because if a sizeable percentage of the student body experiences the curriculum in a way that differs from the educators' intentions, curricular revisions should be implemented, and this can only be learned from further study.

Many of the students remembered stance education occurring outside of their classes. A few named their meetings with thinkers like Yossi Klein Halevi on their Israel trip. Other students remembered the mock-election program held at Gann before the April 2019 Israeli election. Teachers played the role of candidates representing the major ideological camps in Israeli politics. Students asked questions and voted for a candidate. Menachem named this program as effective modeling of stance taking as it offered "a lot of perspectives represented there; we had an element of choice; and it was also really interesting to see how the voting turned out." Menachem, thus, articulated three elements of stance taking that worked for him: multiple viewpoints, authentic choice, and a lack of predictability.

Some students were turned off to stance taking but understood its inherent power. Ayelet linked her lack of connection to Israel to her reluctance toward taking a stance.

> I never really developed my own connection to Israel because the controversial nature of any conversations about Israel were a real barrier to... naturally creating my own relationship. I wasn't able to come into it with a blank page and so it was hard for me to decide for myself what my feelings and opinions were. Instead, there was so much information that I felt like I couldn't start from the beginning and figure it all out.

Ayelet continued:

> It's hard to come into something that you know everyone around you has strong opinions on, has a lot of knowledge about. [It's hard to] try to come into it as a beginner. If I'm trying to develop an opinion about something that I can stand by confidently, I really want to start at the beginning and get all the information... and I think it's difficult to do that when you have people around you that were at the beginning a long time ago. I needed someone to sit down with me one-on-one and give all the basics, all the information.

As Ayelet and others see it, the Israel education paradigm begins with knowledge development, builds then to stance taking, and leads finally to connection development. She also intuits that this knowledge-stance-connection path is not so easy to achieve.

Taken as a whole, Brian, Reza, Menachem, and Ayelet all recognize stance taking as an important component of Israel education and as a tool that can play a crucial role in forming a meaningful attachment to Israel. Concurrent with this understanding is a belief that for some, stance taking in practice was not always recognizable or doable, with both Menachem and Ayelet offering critiques on its implementation alongside recommendations for future improvement.

Stance Taking Beyond Gann

While students recalled stance taking as a powerful tool in their Israel educational experience at Gann, the question remained whether they would continue taking stances beyond the friendly confines of their high school when in college, on social media, or elsewhere.

Brian doesn't see himself as a "political" person but has taken stances on Israel on his college campuses. He sees it as a form of "education."

> I just think it's more than important to stay involved with our side of the story and just to try to educate people and so I go to events with the [pro-Israel campus group] (although I'm not as involved as some of my other friends). I just try to stay involved with the Jewish community and try to have discussions.

He continues, "[I] can count on several hands the amount of times I've had to...explain Jewish things and Israel things to my non-Jewish friends who just didn't understand what exactly was going on."

While some students felt prepared to take stances on Israel after graduating from Gann Academy, others felt less sure-footed. When violence between Jewish Israelis, Arab Israelis, and Palestinians flared in the spring of 2021, Menachem felt comfortable taking stances on the conflict with his sister, but less so on his college campus. Menachem is actively engaged in stance taking around issues like environmentalism but found himself stepping back from political positions on Israel when tensions arose. He reflected, "I tended to...unconsciously recoil or withdraw from a conversation...I was really stressed about everything that was going on [and] didn't really feel like I could engage." Menachem is not sure how to navigate his desire to take stances on college campuses on things he cared about, like fossil fuel divestment, when those conversations steered toward divesting from Israel.

> When a lot of the violence started happening in Israel I felt...torn between my home community and my [college] community and I didn't really feel like I fit in exactly with either because I felt like I was too left-wing for my home community and not left-wing enough for my [college] community.

Brian's and Menachem's reflections about their experiences on college campus reveal their continued interest in learning about Israel and to also remaining connected to Israel. Brian's knowledge and connection clearly led to moments where he felt empowered to take a stance because doing so allowed him to put his knowledge to good use, and the opportunity to transfer that knowledge strengthened his connection and reaffirmed his knowledge. Concurrent with Brian's experiences was Menachem's unwillingness to take a stance because he was unsure how to do so on his politically charged campus. Menachem's continued interest in deepening his knowledge and connection *absent* taking a stance raises future research questions about what the actual relationship is among the three pillars of our pedagogical paradigms and to what extent they are interrelated and interdependent.

The Link Between Stance and Connection

Gann's curriculum-design team began with an assumption that stance and connection are strongly linked, with a student's ability to take stances directly leading to forming deeper connections with Israel. Reza and many of his peers explained that they connected to Israel through forming their "own narrative" of the Israeli–Palestinian conflict based on original and secondary sources. That narrative development took place, for some, in 10th-grade history class. For most, though, it took place in a 12th-grade history elective called the Israeli–Palestinian Conflict (or IPC for short). Reza spoke to the power of that class:

A lot of times different people had different answers... and so just like being immersed in those kind of conversations where different people had different reactions to the different historical events was just like really helpful in shaping like what I thought because maybe I didn't think about those things and then just hearing about them was really helpful.

Connection as a result of stance taking was also evident in places where students found themselves taking a position that disagreed with decisions made by Israel's leaders. For example, Reza said:

It can be very hard for me at least to feel connected to a place when I don't agree with what's going on.... This is true for me in America also. I mean if you asked me how I felt about America during the Trump years it was a very different answer than I felt during the Obama years and so it's not something that's exclusive to Israel.

Notably, Reza never stopped taking stances regarding either the United States or Israel. He was as vociferous about his antipathy to Donald Trump as his adoration for Barack Obama, as vocal about policies that he doesn't like as he is about ones he does. For him, stance taking is an essential element of connectedness. While Reza seems to imply that connection is about feeling emotions that might be coded as positive (and thus his self-described feeling of disconnectedness), we would still consider Reza to be "connected to Israel." Much of this stance taking with teachers and peers came "in 12th grade after having more knowledge [from the IPC course]." This further suggests the importance of knowledge in both stance taking and thus in connection building. Parenthetically, Reza himself seems to see his connectedness to Israel, noting that he feels "more connected to Yom Hazikaron [Israel's Memorial Day] than to American Memorial Day."

Concurrent with the data that showed a relationship between stance and connection, student responses also showed evidence of connections being formed based solely on knowledge irrespective of stance taking. For example, Ayelet rarely engages in political discussions and feels disconnected from campus conversations about Israel. However, she took a class on Israeli film at Gann in which she gained new knowledge and understanding of Israel and developed a sense of connection to the material. Those Hebrew classes weren't

> anything about current events or the conflict or any of that. But I think that felt like the most Israel education to me because I could engage with it.... I was usually just in the advanced [level] and this one was [a mixed-level class] and because I was one of the people that was more comfortable speaking, I think I did a lot of speaking and a lot of writing, and so I got a lot better there.

As opposed to discussions about the conflict, Ayelet felt confident with her mode of expression in this class and more comfortable participating in it.

When Ayelet went to college, the self-perceived foundation of knowledge she'd acquired in her high school class helped her to connect to her Israel-focused college class.

> It was really nice to feel like coming into one of my first college classes [that] I already had all of this knowledge and experience... I felt really prepared... I felt like I belonged there because I was already so familiar with all of these things that we were doing.

For Ayelet, her familiarity with Israeli cinema led to her feeling knowledgeable and thus connected. Unlike with stance taking on political issues, Ayelet felt that in these discussions about culture, she "belonged."

A similar example of connections being formed based on cultural exposure can be found in Reza's reflections on Eurovision. Reza related to us that his first memory of connection was a ninth-grade unit on Eurovision, a song contest in which Israeli performers compete. Reza now follows the contest every year and knows quite a bit about it. Reza's and Ayelet's comments about Eurovision and Israeli film offer an interesting paradigm about the place of arts and culture in Israel education. Their respective interests led directly to new feelings of connection. Reflecting on their experiences, we are struck by the fact that these students experienced increase in connection absent the formation of stances, and we are left wondering whether increased opportunities for stance formation related to cultural events—promoting an Israeli film festival, selecting a student-created piece of artwork about Israel to win a prize—could have increased feelings of connection amongst students who are otherwise disinclined to participate in political encounters.

A further site where connection was frequently felt absent the formation of a stance was on the 10th-grade Israel trip. Rachel (the student who joined the Israeli army) reflected on the moments that may explain her decision to join the Israeli army. She recalled a moment on the trip:

> We stayed at the hostel in Tzfat and we went [to] this underground place where we had like a service or something and we turned off the lights and we're doing kiddush and ... it was just pitch black. We didn't even need to see each other.... It was so loud and everybody was singing and clapping and stomping.... It was the craziest moment of my life, I swear to God. Those moments, specifically within Gann—within our class—even if we all didn't get along, it's like we were all like a big Jewish community.... The only thing that mattered at the end of the day is that we were all believing and celebrating the same exact things. That's something I'll always remember.

Ya'akov describes the Israel trip as having "centered" him. Israel is both a place where he feels "safe" and at home: "You can go up to someone in the middle of the street and get invited for Shabbat. I mean you just have a sense of warmth and welcome that exists nowhere else by wearing a kippah."

Despite identifying two very different moments where they felt connected to Israel while in the country, both Ya'akov's and Rachel's experiences occurred absent stance taking. Instead, they happened at moments where they felt community—either Israeli community or Gann community—and it is community which has facilitated the formation of connection.

In a more explicit rejection of stance taking, Ayelet explained that she found it hard to take stances on the 10th-grade Israel trip. Staking out positions on topics that she felt were "more contentious" led her to fear "the consequences of saying something problematic out of a lack of knowledge." Instead, the trip for her was

> a lot more about bonding with the class and having a vacation and enjoying hikes, meeting people, food, and all of that and a lot less about...

the actual conversations and history.... I didn't feel like I could engage in those parts of it and so [I] turned to the other parts of it.

Indeed, Ayelet would develop her connections to Israel by developing relationships with Israeli culture and people.

Student reflections on stance taking yielded a rich set of data. On one hand, in classes of a political nature like the IPC course, stance taking was a natural outcome of learning about Israel's complex history and its relationship with Palestinians and Arab states, and the opportunity led to increased feelings of connection. Concurrent with this positive outcome was a realization that some students intentionally shied away from courses of a political nature and therefore did not experience stance-taking opportunities because these were not features of other Israel-focused courses. Students shared that they did form connection to Israel in their courses, and we were left wondering whether these classes' providing opportunities for stance taking could have helped form even greater connections.

Transparency of the Trifurcated Paradigm

As an additional challenge for our work, we realized that alumni had trouble defining each of the three key terms and certainly did not do so consistently throughout our interviews. They disagreed on what knowledge meant. (Was it only about the conflict? Could it be about culture too?) What did they think "connection" meant? While Gann educators encourage students to develop relationships with the State of Israel that might be coded as "positive," Gann educators tell students that feelings of anger or disappointment in the state should be considered connections as well. Are alumni cognizant of this?

Reza, for example, sees a link between "connection" and "agreement." As previously noted, Reza voiced how "hard it is to feel connected to a place" whose leaders were making choices with which he disagreed. However, Reza may still be connected to Israel just because he voices strong stances of disapproval with the policies of the Israeli government. Indeed, Reza's assertion led us to wonder whether the opposite of connection is "hatred/disappointment" or, rather, "disengagement." Whichever it is, Reza certainly does not seem disengaged, which highlights the need for educators to be more explicit about what it means to be "connected" to Israel.

Learnings Gleaned and Questions Raised

When the Gann team devised the trifurcated curriculum that would intentionally identify "knowledge," "connection," or "stance" as the primary learning goal of any class, activity, or program, it seemed aligned with the educational mission at Gann Academy of students "doing the intellectual work." In many ways, this is shorthand for connection development through knowledge-informed stance taking.

The study raises the question of how students arrive at their stances and what roles schools play in stance formation. Might proclivities around stance taking be influenced more by other environmental factors beyond the school? Does compelling students to take stances increase their connections or knowledge about Israel? If students take stances that question Zionism or wonder whether Israel's positions in the West Bank might be considered "apartheid," will they ultimately feel less connected to the state of Israel? To the land or people of Israel? What will the impact of such stance taking in high school be on connection development in future years?

Several students felt impeded in taking stances because of a perceived lack of knowledge about the Israeli-Palestinian conflict. This raised the question of whether making the class on the conflict a requirement might be an antidote to this reticence over stance taking and self-perceived lack of knowledge. Students who took the course on the Israel-Palestine conflict believed that it was a foundational class in their formation of connection, knowledge, and stance regarding Israel. They believe that all Gann kids should be required to take this class. Is it possible that the students attracted to such a class were already well on their journey of developing connections, knowledge, and stances on Israel? Might other students find such a class challenging and beyond their zone of proximal development? If so, might such a course impede in the deepening of their knowledge, connection, and stance? These questions linger in our minds as we think about next steps for our school and others committed to stance taking.

Pedagogic Imperatives for Connection-Knowledge-Stance Teaching

Our alumni interviews suggested that a strong predictor of an ongoing feeling of connectedness to Israel was a willingness to take stances on Israel. Some interviewees said that they were taking public stances on Israel in a way they hadn't in high school. They were thus feeling a greater connection to Israel but also regretful that they hadn't acquired more knowledge while at Gann to better equip them when taking those stances. While more data is needed to fully understand the phenomena we have observed, based on the data we have already collected, the teachers on our Israel education team believe that introducing four pedagogic interventions now will help improve the quality of the Israel education program for our future students.

The first teaching intervention we propose is that educators ought more clearly to help students see that meaningful engagement around Israel does not necessarily mean only issues related to the Israeli–Palestinian conflict. Acquiring deep knowledge of Israeli film, religion, or media and then taking stances on those issues (becoming an Israeli film critic, for example) can be an equally powerful path to connection development. As our model has suggested, students will likely gravitate toward whichever field of engagement feels authentic, exciting, and safe for them. It is up to teachers to then overtly explain to them that this exploration of Israel is as important as studying about the conflict. And, finally, because stance taking seems to supply the emotional glue that ensures a long-lasting feeling of connection to Israel, teachers should consider providing students with opportunities to take stances on topics they are learning about.

Relatedly, some students expressed concern that their sense of displeasure with Israel meant that they were not adequately connected to it. This suggests a second teaching intervention: the need to explore with students what it means to be connected to someone or something. Connectedness is complicated, and teachers need to help students understand that sometimes connection takes the form of feelings we might code as warm or affectionate. And connection sometimes can take the form of struggle or feelings we might code as disappointment or anger. Teachers might thereby help students develop a more nuanced and sophisticated sense of their relationship with Israel.

The third intervention acknowledges and embraces the implied critique of students who said that they felt they didn't "know enough about Israel" to take stances (even students who knew quite a bit about other Israel-related topics and took stances on them). As students go into the world beyond high school (particularly in college), the Israel that they will encounter will largely be the Israel engaged in the Palestinian conflict. It is in these settings that many of our graduates expressed feeling regret about not "knowing more." Our research thus suggests the importance of high school teachers providing opportunities for students to learn the basics of the conflict and then to learn the skills (and have the chances) to take stances on what they learned.[2] This also includes requesting that teachers of Israel courses that do not primarily revolve around the conflict modify their curriculum to include increased stance-taking opportunities even in lessons about Israeli culture and society. We hope that students will feel more fluent in the history of Israel (in its many permutations), and fluency, our survey results suggest, is a critical ingredient in connection building.

It may not be enough for students to simply take stances on Israel-related topics, however, and this leads to our fourth teaching intervention. If students take a stance ineffectively (or if students feel as if they did so ineffectively), they may be less likely to emerge with that sought-after feeling of connection (and, indeed, it might backfire, leaving a student less willing to take the emotional risk necessary to take a stance again). Teachers thus ought to consider providing feedback to students on their stance taking and to give them opportunities to try them again (and again). Teachers should offer students opportunities to think about the arguments they made, how they made them, and to explore and practice other possible models for effective stance taking.

Each time that the Gann Academy goals have been presented to educators at other North American Jewish schools, they have been received with nodding heads and deep resonance. While our dataset is small, it provides a compelling portrait of a group of alumni who have been affected by the knowledge-stance-connection model, and who offer both support of our overall approach and challenges to us as we further refine it. We hear in their reflections enough evidence to not only justify further academic study, but also to encourage other Israel educators to give attention to adopting a stance-taking approach to Israel education in their classrooms.

APPENDIX: GANN ACADEMY
ISRAEL EDUCATION OUTCOME GOALS

Connection

Gann helps students cultivate a deep and lasting connection to Israel. We recognize that there are multiple ways for our students to connect to Israel, and below we list seven key ways in which we hope our graduates will connect. Gann graduates will

- Have lasting relationships with Israelis
- Feel at home spending time in Israel
- Feel fellowship with the Jewish people as a whole
- Connect the things that excite them (their interests and passions) to Israel (e.g., Israeli film, Israeli high tech, Israeli sports)
- Feel strong emotional responses to events in Israel's past and present
- Tell stories about the connection between the Jewish people and Israel and find inspiration in those stories
- Derive personal meaning from an ongoing relationship with Israel

Knowledge

Gann supports students in growing their knowledge about Israel. We list four desired outcomes for graduates' knowledge of Israel. Gann graduates can

- Articulate their knowledge of Israeli
    - Geography
    - History
    - Conflict with the Arab world and Palestinians
    - Religious and ethnic diversity
    - Culture
    - Politics
    - Religion
    - Hebrew language
    - Relationships to other Jewish communities
- Use the knowledge listed in real-life situations: Gann graduates feel

prepared to (and do) speak and learn about Israel in a wide variety of contexts (future trips to Israel, college classes, dinner table conversations, conferences, etc). They can connect their knowledge of Israel to other areas of knowledge. They have the knowledge to analyze and explain the significance of information and arguments they encounter, and they can express their personal response.
- Ask and answer authentic questions: Students can synthesize the knowledge listed to answer open-ended questions drawing on a wide range of resources and develop and answer their own questions.
- Explain diversity of perspectives: Students can synthesize the knowledge listed to explain and evaluate opposing viewpoints on topics of central importance to Israel.

Stance

Gann graduates will be able to build on their connection to Israel and knowledge about Israel to develop sophisticated stances on big questions about Israel (even as they realize that stances may be provisional and constantly evolving). Gann students will be able to

- Articulate a stance (confidence): Students will know enough about Israel and feel connected enough to Israel to develop and articulate their own answers to big questions about Israel.
- Navigate internal dilemmas (humility/*anavah*): Students will grapple with the tensions inherent in their viewpoints (as in all viewpoints) in order to further develop and refine their own stances.
- Decide what to do with their point of view: Students' *anavah*-informed point of view will shape their engagement with Israel.

NOTES

1. All alumni names used in this chapter are pseudonyms.

2. This is not meant to replace an inventory approach to learning. Rather, teachers should provide multiple avenues of exploration for students, teach them that those non-conflict-centered topics are equally important, and ensure that students feel confident in their knowledge of the basics of the Israeli–Palestinian conflict.

REFERENCES

Alexander, H. (2015). Mature Zionism: Education and the scholarly study of Israel. *Journal of Jewish Education, 81*(2), 136–161. https://doi.org/10.1080/15244113.2015.1035979

Applebaum, L., Hartman, A., & Zakai, S. (2020). "A little bit more far than Mexico": How 3- and 4-year-old Jewish preschool students understand Israel. *Journal of Jewish Education, 87*(1), 4–34. https://doi.org/10.1080/15244113.2020.1834890

Beška, E., Foster, Z. (2021). The origins of the term "Palestinian" ("Filasṭīnī") in late Ottoman Palestine, 1898–1914. *Academia Letters*, Article 1884. https://doi.org/10.20935/AL1884

Chazan, B. (2016). *A philosophy of Israel education: A relational approach*. Palgrave Macmillan. https://doi.org/10.1007/978-3-319-30779-4

Gorenberg, G. (2006). *The accidental empire: Israel and the birth of the settlements, 1967–1977*. Times Books.

Grant, L. D., & Kopelowitz, E. (2012). *Israel education matters: A 21st century paradigm for Jewish education*. Center for Jewish Peoplehood Education.

Gringras, R. (2006). *Wrestling and hugging: Alternative paradigms for the Diaspora-Israel relationship*. Makom Israel Education Lab. Jewish Agency for Israel. https://makomisrael.org/wp-content/uploads/2016/02/MAKOMWrestlingandHugging.pdf

Hassenfeld, J. (n.d.). *Knowledge and connection as outcomes of Israel education*. Unpublished manuscript.

Hassenfeld, J. (2016). Negotiating critical analysis and collective belonging: Jewish American students write the history of Israel. *Contemporary Jewry, 36*(1), 55–84. https://www.jstor.org/stable/26346515

Hassenfeld, J. (2018). Landscapes of collective belonging: Jewish Americans narrate the history of Israel after an organized tour. *Journal of Jewish Education, 84*(2), 131–160. https://doi.org/10.1080/15244113.2018.1449482

Horowitz, B. (2012). *Defining Israel education*. The iCenter for Israel Education.

Katz, M. (2015). Harnessing teacher potential as Israel education curriculum developers. *Journal of Jewish Education, 81*(2), 162–188. https://doi.org/10.1080/15244113.2015.1034046

Morris, B. (1999). *Righteous victims: A history of the Zionist-Arab conflict, 1881–1999*. Knopf.

Perlman, L. (2008). Commitment and critique: A paradigm shift. *Sh'ma: A Journal of Jewish Ideas, 39*(648), 16–17.

Reingold, M. (2017). Not the Israel of my elementary school: An exploration of Jewish-Canadian secondary students' attempts to process morally complex Israel narratives. *The Social Studies, 108*(3), 87–98. https://doi.org/10.1080/00377996.2021.1954866

Shen, D. (n.d.). *Debate*. Ablconnect. https://ablconnect.harvard.edu/debate-research

Sinclair, A. (2009). A new heuristic device for the analysis of Israel education: Observations from a Jewish summer camp. *Journal of Jewish Education, 75*(1), 79–106. https://doi.org/10.1080/15244110802654575

Sinclair, A. (2013). *Loving the real Israel: An educational agenda for liberal Zionism*. Ben Yehuda Press.

Slekar, T. D. (2005). Without 1, where would we begin? Small sample research in educational settings. *Journal of Thought, 40*(1), 79–86. https://www.jstor.org/stable/42589814

Zakai, S. (2011). Values in tension: Israel education at a U.S. Jewish day school. *Journal of Jewish Education, 77*(3), 239–265. https://doi.org/10.1080/15244113.2011.603070

Zakai, S. (2014). "My heart is in the East and I am in the West": Enduring questions of Israel education in North America. *Journal of Jewish Education, 80*(3), 287–318. https://doi.org/10.1080/15244113.2014.937192

Zakai, S. (2019). From the mouths of children: Widening the scope and shifting the focus of understanding the relationships between American Jews and Israel. *Contemporary Jewry, 39*(1), 17–29. https://doi.org/10.1007/s12397-019-09288-0

PART III

Navigating the Teaching of Politics and the Politics of Teaching

7

Cultivating Critical Inquiry About Israel
Teaching Israel in Our Time

BETHAMIE HOROWITZ

History has a way of lurching forward, with or without us. Shifting tectonic plates reveal previously buried, naturalized, taken-for-granted assumptions, allowing us to see them more clearly, and to possibly reconsider them. And often it is educators who find themselves on the leading edge of digesting these shifts and figuring out how to respond.

A case in point arises regarding how to teach North American Jewish young adults about Israel. For example, Rabbi Michael Paley described what he was seeing in his teaching in Spring 2011:[1]

> We were almost all brought up as liberal, *dash-kova tembel* Six-Day-War Jews.[2] Israel had a big impact on us. Most people who are organizing these things, including myself, were fired up by that. We've never adjusted to the post-Intifada Israel from an ideological and from an educational perspective, and we have to do that. It has a big impact on American Jewish identity. Israel, right now, turns Jews off *from Judaism*. Not [only] off from *Israel*, [but] off from *Judaism*. We have to cope with that in a serious way. [But] we don't cope with it. In fact, we can barely talk about it.[3]

In relating to changes he observed a decade into the 21st century, Paley was basically saying that the tried-and-true conceptual frameworks for teaching about Israel were no longer sufficient. This statement captures the sense that where Israel had served as a bright star in the symbolic constellation of American Judaism through the 1970s, in the years following 2001, it threatened to become a black hole, at least for some.

Leading educational scholars and practitioners—particularly those based in religiously liberal, non-Orthodox Jewish settings—have discussed the new challenges they faced in teaching about Israel, revealing the limits of the prevailing approaches they had employed up to now. It now required "wrestling" with the difficult things about Israel, not only "hugging" its admirable features (Gringras, 2006). It was necessary to move from black-and-white thinking to greater "complexity," to be able to see Israel in higher resolution and finer detail, instead of continuing to rely on simplistic ideas and images (Sinclair, 2003, 2013). There were calls to "complicate" Israel, to move from "naive love" of Israel to "mature love" that would require "critical engagement" in order to foster the "ability to negotiate tensions" arising from encountering Israel (Grant & Kopelowitz, 2012, pp. 22–23, 63, 79). The goal was to enable students to be able to then "forge new connections" and discover "new directions" (Sinclair, 2013; Zakai, 2014). In essence, Paley and these others are saying that for a tougher subject in tougher times, a more complex kind of education is warranted.

Ideally, an educator would want to be able to explain what is important for a young American Jew to know, to understand, and to do in the world today and how that relates to Israel. These pressing questions are very much in flux today in a world that itself is so unsettled, although I expect some readers will view these concerns as extending well beyond the bounds of teaching about Israel. But I accept Paley's consternation, and so in this essay I highlight an educational program that is prepared to address these concerns. Kivunim, whose name means "directions" or "intentions," is an Israel-based gap-year program for recent North American Jewish high school graduates founded by the visionary educator Peter Geffen in 2006.[4] Each year—including a modified form during the pandemic—the program brings together approximately 50 to 60 North American Jewish students for a nine-month course that combines study, volunteering, and exploring Israel, a general rubric that may seem familiar, insofar as this has been and remains the basic shape of any number of well-known gap-year programs operating in Israel for the past decades. In contrast to so many of its gap-year counterparts, the Kivunim program is built around a comparative frame designed to bring Jewish Diaspora perspectives and experiences into view.

The program focuses on two main ideas:

- The importance of learning about society's "Others"—both in places where Jews have been among society's Others and in Israel where Jews form the majority.
- The importance of cultural bridge-building across religious, ethnic, national and other kinds of difference.

These ideas shape the program's educational design in three ways. First, Kivunim's course of study requires not only the study of Hebrew, but also Arabic, a first among the gap-year programs. Then, in addition to extensive travel within Israel—a mainstay of most gap-year programs—Kivunim includes four international trips to key places of Jewish experience (Spain and Morocco, Greece and the Balkans, Central Europe, and India). In this move as well, Kivunim has been a disruptor of existing habits of practice—it was the first of the Israel-based, Jewish gap-year programs to feature international travel to Diaspora Jewish communities around the world as an integral part of its educational program.[5] Finally, the pedagogy of the program is deliberately inquiry oriented, as seen in how the program's educators foster students' question asking and individual and group reflection, viewing them as integral to the work.

I read the Kivunim program as viewing Israel and Zionism as central and significant for Jewish experience, without insisting that Israel is the pinnacle of Jewish experience. By situating the teaching of Israel within a broader frame that allows for different positionings of Israel and Jewish peoplehood, the program design in effect *decenters* Israel (a term not used by Kivunim) and thereby serves to expand the understanding and placement of Israel in the Jewish imagination. This refocusing enables the American Jewish participants to learn about Israel—and to come to understand themselves as American Jews—in a broader historical, sociocultural, and geographic context.

It might seem odd to employ gap-year programs as the best place to investigate new directions in how to teach American Jews about Israel. Gap-year programs are a significant locale for Israel education, but one that has not received much scholarly attention. The overwhelming majority of gap-year participants attend Orthodox, yeshiva-based programs where the focus is on Talmud study, with no explicit attention to teaching Israeli history, society, and culture. In contrast, the non-yeshiva programs attract a much narrower slice of American Jewish high school graduates. Yet, it is precisely this segment of the Jewish world that faces the most pressing questions about the relationship between contemporary Israel and the lives of American Jews. The participants on these programs are typically from the engaged, religiously liberal or secular segments of the Jewish community, for whom the concerns about Israel are the most troubling and where the emotional cross pressures are expected to be strongest.

There are some distinct advantages to looking at how gap-year programs in Israel have handled Israel in their work compared to either short-term educational travel on the one hand (like 10-day Birthright Israel trips) or to teaching about Israel in American Jewish high schools on the other. The first advantage is that in principle the gap-year programs overcome what educators call a "time-on-task" problem: Trips of 10 days or two weeks must necessarily be highly selective in what they can address; in high school (whether Jewish or general/secular), the educational coverage of Israel is also likely to be limited in light of all of the competing academic requirements involved in completing high school and related precollege demands. Compared to these, the gap-year format offers an opportunity for a deeper, more elaborated dive into a rich, extensive, and often complicated subject.

The orientation of these programs is also different. As the term "gap year" suggests, these programs serve as an opportunity to step away from the lockstep of K–12 schooling followed by college. Unlike college, which is a more individualized experience, these programs have the opportunity to cultivate a group experience and a shared ethos as an integral part of their efforts. A second consideration is the way that being on location in Israel might itself animate "critical engagement" (Sinclair, 2012).

In sum, because of Kivunim's particular animating ideas and pedagogical features, I view the program as *a good case to think with* about how to expand the array of possibilities about what teaching about Israel could and perhaps should entail. I hope the analysis will help others reconsider the teaching of Israel in a broader context than what is typically employed, where Israel—typically limited to Jewish Israel—constitutes the sole framework.

Chapter Overview

To set the scene for my analysis, I begin with a brief review of the history of American Jews' relationship with Israel as it relates to the history of teaching about Israel. I highlight the role of travel to and longer-term immersion in Israel as a means of "enchanting" American Jews regarding Israel (i.e., emphasizing the emotional power that experiencing Israel could play for American Jews). I review the ways that Israel educators—Jewish educators who teach Diaspora Jews about Israel—have come to teach about a more complex and complicating Israel. I discuss the various meanings of complexity to consider what is at stake in this work. With this introduction, I turn to Kivunim to see how its educational program widens the framework for teaching about Israel in ways that create space for young American Jews to understand themselves and Israel in fresh ways.

Setting the Scene Historically

There was a long period—at least since 1967—when love of and loyalty to Israel were central in American Jewish civil religion (Woocher, 1986), when Israel galvanized and united most Jews, even those who didn't see themselves as religiously engaged. In this period, American Jews generally viewed Israel as part of "their team," but without being particularly knowledgeable about Israeli life and society (Horowitz, 2010).

By the 2000s Israel had ceased to function as a reliable rallying point for U.S. Jews. Although polls show that a steady majority of American Jews have continued to feel an affinity for Israel, the idealized image of Israel has been replaced by greater realism, if only because American Jews have become more directly acquainted with Israel over the decades. They encounter more of Israeli society, culture, and politics from the steady communications that stream across the media, and also via travel and wider-reaching personal social networks compared to 40 years ago. Across several domains, political scientists have identified new patterns of American Jews' engagement with Israel, including "critical engagement"—defined as questioning, challenging, and criticizing Israel rather than simply accepting or endorsing the state and its policies (Waxman, 2016)—and "direct engagement" arising from personal experience in Israel, in contrast to the prior pattern of mass mobilization (Sasson, 2014). The upshot is that the forms of American Jewish engagement with Israel are changing, becoming more diversified, as mythic images of Israel and idealized expectations have been tempered.

In the realm of educating about Israel, there is a similar contrast to be made between the two time periods. Young people growing up in the American Jewish community in the 1970s and 1980s likely absorbed a positive regard for contemporary Israel from the basic institutional habits and practices that characterized American Jewish synagogues, schools, and summer camps. For most, Israel was a feature within the habitus that undergirded one's American Jewish self-understanding. With the advent of mass travel in the 1970s, some young people would have joined an organized youth trip to Israel, whether for a summer or perhaps for a year. Once the province of an elite cadre of American Jews involved with various Zionist youth movements in the 1950s, spending a year in Israel became more widely embraced beginning in the 1980s. By the 1990s the calculus that Jewish communal and philanthropic leaders made in supporting the "Israel Experience" programs was that immersing oneself in Israeli life for a number of months would convey something powerful about what Israel offers that was not possible elsewhere, because it had the power to "sear the soul" (Ruskay, 1995).

But in the period since 2001, after the failure of the Oslo peace negotiations and with the onset of the Second Intifada, the challenges of teaching about Israel intensified in the face of any number of disturbing developments (e.g., the effects of the Israeli occupation of Palestinian territories, the growing social and economic inequalities within Israel, the Orthodox hegemony regarding how Jewishness is defined in Israel). There was a great deal to be decoded, much of it now explicitly political and consequently more complex to address. For many non-Orthodox American Jews, Israel functioned less as an answer than as a cause for questions, a source of confusions.

Some of these same dynamics play a role in the history of the most significant, massive effort to teach American Jews about Israel. Birthright

Israel, an organization that was founded in 1999, provides free 10-day trips to Israel for Jews ages 18 to 26 on a "journey through Jewish history and the contemporary Jewish state." The wager the funders and founders made was that encountering the vibrancy of Israeli life and society would help to strengthen individuals' sense of themselves as Jews and to bolster their emotional connection to Israel. About 600 thousand American Jews have participated since its inception.[6] This massive effort—with tens of thousands of participants a year—involves multiple trip providers who offer diverse programs that together offer something for everyone. At the same time the program requires all providers to include a core set of experiences during the 10 days, including, among other things, visits to key sites in Jewish history, Zionist history, Israeli national history, and Holocaust history (Birthright Israel, n.d.). In the period beginning in 2017 and continuing through 2019, some participants walked out and protested on some of the trips because they were interested in delving into the politics surrounding Israel in the West Bank and the condition of Palestinians living there, issues that in their own Jewish upbringing had typically been evaded by Jewish educators. The Birthright Israel leaders have been pushed to figure out how the program ought to relate to the ongoing Israel–Palestine conflict (Stockman, 2019). But a 10-day trip is a very limited vehicle for the needed probing educational encounter.

Complexity

In what ways is it complicated educationally to teach American Jews about Israel?

First, making sense of what is transpiring in Israel is itself complex. You might say this about any country, though. But the case of Israel differs from these other cases because most American Jews aren't simply neutral about Israel.

This suggests a second meaning of complexity. At least some teachers and students experience dissonance because they find the policies and directions that Israel pursues to be deeply disturbing, leading them to wonder: "This stuff I'm learning about Israel—how does this affect my relationship to it?" In this context, complexity is a way to flag the contradictions between disturbing features you generally want to avoid or to disavow about your "favored" place. Calling it complex is an attempt to preserve a relationship at risk between Diaspora Jews and Israel.

One other use of complexity is when issues become too hot to handle, leading a community to avoid difficult issues altogether, as in the case of political disagreements about Israel's political and policy directions regarding the West Bank and Gaza (Ariel et al., 2020; Horowitz, 2012; Zakai, 2011). Evading challenging conversations and doubling down on truisms veers in the direction of indoctrination rather than education. The more educative choice is to prepare students to be able to think well and deeply about the challenges today. Here is the final way to employ the term "complexity"—as an educational stance that involves "teaching students to be analysts of information and not just absorbers" (Wineburg, 2012–2013, p. 32) and giving students "the intellectual tools to understand, accept, shrug off, or reject parts of socialization" (Noddings, 2006, p. 106). Teaching for complexity entails preparing students to engage with messy and perplexing aspects of life not only in Israel, but more broadly in the world today.

This brings us back to the centrality of the template of experiential immersion within the educational field of Israel education (Ariel et al., 2020). My conjecture is that *with the presenting questions that students now have, the immersion/experiential model may not be sufficient*. There are more pressing knowledge needs today. In the past, the knowledge needs weren't particularly demanding or deep. There was an expectation that being embedded in Israeli Jewish day-to-day life (e.g., volunteering, touring the country, doing your laundry, managing your time and your various needs in the company of peers, and becoming fluent in Hebrew, for example), along with some regular educational programming, would enable Israel to do its magic.

But in contemporary circumstances, where Israel itself is more complex and the relations between American Jews and Israel are too, teaching about Israel presents new demands. Today the learner needs more input beyond knowledge gleaned from the direct encounter of daily life to decode and grapple with what's going on in Israel. Kivunim employs a critical-analytic pedagogic model across its various modalities, including its formal classes, in travel and cultural encounters. This is essential for getting students to take in new information and ways of thinking, and for teaching students to analyze and assess various narratives and accounts. Coupled with the way that Kivunim reframes and decenters the presentation of Israel to students, this inquiry-oriented approach positions them to think afresh about what they are encountering.

Kivunim: A Case to Think With
The Empirical Study

My portrayal of the Kivunim program is based on a yearlong inquiry that I and my team carried out in 2019. The research included analyses of program materials and its curricular elements, interviews with faculty and staff, and participant observation of the program in Israel and during its travels abroad in 2019.[7] This multi-method inquiry included 1) interviews with program leaders, key faculty, and staff; 2) participant observation of the program in action; 3) documentary analysis of syllabi, academic and student handbooks, program websites, and student artifacts from the course about Israel and Zionism. I employed an abductive approach to data analysis, beginning with provisional hypotheses developed at the outset that I revised over the course of working with the materials. My team and I wrote fieldnotes, summaries, and reflective memos about key themes and emerging questions (Tavory & Timmermans, 2014).

Setting the Scene for Kivunim

Based in Jerusalem for eight months, the students lived at Beit Shmuel, an inviting youth hostel in West Jerusalem. Kivunim has its own small campus, centered around a courtyard, bordered by the program's office, a large meeting room, the hostel's kosher dining hall, plus several smaller classrooms. Students reside, three to four per room, on the floors above the courtyard. Three resident advisors (RAs), all alumni of the program who have since completed college, live there, as well.

Kivunim students take four yearlong courses:

1. Hebrew Language and Literature
2. Arabic Language and Culture
3. Civilization and Society: Homelands in Exile. This is the core humanities course of the program. Each unit is coordinated with one of the

program's international trips and serves to orient students to the Jewish and general history, politics, religion, geography, and culture of that region.
4. Land, People, Ideas: The Challenges of Zionism. This course introduces students to the main themes and concepts that define "the modern Zionist movement, the State of Israel, and the Arab–Israeli conflict."

In addition, there is a special module called Visual Thinking: The Art of Seeing, which is designed to sensitize and orient the students to the aesthetics of what they encounter during the year.

Sundays are devoted to daylong trips around Israel to explore key themes and sites. Students undertake weekly community service during their residence in Israel. Four times a year, approximately every six weeks, the program embarks on an overseas trip of 12–14 days. During all overseas trips, and once a month while in residence in Israel, the entire program joins together for "communal shabbat" programming that accommodates the varieties of Jewish religious orientations among students and staff (ranging from secular to Orthodox).

Kivunim attracts a cross section of students from the mainstream Jewish communities in the United States and Canada (Reform, Conservative, Reconstructionist, Modern Orthodox, and "just Jewish"). Nearly three-quarters of the Kivunim participants over the years have attended Jewish day school at least for part of their schooling prior to the gap year (54% were graduates of Jewish day high schools), and 94% had visited Israel before embarking on this program. Clearly, for the vast majority of those participating, Kivunim is not their first encounter with Zionism or Israel.

One attraction of Kivunim for many students is that they see it as a chance to step out more broadly into the world and to explore Israel and its dilemmas and their sense of Jewish history in ways that may be new to them, that they had not been exposed to as part of their own upbringing or education.[8] As Geffen told me in 2012,

> Among the kids each year there is a marked impatience that they are not "getting the whole story," no matter where we start curricularly. "The whole story" means the Middle East and beyond.... They sense that the Jewish establishment is desperate about loyalty and frightened

about traitors beyond intermarriage. Even discussions of *diaspora* are seen as traitorous to the Zionist outlook. They sense that there are questions not to be posed.[9]

The Program in Action

Kivunim reenvisions the frame within which Israel is considered, in relation to Diaspora Jewish communities *around the world* and to the diverse citizens of *Israel*, without falling back on a conventional Zionist telos. What does this reorientation of the positioning and the representation of Israel look like in practice?

The educators deploy several key concepts in doing their work, concepts that in effect name the capacities that the educators are trying to develop in the students. The first concept relates to the importance of building relationships and finding commonality across cultural differences. Here the notions of "bridge building" and "world consciousness" come into play. A second, related idea is the importance of learning about the "Other" to deepen one's understanding of oneself and one's own group. The third emphasis is a pedagogic one about the importance of encouraging curiosity, inquiry, and reflection in order to step back and take in a wider view.

Bridge Building and World Consciousness

Geffen and his faculty colleagues are deeply committed to teaching the students to have hope and a sense of their own agency in building for the future, which in his view requires deliberately chosen optimism and openness to the world and to others, resisting the lachrymose view of Jewish history that highlights Jews as ever at the mercy of eternal enemies. The optimism is related to bridging differences between different people, leading to developing "world consciousness" and empathy for others. Students explained the meaning of world consciousness as experiencing "the commonalities amidst the diversity" and as "finding commonality with other Jews and being able to appreciate the variations of Jewishness, too," both while traveling abroad and in Israel. In relation to teaching about Israel, the students saw Kivunim itself as engaging in bridge building "because on Kivunim we learn about parts of Israel that most programs don't see."

But it's not about simply touring another country or sightseeing. One of the RAs explained,

> It's not just the travel. If you travel and go to the Greek Islands, you're not building world consciousness. It's about the people we interact with and the kind of travel we do. It's very intensive travel. This is not like chilling for a year. Every day is packed with back-to-back speakers.... [For example] going to Greece and meeting with the people at IsrAID working with refugees,[10] learning about what is going on in those countries, the tensions or relations between Jewish community and non-Jewish community or events that are going on there. I think we're giving the tools to help you learn what's going on.

The tools she refers to are part of the program's pedagogic orientation, addressed later in this chapter.

Learning About the Other

A second concept that program leaders employ is the importance of *learning about the Other* as a means to deepen one's understanding of oneself and one's own group. David Mendelsohn,[11] the dean of academics, said,

> True education is distinct from regurgitation. Students coming from similar upbringings bring a North American bias and a set of assumptions. The point is to recast their views, to re-create their own sense of Judaism, to get them to ask, "What do we share with [the Jewish experience in] Bulgaria or Greece?" The Delphic Oracle says know thyself. We do that by learning about others.

The most palpable way that the program design communicates the importance of learning about the Other is the fact that Arabic is structured into the program. Kivunim is the first program to include Arabic as a requirement (alongside Hebrew) and the first to employ a Palestinian Israeli in a senior staff role. Amal Nagammy, Kivunim's language coordinator, has been a faculty member since Kivunim's inception. She explained that what drew her to work at Kivunim was the program's commitment to equality and coexistence.

> [Kivunim] reflects who I am—open-minded. We grew up in a communist family, with Jews and Christians [in Haifa]. Mixing is normal to me. I decided to teach Arabic for Jews and Hebrew for Arabs.... In 2004 I was working in the [Israeli] Ministry of Education to prepare Arabic teachers to teach languages in high school. No one wanted to teach Arabic in Jewish schools.

Because Israel has separate schools for children from different sectors (i.e., Arab, Jewish, and within the Jewish sector there are separate secular, religious-national, Haredi schools)—Arabs and Jews don't interact in school, and as a result Amal's peers viewed it as a tough assignment. She recalled her own experience in teaching Arabic to sixth graders in a Jewish school.

> The children asked, "What are you? Are you Jewish? Are you Christian?"
> "I'm Muslim."
> A boy called out, "You're Hamas!"

"Finding ways to address equality and freedom in Israel mattered to me," she said. Eventually, when she met Geffen (through the Abraham Fund, an Israeli NGO devoted to coexistence), she shifted her professional focus and began to work with the North American Jewish students on Kivunim. She says, "I believe that they can help with the conflict."

How does she understand Kivunim? Riffing on the meaning of the word *kivunim*, she said it's about "new directions, world consciousness, learning about the Other. I'm here because it's more than [teaching] Arabic. It's about an attitude of openness. The teacher must be open, relate to the students. It's not just about learning the letters and go home. It's about developing a relationship [between the Arabic teacher and the Jewish students]."

The recent study of the alumni from 2006 to 2019 provided respondents with the option of commenting about their experience learning Arabic.

More than half took the opportunity to elaborate, and by far the most prevalent sentiment was their appreciation for being exposed to Arabic and Arabic culture, which they understood and appreciated as key to Kivunim's tenet of coexistence and intercultural bridging. For example, one person wrote,

> I thought learning Arabic was central to understanding Israel as a whole. A vast number of Israeli citizens and those living in the region speak Arabic natively. To fully understand a person and their background it is important to understand their language.
>
> This was the most powerful aspect of my Kivunim education. Language is the key into a culture, a history, and into the human beings who are living out all those realities. It was an integral vehicle into better understanding the relationship between Jews and Muslims AND became the most authentic way of accessing the Palestinian narrative.

Pedagogy of Inquiry

Usually in education, inquiry-oriented work means having students handle original documents and learn to act like historians (Caldor, 2006). But in a gap-year program, where much teaching takes place in settings outside of the formal classroom activity, what inquiry-oriented pedagogies can a teacher employ? During my team's observation, we observed two kinds of regularized practices that the teachers and RAs employed: *question asking* and periodic opportunities for personal and group *reflection* about what students are encountering.

Question asking is the enterprise of cultivating students' inquiry and analysis rather than unthinkingly reproducing longstanding patterns without reflection. The program introduces this approach at a formal session that takes place during the program orientation held during Sukkot, when the entire group and faculty spend two weeks in Sde Boker, a kibbutz in the south of Israel. Mendelsohn told me,

> These kids are used to determining what the teacher wants to hear and then giving it back to the teacher. But what we really want to see is that

they are inquiry-oriented: what do you want to know? What excites you? I tell them not to be afraid, and instead to be vulnerable and to ask questions, even those they think are silly.... The goal is not to steer people, but instead to ask questions, to make people curious, to ask what is the reason for this, to ask why do people feel the way they do.

He described the session he teaches during the program's 10-day orientation, where he offers guidelines for asking questions that are productive for learning, such as, "Listen well to what others are asking in order to advance the questions of the group as a whole, rather than to show off; make sure to think about what the speaker is saying and clarify what you don't understand." One of the alumni commented on this practice:

> [My experience at Kivunim] definitely helped me understand the importance of asking real questions with the intention of listening, not debating or proving myself right. I came away with an appreciation for the value of talking to people I sternly disagreed with and hearing the reasons behind their stances that were different than mine. Granting legitimacy to opinions that differed greatly from my own made it easier to understand how those I disagreed with came to their stances and allowed for a possibility of future understanding. (Reported in Horowitz & Winer, 2020, p. 22)

The discipline of question asking to promote inquiry and build new knowledge was quite palpable in relation to overseas travel, as I saw when I tagged along with the program on its trip to Berlin and Prague for 10 days in May 2019. When I joined the group in Berlin, I noticed that the staff kept referring to a page of "Questions for Reflection Prior and During Our Visit to Germany" that the faculty had prepared together with the students:[12]

1. Is it possible to be freed from responsibility for the past, even after a long time has gone by? What's the "half-life" of historical guilt?
2. Should the grandchildren of Nazis, soldiers, politicians, and silent bystanders see themselves as part of a historical narrative of the Holocaust?

3. Do you think that today's Germans (individually or collectively as a nation) are morally responsible for the Holocaust? If so, how would this moral responsibility manifest itself?
4. One writer once wrote, "It's time for Jews to forgive but not forget." What's your opinion on this statement?
5. Are people destined to see themselves as the descendants of victims or oppressors?
6. To what extent is evil "banal"?
7. To what degree does and should the Holocaust define who we are as modern Jews? Define Germany.

These aren't fact-related questions like "When did such and such happen?" or "What's the history of X?" Rather, the moral-existential questions were the product of an extensive conversation among the faculty and students together. The process of crafting these thoughtful questions collectively in advance of the trip and then having the faculty refer to them at different points while touring to spark short conversations helped students connect what they were seeing to a shared agenda.

Nearly every day during the trip there was a *reflection session* to gather participants' reactions and to process the experience together as a group. In these sessions, led by faculty or the RAs, students had a chance to distill and then share their reactions and to take in the reflections of others. The point was not to look for closure, but to engage in collective sense making about what the encounter had left them with.

Where the "Questions for Reflection" articulated the themes the group planned to address during the visit, the closing reflection session, held at the end of five days in Berlin, focused on the students' own ruminations. Students spoke about their own family linkages or lack thereof to the Holocaust. They discussed the ways they related to present-day Germany. One student gave what I viewed as an excellent coda to the entire visit that embodied the ethos of Kivunim:

> I know the *past*. But I want to know how the *present* is reacting to the past. The Holocaust survivors are dying out and so are the people who are responsible to make sure it doesn't happen again.... Kivunim's motto is, "Remember the past, experience the present, build for the

future." What is our relationship with Germany today supposed to be? I don't blame Germans today for the past. But I do blame them if they don't combat antisemitism today. The rise of the AfD is scary.[13] It's their responsibility and ours, too, to make sure it doesn't happen again.

For this session the students sat or lay on the floor, roughly in a circle, and seemed fully ready and open for engaging in this conversation. It appeared to be a regular practice, one that didn't need to be explained or introduced beyond the RA's particular opening comments and then invitation to share feelings. The group's interchange seemed to be guided by some underlying rules of civility: 1) Students expressed their feelings and spoke only for themselves. 2) Every comment was welcome and there was a very attentive atmosphere. 3) No one debated or criticized another's comment. At one point, one student introduced her comment by saying, "I'm coming from another perspective."

The pedagogic stance of the Kivunim faculty and staff, with its cultivated approach to teaching the art of asking questions, and choreographed opportunities for individual and group reflection is used regularly throughout Kivunim's formal and experiential learning modalities.

How Kivunim Represents Israel and Zionism

The program leaders seek out opportunities for directly encountering many aspects of present-day Israel, in both the formal course about Israel and Zionism and in the program's weekly travel to sites around the country, supplemented by regular cultural programming (attending performances, meeting artists, visiting museums, speaking with experts, and so on).

The Israel represented in these curricular and programming choices includes numerous classic Jewish national sites relevant to Jewish and Zionist history—for example, the program's 10-day orientation is based at Sde Boker, Ben-Gurion's home in the Negev—but Kivunim's staff seeks to widen the students' gaze, to appreciate many facets of contemporary Israeli society that have not been integral to or on the radar of the classic Jewish Zionist itinerary. Kivunim devotes a full day each week to field trips as part of its effort to convey "complexities of Israel." It includes the following broad areas of inquiry: the cultures, demographics, and sociology of "minority populations in Israel, *Yediat ha'Aretz* [knowledge of the Land of Israel by exploring its geography and topography], politics, social, religious and cultural issues."[14]

Mendelsohn explained:

> We're going to Barta'a, Umm Al Fahm, meeting with Said Abu Shakra. We meet artists, we meet elderly [people] who tell their stories. One man was a police detective in Tel Aviv; he has multiple identities as an Arab and Israeli....We go to Givat Haviva. We visit the town in the Galil that is split by the Green Line—Baqa al-Gharbiya and Baqa ash-Sharqiya....We learn about differences—various points of view and experiences—in the Arab community. In the encounter with these people and places, we look for a sense of self-reflection among our students: What did you expect? What bothers you? Why does it bother you? What does that then [reveal]?

Kivunim's educational agenda often ends up challenging students' prior knowledge of Israel. One faculty member said:

> There is an opportunity to be exposed to different voices. Nothing is sacrosanct. There is a political tension, and this feeds into the question of Zionism as well. The Kivunim kids do not end up complaining, "Why haven't you told us...?!" We are doing something right because we're challenging everyone![15]

One student who described herself as a "poster child for [one American Jewish youth movement]," who had also spent a semester in Israel during high school, said she found Kivunim to be refreshing in how it handles hot issues: "Kivunim brings multiple perspectives, even some people who are anti-Israel, and lets us come to our own conclusions."

Letting students come to their own conclusions, indeed celebrating that, emerges from creating a culture of inquiry that encourages students to delve into an issue wherever it may lead. Kivunim cultivates such an atmosphere, where it is not unusual to hear a range of viewpoints and alternative positions.[16] Then students come to experience uncertainties, questions, and confusions as normal rather than off-putting or problematic. That's part of what's required to address the complexities of situations that don't have easy answers.

The goal of Kivunim is not necessarily that the students "become Zionists"; rather, its goal is to make it possible for them to investigate Israel more deeply. My conversation with the RAs in January 2019 addressed this:

> RA 1: Kivunim *wants* you to see the complexities of Israel. That's the main thing. It's not teaching you to hate Israel; it's not teaching you to *not* support Israel. It's teaching you how to love Israel in a critical way.
> RA 2: My hope for the students at the end of the year is that they can become comfortable in different spaces and to be okay in this grey area that exists. I don't care where your politics lie. I truly do not care whether you consider yourself as more right-wing or AIPAC [America Israel Public Affairs Committee] affiliated or J-Street or left. I do not care. Can you be comfortable and respectful and just listen intently, intensely and to learn in these different spaces?
> RA 1: And to understand that you don't know everything; you know nothing!... I feel that I left Kivunim feeling that there's so little that I know and so I have to continue to learn more. Like, I don't have the answers. I don't have the answers and I can't. I'm not willing to go into this "guns blazing" attitude, like "this is how I feel." It's important to be able to listen.

Among the dispositions that the program especially values in its alumni is their ability to listen and learn and to find ways to bridge divides and create space for bridge building. The students spoke enthusiastically about the way the program's teaching had influenced them:

> STUDENT 1: Kids on the Kivunim program are invested in the education. No one's afraid to engage in a conversation with different views.
> STUDENT 2: [But] I've seen someone voicing their view, and then... the politics can get ugly.
> STUDENT 3: I agree, but nowadays in U.S. politics people shut one another down. But we're discussing and learning how to have a conversation. Out in the world it's going to be a great deal worse.
> STUDENT 1: Our conversation is about politics in a way that is atypical.

STUDENT 3: We're learning skills. I wasn't getting confused before, but now I'm getting confused, but in the best way possible. We should be confused. It's a sign of being alert, awake, conscious.

These comments can be read as the fruits of the teachers' efforts to foster a way of relating to others in the group, including question asking, learning to listen to people whose views differ from your own, and keeping an eye on the overall direction of the group discourse.

Kivunim's Relationship to "Zionism"

Kivunim treats the history of Zionism as a central module in its educational program, to understand why Zionism emerged in its time and how different currents have evolved and continue to be played out in Israeli life today. Here is where the program's pedagogical stance can help students address the knottiest aspects of Zionism. It does this in effect by teaching about the *history of Zionism* rather than teaching *Zionist history*. Teaching Zionist history asks the learner to adopt the perspective of Zionism and to use it as a lens for relating to Israel today. Teaching the history of Zionism asks the learner to take stock of the Zionist efforts. Kivunim students wrote essays in response to a teacher's prompt to "compare the views of two or three Zionist (or proto-Zionist or counter-Zionist) thinkers in relation to the broader forces of nationalism and socialism brewing in Europe, in relation to the philosophies and processes that preceded them (i.e., the European Enlightenment and Emancipation)." That assignment illustrates the teacher's interest in contextualizing Zionist thought and analyzing it as a thing to be viewed with some objectivity and not necessarily as resource for building the Zionist identities of the students.

Kivunim has created an intellectual framework that asks students to examine the history of Zionism within a broader comparative framework that encompasses Jewish life and culture in various sociohistorical contexts. It offers what might be called a Diasporic perspective. It states that its goal is to help participants understand Zionism and "the Zionist promise" in ways that allow them to "challenge Zionism and in so doing, to expand it." The program succeeds in conveying a message of resilience and adaptability of Jews and Jewishness in a range of circumstances (Horowitz & Winer, 2020). Against these set of overarching questions, American Jews can ponder the various realities—in Israel, in the United States and Canada, and elsewhere around the world.

Of course, no program can do everything, and indeed there are some things Kivunim does less well than other programs. It does not prioritize cultivating friendships between American Jews and their Israeli peers. It does not have options for premilitary training or in training for emergency medical services or participating in an internship, say, like Young Judaea Year Course. Also, the program's educational ambitions create a tighter daily schedule; its requirement of studying both Hebrew and Arabic may be a barrier for would-be participants who find language learning to be difficult.[17]

Conclusion

As I wrapped up the year of research about Kivunim, Geffen told me a story about Ben-Gurion's relationship to Zionism in his later years, fully two decades after the founding of the state of Israel in 1948:[18]

> A British journalist asked Ben-Gurion, "So, Mr. Ben-Gurion, are you a Zionist?" Ben-Gurion says, "I am not a Zionist. Zionism was over when we created the state." And then the interviewer asked, "Are you a socialist?" He says, "A socialist?! I believe that the movement that Hitler ran was called National Socialism. And I believe that Stalin said that he was a socialist. So, if this is socialism, I am not a socialist." The interviewer asked, "So what are you?" Ben-Gurion says, "I am a Jew who lives in the land of Israel. That's it."

For Geffen, this vignette was significant because it showed how "our thinking as a people actually stopped at '67. We stopped thinking and we just went on to some kind of automatic pilot." In the post-2000 period, there was an opening for thoughtful reconsideration of what should happen next, and Kivunim itself embodies a different conceptualization of the relationship between U.S. Jews and Israel. I see Kivunim's educators as taking

Ben-Gurion's concrete, deceptively simple description about himself, "I am a Jew who lives in the land of Israel," as a formulation upon which to build. Using that formulation, one can then ask, as Kivunim does, what does it mean to be a Jew (or a particular kind of Jew) living in Israel? Or to be a Jew living in the United States, or in Germany, or in India today? What about a Palestinian living in Israel—in Abu Ghosh, in Barta'a, or in the West Bank? What about the perspectives of settlers, of secular Jews in Tel Aviv, of Haredim, of immigrants from Ukraine, or refugees from Africa, and so on? The educational move of reframing or decentering allows for overarching questions to be posed that aren't typically part of the more conventional Israel-experience programs. The Kivunim educators ask the students to consider the following questions:

- What has been the Jewish experience in other countries around the world—historically and today?
- How has the experience of being part of the place and also distinct within it—Other—played out in different contexts?
- Who becomes "Other"? Within Israel itself, what happens to Others? What makes shared society possible?

These kinds of questions essentially *widen the relational frame* so that Israel and American Jewry are part of a broader scene that includes others (and Others) from elsewhere around the world, historically and in contemporaneous terms. Because such overarching subjects are not entirely submerged within contemporary Zionism and the controversies that engulf it, this expanded frame enables educators to craft a different kind of conversation. This approach of decentering and expansion situates Israel in a comparative mode rather than bracketing it off as a mythic exemplar. Coupled with the program's pedagogic inquiry-oriented practices (i.e., question asking and structuring of reflection for both individuals and the group), the Kivunim educators create a lively learning context that fosters students' deeper investigation and enlarges their understanding of Israel, Zionism, and Judaism in forward-looking ways.

ACKNOWLEDGMENTS

This article is based on research supported by a 2018 grant from the Consortium (now "Collaborative") for Applied Studies in Jewish Education (CASJE), entitled "What Are the Terms of Engagement? Israel-Based Gap Year Programs as Sites for Investigating Israel Education for North American Jews." Joshua Krug and Amanda Winer served as research assistants.

NOTES

1. Paley served as founding director of the Bronfman Youth Fellowship in Israel, associate chaplain at Dartmouth College, university chaplain at Columbia University, scholar-in-residence at UJA Federation of NY, and faculty member of Prozdor, the supplementary Jewish high school program at Jewish Theological Seminary.

2. These Hebrew phrases are what would now be called the memes of that era. *Dash* is an abbreviation of *drishat shalom*, meaning "greetings." *Kova tembel* refers to the iconic hats worn by kibbutz members, the quintessential Sabras, in the 1950s to 1970s to ward off the sun as they plowed the fields.

3. I interviewed Paley on June 21, 2011. I followed up with him on January 15, 2022. He affirmed that he still stands by his comment.

4. Geffen founded The Abraham Joshua Heschel School in NYC and served as director of the Israel Experience Program for the CRB Foundation. He received the prestigious Covenant Award in 2012 for his work in Jewish education. The Kivunim program website is www.kivunim.org

5. Shorter-term Jewish heritage and Holocaust-related travel trips predate Kivunim. Kivunim's approach to teaching about Israel includes encounters with various places where Jews have and continue to live, and these are not framed within the ashes-to-redemption narrative that has typically been employed by these shorter-term trips. Finally, Kivunim's international travel is a required, integral feature of its educational conception, rather than an optional add-on (as per other gap-year-in-Israel programs that now include international travel).

6. See Kelner 2010 for a thoughtful examination of Birthright Israel.

7. The data gathering took place during the calendar year 2019 and included more than 30 days of fieldwork in two programs—Kivunim and Young Judaea Year Course—in January, February, May, and November 2019. In this essay I look only at Kivunim. In addition to this CASJE-funded data gathering, in this article I draw on the findings from the study of the Kivunim alumni (Horowitz & Winer, 2020), funded by Kivunim.

8. Horowitz & Winer (2020) offer many examples.

9. Personal conversation with Geffen in August 2012, when we first discussed the possibility of my studying the program.

10. IsrAID is an Israeli NGO that responds to emergencies all over the world with targeted humanitarian help: https://www.israaid.org.

11. Mendelsohn became director of the Kivunim gap-year program in 2020.

12. In preparing the students for encountering their trip, the Civilization course focused on the history and culture of the places that the students would be visiting, and students completed substantial reading assignments and also met with area specialists. Based on this preparation, the teacher guided the group in generating questions to frame their collective inquiry during the trip.

13. AfD—*Alternative für Deutschland*—is the far-right, German populist party. It figured prominently in the news during Kivunim's visit because the EU parliamentary elections were about to take place.

14. Kivunim (2019).

15. His comments echo and respond to the lament of the alumni of Zionist youth programs who created You Never Told Me to call out the major summer camps for failing to teach them about the Israeli occupation of the West Bank: http://web.archive.org/web/20200701000000*/https://younevertoldme.org/

16. This orientation is exemplified throughout the program. One example was a day-long fieldtrip to Gush Etzion in the West Bank, entitled A Close Look at the Israeli Settlement Enterprise from Both Sides of the Spectrum. The group met individually with four speakers: Israeli Jews (from Efrat and Tekoa) and Palestinians (from Khirbet Zakaria) who offered different perspectives and life experiences. The program leaders make a point of working with guides and speakers who can engage with the students genuinely and honestly.

17. The cost of running Kivunim—with its more than 40 days abroad—is very high compared to other gap-year programs that take place only in Israel. For the 2019 year, Kivunim's price tag was $54,000 compared to Young Judaea Year Course's list price of $25,900. The striking difference is related to the fact that Kivunim mandates all travel for all participants, and the program sticker price reflects that. Yet for families that cannot afford that amount, the program offers substantial scholarships and interest-free payment plans. On the other hand, Young Judaea's listed cost does not include the roundtrip airfare to and from Israel or any of the fees for optional overseas trips.

18. Geffen heard this story in the recently discovered audiotapes that led to the recent documentary *Ben Gurion: Epilogue* (2016). See https://www.timesofisrael.com/peace-over-territory-says-israels-first-pm-in-long-lost-footage/

REFERENCES

Ariel, Y., Pomson, A., & Pomson, A. (2020). Educational signposts and pedagogical landmarks: A helicopter view. In J. Ariel (Ed.), *Israel education: The next edge*. Makom/Jewish Agency for Israel.

Birthright Israel. (n.d). *About us*. https://www.birthrightisrael.com/about-us

Caldor, L. (2006). Uncoverage: Toward a signature pedagogy for the history course. *The Journal of American History*, 92(4), 1358–1370. https://doi.org/10.2307/4485896

Grant, L. D., & Kopelowitz, E. (2012). *Israel education matters: A 21st century paradigm for Jewish education*. Center for Jewish Peoplehood Education.

Gringras, R. (2006). *Wrestling and hugging: Alternative paradigms for the Diaspora-Israel relationship*. Makom Israel Education Lab. Jewish Agency for Israel. https://makom israel.org/wp-content/uploads/2016/02/MAKOMWrestlingandHugging.pdf

Horowitz, B. (2010). Beyond attachment: Widening the analytic focus about the American Jewish relationship to Israel. *Contemporary Jewry, 30*(2-3), 241-246.

Horowitz, B. (2012). *Defining Israel education*. The iCenter for Israel Education. https://www.bjpa.org/search-results/publication/13727

Horowitz, B., & Winer, A. (2020). *Kivunim alumni study 2020*. The Kivunim Institute. http://www.kivunim.org/alumni-study

Kelner, S. (2010). *Tours that bind: Diaspora, pilgrimage, and Israeli Birthright tourism*. NYU Press.

Kivunim. (2019). *Kivunim academic handbook 2018-2019*. https://static1.squarespace.com/static/5656c634e4b09e258542f577/t/5ecbce6fe3d0ce7bf206c692/1590414961172/KIVUNIM+Academic+Program+2018-19.pdf

Noddings, N. (2006). *Critical lessons: What our schools should teach*. Cambridge University Press. doi:10.1017/CBO9780511804625

Ruskay, J. S. (1995). From challenge to opportunity: To build inspired communities. *Journal of Jewish Communal Service, 72*(1-2), 22-33.

Sinclair, A. (2003). Beyond black and white: Teaching Israel in light of the *matzav*. *Conservative Judaism, 55*(3), 69-80.

Sinclair, A. (2012). *Loving the real Israel: An educational agenda for Liberal Zionism*. Ben Yehuda Press.

Stockman, F. (2019, June 11). Birthright trips, a rite of passage for many Jews, are now a target of protests. *The New York Times*. https://www.nytimes.com/2019/06/11/us/israel-birthright-jews-protests.html

Tavory, I., & Timmermans, S. (2014). *Abductive analysis*. University of Chicago Press.

Wineburg, S. (Winter 2012-2013). Undue certainty: Where Howard Zinn's *A People's History* falls short. *American Educator, 36*(4), 27-34. https://www.aft.org/sites/default/files/Wineburg.pdf

Woocher, J. S. (1986). *Sacred survival: The civil religion of American Jews*. University of Indiana Press.

Zakai, S. (2011). Values in tension: Israel education at a U.S. Jewish day school. *Journal of Jewish Education, 77*(3), 239-265. https://doi.org/10.1080/15244113.2011.603070

8
Activism and Identity
Teaching (About) BDS in the Israeli–Palestinian Relations Classroom

MIRA SUCHAROV

Although little about Israeli–Palestinian relations goes uncontested, the topic of BDS (boycott, divestment, and sanctions against Israel) presents a set of distinct challenges in the university classroom. On one hand, BDS is a topic like any other. According to this view, educators of Israeli–Palestinian relations should simply apply the same kinds of descriptive, explanatory, and evaluative questions they do to any other issue. This might mean, for example, helping students do the following: trace the history of the BDS movement, which dates from 2005 when Palestinian civil society groups issued a global call; examine the range of activities to which it has given rise in Palestine and abroad; investigate the role of BDS in trade unions and on college campuses; probe why certain types of resistance arise when they do; understand why certain individuals and groups are drawn to particular issues and tactics; analyze Israel's response, including its creation of a government ministry expressly devoted to fighting BDS; and perhaps evaluate whether and to what extent BDS has been effective in moving Israeli policy and shifting international opinion.

But another view of the teaching of BDS sees the topic as mired in pedagogical controversy. Rather than adopt an arm's-length approach, this view sees the teaching of BDS as posing an inherent dilemma. This is for two reasons.

The first reason stems from debates around BDS having captured the academy more broadly, something which has led to tensions across faculty and student bodies on some campuses. Specifically, the academic component of the boycott calls upon educators—including, of course, the very educators tasked with teaching about the conflict—to take a stand within their profession. So one could argue that whether or not they seek to be impartial, educators—especially those in the field of Israeli-Palestinian relations—are necessarily implicated. If they actively participate in an academic boycott, they have taken a stand against a series of Israeli policies and in favor of a certain set of political tactics. If they actively oppose an academic boycott—by going on record as opposing it, signing petitions, participating in groups dedicated to opposing it, and so on—they have taken a different stand. And if they seek to remain aloof, and participate in business as usual, then advocates of BDS might insist that those educators have chosen to side with Israel, even if they haven't done anything overt. So how do educators translate these actual activities—which they may have never consciously engaged in or perhaps consciously or unconsciously avoided—into the classroom?

The second reason that the teaching of BDS may pose an inherent dilemma is that the decision, for a given scholar, whether to engage in BDS—particularly when one is wrapped up in some personal or scholarly way with the dynamics of Israel and Palestine—involves a commitment to a particular set of principles, and perhaps a need to trade off values.

So, while BDS is both a topic about Israeli-Palestinian relations and a topic about academic dynamics on university campuses inside and outside the region, the topic also presents a conundrum: Should those who oppose academic boycotts on principle or oppose the endgame of BDS provide a fair hearing to proponents of such efforts? And if a professor is on record as either supporting BDS or actively opposing it, does this affect the classroom atmosphere? Is it useful to help students assess whether BDS has worked, and is that even possible? And if one asks whether BDS has "worked" and finds it has not (Bahar & Sachs, 2018), is this a sufficient reason to discourage students from engaging in it, given that earlier efforts at peacebuilding and peace talks have yet to bear fruit?

This essay will take readers through the debates over analyzing and assessing the dynamics of BDS with an eye towards helping professors mobilize their own subjectivity in productive ways and towards helping students evaluate the kinds of political activism in their midst. The working assumption I use here is that professors might want to encourage students to engage politically outside the classroom based on the intellectual scaffolding gained in the classroom. While different educators bring different approaches about how to engage with the real world in their classrooms, I situate myself within a tradition that seeks to teach not only subject and disciplinary knowledge, textual and writing literacy, and critical thinking skills—all things that are essential to higher education—but also the skills and sensibility to be and become global citizens. To actively engage in the world once a student leaves the classroom means having obtained the knowledge and skills to do so, and the wisdom to be able to draw on a scholarly understanding of an issue when deciding how to engage politically on it. To that end, this essay further draws on social justice and anti-oppression pedagogy literature to trace opportunities and challenges for generating various modes of questions and for deploying faculty and student activism in ways that model engaged global citizenship.

The Academic and Cultural Boycott

The full extent of the academic and cultural boycott is outlined in the PACBI (Palestinian Campaign for the Academic and Cultural Boycott of Israel) guidelines.[1] When it comes to foreign policy influence, the logic of boycotts generally entails the idea of public pressure. In an economic boycott like the one we see in Israel-Palestine, for example, consumers are urged to avoid buying products from a certain country or company. The logic follows that the producers of that product will be so hurt by the boycott that they will pressure their government to change its policies (so that the producer's products can regain a favorable reception internationally). Part of the BDS call indeed entails an economic boycott by identifying Israeli products that are exported abroad, but the academic boycott's dynamic is broader than these traditional logics. In part, BDS's academic boycott seeks to pressure academics who will in turn pressure their government. But the BDS academic boycott also seeks to punish the Israeli academy itself, viewing it as "profoundly implicated in supporting and perpetuating Israel's systematic denial of Palestinian rights." The drafters of the PACBI (2014) guidelines see "the Israeli academy" as having "cast its lot with the hegemonic political-military establishment in Israel... notwithstanding the efforts of a handful of principled academics."

The PACBI guidelines call on academics outside of Israel to boycott events and conferences sponsored by Israeli academic institutions (or Israel itself), not to serve as an external reviewer or examiner for dissertations and other projects based at Israeli universities, not to engage in research exchanges with Israeli institutions or projects funded by Israel, not to support study-abroad programs in Israel, and to oppose "normalization" projects between Israelis and Palestinians because these projects imply that both sides—the "colonizer" and the "colonized"—are equally responsible for the conflict. The academic boycott shall end, the guidelines state, when Israeli institutions do two things: "recognize the inalienable rights of the Palestinian people as enshrined in international law (including the three basic rights outlined in the 2005 BDS Call)" and "end all forms of complicity in violating Palestinian rights as stipulated in international law." This complicity includes discriminatory policies and practices as well as diverse roles in planning, implementing, and/or justifying Israel's human rights abuses and violations of international law.

There are two sets of criticisms of BDS heard most often. The first is that the *goals* of BDS are antithetical to peace and justice, and perhaps even that they are so anti-Israel as to be antisemitic. What I find most challenging for instructors though, since policy debates like the ones around BDS tend to be familiar ground to tread for anyone used to teaching fields like history and politics, is the debates over the proposed *tactics* of BDS.

The most common criticism of the tactics of the academic boycott—views of Israeli policy aside—has been that it violates the principle of academic freedom, which is a cornerstone of the academy (for articulations of this view, see Berman, 2015; and Nelson, 2015). The logic goes that cutting off scholarly exchange—which is what BDS stipulations would require—and isolating Israeli graduate students reliant on external examiners, and so on, flies in the face of the spirit of scholarship. Yet the PACBI (2014) document explicitly responds to this accusation. The guidelines state that "mere affiliation of Israeli scholars to an Israeli academic institution is... not grounds for applying the boycott." Still, the guidelines go on to try to defend the institutional boycott:

While an individual's freedom of expression should be fully and consistently respected in the context of cultural boycotts, an individual artist/writer, Israeli or otherwise, cannot be exempt from being subject to "common sense" boycotts (beyond the scope of the PACBI institutional boycott criteria) that conscientious citizens around the world may call for in response to what they widely perceive as egregious individual complicity in, responsibility for, or advocacy of violations of international law (such as war crimes or other grave human rights violations), racial violence, or racial slurs. At this level, Israeli cultural workers should not be exempted from due criticism or any lawful form of protest, including boycott; they should be treated like all other offenders in the same category, not better or worse.

Readers, as I do, might find this logic slightly tortuous: Is it, or isn't it, targeting individuals? Omar Barghouti, a prominent BDS spokesperson, has also attempted to defend BDS from academic-freedom-violation accusations. Barghouti argues that critics of the academic boycott confuse academic rights with academic "privileges." He writes:

> Israeli scholars, under the boycott, would still be able to pursue their research, teaching, publishing and participating in international forums, provided that these activities do not involve any institutional links between Israeli institutions on the one hand and international institutions—and academics—on the other. What they do face as a result of the boycott is the *"inconvenience"* of having to seek independent international funding to cover their international academic projects, instead of relying on Israeli state or institutional funding for that. An effective international isolation of Israeli academic institutions will undoubtedly curtail some privileges that Israeli scholars take for granted, from generous travel subsidies to various perks and services that have no bearing on their academic freedom. These privileges are only possible, they forget, due to their universities' lucrative business-as-usual relations with western academia. (Barghouti, 2013)

Barghouti goes on to argue that it is Palestinians, more than Israeli academics, who already have their academic freedom violated by virtue of the Israeli occupation curtailing access to these academics' places of work and study.

When it comes to educational institutions, it is divestment, more than boycott, that has gained the most traction. Some student associations have sought to table divestment resolutions, and some faculty associations have signed onto student-led divestment campaigns, as when, in 2016, Toronto's York University endorsed the campaign to divest from various arms-manufacturing companies apparently complicit in the Israeli military occupation of the West Bank. Of course, some BDS opponents do not even acknowledge that there *is* an occupation (see a discussion in Sucharov, 2017). But the faculty association's president was careful to distance the association from BDS writ large, saying, "Most participants strongly rejected the suggestion that YUFA [York University Faculty Association] would be supporting BDS by supporting YUDivest" (Shefa, 2016). Is that distinction compelling? It's hard to say without knowing the motives behind the vote: If they merely oppose the occupation and do not abide by the other two goals of BDS (refugee return and full equality for Jewish and non-Jewish citizens of Israel), then the president could have a case in claiming that their move differs from BDS. Similarly, if they believe in divestment but not in sanctions or in academic, cultural, or economic boycotts of Israel, then the same could hold.

There have been some particularly controversial academic boycott instances, such as when a professor at University of Michigan declined to write a letter of recommendation for a University of Michigan student seeking to study at an Israeli university, explaining that his decision was based only on the academic boycott (Redden, 2018). The university later disciplined the instructor, denying him a merit raise and blocking him from taking a sabbatical for a subsequent two years (Kozlowski, 2018). While not an example of a direct classroom/pedagogy moment, the incident nevertheless raises questions about the role of professors in deploying their principles in educational settings.

Anti-Oppression and Social Justice Pedagogy

Every educator has an implicit or explicit teaching philosophy: the kinds of beliefs that structure how one seeks to go about teaching. Like any life philosophy, teaching philosophies are not always adhered to in practice, but they can serve as guidelines at times when instructors are trying to be more self-conscious about their methods. One inherent challenge regarding teaching philosophies at the university level is that many professors have not consciously had the opportunity or need to articulate them. The teaching and learning specialist at the Centre for Innovation and Excellence in Learning at Vancouver Island University Kathleen Bortolin (2018), in her lament on the lack of attention in universities to the research area known as SoTL (scholarship on teaching and learning), says, as a research specialty, "SoTL is the party that no one wants to go to." Candidates for academic positions may have been required to include a teaching-philosophy statement in their dossier, but those memories may fade as one's career naturally evolves from the time of appointment. In my case, because I have actively sought out teaching awards and pedagogy grants, I have had to develop and refine my teaching philosophy, a task that I have found rewarding and productive.

Over the last several years, and reflecting the overall shift in society towards discussing issues around structural oppression more fluidly and frequently, I have attempted to confront the various forms of privilege I hold (namely, white, straight, cis, able-bodied, and class privilege—though not gender or nominal-Christian privilege). Accordingly, my own teaching philosophy has broadened to include attention to anti-oppression and social justice topics and methodologies, even if my graduate school training in international relations did not incorporate these issues nearly enough in our coverage of the field. But in many ways, this has been a natural progression from my earlier emphasis on encouraging students to be global citizens and helping them find and hone their public voice—through teaching op-ed writing and social media engagement, for example (Sucharov, 2019a), another mode of engagement that was given less attention as I was training to be an academic. From here, I soon realized that to be engaged prescriptively in the world meant broadening out course questions from merely explanatory ones to normative, values-based ones (Hahn Tapper & Sucharov, 2019; Sucharov, 2019b, 2021). Given that general PhD training in the social sciences does not typically include much, if any, direct pedagogy training, and given that my own discipline of international relations has been slow to confront issues of race and colonialism, my own pedagogical evolution has been self-taught and thus intermittent and unsteady, if enthusiastic. The rest of this essay draws on some of those elements while highlighting ongoing challenges I face in actualizing them. To do so, I interrogate my own teaching practice as an example of what it looks like to seriously engage with the kinds of questions about BDS's place in the classroom like the ones I have posed.

A philosophy of pedagogy that takes oppression seriously can be applied to most any subject, and in fact "critical pedagogy" has sought to challenge the role of the educational institution in society writ large (Berila, 2016, p. 8, drawing on Freire, 1970). More generally, anti-oppression pedagogy takes seriously existing systems of inequality and encourages students to consider themselves both analysts of these systems and potential change-makers. In the words of educator Beth Berila (2016), doing so allows for "unlearning the tools of oppression and dismantling inequitable systems" (p. 4). This approach requires students to consider how their language, framing, discourse, and out-of-classroom activities can serve to bring about justice or to halt it.

In the case of Israel-Palestine, so much of the actual topic is ostensibly about oppression, but without an agreed-upon framework that can determine who holds the power, even that is a controversial claim to some. To lead students toward an anti-oppression framework generally, such that the goal is freedom, equality, justice, emancipation, and so on, I open my course by examining how even the perceived direction of the arrows of oppression—and whether there are actual systems of oppression in place or not—are contested beliefs. The most obvious manifestation of this is in the terminology of the topic, including course and book titles. While many educators, commentators, and certainly the media use the phrase "Arab–Israeli conflict" or "Israeli–Palestinian conflict," I invite students to consider the many criticisms that have emerged of this framing. First, scholars and activists who object to the label "Arab–Israeli conflict" to describe the Palestinian dimension claim it is intended to imply that Palestinian–Israeli tensions are merely a function of the Arab states' rejecting Israel. According to this view, if the Arab states embraced Israel in the region, the Palestinian "issue" would disappear. Second, there are those who criticize the label "conflict" itself. These critics argue that the label "conflict" implies two equal sides, which is certainly not what inheres in the

Israeli–Palestinian relationship. Such critics state that using the term "conflict" effectively "plac[es] blame on Palestinians when they resist Israeli rule" (Dawson et al., 2021). There is much truth to this criticism since it is Israel, of course, who holds the lion's share of the power, and much of Israel's relationship to the Palestinians entails occupying them. However, I also point out to my students a counter critique, which is that the term "conflict" does *not* necessarily imply a power balance: In fact, there is a large field of study that is specifically devoted to asymmetrical conflicts. Moreover, some scholars would argue that the Palestinian–Israeli dimension cannot be understood without taking into account threats towards Israel from other Arab states and from Iran. Assessing the relative threats posed by these states is beyond the scope of this article, but professors may want to encourage their students to attempt to measure actual threats according to the logic of capabilities and intentions.

Perhaps more significantly, critics of the term "conflict" in the context of the Israeli–Palestinian dynamic also argue that the term does not sufficiently account for the settler-colonial or overall systemic dynamics inherent in the Israeli–Palestinian relationship. These dynamics date from before 1948 and span the Nakba (the fleeing and expulsion of Palestinians from their towns and villages from 1947–49), through 1967 and the Naksa (the fleeing and expulsion of Palestinians following the Six Day War/1967 War), to today's occupation of the West Bank and siege on Gaza. Scholars are divided on how well the category of settler-colonialism captures Zionism and the historical and contemporary events in Israel-Palestine, but most argue, given the waves of Jewish immigration beginning in the late 19th century to a land already populated by Palestinians, that there is at least some validity to applying the term in this case. Of course, given that there had been some Jewish presence in Israel for generations, and given that Jews do have ancestral ties—if ancient ones—to the land, the term is not perfect.[2]

By way of a corollary to objections over the term "conflict," I point my students to the phrase "race relations" as having gone out of fashion in the United States, in favor of a view that spotlights systemic racism, white supremacy, and anti-racist imperatives. Similarly, I invite students to consider an anti-patriarchy view versus a formulation that relies on asking how well men and women in society are "getting along." The former, of course, allows for an investigation into systems and structures that shape these microlevel relations. Other professors might disagree with this framing, preferring a more individualist mode of analysis rather than one that spotlights structures.

The other thing I do in the framing of my course is something that I know from conversations with colleagues is not universally done: I invite students to become conscious of their personal subjectivity and positionality. This may entail considering their own religious or ethnic connections to the people and issues, but it need not encompass that. I encourage students to "read" themselves: Do they see themselves as social justice activists, as democratic activists, as Canadians, as allies, and so on—or something else? What do these subjectivities say about their approach to the topic at hand and their response to it? At the beginning of the semester, I offer the same, telling students about my own personal background and evolution. (If students want a deeper dive into understanding the relationship between personal subjectivity and scholarly approach, they can read my memoir [Sucharov, 2021], which was published in an international relations list with a scholarly press, as an example of how the two modes, personal and intellectual, can coexist.)

Writing from the discipline of geography, a discipline which overlaps with international relations in terms of its Western-centric foundational assumptions, Lauren Fritzsche (2021) sees "anti-oppressive pedagogy" as helping to "call into question hegemonic and oppressive forms of knowledge," and thus that type of pedagogy "seeks to facilitate more just learning practices and experiences." Extending this further, she writes that "we need to ground our teachings in histories of place that account for colonialism, displacement, and dispossession" (p. 3).

Fritzsche's specific pedagogical approach relies on contemplative practices, including mindfulness. This might include "spending short periods of time in the classroom to pause, breathe, sit in silence, witness, and acknowledge resistances and emotional reactions" (Fritzsche, 2021, p. 9). I, too, have tried some short moments of guided meditation in order to provide scaffolding for the kinds of difficult conversations involved in teaching about anti-oppression, race, and social justice. In my Israel-Palestine course, I run a five-week simulation (still in the beta stage), where students are randomly assigned a role (either an Israeli Jew living within the Green

Line, an Israeli Jewish settler, a Diaspora Palestinian, a Palestinian citizen of Israel, a West Bank Palestinian, a Gaza Palestinian, a Canadian Jew, or a relevant third-party actor). They are then required to engage in the regular discussion-board forum (whereby students are required to analyze the weekly readings) in the voice of their role. Second, they complete a creative assignment (a piece of visual art, a podcast, a video, etc.) through the lens of their role. Finally, and this is where the contemplative practice comes into play most clearly, I require students to write a short reflection piece placing their character in conversation with their own self. In this piece, they are invited to reflect on how their subjectivity may have shaped their encounter with the character and vice versa.

Through the use of these sorts of inward-seeking exercises, students can imagine themselves as both analysts and out-of-region actors working to understand the motivations of the various parties and to help bring about justice should they continue to be engaged in the issues after their studies. Of course, what justice looks like, and the kinds of tactics that justice seekers deem legitimate, are just as contested. This is especially evident in the context of Israel-Palestine, where the roles of oppressed and oppressor are fiercely debated by the actors themselves and by their coreligionists/ethnic community members, or their allies (formal or informal, state or individual). To reiterate, some scholars and analysts see the arrows of oppression as flowing primarily from the Arab states, Iran, and non-state actors like Hamas and Hezbollah (and to a lesser extent, the Palestinian Authority) towards Israel and Israelis. Others see Israel as the primary driver of injustice and suffering among the Palestinians.

In the next section, I examine these tensions in the case of BDS before turning to how an anti-oppression and subjectivity-aware approach can help students understand what's at stake for individuals and groups in the region and beyond.

BDS: Outcomes and Tactics

In this section I discuss how BDS's endgame implies a certain view of justice—which is itself contested—and how the movement's tactics also are deemed to be just and legitimate by some, and to be unjust and illegitimate by others. But what I'm really interested in is this: Educators have a delicate role. If they feel motivated by justice and anti-oppression in their pursuits, they may feel that only one answer to each of these questions (Who is currently being oppressed? What kind of activism is just and legitimate?) is worth promoting to students (and thus that any other answer simply serves oppressive ends). As such, there may be an inherent tension between shepherding students through an array of arguments and perspectives, on the one hand, and coming down on the side of social justice, on the other.

The BDS movement—whose goals, for the purpose of analysis, I take from its website, are three-fold: end the occupation, promote equality between Jewish and non-Jewish citizens in Israel, and promote refugee return. The BDS website articulates these three demands—or "pillars," in the parlance of the movement—this way:

1. Ending [the State of Israel's] occupation and colonization of all Arab lands and dismantling the Wall
2. Recognizing the fundamental rights of the Arab-Palestinian citizens of Israel to full equality
3. Respecting, protecting and promoting the rights of Palestinian refugees to return to their homes and properties as stipulated in UN Resolution 194 (BDS, n.d.)

Critics of BDS sometimes claim that the demands, as articulated, are disingenuous: that the real goal of BDS, in the words of Shimon Koffler Fogel (2017), head of the main pro-Israel lobby group in Canada, is the "destruction of Israel." Of course, what it means to be a Jewish state is itself contested—does it mean a state that organically has a Jewish majority? A state that engineers a Jewish majority through selective immigration and refusal of Palestinian refugee return? A state whose legal system is informed by *halakha*, Jewish law? A state whose society, and the culture that emerges from it, is shaped by Jewish folkways, including Hebrew language, Hebrew cultural offerings, and Jewish food traditions; and where the weekly day of rest is the Jewish sabbath; and where state holidays are Jewish holidays? Proponents of BDS might agree that the second of these definitions—selective immigration coupled with the barring of Palestinian refugee return—most clearly captures the fundamental criticism that the movement has with Zionism and the policies flowing from it. They may not disagree with the rest. But for us to know this for certain, there would have to be serious dialogue, something that is typically lacking—for various reasons, including anti-normalization commitments (more on this later)—between the most strident proponents of BDS and their most vocal critics.

On the question of tactics—boycott (economic, academic, and cultural), divestment (both direct though more often indirect, namely, divesting from companies perceived to aid and abet the occupation), and (international) sanctions—the issue is particularly sensitive, and sometimes the gulf between positions seems unbridgeable. On the question of consumer boycotts, opponents of BDS often conflate products of Israel, not totally unsurprisingly, with Jews; to boycott an Israeli product, in their mind, conjures up Nazi-era boycotts of Jewish businesses. This was the comparison articulated by German parliamentarians in 2019 when they labeled BDS as antisemitic (BBC, 2019). That just under half the world's Jewish population lives in Israel (47% according to Jewish Virtual Library [2020]) buttresses this view, perhaps.

The question of sanctions comes up much less frequently in everyday BDS debates, especially in classrooms and on campuses. Sanctions (the *S* in BDS), if and when they emerge, would be the purview of governments and international bodies, rather than individuals. While BDS activists can ask voters to pressure their governments to institute such sanctions, the decision to divest or boycott is much more immediate and actionable by individual consumers, student unions, and scholarly associations. And so, while the academic boycott is most relevant for the purpose of this essay, the cultural boycott also rears its head in uncomfortable and quasi-pedagogical ways on campuses. Witness the 2016 brouhaha over the planned screening of Israeli filmmaker Shimon Dotan's feature-length documentary *The Settlers* at a conference at Syracuse University. Not long after Dotan had been invited by one conference organizer, another organizer emailed the filmmaker to rescind the invitation, claiming that "the BDS faction on campus will make matters very unpleasant for you and for me if you come" (M. Gail Hamner, quoted in Friedersdorf, 2016). Cultural offerings like Dotan's film can form an important component of the academic study of Israel-Palestine, and I certainly include many films—including Israeli films, Palestinian ones, and joint ventures—on my syllabus. And it is hard to find an Israeli film that is not financed by the state in some way since the market is simply too small for most Israeli films to succeed without state-based, arts-council funding.

More relevant for the purposes of this essay, since professors, being academics, are most directly implicated, is the question of the academic boycott. One of the main questions that animates this paper is this: Can a university instructor feasibly give a fair hearing to one's opponents within the academic-boycott debate if one feels strongly that either a) the situation in Israel-Palestine is wracked by so much injustice that the only just response is to engage in the kinds of tactics urged by BDS movement, such that actively opposing them, including the academic boycott, is itself an act of injustice, or b) one's view of academic freedom is such that any form of academic boycott necessarily flies in the face of that value, and as such, one sees academic boycotts as being themselves an act of injustice?

Two Views of Israel-Palestine and Two Views of Academic Freedom

The debate over the dynamics of Israeli–Palestinian relations and the role of BDS in responding to them hinges on two issues. First is whether one views the suffering in Israel-Palestine as being characterized fundamentally by Israeli oppression against Palestinians—through barring refugee return, running a state-led system of inequality across ethnic sectors in Israel, running a seemingly endless occupation in the West Bank, operating a siege on Gaza, and so on—as a two-sided conflict, no matter the power differential, whereby the various actors are locked in a mutually reinforcing, bellicose situation; or primarily as a situation of Israel fighting for its life within a region hostile to its very existence.

The second issue on which the debate hinges is that of the place of BDS in the academy. While there are many criticisms levied against BDS by its critics, including its perceived "sheltering" of "avowed antisemites," its "discrimination based on national origin," its "political litmus tests," its harming of the reputation of the profession and the undermining of scholarly standards, and even its inefficacy (Harris & Shichtman, 2018, p. 164), what I'm most interested in here is the value conflict over the perceived stymying of academic freedom.

Whatever their views of the justness of the overall goals of BDS, opponents of the academic boycott on academic-freedom grounds claim that academic channels should never be severed for political reasons, and that doing so flies in the face of the principle of academic freedom. As Tammi Rossman-Benjamin (2019), an outspoken opponent of BDS through her work in the AMCHA organization, writes, "Academic boycotters are certainly welcome to express their political opinions and to pursue political activism, but doing so at the expense of the academic freedom and educational opportunities of their students is not only hypocritical but also morally and professionally reprehensible."[3] The Israel studies scholar Rachel Fish (2019) argues that on university campuses, "BDS prevents constructive and educational conversations" (p. 254). Admittedly, it is hard to find an outspoken critic of BDS who agrees with all the goals, but not the tactics. For example, liberal Zionists, most of whom oppose BDS, tend to agree with the end-the-occupation goal and equality for non-Jewish citizens of Israel, but tend to reject refugee return. These types of academics are represented by the group The Third Narrative. But because they don't agree with all of BDS's goals, it is difficult to assess the motivation for their rejection of the tactics. That said, we can still assess arguments and counterarguments for their inherent worth, and bracket whatever motivations these critics may have.[4]

Proponents of the academic boycott, assuming that they too claim to value academic freedom, see it differently. They argue either that it is a means that is justified by the overall goals or else that Palestinians' academic freedom is curtailed to a greater extent by the occupation than is the academic freedom of Israeli citizens, even were the academic boycott to take root more broadly. Moreover, they claim that Israeli individuals are not harmed (or at least are not supposed to be targeted) by the boycott and that it is merely intended to be used against Israeli academic institutions.

The debates are what they are, but what I find particularly germane, if challenging, is thinking through whether and how a principled framework can accommodate the teaching of both perspectives. If one believes that BDS violates academic freedom, how can, or does, one cover a BDS perspective in the classroom neutrally, allowing students to come to their own conclusions? Conversely, if one believes that BDS is a good and just answer (even if not the *only* answer) to stemming Israeli oppression, how can one cover an *anti*-BDS perspective neutrally?

Of course, in even articulating these two sides here as I do, I present myself standing astride the debate. It is true that I have coedited a volume that brought together various perspectives on this issue (Hahn Tapper & Sucharov, 2019), and I indeed relished cowriting the chapter's introduction, whereby we laid out what is at stake in the BDS debate. In writing that introduction, I certainly did not experience any feelings of compunction in providing "both sides" with a fair hearing. Perhaps it is because, as an active Jew, as someone attached to Israel, and as someone who spent some years debating BDS advocates in the blogosphere as a liberal Zionist (a position I no longer hold in the same way), I hold a certain pride in being able to rise above the fray. But I also see an inherent tension, one which might unravel my position altogether. If I can be neutral on this issue—and at this point I nearly feel that I am—then perhaps I hold to nothing at all. And that, ultimately, is probably a disadvantage for pedagogy, where, although apparent neutrality can seem appealing, ultimately students, I'd argue, are inspired by having a professor with a visible moral core.

A Personal Reflection

The first time I recall going on record talking about BDS was in 2009, when I received a call from a reporter at the *Ottawa Citizen*. An Ontario labor union had recently proposed banning Israeli academics from speaking at Canadian universities or otherwise conducting research with Canadian counterparts—unless they condemned Israel's war on Gaza. Hearing the words "academic" and "boycott" in the same sentence led me to exclaim that I found the move "despicable." I went on to add that "excluding someone is against the entire enterprise of academia" (quoted in Daubs & Greenberg, 2009). When I look back on this a decade later though, I am wondering if my reaction wasn't a bit overblown. I hear imaginary colleagues who align with Palestine solidarity whispering in my ear that what is despicable is what Israel is doing to Palestinians and that this is but a sliver of an inconvenience in comparison.

Not long after that, I was invited to be part of a group of academics who oppose the occupation *and* academic boycotts against Israel. The mission seemed in line with my values—oppose the policies that fly in the face of human rights, and oppose the tactics that seem to contravene the values of open academic exchange. Until, one day, it didn't. Now, I sit on my perch, seemingly with a birds-eye view of the players, not only able to see the perspective of both critics and opponents of BDS, but not wanting to align myself with either.

The "Both Sides" Conundrum in the Classroom

Assuming that at least some educators feel at least some sense of value conflict—something which writers like Lampert (1985 and 2001), Cohen (2011), and Cuban (1992) discuss in educational contexts more broadly—when it comes to the question of BDS, there are several ways one can go about considering the topic in, and for, the classroom:

1. Avoid it. Though I have not researched this definitively, it is my sense that few if any universities require a course on BDS to fulfill a program requirement. At most, some programs (perhaps Middle East studies or Jewish studies) could conceivably require a course on the history or politics of Israel-Palestine. But teaching a course on such a broad topic typically means the precise content is left up to the instructor. Some professors (certainly those teaching more contemporary-oriented material) would seek to cover BDS; others wouldn't. In short, it's normally a choice that falls well within the contours of academic freedom. If it's too uncomfortable to broach, then one could conceivably not cover it at all.
2. Present BDS in a descriptive-analytical way, focusing on the political sociology of the debate, such that the focus is on the discourse itself. In this way, one doesn't need to reveal one's values and political commitments on the topic. This, of course, echoes a long-standing debate in education as to the degree to which education is inherently political (Hess & McAvoy, 2014).
3. Present one's own views, inviting students to disagree with the professor if they wish.
4. Present one's own views without encouraging student debate on the issue.

Each of these options has some merits and some drawbacks: Not encouraging student debate could stifle critical thought; inviting students to disagree could be marred by tricky power relations; avoiding it could feel like an intellectual and political cop-out; planning to present it only descriptively does not equip professors to be prepared if the conversation naturally veers towards normative concerns.

Here I present an alternate framing, one which honors the following instincts: incorporating an educator's own political thinking such that they are modeling what it looks like to be a scholar-activist; using a democracy and human-rights-based framework that, by necessity, takes an absolute stand in favor of rights and against perspectives that would seek to deny rights; and using anti-oppression methods that consider the role of privilege in shaping society. This is what such an approach might look like in teaching BDS.

In the lead-up to the week(s) on BDS specifically, the instructor may wish to spend time scaffolding the idea of privilege. The instructor should invite students to consider the areas in which they do hold privilege, and areas in which they lack it. Peggy McIntosh's (1989) "invisible knapsack" exercise, done privately so as to not to appear to pit students against one another, is useful here. The metaphorical knapsack of white privilege refers to all the social benefits that accrue to white people without them typically realizing it (hence the invisibility), including things like being able to go shopping without being followed, being able to be in the company of people of your own race most of the time if you wish, being able to dress poorly without people attributing immorality to your race, or never being asked to speak for people of your racial group. (Other forms of privilege to discuss could be male privilege, able-bodied privilege, Christian privilege, straight privilege, and so on.) I would not, however, counsel colleagues to use the "privilege walk" exercise popular in some teaching circles—though admittedly it is useful as a cognitive tool—since it can lead students to be singled out.[5] Once students have become practiced in considering their personal privilege, educators can discuss how gaps can be rectified. Rather than see sexism as being the domain of "men" against "women," a classroom discussion might center on how anyone—no matter their gender (male, female, non-binary, gender-fluid, etc.) can help chip away at the patriarchy. Looking at systems, rather than shaming students for their inherited or other identities, helps disarm them and contribute to a more collaborative space. It also makes discussions of privilege less brittle and thus less likely to come up against feelings of emotional fragility. Given the current cultural ethos—on social media, in everyday conversations, and so on—to bring up issues around privilege, this is a helpful skill to impart to students.

Once the BDS topic comes around in the syllabus, students will have been equipped to discuss privilege. For BDS specifically, professors can use a similar method: Rather than merely focus students' attention on "Jews" versus "Palestinians," teachers can invite students to research the following question: In what way do Jews—wherever they live on the globe—possess privilege? In what ways do they lack it? (Where do Jews possess more or less privilege, today and historically?) In what way do Palestinians—wherever they live on the globe—possess privilege? In what ways do they lack it? (Where have Palestinians possessed more or less privilege, today and historically?) Looking at each group in geographic and temporal context, including the many subgroups among them, can help students understand distinct and overlapping systems of oppression and marginalization around issues such as religious hegemony, trauma, human rights abuses, refugee status, race and ethnicity, and so on. Such a list of subgroup actors might include Christians and Muslims within the Palestinian collective, occupied Palestinians, Diaspora Palestinians, Gaza Palestinians, "1948" and "1967" Palestinians, and so on; Diaspora Jews; Mizrahi and Ashkenazi Jews; Ethiopian Jews in Israel and North America; Jews in the West Bank; Holocaust survivors, terrorist victims, Nakba victims, occupation victims, and so on. Professors will need to remind students, however, that collective trauma tends to fan outward, both across the collective and intergenerationally; this means that not only those directly affected may feel the effects of various traumas (Bashir & Goldberg, 2018).

Understanding the various ways in which privilege inheres and is lacking across Israelis and Palestinians can help educators situate the debate over the *goals* of BDS: What kind of endgame is justified? Are the goals of BDS fair? What kinds of current Israeli and Palestinian leadership policies are worthy of criticism?

The next task is to help students trace and evaluate the debate over the *tactics* of BDS. Is it, in its nonviolent approach, fundamentally legitimate? Is it, on the other hand, a violation of academic freedom (as well as the various other criticisms that have been levelled against it)? Once students have obtained a basic fluency in privilege consideration ("checking," in the current parlance), these questions, while seemingly appearing in a different register—since they are about values rather than positionality—can be addressed more fruitfully as well. For example, looking at the array of privilege (and lack of) across Israeli and Palestinian educational systems may lead students to conclude that any impinging on Israeli freedoms is justified in light of Palestinian restrictions already in place. Others might argue that "two wrongs don't make a right" and so no tactics that restrict any form of academic interchange are ever legitimate. Still others, drawing on Omar Barghouti's reasoning (2013), might say that the academic-freedom-violation criticism is itself altogether unfounded.

The comparison of BDS to Nazi-era boycotts of Jewish businesses poses a more delicate problem. Advocates of BDS are not Nazis; their endgame is rights, not racial superiority. This counter critique is easy enough to generate. But collective fears—particularly in traumatized populations—are not only real; they deserve to be honored. In other words, if Israelis or Diaspora Jews are reminded of Nazi-era boycotts when seeing Israeli products boycotted, or even if they think that BDS is aimed at eliminating Israel, then teachers, mediators, and instructors can acknowledge these fears and discuss them. This acknowledgment, in turn, can open up productive discourse. A risk, of course, is that this kind of discourse will be criticized for "normalizing" the status quo. To this, I'd say that with skilled facilitators a trauma-informed discourse can still take place, against the kind of "co-resistance" backdrop that BDS and other Palestine-solidarity activists understandably demand.[6] To explain, "co-resistance" refers to a setting where all parties, whatever their personal or ethnic background, agree to engage in dialogue or other activities with a guiding assumption that together they will oppose systems of oppression. In any event, helping students reason out all these points, even if the discussion ends up toggling between positions, with a basket of proverbial values clearly present in the center of the room, is what can make the educator's job particularly dynamic and rewarding, even—and especially—in cases where justice needs to be served.

NOTES

1. The academic and cultural boycott guidelines are here: https://bdsmovement.net/pacbi/academic-boycott-guidelines; and here: https://bdsmovement.net/pacbi/cultural-boycott-guidelines. PACBI is the group that is understood by the BDS movement to represent its tactics publicly. Individual committee members—the drafters of such guidelines—are not named in promotional materials.

2. For arguments in favor of applying the settler-colonial category to Israel-Palestine, see Ghanem & Khateeb, 2019; Veracini, 2013. For a view that argues that "competing nationalisms" is a better framework than settler-colonialism for understanding Israel-Palestine, see Fleischacker, 2019.

3. AMCHA, which the group capitalizes though it is not an acronym, is a Hebrew word meaning "of the people."

4. For more on The Third Narrative, see https://thirdnarrative.org. Disclosure: I was a founding member of the group but later left, as my own views evolved in favor of refugee return, and to being more ambivalent toward—rather than outright rejecting—BDS.

5. For a description of a "privilege walk," see *Privilege Walk Lesson Plan* (2016).

6. On co-resistance, see Rahman (2012).

REFERENCES

Bahar, D., & Sachs, N. (2018, January 26). *How much does BDS threaten Israel's economy?* Brookings Institute. https://www.brookings.edu/blog/order-from-chaos/2018/01/26/how-much-does-bds-threaten-israels-economy/

Barghouti, O. (2013, December 14). On academic freedom and the BDS movement. *The Nation*. https://www.thenation.com/article/archive/academic-freedom-and-bds-movement/

Bashir, B., & Goldberg, A. (Eds.). (2018). *The Holocaust and the Nakba: A new grammar of trauma and history*. Columbia University Press.

BBC. (2019, May 17). *Germany labels Israel boycott movement BDS anti-Semitic*. BBC. https://www.bbc.com/news/world-europe-48312928

BDS. (n.d.). *Overview*. https://bdsmovement.net/what-is-bds

Berila, B. (2016). *Integrating mindfulness into anti-oppression pedagogy*. Routledge.

Berman, R. A. (2015). The boycott as an infringement on academic culture. In C. Nelson & G. N. Brahm (Eds.), *The case against academic boycotts of Israel* (pp. 49–59). MLA Members for Scholars Rights and Wayne State University Press.

Bortolin, K. (2018, November 29). SoTL: the party that no one really wants to go to. *University Affairs*. https://www.universityaffairs.ca/opinion/in-my-opinion/sotl-the-party-that-no-one-really-wants-to-go-to/

Cohen, D. K. (2011). *Teaching and its predicaments*. Harvard University Press.

Cuban, L. (1992). Managing dilemmas while building professional communities. *Educational Researcher*, *21*(1), 4–11. https://doi.org/10.2307/1176344

Daubs, K., & Greenberg, L. (2009, January 7). Resolution misguided, but not anti-Semitic. *The Ottawa Citizen*. https://www.pressreader.com/canada/ottawa-citizen/20090107/281633891111251

Dawson, B., Cafolla, A., & Waite, T. (2021, May 14). It's not a "conflict": How to talk about Palestine. *Dazed*. https://www.dazeddigital.com/politics/article/52785/1/it-is-not-a-conflict-how-to-talk-about-palestine-israel

Fish, R. (2019). BDS: Binaries, divisions and silencing. In A. J. Hahn Tapper & M. Sucharov (Eds.), *Social justice and Israel/Palestine: Foundational and contemporary debates* (pp. 247–255). University of Toronto Press.

Fleischacker, S. (2019). Interrogating the limits of the settler-colonialist paradigm. In A. J. Hahn Tapper & M. Sucharov (Eds.), *Social justice and Israel/Palestine: Foundational and contemporary debates* (pp. 64–78). University of Toronto Press.

Fogel, S. K. (2017, March 5). *Truth vs. myth in the BDS movement*. HuffPost. https://www.huffpost.com/archive/ca/entry/truth-myth-bds-movement_b_9384642

Freire, P. (1970). *Pedagogy of the oppressed*. Herder and Herder.

Friedersdorf, C. (2016, September 1). How political correctness chills speech on campus. *The Atlantic*. https://www.theatlantic.com/politics/archive/2016/09/what-it-looks-like-when-political-correctness-chills-speech-on-campus/497387/

Fritzsche, L. (2021). Integrating contemplative pedagogy and antioppressive pedagogy in geography higher education classrooms. *Journal of Geography in Higher Education*, 46(2), 167–184. https://doi.org/10.1080/03098265.2021.1946766

Ghanem, A., & Khateeb, T. (2019). Israel in one century—From a colonial project to a complex reality. In A. J. Hahn Tapper & M. Sucharov (Eds.), *Social justice and Israel/Palestine: Foundational and contemporary debates* (pp. 79–91). University of Toronto Press.

Hahn Tapper, A. J., & Sucharov, M. (2019). *Social justice and Israel/Palestine: Foundational and contemporary debates*. University of Toronto Press.

Harris, R. S., & Shichtman, M. B. (2018). BDS, credibility, and the challenge to the academy. *Shofar: An Interdisciplinary Journal of Jewish Studies*, 36(1), 161–182. https://doi.org/10.5703/shofar.36.1.0161

Hess, D. E., & McAvoy, P. (2014). *The political classroom: Evidence and ethics in democratic education*. Routledge.

Jewish Virtual Library. (2020). Vital statistics: Latest population statistics for Israel. *Jewish Virtual Library*. https://www.jewishvirtuallibrary.org/latest-population-statistics-for-israel

Kozlowski, K. (2018, October 9). UM disciplines prof over Israel letter controversy. *The Detroit News*. https://www.detroitnews.com/story/news/local/michigan/2018/10/09/university-michigan-disciplines-professor-over-israel-letter-controversy/1580969002

Lampert, M. (1985). How do teachers manage to teach? Perspectives on problems in practice. *Harvard Educational Review*, 55(2), 178–195.

Lampert, M. (2001). *Teaching problems and the problems of teaching*. Yale University Press.

McIntosh, P. (1989, July/August). White privilege: Unpacking the invisible knapsack. *Peace and Freedom Magazine*, 10–12. https://nationalseedproject.org/images/documents/Knapsack_plus_Notes-Peggy_McIntosh.pdf

Nelson, C. (2015). The fragility of academic freedom. In C. Nelson & G. N. Brahm (Eds.), *The case against academic boycotts of Israel* (pp. 60–74). MLA Members for Scholars Rights and Wayne State University Press.

Palestinian Campaign for the Academic and Cultural Boycott of Israel. (2014). PACBI guidelines for the international academic boycott of Israel. *BDS Movement*. https://bdsmovement.net/pacbi/academic-boycott-guidelines

Privilege Walk Lesson Plan. (2016) Peace Learner. https://peacelearner.org/2016/03/14/privilege-walk-lesson-plan/

Rahman, O. H. (2012, January 3). Co-existence vs. co-resistance: A case against normalization. *+972 Magazine*. https://972mag.com/co-existence-vs-co-resistance-a-caseagainst-normalization/32076/

Redden, E. (2018, September 19). The right to a recommendation? *Inside Higher Ed*. https://www.insidehighered.com/news/2018/09/19/professor-cites-boycott-israeli-universities-declining-write-recommendation-letter

Rossman-Benjamin, T. (2019, March 20). Academic BDS and the calculus of hypocrisy. *Inside Higher Ed*. https://www.insidehighered.com/views/2019/03/20/scholars-who-support-bds-are-denying-academic-freedom-students-opinion

Shefa, S. (2016, March 4). York University Faculty Association joins YUDivest campaign. *Canadian Jewish News*.

Sucharov, M. (2017, May 10). In Diaspora Jewish communities, just don't call it the occupation. *Haaretz*. https://www.haaretz.com/opinion/.premium-in-diaspora-jewish-communities-just-don-t-call-it-the-occupation-1.5470414

Sucharov, M. (2019a). *Public influence: A guide to op-ed writing and social media engagement*. University of Toronto Press.

Sucharov, M. (2019b). Letting politics into the Israeli-Palestinian relations classroom. In R. S. Harris (Ed.), *Teaching the Arab-Israeli conflict* (pp. 282–287). Wayne State University Press.

Sucharov, M. (2021). *Borders and belonging: A memoir*. Palgrave Macmillan.

Veracini, L. (2013). The other shift: Settler colonialism, Israel, and the occupation. *Journal of Palestine Studies*, 42(2), 26–42. https://doi.org/10.1525/jps.2013.42.2.26

9
Barriers to Entry
Exploring Educator Reticence for Engaging With the Israeli–Palestinian Conflict

KEREN E. FRAIMAN

Israel is a touchy subject [for] a lot of American Jews... if we are trying to build an affinity or a connection between Diaspora American Jews and Israel... it does a disservice to teach a narrative that is one sided or rosy or covers up some of the more controversial aspects of the conflict. To give students context and information they can use so they can make meaning out of it is hugely important.

I received this candid response from Maya (pseudonym), a teacher and curriculum writer at a California Jewish day school. I had asked her to describe the value of conflict education, an educational practice focused in this context on engaging with and educating about the Israeli–Palestinian conflict. Her response was clear, on point, unwavering, and emphasized enthusiastically how important this type of educational engagement was for her learners.

When I asked Maya to describe on a scale of 1 to 10, with 1 being very uncomfortable and 10 being very comfortable, her own comfort level with engaging in conflict education, broadly defined, she hesitatingly labeled it as a 3. This answer and her critical self-assessment of comfort was common among the educators that I interviewed. Maya, like many of the educators with whom I spoke, had participated in several professional-development opportunities about Israel and had spent significant time living in and visiting Israel. She believed in the importance of conflict education, and yet she herself felt unprepared to facilitate conflict education in her school. Maya exemplifies the experiences of so many Jewish educators whose work I have investigated. Despite an overwhelming commitment to conflict education and belief in its importance and urgency for their learners, many educators still expressed significant reticence about teaching conflict.

The central puzzle this chapter addresses is why Jewish educators who can clearly articulate the importance of conflict education are nonetheless reticent to engage in it?[1] What do Jewish educators name as the barriers that prevent them from engaging in the work that they believe is so crucial for their learners?

Through a survey of educators at formal and informal Jewish educational institutions, as well as in-depth interviews, this chapter will uncover what educators identify as their biggest challenges with conflict education. By developing a typology of barriers to entry, this chapter aims to identify potential interventions to bolster educators as they enter this challenging space.

This chapter identifies four distinct types of barriers to teaching the conflict:

1. Knowledge: Knowing enough about the conflict and its context
2. Pedagogy: Facilitating challenging conversations more generally
3. Emotions: Supporting students' emotions that emerge when learning about and discussing the conflict
4. Communal pressures and institutional support (or lack thereof): Understanding the external forces that educators navigate when tackling this topic

All 14 of the participants in the sample mentioned confronting at least two of these barriers, and three participants mentioned all four. Each of these categories are intertwined but present distinct challenges and require specific interventions to support educators. Furthermore, due to each educator's unique circumstances, educators' reticence can vary tremendously across each of these categories. When educators identify the obstacles preventing them from engaging with conflict education, the field can properly support these educators and create an ecosystem that addresses the needs of educators in this space.

Literature Review

This chapter situates conflict education—teaching and learning focused on helping learners understand the history, context, and structures of societies engaged in intractable conflict—as one key pillar of a larger approach to Israel education. There is a growing consensus among scholars, and increasingly, educators, that successful and holistic Israel education demands a sophisticated and nuanced engagement with critical questions within Israel, and in particular, the Israeli-Palestinian conflict. As the Israel education scholars Robbie Gringas and Alex Pomson (2021) observe in their evaluations with young adult learners, "The research suggests that rather than being overwhelmed by the multidimensionality, participants were liberated by it" (Gringras & Pomson, 2021, referencing Pomson et al., 2014). Israel education lives within these disagreements. Rather than frustrating learners in their disagreements and perspectives, an engagement with diversity can place the learner within the content in a more meaningful and resonant manner (Fraiman & Bell, 2021). While Israel education broadly encompasses engagement with the many facets of Israel, its histories, cultures, peoples, and more, this growing consensus suggests that it is crucial to also incorporate an intentional engagement with conflict education as part of a larger approach to Israel education.

In educational literature and practice, conflict education—education that "addresses conflict" (Bickmore, 2017, p. 286)—may be distinct from or a central component of another form of education often called peace education (e.g., Harris & Morrison, 2013; McGlynn et al., 2009). The former is devoted to helping learners understand conflict, and the latter to helping learners prevent, resolve, alleviate, or transform conflict (Almanza, 2022). Though the language and educational commitments of peace education were, briefly, a central focus of Jewish education in the years after the assassination of Israeli Prime Minister Yitzhak Rabin in 1995, conflict education has been much more prevalent in Jewish educational institutions in the intervening decades (Zakai, 2014).

The focus on conflict education can be explained, in part, because it is increasingly clear that Jewish learners are aware of the political realities in Israel—including its role in ongoing and intractable conflict—from a young age, and as they mature, they are increasingly dissatisfied with the Israel educational opportunities at Jewish educational institutions (Pomson et al., 2014; Zakai, 2011, 2019). An educator I interviewed explained that "the Seth Rogen effect is real," referring to the Canadian comedian and actor Seth Rogen's remark that "as a Jewish person, I was fed a huge amount of lies about Israel my entire life" (Rogen quoted in Angel, 2021; Brownfeld, 2020; Tracy, 2021). Thus, there is a critical need for more nuanced discussions about Israel, including an explicit focus on conflict education.

Much of the existing research has focused on the needs of learners in the Israel education space (Hassenfeld, 2016; Pomson et al., 2014; Reingold, 2017; Reingold, 2018; Zakai, 2019). This chapter seeks instead to shift the focus to the *educators* who are charged with providing conflict education as a central component of Israel education. A nuanced understanding of these educators, their backgrounds, and their hesitancies to engage in conflict education despite their commitment to it can provide a valuable window into their needs within this complex, political, and educational space. Engaging with the Israeli–Palestinian conflict, and conflict more broadly, is qualitatively different than many areas of Jewish education that are not political or perceived as controversial. Education around the conflict shares many of the characteristics of engaging with other controversial political issues about which there is collective disagreement (Hess, 2009).

Importantly, and as will be seen later, many educators understand the value and urgency of bringing these conversations to their learners while they are still within the Jewish educational landscape. However, despite this critical need, many educators continue to express reticence to engage in education about the Israeli–Palestinian conflict and other conflict areas within Israel education.

Methodology and Participants

The initial data for this project emerged from a series of workshops that I conducted as part of the iFellows concentration in Israel education over a 2-year period. The iFellows Masters Concentration in Israel Education, offered by the iCenter, is a program that aims to nurture and challenge knowledgeable and passionate educational leaders committed to the integral role of Israel in contemporary Jewish life. The goal of the initiative is to create systemic change in how Israel education is defined, approached, and integrated into every area of Jewish education throughout North America. During the period of study, I served on the faculty of the iFellows program and conducted workshops on conflict education.

During these workshops, I asked participants to use a notecard to describe the greatest challenges they face within conflict education. In reviewing the 69 notecards containing a total of 154 challenges, I found that a typology of reticence emerged, with each challenge falling into one or more of the categories described previously: knowledge, pedagogy, emotions, and communal pressures and institutional support.

To dig deeper, I invited the iFellows who filled out the notecards to participate in these research interviews. Over several months, I interviewed 14 of the educators who volunteered to participate.[2] This sample included educators with a diversity of backgrounds, perspectives, roles, and institutional contexts that represented the broader pool of iFellows alumni. Participants were scattered across North America and worked in a range of institutions, including day schools, synagogues, supplemental schools, Jewish Federations, Jewish Community Centers (JCCs), Hillels, and Israel tour companies, and which had both denominational and nondenominational affiliations. The participants served in a variety of roles, including education directors, program chairs, Jewish studies teachers, rabbis, curriculum writers, and Israel programming chairs at day schools and a Hillel.

Each semi-structured interview followed a scripted interview protocol while also leaving space to explore educators' responses in more depth. Through the first half of the interview protocol, I sought to obtain information about each participant's background and education, as well as their approaches to and comfort level with teaching about the conflict. Before delving into the challenges each educator faced, I assessed their comfort level by asking them about how they value and understand conflict education and how they would numerically rank their own personal comfort level for teaching or engaging with the conflict. In the second half of the interview, I asked educators to identify the greatest challenges to their engagement in conflict education.

The interviews were conducted on Zoom and were transcribed using transcription software. The interviews were conducted on condition of confidentiality, as these questions probed areas of significant professional vulnerability for the participants, and all those who are quoted in the chapter are named with a pseudonym.

As I learned during the interviews, all of the participants had advanced degrees in addition to successfully completing the iFellows program and had spent significant time learning and/or traveling in Israel. Many had actively pursued a range of professional-development opportunities in Israel education. All of the educators had extensive experience in Israel education, and all had some experience teaching and facilitating conflict education.

In considering the backgrounds and training of these educators, it is worth noting that these educators may be described as having a high degree of preparedness for engaging in conflict education. Thus, while the second phase of this research is based on a relatively small sample size of in-depth interviews, the diversity of the participants' personal and geographic backgrounds, sites of employment, and ages and stages of life makes them particularly good informants for reflecting the range of challenges and barriers within the broader field. Despite their richer-than-average backgrounds, the fact that these specific educators continued to express significant reticence to doing the work of conflict education underlines the contours of the challenges in this space.

The Purpose: Why Teach About the Israeli–Palestinian Conflict?

In *Teaching History for the Common Good*, Barton and Levstik (2004) emphasize the importance of a teacher's intentionality, even more than pedagogical content knowledge, for adjusting their educational practice to create space to teach about controversial issues and to develop a more sophisticated approach to that work. They explain that educators are far more likely to engage in highly politicized educational experiences when they have clarity of purpose. In exploring educator reticence to teaching about the conflict, therefore, one reasonable hypothesis was that one key area of reticence might be a lack of clarity about the purpose and value of engaging with the conflict. Thus, it was essential to gauge how educators perceive and articulate the value of teaching about the Israeli-Palestinian conflict, separate from their willingness or reticence to engage in it.[3]

All of the interviewees clearly articulated, in their own ways, the value of teaching the Israeli-Palestinian conflict to their learners, regardless of their own personal readiness or confidence with conflict education.[4] While one cannot assume that all educators who see value in addressing the conflict are necessarily highly motivated to teach it, the selection effect makes such educators more likely to lean into this type of education.

There is a robust literature that highlights the importance and benefits of engaging in controversial topics within the classroom (Hess, 2009; Levinson & Fay, 2019; Noddings & Brooks, 2017). Importantly, the educators that I interviewed were able to reflect on both the proximate needs and more global benefits of these types of conversations within their own educational institutions. They consistently emphasized the importance and urgency of educational experiences that engaged with the conflict, and it was clear that a pedagogy that sought to engage diverse narratives and complexity was significant in their thinking.

Educators identified several reasons why they believed it was important to engage with learners about the Israeli-Palestinian conflict, regardless of the learners' age. First, educators articulated that it was important to address the current realities and complexities of contemporary Israel, which both reflect and sharpen aspects of the conflict. This observation is supported by the work of the Israel education researcher Sivan Zakai, who demonstrates that even very young learners are quickly tuned into the challenges of the region (Zakai, 2011, 2014, 2015, 2019; Zakai & Cohen, 2016). Many educators highlighted the need to address these issues within their Jewish educational settings or institutions, providing opportunities for students to make meaning for themselves within a safe and supportive environment. Malka, an associate director of Jewish studies at an Ontario day school, for example, explained:

> [The conflict] is something they see all around them and they hear it... all you have to do is open, really, any social media platform that you had. All you saw was posts about Israel and Palestinians and both sides, and celebrities that were talking about and posting about it. There are so

many reasons to teach about the conflict, but I think the fact that our world is so easily accessible to our students, just one click of a finger away, means that it's so important that they have an understanding of what's out there and how they feel about it.

Malka, like many of the interviewees, saw the importance of contextualizing and discussing the conflict within Jewish educational settings as a way to help learners understand what they might encounter outside the classroom and to develop their own opinions and feelings about it.

Second, beyond the immediate realities, the educators interviewed explained that their students were increasingly skeptical and disillusioned by the oversimplified narrative of Israeli history that had been presented to them in the past and that it was, therefore, important to mitigate or prevent this disillusionment moving forward. Teens expect authentic and open education that includes engagement with the diverse narratives and realities that exist in the region. One educator noted that teens regularly have political or controversial educational experiences in other settings, where, for example, they engage with the implications of slavery and race relations within the United States.[5] The concern expressed consistently, and mirrored in both research and the popular press, is that when learners leave their Jewish settings and encounter a wholly different accounting of Israel and of the conflict, they feel unprepared, confused, and, at worst, deceived or betrayed (Beinart, 2010; Brownfeld, 2020; Goldenberg, 2020; Reingold, 2017). Rachel, a synagogue education director in Oklahoma, explained that "our late high schoolers or college students...they come back and they say 'you lied to us. You didn't tell us the truth. You taught us the wrong thing....' This teen is looking at their institutions and Judaism as having let them down." Isaac, a director of Israel programs at a college Hillel, similarly rued: "When [learners] ask Israelis or Israel educators... about the conflict and they get answers that they can sense are either too short or too simple, and that don't address the other things they're hearing, then they learn that [Israel] is brittle and it can't withstand scrutiny."

Lastly, some educators indicated that beyond knowledge of the conflict, engaging with conflict education can lead to greater civic engagement and can foster the acquisition of skills with which they hope Jewish learners enter adulthood, such as critical thinking, listening empathically, talking across differences, gaining comfort in uncertainty, and developing tools for global citizenship. In this way, engaging with the conflict not only provided an opportunity to develop a deeper and more nuanced relationship with Israel, but it also provided a Jewish laboratory for honing invaluable life skills as students entered adulthood.

Among the educators interviewed, all could clearly articulate the essential value of and purpose in engaging with the conflict, and many expressed great urgency to provide this type of educational experience for their learners. Ultimately, not a single educator in this study minimized the importance of conflict education. Instead, each clearly described its value for their learners. Despite seeing this value, these educators were also hesitant, to different degrees, to engage in this work.

Barrier 1: Knowledge—The Content of the Israeli–Palestinian Conflict

When asked about the causes of their reticence to engage with the conflict, 10 of the 14 educators in the interview portion of the study expressed concerns about their own level of knowledge and that of their learners. When the topic was probed more deeply, educators revealed significant differences in their own perceived knowledge gaps. In some cases, the educators felt that they lacked mastery of the content of Israeli history and the conflict specifically. Other educators felt that they knew the broad contours of the conflict but lacked the knowledge to fully understand current events and, in turn, relay or discuss them with their learners. Another group of educators felt that they knew enough, but were concerned about what their learners knew, and they lacked an approach for how to engage in these conversations with their learners. Finally, despite having a solid foundation of knowledge and training, some still felt uncomfortable with their level of mastery, and/or they lacked confidence in what they already knew.

An essential component of teaching conflict education is mastery of the content area and confidence in one's knowledge about the context and subject matter. The educators noted that the conflict is layered, has extended over a significant period of time, has many protagonists, and is highly political. Knowing where to start and how to untangle the layers, let alone educate others, can be extremely daunting. Additionally, the conflict continues to unfold in present time. The evolving dynamics require facility with the material and timely responses to crises. When hostilities flare up, there are many unanswered questions, and keeping up with the news cycle can feel overwhelming for educators.

Knowledge of the Conflict Itself

In describing their lack of knowledge, eight educators remarked that they don't know enough about the history and different sides of the Israeli-Palestinian conflict. Some educators explained that they faced information overload and were uncertain where they could get "reliable and trustworthy" information or how to sort through the vast resources on the subject.

Reflecting several core concerns, Emily, an education director of a Jewish day school in California, explained:

> I often feel like I come into the middle of the story. I read the news and that this happened and then this happened, but I know that there is a lot of history that may explain how we got here...I just feel like you drop into the middle of the thing, and somebody can always refute you as to why you were there first or they were...when I want to have these discussions, I feel personally like I start losing ground when I don't know all of the backstory.... It's hard for me as an educator to wrap my arms around all of these layers...I don't even know where to start.

Even after participating in educational opportunities and professional-development workshops in Israel education, Emily was still uncomfortable with the subject matter. This reality is even more challenging when considering that the vast majority of the educators that Emily supervised had a far more limited Jewish education broadly and, in particular, with regards to Israel.

Interestingly, some educators were not as concerned with specific knowledge, but rather with formulating their own stance on challenging questions or issues on Israel. They described not feeling comfortable or settled themselves in this area. In these cases, it seemed the educators were not only looking for content, but for a deeper understanding of the content. Some educators sought the opportunity to make sense of the content for themselves, assimilate it within their own values, and assess its importance or impact. For example, Rachel—a synagogue education director early in her career—explained, "[I don't] feel comfortable yet with my own stance about it," and she is therefore "[not ready] to engage with" her learners about it.

Regardless of their own knowledge—or, for education directors, that of their educators—some educators worried about the challenges of engaging with the conflict when their own learners did not have a solid foundation on the subject. They were concerned that their students didn't know a lot about Israel in general, let alone the conflict. For example, Tanya, an education director at a synagogue in Florida, worried that "when their first interaction was like 'ooh we're bad' because everyone on campus seemed to be aligning with the Palestinian students.... It's very hard to start that education when you're 20 or 19 and you don't have that foundation."

Confidence in Their Knowledge

Some educators did not feel fully prepared for engagement with conflict in their teaching even though they participated in a variety of professional-development opportunities. Such feelings appeared to be less related to content knowledge than to their confidence in relaying that content. For example, Anat—an alumni-engagement manager for an Israeli educational tour company—said, "I am not Israeli. I have only lived there for a year at a time and was not super enmeshed in it. So, I don't feel like I have much clout." The use of the word "clout" suggested something beyond what Anat knew or didn't know, but rather the confidence or authority that she felt she had. Yosef, a JCC program director in Ontario, used the words "intimidated" and "scary" to describe teaching the subject. He followed these words by suggesting that "maybe I don't know enough." He appeared to suffer not from a lack of knowledge, but from a lack of confidence about teaching the material.

These interviews raise the question of what knowledge might be needed to provide educators with the foundation for teaching about the Israeli-Palestinian conflict. Interestingly, educators could rarely point to the specific knowledge they wanted to acquire in order to engage with the topic more freely. Further research would be required to identify an impactful teacher-education curriculum to serve as the foundation for these critical conversations. Similarly, it is important to consider how educators can gain the confidence to engage in these conversations despite acknowledging that they may not know "everything." How can educators achieve a baseline level of knowledge while also gaining greater comfort in uncertainty and changing conditions?

Barrier 2: The Pedagogy of Navigating Difficult Conversations

Across my interviews, educators consistently expressed a fear of the classroom getting out of control or being "hijacked" by students with strong opinions. Regardless of their comfort with the content knowledge, 10 of the 14 educators in the study acknowledged they lacked the skill to facilitate these charged learning experiences. As will be seen, these attitudes were sometimes born out of past negative experiences. In other cases, it was a preemptive fear of this occurrence which led to a disengagement from controversial topics.

Emily, an education director at a day school in California, described an instance when her class of teens had the opportunity to discuss the Israeli military with an Israeli guest speaker. The conversation quickly spiraled out of control, and Emily reported that "I couldn't navigate that. I felt like I was refereeing. I was trying to [have a constructive conversation], but they weren't understanding each other.... It was an opportunity lost. I don't even know how I could have handled that better." Emily's dismissive statement about her ability to handle this scenario differently in the future highlights the shallow toolbox that she felt she had for navigating this escalating conversation.

Marissa, who had formerly worked with university students across Canada, mentioned the "hidden agendas" of some learners, saying, "You may have a student that would say they are open-minded... and quickly realize that, no, they have their own agenda coming into it. They just want to fight as opposed to really think through and hear other perspectives." Many educators spoke explicitly about their need to develop better facilitation techniques and create a space for students to hear other perspectives and avoid shutting down conversations when they become difficult or heated. Lacking the tools to navigate these tensions, educators felt their only options were disengagement or avoidance. Importantly, these educators emphasized that the challenge was not the charged opinions themselves, but rather how to create a dynamic that allows constructive conversation and listening across differences. In all these cases, the barrier was the inability, or the perceived inability, to facilitate constructive conversations about the conflict. The fear of the classroom spiraling and getting heated has prevented educators from engaging with important questions and issues.

Barrier 3: Love, Anger, Apathy, and Exhaustion— The Role of Emotions

Another category consistently raised by 10 of the 14 educators was the emotional impact for their learners—love, anger, apathy, fear, exhaustion, among others—of engaging with the conflict. These educators explicitly worried that engaging in conflict education and revealing challenging issues in contemporary Israel could diminish the love and connection that some students felt, and that educators felt was their responsibility to support (see also Zakai, 2011). Nine of the 10 educators also worried that students were entering the educational space already highly emotional and that teaching about the subject would further enhance or exacerbate these feelings. These concerns are not unique to teaching about Israel, as Nel Noddings and Laurie Brooks (2017) note in *Teaching Controversial Issues*. They argue that "when we encourage full and open discussion of controversial issues, we may unintentionally induce demoralization.... We want students to recognize the wrongdoings of their own country or group, but we also want them to see the best in their various traditions, and find hope in the work of restoring, maintaining, and extending that best" (pp. 2-3). One of the challenges of engaging in conflict education is that educators may enter a morally ambiguous, emotive space that involves many values in tension.

Maya, a teacher and curriculum writer at a California day school, shared that:

A lot of the educators just love Israel so much and they want to pass on that pure love to their students. The fear is that students will be too critical of Israel and they will discover unpleasant truths about Israeli history and the things that it does to Palestinian groups and turn against Israel...the Jewish People and Judaism. This is the doomsday scenario that we fear...it's going to ruin the love.

Some educators may feel vulnerability in introducing complex narratives when they feel that one of the explicit educational goals is love of Israel. These educators express this concern despite the fact that research has demonstrated that engaging with diverse and morally complex narratives does not generally have this impact (Reingold, 2017). Whether real or imagined, there is a fear that new knowledge of the complexity of the conflict and the moral dilemmas inherent in it will lead young Jews to stray not only from Israel, but from the Jewish people more broadly.

A different set of pedagogical challenges emerge when working with learners who enter the conversation with anger that has been evoked for a range of reasons, often during violent outbreaks in the region. For example, the highly charged social media environment that is created, especially during outbreaks of violence, can be highly impactful for teens and produce angered reactions (on all sides) about the conflict. Malka, an associate director of Jewish studies at an Ontario day school, asserted that when there is so much anger before the conversation even begins, it's hard to create a productive learning environment. This anger stifles the conversation and precludes conflict education. She explained that the most stressful thing for her is "calming down the emotions and bringing students and teachers to a space where they are comfortable sharing without feeling attacked, and where they are comfortable hearing someone else's opinion without kind of saying no."

In addition to the emotions of their learners, educators opened up about the role their own emotions play as a barrier to entry. Rebecca, a director of education at a New York synagogue, explained that many educators she works with "had not reconciled their own connection to Israel to be comfortable teaching it. Like, 'how can I still love Israel, if it's true that Israel has done these things? I don't know how I can reconcile that or how I fully feel about that, let alone teach my students about that.' I think it's scary for people to have to do their own reckoning." Rebecca also mentioned, "[A] lot of my teachers are Israeli and have complicated feelings; all of them, for one reason or another, are not currently living in Israel. I think some of those conflicting emotions play a role in this space." Similarly, educators frequently discussed the emotional toll that engaging with the conflict took on them. Many educators used words like "exhausting," "challenging," "tiring," "encompassing," and "lacking energy" to describe how they felt when teaching about the conflict. Benjamin, an Israel education chair at a California day school who confidently taught about the conflict with institutional support, nevertheless described the feeling of being "on a knife's edge at all times" and said that when the school year ended, he had to tune out Israeli news. Many others felt burdened by these emotions, and, as a result, some sought to avoid them. It was taking a significant toll on these educators.

Clearly, both the emotions of the learners and the educators play a crucial role in creating barriers to engagement with conflict education. Whether educators are managing positive or negative emotions, the abundant presence of emotions restrains some educators from engaging with the conflict and controversial issues relating to Israel.

Barrier 4: Community Reactions and Institutional Support

While knowledge, pedagogy, and emotions are primarily associated with the individual educator's experiences within their settings, this last category looks outside the "classroom" to include environmental factors beyond their control that impact their willingness to engage in conflict education. Even amongst educators who felt better prepared to address the first three challenges, this final category often emerged as a constraint on their teaching. All 14 of the interviewees expressed concern about their community members' reactions to engaging in conflict education and the institutional support they would receive. In many cases, educators cited specific moments when they, or close colleagues, experienced a backlash from the community or lacked institutional support. These experiences, including accusatory phone calls from parents, programs being canceled, and people losing jobs due to conflict education, significantly chilled educators' appetites for engaging in these topics. The educators' concerns were primarily centered around the relationship of the educator towards the administration or leadership of the institution and, simultaneously, parental responses. At times, the question of institutional support is about fear. At other times, it is about guidance. The conflict can be a dicey and politicized arena, so obtaining clarity and transparency about what is okay (or not okay) to teach is an important mechanism for handling a potential parental or communal "phone call." These concerns are certainly intertwined, yet each presented different kinds of challenges.

The importance of institutional support for enabling education around controversial topics is well documented. A report by the Carnegie Corporation and the Center for Information and Research on Civic Learning and Engagement (CIRCLE, 2003), underscored that "teachers need support in broaching controversial issues in classrooms since they may risk criticism or sanctions if they do" (p. 6). The civic-engagement scholar Diana Hess and the scholar of social studies education Paula McAvoy (2014) explain further that educators who don't receive pushback for engaging with controversial political issues are those who have support from their department chairs and principals, "who could then serve as a front line of support" (p. 209). Ultimately, as is documented in this study, even educators who may be prepared and demonstrated readiness for engagement in controversial topics are far less likely to do so when the environment doesn't support this kind of "risk-taking."

General Institutional Support

Institutional support can take many forms. Eight educators felt that their institutions were not interested in probing controversial issues relating to Israel. Ten educators expressed uncertainty about what was expected and allowed by their institutions, and importantly, where red lines were drawn. When probed, many educators could not identify a specific red line or taboo topic but still felt that these existed and avoided topics that could be controversial. Some educators discussed experiences where programs or initiatives were canceled by the administration or through board interference. These signals demonstrated the institutional stance and often negated efforts to foster more dynamic conversations. When probed, many expressed fear, and some educators worried about sanctions or even job loss on account of these issues.

For example, Sarah—a Jewish history teacher at a day school—noted, "My largest barrier is the ability to gauge what will be viewed as appropriate." When asked by whom, Sarah answered, "Mostly parents, but also colleagues.... I know that my institution prides itself on its Zionism and pro-Israel stance, and that was part of my trepidation at first for taking this job.... There is always a feeling like am I going to say something offensive or be construed as offensive." Whether directly or indirectly, some educators receive the message from their administration that engaging with the conflict is either forbidden, or, at the very least, risky. In the interviews, the concern raised by these educators was palpable; it took a significant toll and was clearly an inhibitor in their educational practices.

Lack of institutional support was communicated through the interference or canceling by the administration, either preemptively or in response to communal pressures. Tanya, the director of youth education at a Florida synagogue, described the direct manner in which her efforts to engage with the conflict were shut down by the Rabbi. After developing a family-education program that was intended to provide an opportunity to "struggle" with Israel, the senior Rabbi informed Tanya, "Yeah, we don't struggle with Israel here. We are all pro and that's it." Despite Tanya's willingness to engage in conflict education, this rabbinic edict canceled the program.

Yosef, a JCC program director in Ontario, emphasized that managing competing interests from various internal and external stakeholders was his biggest barrier. When Yosef planned a conflict educational program, he asked, "Who do I align with? Who's got more weight in terms of the agenda? The agenda [of these stakeholders] influences what you do, whether or not it is actually relevant to the situation or whether you think it is best from an educational perspective."

Emily, an education director at a California day school, highlighted the personal shift that emerged when she moved from an institution where she felt supported to one where she felt there was no institutional prioritization or support. Environmental conditions, therefore, can often supersede the readiness and preparation of the individual educator. These negative experiences deter educators from engaging with the conflict in the future.

Parents

Twelve educators expressed significant concern about harsh parent reactions to teaching about the conflict when the Israel educational content or approach didn't align with the parents' views or expectations. The concerns ranged from handling unprofessional communication from parents to some parents even withdrawing their children from the school. This parental resistance is consistent with what is seen in other educational arenas around controversial or political subjects (e.g., Hess, 2009, pp. 23–24).

Some educators worried about parents who have a strong connection to Israel and might become upset about things that their children are learning. In other cases, parents who prioritize balance might be concerned about Israel being taught only from one perspective. Complicating matters, educators often have students with parents with diverging opinions and expectations within the same class, creating pressures on the educator from both sides.

Rebecca, an education director at a New York synagogue who was confident in her knowledge and ability to engage with the conflict, revealed how communal responses can reduce educator confidence and impose constraints on what is taught and how. When asked to rank her confidence on a scale of 1 to 10, Rebecca reported that it ranged from 7 to 10. When asked about the difference, she responded, "I am very comfortable with what I am trying to teach, but when I am not sure that I'll be able to predict the parental response if they bring it up at home, [it lowers my confidence]." Similarly, Emily, an education director at a California day school, reported her confidence level as a 2, citing her concern about being new in her role and potentially offending community members and getting unpleasant "pushback."

Parental concerns not only generate fear but also have implications for the broader school environment. As Rebecca stated, "The worst-case scenario for me is that the parents pull their kid from the synagogue and potentially take their friends with them. Another worst-case scenario for me, and I don't know how likely it is, but if enough board members get mad about what has been happening in Israel education, would I get my contract revoked." Even if improbable, parental response can have a significant chilling effect on an educator's willingness to engage in conflict education. Rebecca's comment highlights how the issues of institutional support and parental response can be intertwined and often reinforce one another, further elevating educators' fears.

Across both institutional and parental challenges, there was a feeling among educators that concern with navigating these issues superseded any individual educator's knowledge and skills, and consequently impacted their inclination to engage in conflict education. When educators felt that they lacked institutional or communal support, the risk of engagement felt untenable.[6]

Conclusion and Recommendations

Understanding why many educators are reticent to engage with the Israeli–Palestinian conflict is critical to unlocking a more nuanced and comprehensive approach to Israel education in general, and conflict education in particular. Despite a growing consensus about the importance of tackling the conflict and the long-term negative impact of avoiding the subject, my research highlights the barriers for those on the front lines of this critical work.

Ultimately, this research identifies four distinct yet interrelated areas of reticence that educators encounter in this field. Each of these categories—knowledge, pedagogy, emotions, and communal pressures and institutional support—presents distinct challenges for educators, and, in turn, requires a different kind of preparation so that educators can confidently enter this politicized area of conflict education. Digging underneath the surface of this reticence reveals a nuanced picture that recognizes the nature of the challenges that educators face.

To prepare educators to enter this arena, it is necessary to develop robust professional development that directly addresses these challenges. Particularly in the three categories of knowledge, pedagogy, and emotions, educators lamented the scarcity of readily available resources and training designed to increase their competence and confidence with the topic. For example, a graduate-level program could delve into the often uncomfortable and political aspects of the conflict, allowing educators to first grapple with the issue among peers, then equip them to bring these concepts back to their learners. Such a program should toggle between timeless key historical context and timely current realities of the conflict, addressing educators' concerns about both kinds of knowledge while emphasizing the conflict's recurring themes and essential questions.

Second, most of the educators that I interviewed had not participated in training for leading difficult or critical conversations. These tools and techniques extend beyond the content of the conflict and would provide educators with a toolbox for creating a productive space for navigating these and other difficult conversations. Learning how to handle a conversation that has "spun out of control" or creating environments conducive to empathetic listening across differences are crucial skills for educators and increase the chances for successful engagement. Leaning on the best practices from adjacent fields, including teaching controversial histories, mediation, and conflict resolution, can provide a robust framework for educators (Hess, 2009; Hess & McAvoy, 2014; Levinson & Fay, 2019; Noddings & Brooks, 2017). Providing educators with facilitation training and experience will enable them to leverage these skills at their own institutions.

Third, addressing the psychology of the conflict requires greater awareness of how to channel the volatile emotions expressed in a classroom. Educators need to be trained in how to identify and address potential triggers for their learners. This includes tools for addressing issues or content areas that trigger difficult feelings on the part of students or preclude students from engaging in classroom-appropriate norms for discourse. They also need to learn ways to create space that recognizes and allows for emotions, without driving or detracting from important educational conversations.

Removing or at least reducing these barriers requires a deep investment of time and energy. This type of training requires repeated and sustained exposure to the topic, which cannot be achieved through a large group, single seminar offering, a quick and pointed intervention, or even a briefing on the latest round of violence. Professional development in this area must be reimagined to create a substantively different experience than anything these educators have already encountered. For educators to bring an educationally impactful discussion of the conflict (and other complex topics) to their learners most effectively, a multilayered intervention is required. This approach would not be "one size fits all," as the needs of educators vary dramatically.

Finally, the fourth and final category, regarding institutional support and communal pressures, points to a different type of intervention, one that addresses the ecosystem in which these educators operate. As demonstrated in some of the previous examples, even if an educator is willing and eager to enter into the conflict-education arena with their learners, they are unlikely to do so if they feel that they lack the backing of their institution and, potentially, of the community.

Therefore, educational opportunities for lay and professional educational leadership are also necessary. This intervention would provide avenues for lay leaders and professionals to nurture the leadership skills required to navigate the political arena of Israel education. This opportunity would allow them to identify their goals and craft a plan for providing and communicating their support to their educators. As noted previously, educators are seeking both support and direction from their institutional leaders. A formal environment for lay and professional leaders to discuss, debate, and determine their own position on these issues, as well as critically and courageously explore multiple narratives and perspectives, would create a far more permissive and supportive environment for educators. Empowering educational leaders to reimagine this space will help educators meet the needs of young Jews who demand that we bring these conversations into our settings (Zakai, 2011).

Similarly, educational opportunities that engage parents are fundamental to the partnership model that is required for successful engagement in conflict education. Parent education should focus explicitly on both the what and why of conflict education. This approach would provide space for learning about many of the same issues their children are thinking about and engaging with in their settings. Equally important is explaining to parents why conflict education is essential for their children to experience in their Jewish settings, even, or perhaps especially, when some of the opinions presented may not fully align with their own. Parents need to better understand the educational and pedagogical benefits of engaging with complexity, and assuage their concerns, whatever they may be, about the potential damaging impact of this type of educational experience on their children.

The topic of Israel is extremely complicated and nuanced in itself, the Israeli–Palestinian conflict all the more so. All of the challenges associated with developing educators' toolboxes and navigating communal complexities only highlight the pressing need to engage with the conflict in a holistic and thoughtful manner. Irrespective of their individual comfort level, geographic location, and institution type, all of the interviewees provided a clear statement of purpose articulating why conflict education was worth pursuing. In this regard, while this chapter highlights the myriad of challenges educators face, it also highlights educators' eagerness for an intervention. Consequently, an investment of educational resources in this realm has the potential to have a tremendous impact.

ACKNOWLEDGMENTS

I would like to thank Scarlett Andes for her research assistance on this project; Dean Bell for his thought partnership and insights; and my home institution, Spertus Institute for Jewish Learning and Leadership, and the iCenter, for enabling this project. I would also like to thank all of the iFellows who agreed to participate in these interviews. Finally, I would like to thank Lauren Applebaum, Miriam Heller Stern, Benjamin Jacobs, Ezra Kopelowitz, Anne Lanski, Jon Levisohn, Matt Reingold, Michael Soberman, Eitan Stieber, and Sivan Zakai for their excellent comments and suggestions. They have all sharpened my thinking and provided important lenses for this work. I am truly grateful. I welcome all comments, critiques, and questions.

NOTES

1. There are invariably educators that are not reticent to engage and have masterfully taught this content. For example, see Reingold (2017). However, my research focuses on those that are reticent to engage in order to better understand their barriers to entry.

2. While small samples have some limitations, including the inability to draw far-reaching conclusions, conducting in-depth interviews with a smaller, representative sample has proven to be an effective methodology in this and related fields. See for example, Reingold (2017); Reingold (2018).

3. While Israel is engaged in many different types of conflicts, the Israeli–Palestinian conflict has been an area of central and persistent focus in Israeli politics and within the news. For this reason, I chose to focus on this enduring and intractable conflict. Some of these broader lessons, however, may be relevant in considering other conflicts that involve Israel.

4. This finding does not preclude that there may be educators who do not have clarity of purpose or feel that a focus on the conflict is not essential for their work in Israel education. In future work, it would be important to better ascertain the prevalence of these attitudes towards conflict education. For the purposes of this chapter, 100% of educators, regardless of their personal comfort or readiness, expressed clear purpose.

5. The trend of oversimplifying historical experiences is not unique to the context of Israel. As Barton and Levstik (2004) note, "Very often the complexity of the past is simplified to such an extent that students are presented with an utterly false portrait of history, usually one of happy consensus" (p. 216).

6. In some cases, there were educators who could describe some instances of great institutional support, but this was not consistent in all settings in which they worked. This seemed to permit them to experiment and take risks within the subject matter. As this chapter focused on reticence and barriers, I have not expanded on these experiences as they fell outside of the scope of the chapter. However, further research is needed to explore the ways in which institutional support is communicated and felt, and how it enhances educator experiences in this arena.

REFERENCES

Almanza, M. (2022). Six educational approaches to conflict and peace. *Journal of Peace Education*, *19*(2), 205–225.

Angel, A. (2021, May 22). Jewish Americans are at a turning point with Israel. *The Guardian*. https://www.theguardian.com/commentisfree/2021/may/22/jewish-americans-israel-palestine-arielle-angel

Barton, K. C., & Levstik, L. S. (2004). *Teaching history for the common good*. Routledge.

Beinart, P. (2010, June 10). The failure of the American Jewish establishment. *The New York Review*. https://www.nybooks.com/articles/2010/06/10/failure-american-jewish-establishment/

Bickmore, K. (2017). Conflict, peace-building, and education: Rethinking pedagogies in divided societies, Latin America, and around the world. In K. Bickmore, R. Hayhoe, C. Manion, K. Mundy, & R. Read (Eds.), *Comparative and international education: Issues for teachers* (2nd ed., pp. 268–299). Canadian Scholars Press.

Brownfeld, A. C. (2020). Peter Beinart and Seth Rogen reflect Jewish disillusionment with Israel. *Washington Report on Middle East Affairs*, *39*(6), 16–28.

Carnegie Corporation of New York & CIRCLE. (2003). *The civic mission of schools*. https://www.carnegie.org/publications/the-civic-mission-of-schools/

Fraiman, K. E., & Bell, D. P. (2021). A new approach to education and peoplehood: Diversity as a key to a sustainable model of peoplehood. *The Peoplehood Papers*, *30*, 42–50.

Goldenberg, T. (2020, August 7). Seth Rogen's Israel comments highlight fraught diaspora ties. *AP News*. https://apnews.com/article/israel-ap-top-news-media-middle-east-entertainment-cd8614d0afeee761ae5dd9ba0b518f7e

Grant, L. D., & Kopelowitz, E. (2012). *Israel education matters: A 21st century paradigm for Jewish Education*. Center for Jewish Peoplehood Education.

Gringras, R., & Pomson, A. (2021, June 8). Disagreeing over much more than we thought possible. *eJewish Philanthropy*. https://ejewishphilanthropy.com/disagreeing-over-much-more-than-we-thought-possible/

Harris, I. M., & Morrison, M. L. (2013). *Peace education* (3rd ed.). McFarland.

Hassenfeld, J. (2016). Negotiating critical analysis and collective belonging: Jewish American students write the history of Israel. *Contemporary Jewry*, *36*(1), 55–84. https://doi.org/10.1007/s12397-016-9157-6

Hess, D. E. (2009). *Controversy in the classroom: The democratic power of discussion*. Routledge.

Hess, D. E., & McAvoy, P. (2014). *The political classroom: Evidence and ethics in democratic education*. Routledge.

Levinson, M., & Fay, J. (2019). *Democratic discord in schools: Cases and commentaries in educational ethics*. Harvard Education Press.

Levisohn, J. A. (2016). *Ekev and resilient listening*. Jack, Joseph and Morton Mandel Center for Studies in Jewish Education at Brandeis University. http://www.encounterprograms.org/wp-content/uploads/2017/12/EkevandListening2016.pdf

Levstik, L. S., & Barton, K. C. (2018). *Researching history education: Theory, method, and context*. Routledge.

McGlynn, C., Zembylas, M., Bekerman, Z., & Gallagher, T. (Eds.). (2009). *Peace education in conflict and post-conflict societies: Comparative perspectives*. New York: Palgrave Macmillan.

Noddings, N. (2011). *Peace education: How we come to love and hate war*. Cambridge University Press.

Noddings, N., & Brooks, L. (2017). *Teaching controversial issues: The case for critical thinking and moral commitment in the classroom*. Teachers College Press.

Nortey, J. (2021, May 21). U.S. Jews have widely differing views on Israel. *Pew Research Center*. https://www.pewresearch.org/fact-tank/2021/05/21/u-s-jews-have-widely-differing-views-on-israel/

Pomson, A., Wertheimer, J., & Hacohen Wolf, H. (2014). *Hearts and minds: Israel in North American Jewish day schools*. The Avi Chai Foundation in cooperation with Rosov Consulting. https://avichai.org/knowledge_base/hearts-and-minds-israel-in-north-american-jewish-day-schools/

Ravid, S. (Ed.). (2021). *Peoplehood education—Goals, pedagogy, and outcomes* (Vol. 30). The Center for Jewish Peoplehood Education.

Reingold, M. (2017). Not the Israel of my elementary school: An exploration of Jewish-Canadian secondary students' attempts to process morally complex Israeli narratives. *The Social Studies*, *108*(3), 87–98. https://doi.org/10.1080/00377996.2017.1324392

Reingold, M. (2018). Broadening perspectives on immigrant experiences: Secondary students study the absorption difficulties faced by Mizrachi immigrants in Israel. *Journal of Jewish Education*, *84*(3), 312–329. https://doi.org/10.1080/15244113.2018.1478531

Tracy, M. (2021, November 2). Inside the unraveling of American Zionism. *The New York Times*. https://www.nytimes.com/2021/11/02/magazine/israel-american-jews.html

Zakai, S. (2011). Values in tension: Israel education at a U.S. Jewish day school. *Journal of Jewish Education*, *77*(3), 239–265. https://doi.org/10.1080/15244113.2011.603070

Zakai, S. (2014). "My heart is in the East and I am in the West": Enduring questions of Israel education in North America. *Journal of Jewish Education*, *80*(3), 287–318. https://doi.org/10.1080/15244113.2014.937192

Zakai, S. (2015). "Israel is meant for me": Kindergarteners' conceptions of Israel. *Journal of Jewish Education*, *81*(1), 4–34. https://doi.org/10.1080/15244113.2015.1007019

Zakai, S. (2019). From the mouths of children: Widening the scope and shifting the focus of understanding the relationships between American Jews and Israel. *Contemporary Jewry*, *39*(1), 17–29. https://doi.org/10.1007/s12397-019-09288-0

Zakai, S., & Cohen, H. T. (2016). American Jewish children's thoughts and feelings about the Jewish state: Laying the groundwork for a developmental approach to Israel education. *Contemporary Jewry*, *36*(1), 31–54. https://doi.org/10.1007/s12397-016-9160-y

PART IV
When Teachers Learn

10
"What Are We Doing?"
The Pedagogical Questions of Jewish Early Childhood Educators and Teacher Educators

SIVAN ZAKAI and LAUREN APPLEBAUM

In the early childhood center that Randi directs,[1] children and teachers have been preparing for a special day. The classroom has been transformed into an airplane, with chairs set up in two rows facing the front of the room and a large aisle in between. One teacher, dressed as a flight attendant, distributes snack service as the children clutch their new passports, made with cardboard and paint. After the children have finished eating, another teacher, acting as a pilot, calls out, "Welcome to Israel!"

After the trip has ended and the happy children have returned to their classrooms back in the United States, Randi reflects with us about her role as travel agent and tour guide. "I've done all this work," she explains, "and I still don't feel whole...I realized that I had all these freakin' meetings [to plan for the trip] and I never asked, 'What do we want the children to walk away with from this?'"

As teacher educators working to support Randi's professional learning about the teaching of Israel, we also had questions. What new knowledge and experiences might Randi need in order to clearly articulate her goals for children's learning, plan with her faculty to meet those goals, assess their collective work, and replan for the future? Which concepts and language from the fields of early childhood education and Israel education might help her? And how should we think about both helping Randi articulate and meet *her* goals while also meeting *our* goals as teacher educators and scholars of Israel education who hold particular beliefs about what constitutes good practice? In short: What do we want Randi to walk away with from her time with us?

This chapter explores the pedagogical questions that educators working in Jewish early childhood institutions ask about their work, and the pedagogical questions that we, as facilitators of teacher learning, ask about our own work to support and challenge these educators. We focus in particular on pedagogical questions regarding pretend trips to Israel, a common approach to teaching Israel in Jewish early childhood settings (Applebaum & Zakai, 2020). We use these pretend trips as a prism for understanding the questions of early childhood educators attempting to navigate their multiple educational commitments and our own questions as we do the same. We argue that the pedagogical questions that both early childhood educators and teacher educators ask about their *own* work in the field of Israel education require navigation of competing pedagogical priorities. The pedagogical questions that we ask about *each other's* work, by contrast, function as a way of sharpening all of our initial pedagogical dilemmas. In making this argument, this chapter rests on a premise that articulating and focusing on the *questions* that both teachers and teacher educators voice about their own and one another's pedagogical practices are a necessary step towards understanding and, ultimately, improving the work of teaching and learning about Israel.

The Context

In the fall of 2017, we launched a multiyear collaboration with early childhood educators working in a range of Jewish educational settings in two large metropolitan areas. In each city, the educators had formed a Community of Practice (CoP; Wenger, 1998) to think together about the work of early childhood Israel education. The CoPs were supported by local funders and directed by local educational leaders who selected participants and invited us to facilitate their learning.

The educators hoped to learn from us about the broader field of Israel education and, in particular, about how young children learn about Israel. We hoped to learn from them about the early-childhood-specific practices at the heart of their work and the questions that animated their professional learning and wondering. Over the course of our sessions together, the group studied current literature and debates about the field of Israel education (e.g., Horowitz, 2012; Sasson, 2014; Zakai, 2015) and engaged in structured reflection about their own educational practice. As we prepared for and debriefed from the sessions, the two of us reflected on our own work as teacher educators and facilitators.

The early childhood educators held a range of views about both early childhood education and about Israel education. Some worked in institutions that embraced constructivist approaches to early childhood education (Muller, 2013), while others were situated in preschools that attempted to balance progressive pedagogies with more teacher-directed approaches. Some expressed strong ideological positions about how and why Israel ought to be taught to Diaspora Jews, while others had philosophies of Israel education that they were beginning to develop. See Table 10.1 for basic demographic information about these educators and the institutions in which they worked.

Over the course of several years, we collaborated with these early childhood educators—at times as a group and at times with members of the CoP in concert with additional colleagues from their institutions—to investigate a series of questions about early childhood Israel education (see Applebaum & Zakai, 2020) and early childhood learners' thinking about Israel (see Applebaum et al., 2020). Drawing upon data we collected as part of this collaboration, this chapter interrogates the kinds of questions that these early childhood educators asked about their own pedagogies of teaching Israel and the questions that their work elicited for us as teacher educators seeking to both support and challenge their work in the field.

Pedagogical Questions as a Core Educational Practice

Educators ask questions of their practice in order to understand it better, to change it, and to improve it. In the words of Shagoury and Power (2012), sometimes "a question suddenly snaps into consciousness" when a teacher is reflecting on her day in conversation with colleagues or perhaps in a journal (p. 20). In other cases, questions about pedagogy and practice surface when a teacher engages in collaborative reflection (Dana & Yendol-Hoppey, 2008; Darling-Hammond & Oakes, 2019), joins a curriculum study group

(Grossman et al., 2001), or participates in mentoring experiences (Drago-Severson, 2009). Questions can come from "felt difficulties" (Sherman & Webb, 1997) or tensions in practice, and also from successes and strengths (Dana & Yendol-Hoppey, 2014).

One kind of pedagogical question that teachers often ask about their own work is called a teaching dilemma (Lampert, 2001). In articulating teaching dilemmas, educators are able to surface challenges in teaching that seem intractable because they balance competing aims and goals (Lampert, 2001). Such dilemmas "arise reasonably from competing and worthwhile aims and from the uncertainties inherent in striving to attain them" (Ball, 1993, p. 373). Because any decision that privileges one priority means sacrificing another, teaching dilemmas can never be satisfactorily resolved but instead can only be "managed" (Cuban, 2001).

Surfacing and investigating teaching dilemmas is one core practice that is part of a suite of activities that lies at the heart of meaningful teacher professional development (Ball & Cohen, 1999; Darling-Hammond & Oakes, 2021; Drago-Severson, 2009). Although it is difficult to draw a direct link between asking a pedagogical question and gracefully managing the dilemma at the heart of the question in everyday practice, the twin acts of naming a dilemma and beginning to investigate how it functions in practice are necessary first steps in a larger process of pedagogical tinkering. The theory of change that undergirds this approach assumes that teachers cannot change their practice if they do not investigate it, and the process of investigating begins with the surfacing of deep-seated questions about it (Dana & Yendol-Hoppey, 2008, 2014).

Situating Pedagogical Questions and Dilemmas in the Pedagogy of the Pretend Israel Trip

This chapter highlights the questions and dilemmas that early childhood educators and we as teacher educators ask about one particular pedagogical practice: the pretend trip to Israel. Pretend trips, like the one described in the opening anecdote of this chapter, are carefully constructed experiences that educators create for young children as a simulated experience of traveling to and touring around Israel. Just as travel to Israel has become a central feature of Jewish education for young adults and teenagers (Ezrachi, 2015;

TABLE 10.1. Participants in the Study

Participant*	Professional Position	Institution Type	Institution's Denominational Affiliation
Addie	Education director	Synagogue education department	Reconstructionist
Amy	Director of early childhood	Day school ECC	Community/trans-denominational
Bina	Teacher	Synagogue ECC	Conservative
Carmella	Director of early childhood	Synagogue ECC	Conservative
Daniella	Director of early childhood	JCC ECC	Nondenominational
Elka	Education director	JCC ECC	Post-denominational
Hadas	Teacher	BJE ECC	Nondenominational
Hana	Teacher	Day school ECC	Community/trans-denominational
Heather	Assistant director of early childhood	JCC ECC	Nondenominational
Jocelyn	Director of young family education	Synagogue education department	Conservative
Mandy	Teacher	JCC ECC	Nondenominational
Michelle	Teacher	Synagogue education department	Reform
Mina	Director of early childhood	JCC ECC	Nondenominational, primarily Orthodox students
Natalie	Director of early childhood	BJE	Nondenominational
Ohr	Israeli shlicha (emissary)	Synagogue education department	Reform
Randi	Director of early childhood	Synagogue ECC	Conservative
Rebecca	Program director	PJ Library	Nondenominational
Renae	Teacher	JCC ECC	Nondenominational
Rivka	Director of young family education	Day school ECC	Modern Orthodox
Shifra	Teacher	Synagogue ECC	Conservative
Shosh	Director of early childhood	Day school ECC	Sephardic/Orthodox
Talia	Teacher	Synagogue ECC	Conservative

*Pseudonyms have been used

Kelner, 2013; Saxe & Chazan, 2008; Saxe, et al., 2013), so too does pretend travel to Israel function as a common experience of young Jewish children, whose teachers guide them through an elaborate imagined journey.

A pretend trip almost always begins with the travel experience. The children "pack" imaginary suitcases and board the "plane." As Randi describes, "The chairs are set up.... There's a pilot. There's music that's playing when they're on the plane. There's Israeli crackers or cookies that are passed out by the flight attendants. Someone's dressed as the pilot." Upon arriving in Israel, children usually have their passports stamped. The first stop for nearly all trips is Jerusalem and a visit to the Western Wall. In most settings, children prepare by building the Western Wall out of shoeboxes, classroom blocks, or cardboard painted with gold glitter. Tel Aviv is usually the location for either a beach trip or a *shuk* (open-air market) experience. Children use photocopied Israeli money to buy and sell a mix of real fresh fruits and vegetables or prepare simple Israeli foods like cucumber and tomato salad. Children also visit the desert, often located in the school sandbox, where they might participate in an archeological dig or pose for pictures atop a cutout of a camel. In order to create a fully immersive experience, early childhood educators invest painstaking effort into constructing interactive experiences that allow young children to "visit" Israel.

Elsewhere (Applebaum & Zakai, 2020), we have demonstrated that these pretend trips to Israel are widely prevalent, deeply embedded in the "grammar" of Jewish early childhood education (Tyack & Cuban, 1995; Tyack & Tobin, 1994), and remarkably consistent across different early childhood institutions. After having previously explored how this "signature pedagogy" (Shulman, 2005) of Jewish early childhood education is simultaneously beloved and unsatisfying for the Jewish early childhood educators who engage in this work, in this chapter we investigate a series of questions that Jewish early childhood educators and we as teacher educators have about this common practice.

Pretend trips to Israel sit at the nexus of three educational domains that matter for the work of early childhood educators who work in Jewish institutions: Israel education, educational simulation, and dramatic play. *Israel education*, a subfield of Jewish education, situates teaching and learning about Israel as integral to Jewish life (Grant & Kopelowitz, 2012) and a core aspect of the education of Jewish children in particular (Zakai, 2022). *Educational simulations* offer learners an opportunity to encounter a "quasi-real" situation (Claudet, 1998) that imitates but does not fully reproduce reality. Commonly used in both Jewish (Katz & Kress, 2018) and social studies education (Gehlbach et al., 2008; Lo, 2017), simulations are often seen as a pedagogical practice particularly well suited to teaching geography (Conolly, 1982; Tansey, 1971). *Dramatic play* is an early-childhood-centered practice that recognizes the essential nature of play for children's development (Bergen, 2002; Piaget, 1962; Vygotsky, 1967) and situates play at the center of children's learning (Fragkiadaki et al., 2021; Robertson et al., 2018). While play is typically generated by children themselves, "tutored dramatic play" (Mellou, 1994) offers a way for adults to offer guidance, directions, and participation in children's play (Hakkarainen et al., 2013). Thus pretend trips to Israel are—all at once—a form of Israel education, a type of educational simulation, and a space for children's and adult's co-constructed dramatic play.

Despite the rich opportunities that pretend trips to Israel afford, they also raise profound questions about the goals of Jewish and Israel education and the pedagogical decisions that educators might make in order to meet those goals. In this chapter, we focus on the questions that lay at the heart of this common practice—questions voiced by early childhood educators about their own work, and questions that arise for our own work as teacher educators who are committed to collaborating with early childhood educators.

Methods

To understand the educators' pedagogical questions, we used two primary methods: interviews and seminar records. We interviewed the early childhood educators about their developing beliefs about Israel education and early childhood education. The interviews were semi-structured, based on a prewritten script but allowing for fluid conversation and follow-up probes (Gillham, 2005; Miles & Huberman, 1994). We asked questions about the educators' backgrounds, about their practices, and about their beliefs and questions about those practices. Once we realized that pretend trips to Israel were a core and common part of their practice, we also asked them to describe their pretend trips, explain their decision-making processes in crafting and running the trips, reflect on what they believed that the children they teach might learn from these trips, and share their successes, concerns, questions, and next steps. These semi-structured interviews allowed us to better understand the practices and beliefs of the educators and offered the educators themselves both a voice in the research and an opportunity to better understand their own practice.

We also examined the records from the seminars that we facilitated. These included transcripts of highly structured protocols that we used to surface, examine, and probe the challenges and dilemmas that arise in teaching (Bambino, 2002; Lampert, 2001; McDonald et al., 2013). In addition, some of the educators brought to these conversations artifacts of practice (Ball & Cohen, 1999) and/or documentation (Katz & Chard, 1996). For example, one participant brought a storybook that she and her students created as they "visited" different sights in Israel. Other educators, for whom documentation is a regular part of their teaching practice (Thornton & Brunton, 2007), brought photographs and written descriptions of their work. We examined both the artifacts and the transcripts of the educators' reflections about this documentation.

To understand our *own* pedagogical questions, we drew upon two additional methods from the tradition of practitioner research. We collected data of our facilitation practice by audio-recording and transcribing each session and kept careful notes of the co-planning process before sessions and the joint debriefing and reflection sessions after each session (Raider-Roth et al., 2012).

Data Analysis

To analyze these sources of data, we generated some conceptual categories using what Robert Weiss (1994) calls issue-focused analysis. We searched for patterns in the way that educators framed their pedagogical practices and their questions about those practices. We also sought parallels between the types of questions that they were asking about their teaching and the kinds of questions we were asking about our teaching of them.

Other conceptual categories were generated using selective open coding to search for emergent themes (Emerson et al., 1995). In the tradition of grounded theory, these codes emerged from the thoughts and reflections of the participants (Charmaz, 2014; Glaser & Strauss, 1967). For example, the theme of "child-centered" was repeated in a variety of ways by participants, so we searched specifically for the times they asked questions about the child-centered nature of their work. Similarly, the records of our own practice show that we often asked questions about the goals of early childhood Israel education, so we searched our records for examples of these questions.

Taken together, careful analysis of the data offered multiple windows into the assumptions, questions, doubts, fears, hopes, and accomplishments that early childhood educators articulated as they examined their own work and the work of their peers and the ways that their work has raised questions for our own pedagogical practices as teacher educators.

Pedagogical Questions of Jewish Early Childhood Educators

As the early childhood educators with whom we collaborated investigated their teaching, they asked a series of pedagogical questions about their own work: How can I weave Israel into the culture of the early childhood classroom (Mina)? How can I represent for young children a faraway physical place if they've never been there before (Daniella)? How can I represent for children a place that *I've* never been before (Heather)? How can I help young children build an emotional attachment to Israel in a way that is meaningful to them (Hana)? Is it even an appropriate pedagogical goal to direct children's gaze towards Israel just because adults situate Israel as important in our own lives (Talia)?

All of the early childhood educators in this study were able to voice questions about their own pedagogical practices; in many cases, these questions were the very impetus behind them deciding to join the groups in the first place. Yet upon further investigation and reflection, it turned out that in addition to the questions that initially brought them to the work of the CoP, they also had a *shared* question that cut across institutions, contexts, and cities: *What pedagogical practices would allow us to balance a commitment to developmentally appropriate early childhood education with a commitment to Israel education?* Each of the early childhood educators in this study asked versions of this question in one-on-one interviews and/

or in group seminars, and each voiced a belief that this question was, in Jocelyn's words, "the main thing for me to figure out how to balance." As Hana explained, the educators viewed this question as "important [in order] to know: What are we doing?"

To understand this shared question, it is necessary to recognize that all of the educators in this study embraced two distinct and deeply held beliefs: the importance of developmentally sound practices for young learners and the importance of teaching young Jews about Israel. As early childhood educators, they know and love the physical, emotional, and intellectual lives of two-, three-, and four-year-olds, and they are committed to developmentally appropriate pedagogical practices (Copple & Bredekamp, 2009; Copple et al., 2013). As educators at Jewish institutions, they believe Israel is an integral part of Jewish life and learning (Grant & Kopelowitz, 2012). While on the surface these dual commitments make sense for educators who teach young learners in Jewish institutions, for the educators themselves, it was clear that the dual commitments give rise to two tensions in their pedagogical practices.

First, the teachers' own desire to impart knowledge of and connection to Israel must contend with their firmly held belief in child-directed learning, where children's own interests and passions direct the play. In recent years, many Jewish early childhood institutions have adopted or adapted the philosophy of the schools of Reggio-Emilia, which are associated with a range of constructivist pedagogical approaches (Ben-Avie et al., 2011; Edwards et al., 2011; Muller, 2013; Muller et al., 2018). While in practice the educators vary in their level of fidelity to these principles, there was consensus among most participants that child-centered practices ought to guide their teaching. In a child-centered classroom, an educator offers provocations or invitations to explore, but it is the children who decide if and how they will direct their play and learning in response.

In this type of child-centered learning environment, there is no guarantee that the children in any particular classroom will select to explore any particular topic. Thus it is not hard to imagine a situation in which there was no learning about Israel at all, if children did not show interest. A firm commitment to Israel education, therefore, requires a more teacher-directed approach, which sits in tension with the educators' own espoused pedagogic commitments.

Many of these educators gravitate towards the practice of the pretend trip to Israel because they understand it to be a compromise between the competing priorities of child-centered learning and teaching about Israel. As Shosh somewhat ruefully explains, it is "a child-centered-*enough* activity." Renae describes how she attempts to strike a balance by asking children, "What would you like to learn *about Israel*?" (rather than simply, "What would you like to learn?") and then using those responses to "direct what we did [in the trip]." Some educators, like Renae, comfortably embrace the pretend trip as a reasonable balance between competing priorities; other educators, like Shosh, remain dissatisfied by the sacrifices it requires of children's agency.

Just as they reflect on the tensions between child-directed play and a commitment to teaching about Israel, so too do the educators acknowledge the tensions between teaching about a faraway place and recognizing children's limited ability to understand geographic concepts. Even as they stamp their students' "passports," educators with a keen sense of the developmental needs of young children understand that children's conceptual understanding of geography is quite limited. Although children begin to map the environment from a very young age (DeLoache, 1989; Matthews, 1992), preschool-aged children often find it challenging to conceive of larger geographical concepts related to space and have particular difficulty with the nomenclature used to discuss geography (Platten, 1995).

Many of the educators are thoughtfully skeptical about whether a simulated trip through the geography of another country is within the developmental grasp of young children. As Shifra explains, "I think that preparing for this trip and going on the airplane is fun, but do they really know where they are going? I'm not so sure that the children really understand it." Similarly, Rivka wonders, "Are they really getting that when they make colored sand bottles...they're in Israel doing it? Probably not."

The educators' concern here is not that pretend play is developmentally inappropriate, but rather that the pretend trip does not improve children's limited ability to understand a remote place on the globe. As a way of checking that hypothesis, Randi had asked some four-year-olds in her institution what they knew and remembered about Israel. She ruefully reports, "I could've been asking them about Brazil. It hadn't resonated."

All of the educators in this study were aware of the tension between their desire to allow children to direct their learning and their desire for children to direct their attention towards Israel, as well as the tension between their desire to capitalize on the joy of hands-on "travel" experiences with their knowledge that young learners have difficulty conceptualizing geographic space and distance. The central pedagogical question that animated their work—*What pedagogical practices would allow us to balance a commitment to developmentally appropriate early childhood education with a commitment to Israel education?*—was a rich and complicated teaching dilemma that they could work to manage but not resolve.

Next-Step Pedagogical Questions for Jewish Early Childhood Educators

In our collaborative conversations, the educators readily articulated the thoughtful questions about their own work discussed in the previous section. As teacher educators attempting to navigate our own dual commitments to supporting and challenging teachers in their work (Drago-Severson, 2009; Martin, 1996), we have additional questions that we have begun to ask about the practice of the pretend trip to Israel. We call these "next-step questions" because we think that a serious attempt to engage with them would allow early childhood educators to gain additional conceptual clarity about the purpose and nature of their work in order to navigate and "manage" their shared pedagogical dilemma with the kind of excitement with which they initially investigated their practice and not with, as Randi describes, a "big horrible epiphany" about the intractability of competing commitments.

Our next-step questions for early childhood educators focus on the ways that the youngest Jewish learners might be taught to think about Israel. We ask: When the children disembark from the "plane," where are they pretending to visit? And who are they pretending to be while there? Asking these questions offers early childhood educators who design pretend trips a next step towards aligning the trips they so carefully plan with their own goals.

» Where Are the Kids Pretending to Visit?

The practice of pretend trips raises questions about which aspects of Israel very young children should learn about and why. Israel can be framed as contemporary and/or historical, real and/or symbolic, Jewish and/or multiethnic (Avni et al., 2012). In theory, educators could make a wide range of choices about how to frame Israel for children.

In reality, these multiple options mean that many children are introduced to an amalgamation of different versions of Israel on their "trip": Biblical, contemporary, and symbolic. In many cases, early childhood pretend trips blur the lines between ancient and contemporary Israel from the moment that they "fly" to an Israel they know from the stories of the Bible and the rituals of Jewish holidays. For example, in Renae's class, "We had just talked about the desert because of Passover. The kids tied that together. Then we created a map of Israel." While in some cases the connections flow from one to the next, in other classrooms they are comingled, as most educators are readily willing to abandon fidelity to details of contemporary life in Israel in order to help children connect the concept of Israel to Jewish culture and stories. For example, in Hadas's class, the children visit an archeological dig site where they excavate a variety of objects, including contemporary Sabbath candles. "Why a [Sabbath] candle?" she explains. "Because we celebrate [the Sabbath] every week. I guess that's more of a Jewish lens, I think, than Israel." Hadas knows that archeologists wouldn't find these candles at a dig site, but when asked, she readily embraces the anachronism. "I see the importance of everything," she says. "The history, the modern, the ways to make it fun for young children."

By knowingly blurring the boundaries between ancient and contemporary, real and symbolic, early childhood Jewish educators toggle between "visiting" Israel to serve the role of Israel education and using a pretend trip to Israel as a site for other educational goals. This flexibility offers them a chance to reinforce concepts unrelated to Israel education that are nonetheless important to them as educators while muddying details about the contemporary state of Israel. We ask early childhood educators to consider the question "Where are the children pretending to visit?" as a way of helping them to clarify their visions of Israel education for young children and to make curricular and pedagogical choices that align with those visions.

» Who Are the Kids Pretending to Be?

Another central question raised by the pedagogical practices of the pretend trip is that of the role of the children themselves vis-à-vis the place they are pretending to visit. As early childhood educators design a pretend trip, how are they situating the children in relation to Israel? Are the children traveling as tourists to a foreign vacation destination? Are they simulating the experiences of an Israeli citizen? Or are they visiting as Diaspora Jews who take on some citizen-like behaviors as they engage with their symbolic homeland (Sasson, 2014)? A pretend trip has the potential for any of these, yet in many instances the experiences that early childhood educators produce for children blend these categories in ways that are—at once—playful and potentially confusing.

The blurring of the children's status as they visit Israel is particularly pronounced as educators design and use "passports." In many early childhood settings, as children "travel" to Israel, they receive a passport, often an Israeli one. Traveling on an Israeli passport might indicate that the children are to play Israeli citizens, yet the role quickly shifts upon arrival, as their passports are stamped and they are welcomed as if they were tourists visiting from abroad.

The itineraries of the pretend trips also offer inconsistent messages about the roles that the children themselves are to play. In several early childhood centers, children visit a mock *shuk* (open-air market) where they make Israeli salad or other food. Yet, as Jocelyn reflects on the Israeli salad-making experience, "[On a real trip], you're not going to go to a *shuk* and make Israeli salad. That's not what a trip to Israel would be at all." Israelis may shop at a *shuk* to buy ingredients for their salad, yet visitors to the *shuk* would be unlikely to prepare their salads there. In conflating the experiences of *shopping for* Israeli salad, which might occur by a visitor to the *shuk*, and *making* Israeli salad, which is a task generally associated with a vendor in the *shuk* or a resident of the city, children are inhabiting the role of tourist and citizen at once.

As early childhood educators prioritize experiences that allow the children to touch, taste, hear, and smell what it might be like to be in Israel, they often situate children in an amalgamation of roles: (generic) tourist, Diaspora Jewish visitor, and Israeli citizen. This playfulness allows educators maximum flexibility in planning hands-on learning experiences, and at the same time it obscures from view why the children are being invited to fly to Ben Gurion airport. We ask early childhood educators, "Who are the kids pretending to be?" as a way of helping educators clarify—for themselves and for the children whose play they are directing—an answer to an even more fundamental question. Why should Jewish children in the United States be learning about Israel?

» Asking Next-Step Questions for Teachers' Professional Learning

As we learned to identify these next-step questions through our partnership with early childhood educators, we have begun to ask, "Who are the children?" and/or "What Israel are they visiting?" in a variety of ways. Sometimes we pose them as clarifying questions in response to a shared story or artifact that an educator might bring into a group seminar. At other times we ask them as probing questions in individual semi-structured interviews. On a field-wide level, we engage early childhood educators in these questions through presentations and engagement at early childhood conferences and through our published writing. In all of these contexts, we ask these "next-step" questions to invite early childhood educators to investigate their own practice, in the spirit of helping them better align their own teaching with the larger goals they have developed for Israel education in their early childhood centers.

While we believe in the power of *asking* these questions of early childhood educators, we do not suggest that a direct line can be drawn between the process of pedagogical questioning and substantive change in teachers' classroom practice. There is no simple causal relationship between professional-learning opportunities for teachers and changes in teachers' pedagogy in other fields (Garet et al., 2001; Jacob & McGovern, 2015), and we have no reason to believe otherwise when it comes to Israel education. In our work with early childhood educators, we have found that at times educators leave our professional-learning seminars and report that they return to their classroom and make next-day changes. For example, Hana regularly committed to "try to incorporate that" in response to our questions. But more often, there is no immediate visible change to teachers' work. In these cases, we view our questioning of the educators as akin to planting seeds that may (but also may not) germinate over a long-time horizon (Dorph & Holtz, 2000). While asking questions may not always directly lead to change in the classroom, we believe that changing minds and changing practice always *begins* with questions.

Pedagogical Questions of Teacher Educators

Our articulation of these next-step questions as essential for both honoring and helping to change teachers' work forces us to confront a pedagogical dilemma that sits at the heart of our own teaching practice. Just as the educators situate as central to their work two core beliefs that at times compete with one another—a fidelity to developmentally appropriate practice for young learners and a commitment to teaching young Jews about Israel—we, too, have two priorities that do not always easily coexist.

On the one hand, we view our role as supporting educators so that they can make pedagogical and curricular choices that align with their educational goals and those of their institutions. This belief—rooted in our deep commitments to both adult learning and autonomy, and to Jewish pluralism grounded in an understanding that different Jewish communities situate Israel in different ways—means that we strive to help educators articulate *their* goals for the children in their institutions, and we attempt to help them align their curricular and pedagogic decisions to those goals. One of the reasons we ask educators to consider not only the questions that they can readily identify about their own practice but also the "next-step" questions that *we* raise about their work is because we believe that addressing these questions can help educators more clearly articulate their own educational goals.

On the other hand, we see our role as teacher educators as part of our commitment to shaping the field of Israel education, and in that regard, we have *particular* beliefs about what "good" Israel education for children might look like. In a field that has a range of articulated possible goals for Israel education (e.g., Chazan, 2016; Grant & Kopelowitz, 2012; Sinclair,

2013), we are not neutral observers but active participants in shaping conversations about what Israel education could be. We privilege the thinking and questions of children in shaping educational experiences (see Applebaum et al., 2020; Zakai, 2022), and we prioritize an educational approach that attempts to foster children's understanding of the collective Jewish experience over attempts to facilitate children's affective connections to Israel (see Winer, this volume).

Our beliefs—and thus the pedagogical choices we make about how to frame professional-learning opportunities for educators—are, at once, rooted in commitments to teachers' agency in creating rich and educative classroom environments, and to children's agency in shaping their own worldviews. We strive to make room for a plurality of beliefs and approaches to Israel while simultaneously upholding particular visions for Israel education. Like the early childhood educators, we understand that these commitments compete with one another, and we seek "good enough" ways of managing these tensions, at times providing opportunities for educators to encounter and reflect upon a range of articulations about Israel education and its purposes, and at times focusing on a process of inquiry that highlights our own commitments to situating children's genuine questions at the heart of educational work (Wells, 1999). Drawing upon Magdalene Lampert's (1985) framing of teaching dilemmas as an "argument with oneself" (p. 182), we view ourselves as being in a constant process of negotiating with ourselves as we attempt to consider the question: *What pedagogical practices would allow us to manage our competing commitments to helping teachers articulate and work towards their goals, and articulating and working towards our own vision for the field?*

Next-Step Pedagogical Questions for Teacher Educators

Just as we hold a mirror to the work of early childhood educators, posing next questions that they may not have initially considered but that are nonetheless important for their own work, so too do the early childhood educators ask us to think about questions that we hadn't initially considered. We frame these as our own "next-step questions" because we hear the early childhood educators asking them as a way of sharpening our own work and a larger set of practices in the field. Like the "next-step questions" that we ask of early childhood educators, their "next step questions" for us are ultimately important to address as we attempt to cultivate pedagogical practices that align with a larger vision for teaching and learning in the field.

» What Constitutes "Best Practice" in Early Childhood Israel Education?

As we design professional learning experiences for Jewish early childhood educators, we often hear them asking us to more clearly articulate a vision for Israel education appropriate for the particular context of early childhood education. As Amy asked, "How could and should best practices look like?" In Daniella's words, "I think there is a general feeling of importance and value of Israel, but no... specifically stated direction of 'you should be doing this. This is the way.... This is what we want of you....' What *is* best?"

The urgency of articulating a clear vision for Israel education in the particular context of early childhood education often felt especially pressing as we considered the tremendous amount of work and preparation required to, as Mandy noted, cart "40 pounds of sand into the classroom" to create a desert landscape. The educators who expressed pride at their efforts also expressed profound reticence about the compromises required of them as they balanced their competing priorities. In thinking about this tension, Jocelyn turned to us and said, "I don't know that it [the pretend trip] is our best entry point... [but] what would replace it?" Her question lingers in our minds.

We view Jocelyn's charge—and the pointed questions of other educators including Amy and Daniella—as essential for helping us refine our own work. We understand the practice of teaching not as one in which the teacher has the answers to important questions and conveys those answers to students, but rather as a practice in which the teacher facilitates a process of co-investigation—even, or perhaps especially, when the answers are not yet known. In that light, we view the early childhood educators' questions of us, their teachers, as the starting point for our next joint inquiry. Just as their question "What do 3- and 4-year-olds understand about Israel?" became the basis for our collaborative investigation into children's thinking about Israel (Applebaum et al., 2020), so too do we view their question about best practices in early childhood Israel education as the starting place for further collaborative work.

What might that collaborative work entail? We suggest beginning with an investigation into pedagogical practices—beyond the pretend trip—that are already central to Israel education or already present in early childhood education in order to learn together about the possibilities and challenges they afford for developing a richer understanding of developmentally appropriate Israel education in the early years.

If the pretend trip can be understood as an early childhood corollary to actual trips to Israel taken by teens and young adults (Applebaum & Zakai, 2020), it may be possible to draw other Israel education practices into early childhood settings. For example, the *mifgash*, a structured encounter between Israelis and Diaspora Jews, is a core pedagogical practice of Israel education in other Jewish educational settings (Lanski et al., 2015; Sasson et al., 2011). Early childhood educators could experiment with opportunities for young children to encounter Israelis who already live in or are visiting their communities. These encounters are likely to create challenges unique to the early childhood context, as young learners are only beginning to develop a conceptual understanding of what constitutes "Israeli," but they also may afford substantive opportunities for authentic learning rooted in children's curiosity.

In addition to "drawing down" Israel education practices into the early childhood context, another worthy experiment might "draw out" from other early childhood core pedagogies. For example, the robust tradition of supporting second language development in the early years (e.g., Akcan, 2005a, 2005b; Payesteh & Fortune, 2016) suggests that a focus on Hebrew-language education may be beneficial not only for children's linguistic development but also for their understanding of Israeli culture and its similarities and differences to American Jewish culture.

Like pretend trips, experimentation with *mifgash* and creating Hebrew-rich early childhood classrooms will not "solve" early childhood educators' dilemmas as they attempt to balance commitments to Israel education and children's self-directed learning. Nor will these practices "solve" our own dilemmas about supporting and challenging teachers in their work. Nonetheless, by extending educators' understanding of possible approaches that may be both developmentally appropriate and Israel focused, we can expand the playing field on which both the educators, and we as their supporters and challengers, can do the complex work of managing these dilemmas.

Conclusion

For Jewish early childhood educators who care deeply about Israel education and about developmentally sound practices for young learners, pretend Israel trips offer an interlocking set of educational dilemmas: How should children's limited geographic understanding factor into attempts to teach them about a faraway place? How ought the goals and priorities of Israel education be weighed against the interests and passions of students? How should different portrayals of Israel—past and present, real and symbolic—factor into children's learning? Some of these questions are clear and apparent as early childhood educators investigate their own work, and some require the outside eyes of teacher educators holding a mirror to the work of early childhood educators.

For us as teacher educators committed to supporting and challenging the work of these educators, pretend trips also offer a complex set of pedagogical questions: How can we help educators learn to better articulate and plan towards the educational goals of their institutions while also giving them space to consider and experiment with new ways of thinking about the field? How can we provide support and encouragement to build upon the considerable strengths and successes of our colleagues in the field while also offering new "visions of the desirable and the possible" (Shulman & Shulman, 2009)? How can we raise up the genuine questions of children, early childhood educators, and our own questions as teacher educators while allowing room for autonomy, agency, and joint inquiry of all three groups? As is true for the early childhood educators, some of these questions have animated our work from the start, while others we have learned to articulate in conversation with the early childhood educators who held up mirrors to our thinking.

Thus the pedagogical questions of early childhood educators and teacher educators are in many ways parallel. In both instances, thoughtful educators are able to identify a core dilemma that sits at the heart of their practice and provokes their curiosity with great regularity. These dilemmas are made more complex—and more interesting!—only in the presence of external thought partners who help revisit, refine, and sharpen these questions. The process of pedagogical questioning—at times parallel and at times in explicit dialogue with one another—remind us that teacher development and field development are inextricably linked.

NOTES

1. All early childhood educators in this chapter are referred to by pseudonyms.

REFERENCES

Akcan, S. (2005a). Puppet theater time in a first grade French-immersion class. *Young Children*, 60(2), 38–41.

Akcan, S. (2005b). Supporting oral second language use: A learning experience in a first grade German immersion class. *Early Childhood Education Journal*, 32(6), 359–364. https://doi.org/10.1007/s10643-005-0005-7

Applebaum, L., Hartman, A., & Zakai, S. (2021). A little bit more far than Mexico: How 3- and 4-year-old Jewish children understand Israel. *Journal of Jewish Education*, 87(1), 4–34. https://doi.org/10.1080/15244113.2020.1834890

Applebaum, L., & Zakai, S. (2020). "I'm going to Israel and all I need to pack is my imagination": Pretend trips to Israel in Jewish early childhood education. *Journal of Jewish Education*, 86(1), 94–119. https://doi.org/10.1080/15244113.2019.1696659

Avni, S., Kattan, S., & Zakai, S. (2012). *Purposes and practices of Israel education and Hebrew education: Towards a joint agenda for applied research*. The Consortium for Applied Studies in Jewish Education.

Ball, D. L. (1993). With an eye on the mathematical horizon: Dilemmas of teaching elementary school mathematics. *The Elementary School Journal*, 93(4), 373–397. https://doi.org/10.1086/461730

Ball, D. L., & Cohen, D. K. (1999). Developing practice, developing practitioners: Toward a practice-based theory of professional education. In L. Darling-Hammond & G. Sykes (Eds.), *Teaching as the learning profession* (pp. 3–32). Jossey Bass.

Bambino, D. (2002). Critical friends. *Educational Leadership*, 59(6), 25–27.

Ben-Avie, M., Vogelstein, I., Goodman, R. L., Schaap, E., & Bidol-Padva, P. (2011). Early childhood education. In H. Miller, L. D. Grant, & A. Pomson (Eds.), *International Handbook of Jewish Education* (pp. 749–766). Springer.

Bergen, D. (2002). The role of pretend play in children's cognitive development. *Early Childhood Research & Practice*, 4(1). https://files.eric.ed.gov/fulltext/ED464763.pdf

Charmaz, K. (2014). *Constructing grounded theory* (2nd ed.). Sage.

Chazan, B. (2016). *A philosophy of Israel education: A relational approach*. Palgrave Macmillan.

Claudet, J. G. (1998). Using multimedia case simulations for professional growth of school leaders: Administrator case simulation project. *T.H.E. Journal, 25*(11), 82–86. https://www.jstor.org/stable/42589856

Conolly, G. (1982). Games in geography: Development in technique. *Journal of Geography, 81*(3), 112–114. https://doi.org/10.1080/00221348208980860

Copple, C., & Bredekamp, S. (2009). *Developmentally appropriate practice in early childhood programs serving children from birth through age 8*. National Association for the Education of Young Children.

Copple, C., Bredekamp, S., Koralek, D. G., & Charner, K. (Eds.). (2013). *Developmentally appropriate practice: Focus on preschoolers*. National Association for the Education of Young Children.

Cuban, L. (2001). *How can I fix it? Finding solutions and managing dilemmas: An educator's road map*. Teachers College Press.

Dana, N. F., & Yendol-Hoppey, D. (2008). *The reflective educator's guide to professional development: Coaching inquiry-oriented learning communities*. Corwin Press.

Dana, N. F., & Yendol-Hoppey, D. (2014). *The reflective educator's guide to classroom research: Learning to teach and teaching to learn through practitioner inquiry*. Corwin Press.

Darling-Hammond, L., & Oakes, J. (2019). *Preparing teachers for deeper learning*. Harvard Education Press.

DeLoache, J. S. (1989). Young children's understanding of the correspondence between a scale model and a larger space. *Cognitive Development, 4*(2), 121–139. https://doi.org/10.1016/0885-2014(89)90012-9

Dorph, G. Z., & Holtz, B. W. (2000). Professional development for teachers: Why doesn't the model change? *Journal of Jewish Education, 66*(1–2), 67–76. https://doi.org/10.1080/0021624000660107

Drago-Severson, E. (2009). *Leading adult learning: Supporting adult development in our schools*. Corwin Press.

Edwards, C., Gandini, L., & Forman, G. (Eds.). (2011). *The hundred languages of children: The Reggio Emilia experience in transformation* (3rd ed.). ABC-CLIO.

Emerson, R. M., Fretz, R. I., & Shaw, L. L. (1995). *Writing ethnographic fieldnotes*. University of Chicago Press.

Ezrachi, E. (2015). Educational travel to Israel in the era of globalization. *Journal of Jewish Education, 81*(2), 212–225. https://doi.org/10.1080/15244113.2015.1036351

Fragkiadaki, G., Armeni, A., Zioga, S., & Ravanis, K. (2021). Dramatic play as a means to explore and support preschool children's thinking about thermal insulation. *Journal of Childhood, Education & Society, 2*(3), 220–234. https://doi.org/10.37291/2717638X.20212395

Garet, M. S., Porter, A. C., Desimone, L., Birman, B. F., & Yoon, K. S. (2001). What makes professional development effective? Results from a national sample of teachers. *American Educational Research Journal, 38*(4), 915–945. https://doi.org/10.3102/00028312038004915

Gehlbach, H., Brown, S. W., Ioannou, A., Boyer, M. A., Hudson, N., Niv-Soloman, A., & Janik, L. (2008). Increasing interest in social studies: Social perspective taking and self-efficacy in stimulating simulations. *Contemporary Educational Psychology, 33*(4), 894–914. https://doi.org/10.1016/j.cedpsych.2007.11.002

Gillham, B. (2005). *Research interviewing: The range of techniques: A practical guide.* McGraw-Hill Education (UK).

Glaser, B. G., & Strauss, A. L. (1999/1967). *The discovery of grounded theory: Strategies for qualitative research.* Adline Transaction.

Grant, L., & Kopelowitz, E. (2012). *Israel education matters: A 21st century paradigm for Jewish education.* Center for Jewish Peoplehood Education.

Grossman, P., Wineburg, S., & Woolworth, S. (2001). Toward a theory of teacher community. *Teachers College Record, 103*(6), 942–1012. https://doi.org/10.1111/0161-4681.00140

Hakkarainen, P., Brėdikytė, M., Jakkula, K., & Munter, H. (2013). Adult play guidance and children's play development in a narrative play-world. *European Early Childhood Education Research Journal, 21*(2), 213–225. https://doi.org/10.1080/1350293X.2013.789189

Horowitz, B. (2012). *Defining Israel education.* The iCenter for Israel Education.

Jacob, A., & McGovern, K. (2015). *The mirage: Confronting the hard truth about our quest for teacher development.* The New Teacher Project.

Katz, L. G., & Chard, S. C. (1996). *The contribution of documentation to the quality of early childhood education.* ERIC Digest and Office of Educational Research and Improvement (ED).

Katz, M. L., & Kress, J. S. (2018). Jewish history engagement in an online simulation: Golda and Coco, Leah and Lou at the Jewish Court of All Time. *Journal of Jewish Education, 84*(2), 196–221. https://doi.org/10.1080/15244113.2018.1450545

Kelner, S. (2010). *Tours that bind: Diaspora, pilgrimage, and Israeli birthright tourism.* New York University Press.

Kelner, S. (2013). Historical perspectives on diaspora homeland tourism: "Israel experience" education in the 1950s and 1960s. *Diaspora, Indigenous, and Minority Education, 7*(2), 99–113. https://doi.org/10.1080/15595692.2013.763788

Lampert, M. (1985). How do teachers manage to teach? Perspectives on problems in practice. *Harvard Educational Review, 55*(2), 178–195. https://doi.org/10.17763/haer.55.2.56142234616x4352

Lampert, M. (2001). *Teaching problems and the problems of teaching.* Yale University Press.

Lanski, A., Stewart, A., & Werchow, Y. (2015). Relating and relationships. In *The Aleph Bet of Israel education.* iCenter.

Lo, J. C. (2017). Adolescents developing civic identities: Sociocultural perspectives on simulations and role-play in a civic classroom. *Theory and Research in Social Education, 45*(2), 189–217. https://doi.org/10.1080/00933104.2016.1220877

Martin, S. (1996). Support and challenge: Conflicting or complementary aspects of mentoring novice teachers? *Teachers and Teaching, 2*(1), 41–56. https://doi.org/10.1080/1354060960020104

Matthews, M. H. (1992). *Making sense of place: Children's understanding of largescale environments.* Harvester Wheatsheaf.

McDonald, J., Mohr, N., Dichter, A., & McDonald, E. C. (2013). *The power of protocols: An educator's guide to better practice.* Teachers College Press.

Mellou, E. (1994). Tutored-untutored dramatic play: Similarities and differences. *Early Child Development and Care, 100*(1), 119–130. https://doi.org/10.1080/0300443941000109

Miles, M. B., & Huberman, A. M. (1994). *Qualitative data analysis: An expanded sourcebook*. Sage.

Muller, M. (2013). Constructivism and Jewish early childhood education. *Journal of Jewish Education, 79*(3), 315–334. https://doi.org/10.1080/15244113.2013.816116

Muller, M., Gorsetman, C., & Alexander, S. (2018). Struggles and successes in constructivist Jewish early childhood classrooms. *Journal of Jewish Education, 84*(3), 284–311. https://doi.org/10.1080/15244113.2018.1478533

Payesteh, B., & Fortune, T. (2016). *Preschool immersion education in Persian*. Center for Advanced Research on Language Acquisition.

Piaget, J. (1962). *Play, dreams, and imitation in childhood*. W. W. Norton & Company.

Platten, L. (1995). Talking geography: An investigation into young children's understanding of geographical terms Part 1. *International Journal of Early Years Education, 3*(1), 74–92. https://doi.org/10.1080/0966976950030108

Raider-Roth, M., Stieha, V, & Hensley, B. (2012). Rupture and repair: Episodes of resistance and resilience in teachers' learning. *Teaching and Teacher Education, 28*(4), 493–502. https://doi.org/10.1016/j.tate.2011.11.002

Robertson, N., Yim, B., & Paatsch, L. (2018). Connections between children's involvement in dramatic play and the quality of early childhood environments. *Early Child Development and Care, 190*(3), 376–389. https://doi.org/10.1080/03004430.2018.1473389

Sasson, T. (2014). *The new American Zionism*. New York University Press.

Sasson, T., Mittelberg, D., Hecht, S., & Saxe, L. (2011). Guest-host encounters in Diaspora-heritage tourism: The Taglit-Birthright Israel mifgash (encounter). *Diaspora, Indigenous, and Minority Education, 5*(3), 178–197. https://doi.org/10.1080/15595692.2011.583521

Saxe, L., & Chazan, B. I. (2008). *Ten days of Birthright Israel: A journey in young adult identity*. UPNE.

Saxe, L., Fishman, S., Shain, M., Wright, G., & Hecht, S. (2013). *Young adults and Jewish engagement: The impact of Taglit-Birthright Israel*. Cohen Center for Modern Jewish Studies.

Shagoury, R., & Power, B. M. (2012). *Living the questions: A guide for teacher-researchers*. Stenhouse Publishers.

Sherman, R. R., & Webb, R. B. (1997). *Qualitative research in education: Focus and methods*. Falmer.

Shulman, L. S. (2005). Signature pedagogies in the professions. *Daedalus, 134*(3), 52–59.

Shulman, L. S., & Shulman, J. H. (2009). How and what teachers learn: A shifting perspective. *Journal of Education, 189*(1–2), 1–8. https://doi.org/10.1177/0022057409189001-202

Sinclair, A. (2013). *Loving the real Israel: An educational agenda for liberal Zionism*. Ben Yehuda Press.

Tansey, P. J. (1971). *Educational aspects of simulation*. McGraw-Hill Publishing.

Thornton, L., & Brunton, P. (2007). *Bringing the Reggio approach to your early years practice*. Routledge.

Tyack, D. B., & Cuban, L. (1995). *Tinkering toward utopia*. Harvard University Press.

Tyack, D., & Tobin, W. (1994). The "grammar" of schooling: Why has it been so hard to change? *American Educational Research Journal, 31*(3), 453–479. https://doi.org/10.3102/00028312031003453

Vygotsky, L. S. (1967). Play and its role in the mental development of the child. In M. Cole (Ed.), *Soviet developmental psychology* (pp. 76–99). M. E. Sharpe.

Weiss, R. S. (1994). *Learning from strangers: The art and method of qualitative interview studies*. Free Press.

Wells, G. (1999). *Dialogic inquiry*. Cambridge University Press.

Wenger, E. (1998). *Communities of practice: Learning, meaning, and identity*. Cambridge University Press.

Zakai, S. (2015). "Israel is meant for me": Kindergarteners' conceptions of Israel. *Journal of Jewish Education, 81*(1), 4–34. https://doi.org/10.1080/15244113.2015.1007019

Zakai, S. (2022). *My second-favorite country: How American Jewish children think about Israel*. NYU Press.

11
Teaching Who They Are
Understanding Teachers' Connections With Israel and How Those Enter Into the Classroom

LAURA NOVAK WINER

Sitting in the circle of chairs in a congregation's social hall were 15 synagogue supplementary school teachers and three workshop facilitators. We gathered for a professional-development workshop on Israel education and were engaging in a conversation about the teachers' relationships with Israel. The teachers and facilitators were of varying genders and ages, American and Israeli born. One American-born teacher tentatively and bravely commented: "I find it really hard to teach about Israel. I'm ambivalent about my relationship. I've never been to Israel. I don't agree with the Israeli government's positions on the Palestinians and the settlements." As she continued to articulate her struggles, an Israeli-born teacher sitting across the circle interrupted, "What's so hard? It's Israel. You teach it."

These two teachers clearly view teaching Israel differently. Their perspectives are informed by their connections to Israel, as illustrated by the American-born teacher who frames her challenges through the lens of her ambivalent relationship with it. The American educator Parker Palmer (1998) offers insight into this phenomenon when he asserts that teachers must recognize how their own experiences and psyche impact how they address the complexities of their teaching practice. "As I teach," Palmer explains, "I project the condition of my soul onto my students, my subject and our way of being together" (p. 2). In this way, teachers "teach who we are" (p. 2). As this powerful interaction between two teachers reveals, the stance of "teaching who we are" is acutely germane to Israel education.

For decades and despite a variety of challenges, Israel education in the United States has focused on developing American Jews' personal connections to Israel (Chazan, 2016; Horowitz, 2012)—the ancient land, the modern state, and the Jewish people, who are referred to as the people of Israel. This is often condensed down to the terse yet immensely complex aim that is anecdotally described as "developing a love for Israel." This goal was both evident and contested in the two congregational supplementary schools that are the settings of the study described in this chapter. In one school (Beit Am),[1] the stated goal was "to teach [the students] *ahavat tzion* [love of Zion]." The director of education at that school explained, "I want the kids to love Israel [like] an old school *halutzim* [pioneers'] love of the land and love of the people and love of the language." In the other school (Temple Israel), the director of education said, "It is very hard to have a personal connection to Israel without going there. That's not something I can teach kids.... You can't have a personal connection with something you've never experienced." In this school, the director of education believed that the goal of developing love was unattainable given the limitations of the setting and the learners' experiences with Israel as a place.

This debate over the goal of Israel education, and my experiences with Israel educators such as the ones illustrated, led me to wonder about the role of the teacher in helping students develop connections with Israel. If the students are to develop a connection with Israel, then shouldn't the teacher have done so as well? The teacher educator Gail Dorph (2010) explored a similar question in her study of prospective Jewish teachers of Torah (Five Books of Moses). Dorph found that when the teacher held a certain stance toward the study of Torah, the students could develop that same stance. This led me to wonder what kinds of connections with Israel Israel education aims to inspire in students and in what ways a teacher's own connection with Israel might enter into the classroom.

This chapter presents findings from a study of three part-time teachers in two synagogue supplementary schools. It investigates three questions:

1. How do scholars and educators articulate the goals of Israel education?
2. How do teachers articulate their personal connections to Israel?
3. In what ways does the teacher's own relationship with Israel surface during the teaching process?

In answer to the first question, this study uncovers a new way of mapping the field of Israel education according to two different sets of goals, one which addresses the development of the Jewish self, and the other which addresses building a connection to the Jewish collective. The findings of this study suggest a typology for conceptualizing connections with Israel, which provides answers to the second question. This typology is simultaneously confirmed by the mapping of the field and emerges from the informants of this study. The third question is explored through the examination of cases that demonstrate how there is a difference between how teachers *describe* their personal connections to Israel and what they *present* about those connections in the classroom. Finally, I will discuss the implications of these findings for the alignment of curricula, teacher selection, and the professional development of Israel educators.

Study and Methods

The study's primary informants are three American-born Israel educators. The focus on American-born teachers enables a close look at how they developed their own understandings about and connections with Israel in that societal milieu. These teachers are cisgender females who share several biographical commonalities: All of them were in the process of completing or had completed graduate-level education; all have spent extended periods of time in Israel; all have basic fluency in modern conversational Hebrew; and finally, all have deep knowledge about Israel's history, politics, and culture. The commonalities between the three informants end here.

Miriam teaches fourth grade part-time in Beit Am's supplementary school.[2] She is the oldest of the informants and has the most extensive teaching experience (36+ years) among them and also has a graduate degree in Jewish education. The youngest of four children in a progressive, ardently Zionist, rabbinic family, Miriam grew up immersed in Jewish learning in a multiplicity of settings and in the Jewish community. Her life story reveals a woman who is energetically creative and lives life passionately.

Ashley and Yael are both part-time teachers at Temple Israel and are using the same curriculum in their fourth- and fifth-grade classes. Ashley has a quiet and strong presence which is grounded in a resilience that has sustained her through a challenging childhood in which her parents frequently moved the family, and she experienced loneliness as a Jew in a series of homogenous, white, Christian communities. She is a novice when it comes to teaching, which she does while pursuing a graduate degree in speech-language pathology.

Yael, the oldest child of an American father and Israeli–Yemenite mother, was teaching supplementary school as a requirement for her graduate studies in Jewish education along with pursuing a concurrent degree in nonprofit management. Growing up in both Israel and the United States, Yael had no exposure to American Jewish education until her high school years, when she joined a nondenominational Jewish youth movement.

To develop an understanding of each teacher's personal biography and connection to Israel, I designed a multilayered study that allowed me to create rich and thick profiles and cases of the informants. Three primary strategies were employed: life history, intellectual biography, and case study. Moving beyond the teacher's intellectual knowledge, a life history situates the teacher's biography in the social, political, and cultural contexts into which their life story takes place (Ben-Peretz, 1995; Goodson, 2008). An intellectual biography is a record of what a teacher knows about an area of content or practice, how they came to know it, and how that shapes their current understanding of that content or practice (Clandinin & Connelly, 1986; Grossman, 1990; Lortie, 1975; Salinas & Bevins, 2013; Shulman, 1986; Wilson et al., 1987). A case study "is a way of organizing social data so as to preserve the unitary character of the social object being studied" (Goode & Hart, 1952, as cited in Punch, 2009). These were combined in a holistic and overlapping way, with a logical sequence of interactions with the informants, based on a cycle of planning-observation-reflection (Clark & Yinger, 1987; Wilson et al., 1987; see Figure 11.1).

Mapping the Field of Israel Education

In examining the goals of Israel education within the contemporary discourse of Jewish education, I found that the field can be mapped into two primary philosophical stances. The relational approach focuses on the Jewish self and the formation of the individual's Jewish identity. The complexify approach focuses on the Jewish collective and on the formation of bonds between Jews in America and Israel.³ Both approaches endeavor for Jews to build connections to Israel, and both approaches want Jews to know "the real Israel" (Sinclair, 2013) in all its complexities—as opposed to a mythic or romanticized Israel—through those connections. The distinctions between the two approaches arise out of the focused meaning they ascribe to that connection—either enhancing the sense of Jewish self or enhancing bonds to the Jewish collective. The following sections will examine each of these philosophical stances toward Israel education and offer illustrations of how they are enacted in the congregations and teachers studied.

The Relational Approach: A Focus on the Jewish Self

The goal of Israel education according to the relational approach is to "educate people to think, feel and integrate Israel into their overall character as Jews and as human beings" (Chazan, 2016, p. 11).⁴ This approach, put

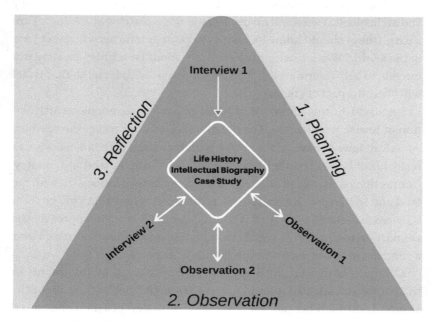

FIGURE 11.1. Data collection process

forth most prominently by the educational philosopher Barry Chazan, is grounded in theories of "relational education," which "believes that the ultimate focus on education is on the kind of life a person leads and the core values which shape that life" (Chazan, 2016, p. 7).

The relational approach conscientiously prioritizes learners and how a relationship with Israel informs their self-understanding as Jews. "The individual—not Israel—is the center of Israel education" (Chazan, 2016, p. 7). This is a new way of thinking about the goal of Israel education. In the 20th century, "great emphasis was placed on telling children *that* Israel was important; however little emphasis was placed on explaining *why*" (Chazan, 1984, p. 10).[5] A relational Israel education aims to nurture students' development of their own meaning and connection to Israel as a means of defining their individual Jewish identities. In my analysis of the relational approach, the answer to the *why* question becomes "because when I have a connection to Israel, I come to know more about who I am as a Jew."

I saw the relational approach embraced at Beit Am, as well as in Miriam's personal beliefs about Israel education. The Beit Am director of education explained that she wants the children "learning Israeli history and archeological sites and places because it is a place of which [they] are a part; [they] should know its history because it informs who [they] are in the world." When teaching her students about Israel, Miriam similarly intends to help them develop their relationships with Israel so that Israel will "become part of [them]."

Importantly, this approach to Israel education abandons an articulation of Jewish peoplehood. The definition clearly addresses the need for American Jews to have relationships with Israel and with Israelis who, as residents of Israel, have their own relationships with the land and country. Connections to Israel are navigated through narratives associated with the land and the Jewish life, language, culture, and values that emerge from it or are associated with it (Raviv, 2015). In the relational approach, the connection to the land of Israel is foundational and thus prioritized over a connection to a global community of Jewish people.

Critiques of the relational approach are articulated by informants in this study and are also found in recent research. Yael learned about the approach through her participation in a fellowship program sponsored by the iCenter, an organization whose mission is to provide professional development for Israel educators by specifically providing them with a relational-approach focus. She believed that this approach otherizes and objectifies Israel as an instrument of the learner's process rather than encouraging the learner to create, in the words of the Jewish theologian Martin Buber (1958), an I-Thou relationship with Israel. As mentioned earlier, the director of education at Temple Israel questioned the achievability of relational-approach goals given the limitations of the setting and the learners' experiences with Israel. The social scientist Sivan Zakai's (2021) longitudinal research on children's relationships with Israel over time reveals that "they do not have 'a relationship' or 'a connection' with Israel but rather many different relationships to Israel, depending on the moment and circumstance" (p. 136).

The Complexify Approach: A Focus on the Jewish Collective

An Israel education that adopts the complexify approach addresses the complexities of life in Israel and of the American Jewish relationship with Israel as a means of building connections and shared obligation among American and Israeli Jews.[6] This willingness to lean into rather than ignore the most challenging aspects of Israel today is supported by a foundational philosophical belief that American Jews need to view themselves and act as empowered, mutual participants in the global Jewish community. As members of the Jewish people, American Jews who are knowledgeable about Israeli society, Jewish history, and Jewish values can play a meaningful role in the moral conversations taking place in Israel and throughout the world. As an example of this approach, the philosopher of education Alex Sinclair (2013) proposes a model in which American Jewish engagement with Israel entails a series of conversations about the complexities of Israeli society, requiring American students to be empowered to dialogue and disagree with Israelis about a variety of issues, including political ones. The complexify approach seeks an outcome in which students have robust connections to the Jewish people, so that they—Americans and Israelis—can enrich and be enriched by each other (Sinclair, 2013).

Like the first approach, the complexify approach creates space for personalized connection and articulations of one's relationship with Israel. But, in contrast with the relational approach, this personalized connection is meant to both come from and lead to a place of belonging and mutual commitment to the Jewish people. This approach was encapsulated in Temple Israel's Israel education curriculum, which focused on the essential question "What does it mean to be part of a Jewish community?"

A common critique of the complexify approach is that it is not necessarily applicable to students at all ages and developmental stages. Some suggest that Israel education should begin with building a love for Israel in the youngest students because those students will not be able to both "hug and wrestle" with Israel at the same time (Gringras, 2006). This attitude was expressed by the Beit Am director of education, when she reiterated, "I want [the students] to have a foundation of love so when it comes to critique [of Israel] it comes from a place of love and connection." This viewpoint relies on the presumption that only once that love of Israel is firmly established and the students become more cognitively capable of dealing with the complexities should complexities be introduced (Grant, 2008; Yoffie, 2015). Zakai (2015a, 2015b, 2021, 2022) has demonstrated that those concerns are unfounded.

Two Approaches in Practice

On close examination, these two approaches to Israel education may differ in their primary ideological commitments but are not always that different from each other in practice. Both agree that Israel education should no longer focus on the mythic, idealistic Israel. Both expect Israel educators to have deep content knowledge about Israel. The two approaches employ similar learner-centered pedagogies, such as creating *mifgashim* (face-to-face encounters) between Americans and Israelis and the exploration of multiple narratives. Yet, there are also some striking differences in the types of subject matter to be taught, and additional qualities required in the Israel educator (see Table 11.1).[7] The differences in these two approaches emerge from their foundational philosophical understandings about why Israel education is important. They also diverge in their desired outcomes; they aim for very different impacts on the learner.

A Typology for Understanding Connections to Israel

The teachers in this study were asked to tell me about their relationships with Israel, how those were developed, and what those relationships mean to them, as well as about their personal goals for Israel education. These questions enabled me to understand more about their personal connections with Israel and their identities as Israel educators. The dynamics of teacher identity and beliefs are relevant to teachers of Israel who themselves learned about Israel in particular ways and under certain societal or communal influences.

TABLE 11.1. Comparison of Approaches to Israel Education

	Relational Approach: A Focus on the Jewish Self	Complexify Approach: A Focus on the Jewish Collective
Aims	To help the learner shape their self-understanding as a Jew. To initiate a relationship with the Land of Israel as a value and a portal into Jewish life.	To enculturate the learner toward the construction of content knowledge and thus be able to engage in dialogue with the global Jewish people.
Types of Subject Matter	The individual's relationship with Israel is the content. The focus is on values and on aspects of Israel's history and culture that are attractive to the learner. Hebrew is of particular importance to entering Israeli culture.	All aspects of Israel's history, society, and culture become the content.
Qualities of the Israel Educator	Teaches from within and can access their own emotions and beliefs about Israel. Is a model for developing a personal relationship with Israel. Has skills in relationship-building, questioning, group-dynamics.	Can hold multiple narratives at once, has a high tolerance for ambiguity, and allows for varying points of view. Commitment to meaningful engagement about Israel with the students.
Outcomes	Finding the "I" in Israel: The individual finds their personal Jewish identity.	Mutuality and dialogue: The individual finds their connection to the global Jewish people and is a moral voice in the conversation.

Teachers' personal beliefs, biography, life experiences, and memories inform their identities as teachers, their beliefs about teaching and learning, and their beliefs about the subject matter they teach (Grossman, 1990; Holtz, 2003, 2009). Additionally, the sociologist Dan C. Lortie (1975) determines that one's "apprenticeship of observation," one's memories of the subject matter and strategies experienced as students themselves, act as a powerful influence on a teacher's identity. I found that the teachers' own life experiences, biography, and apprenticeship of observation contributed to shaping their identity and beliefs about Israel and about teaching Israel.

The findings from the study suggest a typology for conceptualizing connections with Israel. There are two continuums of relationships, corresponding to four types of connections a teacher may have to Israel.[8] I call one the Jewish Collective–Jewish Self Continuum. This continuum aligns with the approaches to Israel education described previously and situates teachers based on how they conceptualize their own connection with Israel and their beliefs about Israel education. I call the other the Insider-Outsider Continuum, which situates teachers based on how they view their own relationship with the modern State of Israel and Israelis. This typology helps to understand a teacher's personal identification with Israel.

Jewish Collective–Jewish Self Continuum

The Jewish Collective–Jewish Self Continuum (see Figure 11.2) relates directly to the differing foundational principles of the relational approach and the complexify approach. While these are understood as schools of thought about Israel education, it became clear through this study that the types of connections each approach prescribes can also be applied in a descriptive manner to the informants' conceptualizations of their connections to Israel and their beliefs about teaching Israel.

FIGURE 11.2. Jewish Collective–Jewish Self Continuum

At one end of this continuum of connections to Israel, teachers see themselves as being part of a greater Jewish collective—part of a family of Jews across time and space—and want the same for the students.[9] This type of connection to Israel reflects the same concepts as the complexify approach.

Ashley describes her connection to Israel by articulating notions of Jewish heritage and history, greater Jewish family, Jewish community, and Jewish homeland. Beginning with her earliest memories of reciting the bedtime *Shema* prayer, the Jewish statement of faith, Ashley has viewed herself as being part of a greater Jewish collective. When she says the words "*Shema Yisrael*" ("Hear, Israel") she sees herself as part of a "community...a child of Israel."[10] As she grew, she got to know her "Israeli family." She learned about Israel as a haven for Jews from around the world, a place Jews can call home, and she wants her students to learn that as well. After an unstable childhood with her family of origin, a socially isolated and lonely high school experience, and experiencing a sense of purposelessness during her early college years, Ashley moved to Israel and soon after made *aliyah* (immigrating to Israel). She found direction and purpose in Israel. She found stability in a place where "everybody becomes your family," and she found a life partner. Ashley's primary conceptualization of her connection to Israel is that it is a place that Jews "can call home, that is a community for them as [Jews]."

At the other end of this continuum, informants see their connection with Israel as enriching their Jewish self—their own sense of themselves as Jews. This type of connection to Israel is firmly grounded in the relational approach. When a Jew has a personal connection to Israel in the relational-approach sense, it helps them understand who they are and where they fit in the world (Chazan & Bryfman, 2015). Miriam describes her relationship to Israel in this way.

Miriam primarily speaks about Israel as a place of personal transformation and unlimited potential. Her frequent visits to Israel beginning at age three, and occurring every two to three years until very recently, allowed her to continuously learn, grow, and "explore." As a person who asserts that she learns through experience, her time in Israel provided those lived experiences that shaped her identity and sense of self. She "wanted everything that Israel had to offer." She treasured the time to connect with her "favorite human beings." With the influence of these "very good people," and inspired by the natural beauty of the land, she personally experienced and came to see Israel as a place where change and transformation are possible. Reflecting on spending the whole of 10th grade in Israel, she said,

> The independence and strength that I have as a human being came from [that year], out of [America] on your own. Realizing that I was not the baby sister, but I was a person. It was my first experience with power, with independence, [with] not being in someone else's shadow. So, Israel was a lot of good, good stuff for me.

There she began to step out of the "shadow" of being the youngest sibling and the daughter of two very publicly visible parents. Israel is the place where she was able to develop her own identity.

While Ashley and Miriam were each fully on one or the other side of the continuum, Yael was firmly in the center of it (see Figure 11.2). Her relationship to Israel is conceptualized both by a sense of connection to a Jewish collective and as a way of understanding her own Jewish self. Intellectually, Yael describes her connection to Israel in the language of the Jewish-collective approach. She speaks about having a strong sense of obligation to the greater Jewish community. She believes Israel is the "locus of Jewish peoplehood" and is a homeland and wants her students to understand that as well.[11] "It's tied to our Scripture, and we come from there. It's important for historical [reasons], also contemporary [ones].... It's important for us to know [both] because as a Jew, Israel is a homeland for the Jews, and I think it is unique and special." Yet, when I look at Yael's relationship with Israel through her emotional experience of it, I find her expressing feelings evocative of both being part of the Jewish collective and being shaped as a Jewish self. While fully American, she feels a deep connection to her Israeli and Jewish heritage and history, as well as loyalty to Israel as a homeland and a haven for Jews who have been victims of oppression, including members of her own family. In addition, Yael's emotions reflect what a connection through Jewish self can look like. She has spent equal time in each country. Yael describes Israel as a place where she feels like her whole self. She is fully bilingual in Hebrew and English. When in Israel she is fulfilled by time with dear family members, especially her grandmother, and she is able to immerse herself in the tempo of Israeli life. She struggles with how to find that wholeness in the United States. Yael asks, *eyfo yoter tov*, where is it better for me? She doesn't know where she fits in, is struggling to figure it out, and thus sits in the middle of the Jewish Collective–Jewish Self Continuum.

Insider–Outsider Continuum

The second continuum relates to individuals' perceptions of themselves and reflects how they situate themselves in relation to current-day Israel and Israelis. The Insider–Outsider Continuum (see Figure 11.3) emerges out of the informants' uses of the terms "insider" and "outsider" when speaking about their connections to the modern State of Israel and when describing their self-understanding of their place within Israeli society.

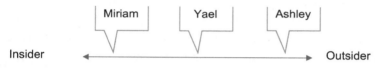

FIGURE 11.3. Insider–Outsider Continuum

Insider/outsider standing does not have to do with one's legal or Jewish status; citizenship is not a factor. Expressions of insiderness and outsiderness were voiced by the informants themselves. They each situated themselves as insiders or outsiders in Israel in three ways:

1. Understanding of the country and the culture: An insider is deeply familiar and fluent with and immersed in Israeli society and culture. An outsider feels like, behaves like, or believes they are perceived by Israelis as a tourist.
2. Knowledge of Hebrew: An insider is fluent in Hebrew and speaks it with an Israeli accent. An outsider either doesn't know Hebrew or is still in the process of learning it. Those who are fluent in Hebrew but speak it with an American accent self-perceive themselves as outsiders.
3. Service in the Israeli Defense Forces (IDF): Someone who has served in the IDF is an insider. Those who have not served—even if they made *aliyah* after the age of enlistment—view themselves as outsiders.

The teachers may be at either end of the Insider–Outsider Continuum or anywhere in between (see Figure 11.3).

Miriam speaks about her connections with Israel as an insider. She feels like and speaks like she "owns" it. She is fluent in Hebrew, speaks it with an Israeli accent, and claims to know the streets of Jerusalem like the back of her hand. She calls Jerusalem "my stone city." She takes personal affront to the modernization of the city with the development of the Jerusalem Light Rail.

Now that she and her husband are living in Los Angeles, Ashley calls herself an Israeli-American. She sees herself as a "representative" of Israel to her students. So, one might think that she would view herself as an insider. Ashley found the transition from outsider to insider to be quite challenging because when she first made *aliyah*, she didn't yet know Hebrew, didn't understand Israeli culture, and didn't even like Israeli food. She struggled with mixing her "American-ness with being Israeli." Through her perseverance, resilience, and her ability to learn from her experiences, she feels like she was able to move closer to becoming an insider. "I have a place in me now that is Israeli." Nevertheless, in her own words and self-understanding, Ashley is forever an outsider because she did not serve in the IDF.

Yael views herself as both an insider and an outsider. She identifies Hebrew as a primary marker of her insider standing. She speaks Hebrew like a native, and she has deep familiarity with Israeli culture, much of which developed during her elementary school years living there. However, at the same time, Yael feels like an outsider. Recalling a trip to Israel when she was a young child, she says, "I have this memory of all my cousins doing *birkat hamazon* [grace after the meal] and I didn't know the words and that made me aware of my difference from them." As the child of an Israeli, she could have enlisted in the IDF but chose not to. Thus, like Ashley, she feels she can never be a complete insider. Furthermore, Yael questions her right to give voice to important matters in Israeli current events. While Sinclair (2013) suggests that all Jews should be empowered to engage in "deep conversations together" (p. 109), Yael feels that she has no place in those conversations because she doesn't live there and didn't serve in the IDF.

Understanding the Continuums

These two continuums offer multiple different ways of describing the features of a personal connection to Israel. A teacher may be insider-collective, feeling both personally situated "inside" the life of Israel and connected to Israelis and the Jewish people. Teachers may be insider-self, feeling a personal sense of being inside the "intimate discourse" of Israelis (see Schuster, this volume), and have a strong sense of themselves as Jews because of that connection. Teachers may also be outsider-collective, situating themselves "outside" of Israeli life and simultaneously committed to the greater Jewish collective. Or a teacher may be outsider-self, self-identifying as an "outsider" to Israel even as they attempt to foster their own personal connections to it as an expression of their Jewishness. And, because the teacher might fall in any place along a continuum that doesn't function as a simple binary, a teacher may self-identify as both insider and outsider, committed to both individual and collective expressions of Judaism.

In mapping these four distinct features, I am certainly not the first to think about connections to Israel in terms of continua. The "Makom Matrix," a heuristic device, proposes prescriptive outcomes for Israel education experiences, aiming for learners to develop "high-res and connected" relationships with Israel, which are deeper and more nuanced than "low-res and disconnected" ones (Sinclair, 2003, 2009, 2013).[12] Other scholars have offered potential correctives to Sinclair's matrix (e.g., Applebaum et al., 2020; see also Golden and Kadden in this volume), but the ideas that more or less "connection" and more or less "knowledge" are essential ways of mapping the learning process have remained.

This typology of the Insider–Outsider and Jewish Collective–Jewish Self Continuums is distinct from the Makom Matrix in three ways. First, it is descriptive rather than prescriptive. I provide a framework for neutrally analyzing or classifying connections to Israel, rather than prescribing what those connections should look like. Second, the focus here is on teachers, not learners. This typology assumes that knowledge of the self, of one's beliefs and identities, and the impact those have on them as Jews and as teachers, is essential to being a good teacher. And finally, as will be illustrated, this typology provides a framework for examining pedagogic choices and challenges that teachers face when planning for and during teaching.

How Teachers' Connections to Israel Enter Into the Classroom

In this section, I compare the informants' personal connections to Israel and their beliefs about Israel education, as described earlier, to how they express their connections with Israel *in their teaching*. In order to make such comparisons, I once again draw upon research on teachers' identity and beliefs and how these inform teachers' practice.[13] Teachers' identity and beliefs inform each step of the teaching process, including how teachers navigate and interpret curriculum, select what and how they plan to teach, make decisions in the classroom, and interact with students. Through an examination of cases, I demonstrate that there are differences in the ways teachers present themselves in the classroom and explore the factors that lead to those differences.

The cases will illustrate three different ways in which teacher connections to Israel enter into the classroom. Miriam is very clear about her connection with Israel and is able to enact that connection in her teaching. Alternatively, while Ashley is also very clear about her connection with Israel, she is not able to represent her connection in the classroom. And finally, Yael, while not personally clear about her connection with Israel, enacts a version of a connection with Israel for her students when they are together in the classroom.

Miriam: The Case of a Teacher Whose Connection to Israel Permeates the Class Atmosphere

Miriam reveals both her Jewish self and insider connections with Israel to her students. She wants her students to "join in [her] excitement for wanting to know Israel" and to develop connections to Israel that are similarly very personal. She imagines these connections evolving over time. She describes it like a parental relationship: one's relationship with Israel should transform as one matures and learns more about it and about oneself.

As a teacher at Beit Am, Miriam is expected to create memorable learning experiences for her students that will build their connections to Israel; she is given the autonomy to make her own educational decisions about how to accomplish that. A veteran teacher, the latitude given her enables Miriam to create a classroom culture in which her deeply personal love for Israel and her self-understanding as an insider permeates the classroom atmosphere. Her self-understanding informs the content she teaches and the way she teaches it. When describing Jerusalem to her students, Miriam talks about it as if it is hers:

> So just to show you, in the Jerusalem section, they're very proud of their new silver train that goes through town, and this is what it looks like.... You get to see the old city with all of the stone and then all of a sudden, this bright, shiny, silver train. My very least favorite, but if you live there, I can understand why you would want it, it makes getting around a lot easier. So, I get it, but... I still like my stone city.

She is frank and outspoken when she talks about her connections to Israel. She tells stories of her experiences there, such as bemoaning the changes in Jerusalem, "my stone city." Miriam's connections to Israel as encapsulated by both the Jewish self and insider are clearly visible in her teaching.

Ashley: The Case of a Teacher Who Is Bound to the Lesson

Ashley describes herself as one connected to the Jewish collective and an almost-insider, but it is hard to see that enacted in her teaching because of her inexperience as a teacher. A novice, she does not yet have the experience or skills to identify worthwhile opportunities to veer off the lesson-plan script, and she forgoes chances of revealing her own beliefs about Israel that would enrich the students' learning.

All teachers at Temple Israel are provided with a sequenced, semi-scripted curriculum that was developed by the director of education. Teachers are expected to follow the guidelines provided in the curriculum for how and what to teach. The lesson that I observe Ashley prepare and teach is entitled "Israeli Street Party" and aims to explore the diversity of the Jewish people and of Israel. It is squarely situated in the complexify approach, with its focus on the Jewish collective.

As I observe Ashley prepare her lesson, I notice that she embodies a connection to Israel that is firmly at the Jewish-collective end of the continuum. In her framing of the content of her lesson, Ashley explains that she wants the students to "understand who's in Israel and what brought them there and different reasons why people go and pick up their whole lives from whatever life they were living before." But she does not fully represent that in a personal way during the lesson, though she has her own personal story of immigrating there. The students know that Ashley used to live in Israel, but when one asks Ashley about her decision to make *aliyah*, Ashley pushes off the question. Later, Ashley explains that she wanted to "keep on track. They had their momentum going with [the lesson] and I think it would have distracted them from completing the activity."

Ashley envisions herself as a "representative" of Israel for her students, and she wants them to see her as an insider. But she does not share her self-identity as an Israeli American and holds back on sharing personal stories with the students. It would have been entirely appropriate to share her own immigration story during this lesson and probably would have enriched the students' learning. So, while the curricular content of the lesson aligns with her connection to Israel and her own experience of it, Ashley's inexperience as a teacher prevents her from having the pedagogic skills to navigate between sticking to a scripted lesson and finding moments in which there is educative value in making space to improvise. Ashley's connections to Israel, while clear for her, are not visible to the students in the classroom.

Yael: The Case of a Teacher Who Is a Symbolic Exemplar

Yael sits in the middle of both continuums. She speaks about being part of the Jewish collective and also expresses an identity aligned with the Jewish self. She is both an insider and an outsider. But as a teacher, Yael presents as someone with a strong identity that exemplifies a commitment to the Jewish collective and being an insider. Yael shares these aspects of her personal connection to and experiences with Israel in symbolic ways.

Yael exemplifies her Jewish collective connection with Israel by creating an opportunity for her students to meet over the phone an Israeli family member who was an active player in the 1991 Operation Solomon, a significant moment in Israeli and Jewish collective history when over 14,000 Jewish Ethiopians were rescued and covertly flown to Israel. She demonstrates insider standing through expressions of her connection to Israel and Israelis, like speaking with this family member in fluent, Israeli-accented Hebrew, translating his words back into English for the students, and being able to draw a freehand map of the Middle East.

Despite her internal struggles with her connection to Israel, Yael presents a strong Jewish collective and insider identity to her students. They see and hear her deep familiarity with the land, the country, the Hebrew language, her family, and Jews around the world.

We see from these three cases of teaching that the informants do take their own identity and beliefs about Israel into account while teaching. Their beliefs inform their planning and design of lessons and the choices they make in the classroom. At times those connections are revealed to their students, and at times they are not. Factors that either enhance or hinder the teachers' choice to share their personal connections with the students include the curriculum, the pedagogic skills of the teacher, and the teachers' personal clarity or confusion about their connection to Israel. In light of these three factors as influences on teachers' ability to share themselves with their students, it becomes clear that sometimes the type of connection shared with the students aligns with a teacher's personal conceptualization of said connection—as in the cases of Miriam and Ashley—and sometimes the connection shared with the students is different than the teacher's personal conceptualization—as in the case of Yael.

Ultimately, an understanding of how teachers make decisions and then comport themselves in the classroom is valuable for considering the impact it may have on the students' learning.

Theoretical and Practical Implications for the Field of Israel Education

The findings of this study provide new lenses through which the field of Israel education may continue to develop. They have theoretical and practical implications. In this final section, I explore how this study suggests a reconsideration of how Israel education's aims and goals are articulated. Additionally, the findings offer new ways for thinking about how institutions could approach the selection of Israel educators and about the professional development of Israel educators.

Aims and Goals of Israel Education

This study has implications for Israel education's aims and goals, and for the efforts to further articulate them. The two common approaches to Israel education, the Relational Approach and the Complexify Approach, agree that Israel education should ultimately inspire a connection with Israel, but both schools of thought are imprecise about how exactly that connection is meant to be conceptualized or described. This typology of connections with Israel offers vocabulary and framing about the various ways that teachers, and often by extension their students, conceptualize connection.

Although I have used these continuums descriptively, some may choose to apply the typologies of connections to Israel in a prescriptive way. Specific Jewish educational settings, such as day schools or congregational supplementary schools, which have unique cultures and educational visions, may use the typology to pinpoint ideal types of connections they would seek to nurture in their communities and students. Such a clarification of goals could then lead to the refinement and selection of curricular materials and design of education programs that would align with those goals.

Teacher Selection

Jewish educational settings that have clear visions of the types of connections and relationships with Israel they seek to nurture in their students would benefit from hiring Israel educators who align with those visions. Educational leaders could design selection processes in which prospective teachers are invited to reflect upon how they describe their connections with Israel, how they articulate goals for Israel education, and how those goals would be enacted. If, as the data shows, when unimpeded by limiting factors, teachers can reveal their own connections with Israel to their students, it would make sense to employ Israel educators whose connections with Israel align with the ideology and educational aims of the institution, as is evident in the cases of Miriam and Ashley.

Professional Development of Israel Educators

The findings of this study suggest the continuing need for, and a particular direction for, professional development for Israel educators.[14] Drawing from similar recommendations (Dorph, 2010; Kopelowitz & Wolf, 2013), this study suggests a professional-development strategy that enables a close examination of teachers' own connections to Israel, exploration of the questions they ask themselves in planning to teach and during interactions with students in the classroom, as well as an investigation of challenges they face in teaching about Israel. All of these strategies provide fruitful matter for inquiry and growth as teachers. For example, since teacher identity and beliefs inform how they navigate curriculum, Israel educators who can consider their personal beliefs about Israel as a precursor to their interpretation and implementation of curricular materials will be more successful in their teaching (Ben-Peretz, 1990, 1995; Brady, 2014; Dorph, 2010). The case of Ashley, an inexperienced teacher who feels bound by the lesson plan and does not know how to effectively navigate away from it when teachable moments arise, provides an example of a teacher who could benefit from such a model of professional development. There is a need for professional development that addresses the development of teaching skills, enables teachers to refine their visions for Israel education, and increases knowledge and awareness of their teacher identity and its impact on student learning.

Conclusion

The process of creating this study began with a critical moment in my own teaching. While facilitating a professional-development workshop for supplementary-school Israel educators, an American-born teacher bravely explained to the mixed group of Americans and Israelis that she found "it really hard to teach about Israel" because she was "ambivalent" about her relationship with Israel. Palmer (1998) suggests that teachers need to teach who they are. In the context of Israel education, teaching who you are means two things: 1) knowing how you connect with Israel, and your experiences of Israel itself, and 2) knowing what you believe about the purposes of Israel education. Yet, "knowing who you are" is not yet enough. There are educational constraints that can inhibit teachers' ability to bring themselves into the classroom (as with Ashley). This examination of teaching cases identified ways in which teachers share their connections to Israel with their students and featured factors that enabled or prevented them from doing so. Ultimately, an awareness of how teachers' identity and beliefs impact teaching practice is a valuable piece of the puzzle in Israel education.

NOTES

1. Both synagogue names are pseudonyms.

2. All names used in this article are pseudonyms.

3. "Relational approach" is a term coined by Chazan (2016). "Complexify approach" is my term. The literature refers to an approach which proposes that Israel education addresses the complexities of life in Israel and the relationship between Israel and American Jews as the "complexity hypothesis" (Sinclair et al., 2013).

4. The primary proponent of this approach is Chazan (2016). The iCenter (https://theicenter.org/) and its founding CEO, Anne Lanski, sit squarely within this school of thought, as do Katzew (2007) and Raviv (2015).

5. Emphasis in the original.

6. Proponents of this approach include Alexander (2015), Backenroth & Sinclair (2014, 2015), Eisen and Rosenak (1997), Grant (2008), Grant & Kopelowitz (2012), Gringras (2006), Sinclair (2003, 2009, 2013), and Zakai (2015a).

7. Chazan (2016), Grant & Kopelowitz (2012), Sinclair (2013), The iCenter (2015).

8. The limited scope of this study raises questions about further refining the definitions of each connection type. I cannot claim the informants are representative of the full set of experiences or conceptualizations of these types of connections. Questions remain about what would emerge from further study that would expand or clarify the definitions.

9. Though conventionally and historically, the concept of connection to a greater Jewish People has been called Jewish Peoplehood, only once did one informant use this term.

10. As a "child of Israel," Ashley signals that as a child she saw herself as a member of the greater Jewish community, the people of Israel.

11. This is the only time the word "peoplehood" is articulated by the informants.

12. While published by Sinclair, the Makom Matrix resulted from the collaborative work of Alex Sinclair, Robbie Gringras, and Esti Moskowitz-Kalman, as noted in Sinclair (2009).

13. Ball (1996), Ben-Peretz (1990, 1995), Brady (2014), Dorph (2010), Grossman (1990), Holtz (2003, 2009), Kansteiner (2002), Kiel et al. (2016), Lortie (1975), Palmer (1998), Sexton (2008), and Thorne (2000) each offer support for this notion.

14. Applebaum (2016), Kopelowitz (2013), Kopelowitz & Wolf (2013), Sinclair et al. (2013), and Zakai (2014) also speak to the continuing need for professional development of Israel educators.

REFERENCES

Alexander, H. (2015). Mature Zionism: Education and the scholarly study of Israel. *Journal of Jewish Education*, 81(2), 136–161. https://doi.org/10.1080/15244113.2015.1035979

Applebaum, L. (2016). *"When you change me, you change what I do": Challenges and possibilities in transformative learning for teachers* [Doctoral dissertation, Jewish Theological Seminary]. ProQuest Dissertations Publishing. https://www.proquest.com/openview/d55c50d982a0fcd5fc44317afaa6cc92/1?pq-origsite=gscholar&cbl=18750

Applebaum, L., Hartman, A., & Zakai, S. (2020). A little bit more far than Mexico: How 3- and 4-year-old Jewish children understand Israel. *Journal of Jewish Education*, 87(1), 4–34. https://doi.org/10.1080/15244113.2020.1834890

Backenroth, O., & Sinclair, A. (2014). Vision, curriculum, and pedagogical content knowledge in the preparation of Israel educators. *Journal of Jewish Education*, 80(2), 121–147. https://doi.org/10.1080/15244113.2014.907013

Backenroth, O., & Sinclair, A. (2015). Lights, camera, action research!—Moviemaking as a pedagogy for constructivist Israel education. *Journal of Jewish Education*, 81(1), 64–84. https://doi.org/10.1080/15244113.2015.1003480

Ball, D. L. (1996). Teacher learning and the mathematics reforms: What we think we know and what we need to learn. *Phi Delta Kappan*, 77(7), 500–508.

Ben-Peretz, M. (1990). *The teacher curriculum encounter: Freeing teachers from the tyranny of texts*. State University of New York Press.

Ben-Peretz, M. (1995). *Learning from experience: Memory and the teacher's account of teaching*. State University of New York Press.

Brady, K. (2014). Toward a fresh understanding of the relationship between teacher beliefs about mathematics and their classroom practices. In J. Anderson, M. Cavanagh, & A. Prescott (Eds.), *Curriculum in focus: Research guided practice (proceedings of the 37th Annual conference of the Mathematics Education Research Group of Australasia)* (pp. 103–110). MERGA.

Buber, M. (1958). *I and thou*. Scribner.

Chazan, B. (1984). Israel in American Jewish schools in the mid-70's. *Jewish Education*, 52(4), 9–12. https://doi.org/10.1080/0021642840520404

Chazan, B. (2016). *A philosophy of Israel education: A relational approach*. Palgrave Macmillan.

Chazan, B., & Bryfman, D. (2015). Israel as a cornerstone of Jewish identities. In *The aleph bet of Israel education* (2nd ed., pp. 17–27). The iCenter for Israel Education.

Clandinin, J. D., & Connelly, M. F. (1986). *On narrative method, niography and narrative unities in the study of teaching*. Calgary University, Ontario Institute for Studies in Education.

Clark, C. M., & Robert J. Yinger. (1987). Teacher planning. In J. Calderhead (Ed.), *Exploring teachers' thinking* (pp. 84–103). Cassell Education.

Dorph, G. Z. (2010). Investigating prospective Jewish teachers' knowledge and beliefs about Torah: Implications for teacher education. *Religious Education, 105*(1), 63–85. https://doi.org/10.1080/00344080903472733

Eisen, A., & Rosenak, M. (1997). Teaching Israel: Basic issues and philosophical guidelines. In *Israel in our lives* (pp. 1–39). http://www.bjpa.org/Publications/details.cfm?PublicationID=6090

Goodson, I. (2008). *Investigating the teacher's life and work* (Vol. 1). Sense Publishers.

Grant, L. (2008, May 28). *A vision for Israel education* [Paper presentation]. The Network for Research in Jewish Education Conference, Jerusalem, Israel. http://www.bjpa.org/Publications/details.cfm?PublicationID=20968

Grant, L., & Kopelowitz, E. (2012). *Israel education matters: A 21st century paradigm for Jewish education*. Center for Jewish Peoplehood Education.

Gringras, R. (2006). *Wrestling and hugging: Alternative paradigms for the Diaspora-Israel relationship*. Jewish Agency for Israel (JAFI), Makom: Renewing Israel Engagement. Retrieved from http://makomisrael.org/wp-content/uploads/2011/11/MAKOMWrestlingandHugging.pdf

Grossman, P. (1990). *The making of a teacher: Teacher knowledge and teacher education*. Teachers College Press.

Holtz, B. (2003). *Textual knowledge: Teaching the Bible in theory and practice*. Jewish Theological Seminary of America.

Holtz, B. (2009). Making choices: Teachers' beliefs and teachers' reasons. *Journal of Jewish Education, 75*(3), 304–309. https://doi.org/10.1080/15244110903079292

Horowitz, B. (2012). *Defining Israel education*. The iCenter for Israel Education. https://www.bjpa.org/bjpa/search-results?search=Defining+Israel+education

The iCenter for Israel Education. (2015). *The aleph bet of Israel education* (2nd ed.). The iCenter.

Kansteiner, W. (2002). Finding meaning in memory: A methodological critique of collective memory studies. *History and Theory, 41*(2), 179–197. http://jstor.org/stable/3590762

Katzew, J. (2007). Is there part of me in the East? *CCAR Journal, 54*(2), 52–68.

Kiel, E., Lerche, T., Kollmannsberger, M., Oubaid, V., & Weiss, S. (2016). The pedagogic signature of the teaching profession. *Journal of Education and Learning, 5*(4), 201–220. http://dx.doi.org/10.5539/jel.v5n4p201

Kopelowitz, E. (2013). *Nurturing master Israel educators*. The iCenter. http://www.bjpa.org/Publications/details.cfm?PublicationID=21099

Kopelowitz, E., & Wolf, M. (2013). *Israel education in practice: Growth of the field from the educator's perspective*. The iCenter. http://www.bjpa.org/Publications/details.cfm?PublicationID=21098

Lortie, D. C. (1975). *School-teacher: A sociological study*. University of Chicago Press.

Palmer, P. (1998). *The courage to teach* (1st ed.). Jossey-Bass.

Punch, K. (2009). *Introduction of research methods in education*. Sage.

Raviv, Z. (2015). Eretz, medina, am yisrael: Navigating multiple landscapes. In *The aleph bet of Israel education* (2nd ed., pp. 41–48). The iCenter for Israel Education.

Salinas, C., & Blevins, B. (2013). Examining the intellectual biography of pre-service teachers: Elements of "critical" teacher knowledge. *Teacher Education Quarterly*, 40(1), 7–24. https://www.jstor.org/stable/23479660

Sexton, D. M. (2008). Student teachers negotiating identity, role, and agency. *Teacher Education Quarterly*, 35(3), 73–88. https://www.jstor.org/stable/23478982

Sinclair, A. (2003). Beyond black and white: teaching Israel in light of the matzav. *Conservative Judaism*, 55(4), 69–80.

Sinclair, A. (2009). A new heuristic device for the analysis of Israel education: Observations from a Jewish summer camp. *Journal of Jewish Education*, 75(1), 79–106. http://doi.org/DOI: 10.1080/15244110802654575

Sinclair, A. (2013). *Loving the real Israel: An educational agenda for liberal Zionism*. Ben Yehuda Press.

Sinclair, A., Solmsen, B., & Goldwater, C. (2013). *The Israel educator: An inquiry into the preparation and capacities of effective Israel educators*. The Consortium for Applied Studies in Jewish Education. http://www.casje.org/sites/default/files/docs/the-israel-educator.pdf

Shulman, L. (1986). Those who understand: Knowledge growth in teaching. *Educational Researcher*, 15(2), 4–14. https://doi.org/10.3102/0013189X015002004

Thorne, A. (2000). Personal memory telling and personality development. *Personality and Social Psychology Review*, 4(1), 45–56. http://people.ucsc.edu/~avril/PDFs/Pdf.5.pdf

Wilson, S. M., Shulman, L. S., & Richert, A. E. (1987). "150 different ways" of knowing: Representations of knowledge in teaching. In J. Calderhead (Ed.), *Exploring teachers' thinking* (pp. 104–124). Cassell Education.

Yoffie, E. (2015, November 6). *Israel panel: Jodi Kantor, Stav Shaffir, Ari Shavit and Rabbi Eric Yoffie – URJ Biennial 2015* [Video]. Youtube. https://www.youtube.com/watch?v=duOVyCtj_zs

Zakai, S. (2014). "My heart is in the East and I am in the West": Enduring questions of Israel education in North America. *Journal of Jewish Education*, 80(3), 287–318. https://doi.org/10.1080/15244113.2014.937192

Zakai, S. (2015a). "Israel is meant for me": Kindergarteners' conceptions of Israel. *Journal of Jewish Education*, 81(1), 4–34. http://doi.org/10.1080/15244113.2015.1007019

Zakai, S. (2015b, December 2). *Miles from where I live and near to my heart* [Presentation]. The iCenter iCamp, Las Vegas, NV.

Zakai, S. (2021). "It makes me feel many different things": A child's relationship to Israel over time. *Journal of Jewish Education*, 87(2), 120–143. https://doi.org/10.1080/15244113.2021.1926375

Zakai, S. (2022). *My second favorite country: How American Jewish children think about Israel*. NYU Press.

12
Nurturing Jewish Consciousness
Utilizing Values at Synagogue Supplementary Schools to Teach Israel

EZRA KOPELOWITZ and ABBY PITKOWSKY

Jason, a director of a Conservative synagogue supplementary school, wants his students to see Israel as important to them. He explains,

> I've moved away from the outcome about how my learners feel about certain topics and issues and think more about the extent to which that matters to them at all. I am less concerned about their stance on a certain topic or issue and more concerned that the topic itself has some importance to them.

Jason participated in the Qushiyot Fellowship, a professional-development program in the New York area that seeks to enable synagogue educators to grapple with what the program's sponsors and participants view as two major barriers to Israel attachment: 1) apathy or indifference towards Israel and 2) the heightened politicization and contentiousness that teaching Israel can trigger in their synagogue communities. The other synagogue educators in the fellowship share Jason's goal; they, too, want to strengthen their students' personal sense of connection to Israel.

The organizers of the Qushiyot program and the synagogue educators who participated in it frame their focus on connection in response to a steady stream of survey data showing that younger American Jews have a weaker sense of attachment than previous generations (Cohen & Kelman, 2007; Cohen & Kelman, 2010; Wertheimer, 2022).[1] A recent example is found in the 2020 Pew Study, which shows that American Jews 18 to 29 years of age express less attachment and greater criticism of Israel in comparison to older generations. The study shows just 24% feeling "very attached" to Israel, while 51% feel "not so attached, or not attached at all." The study found that 35% state that Israel is an "essential part of what being Jewish means to them," compared to those who state Israel is "important, but not essential" (37%) or "not important" (27%; Pew Research Center, 2021, pp. 137–149). Despite the fact that other researchers have suggested that the assumption that younger generations of Jews have a weaker connection to Israel than previous generations should be viewed in a more nuanced fashion,[2] the synagogue educators whose work is at the heart of this chapter fear that their students, and young American Jews in general, are less likely than their parents' and grandparents' generations to view Israel as a special place for the Jewish people, a "homeland," or identify with the idea of the need for an independent Jewish state as relevant to their personal sense of Jewishness.

The work of these educators, whom we have studied extensively, frames Israel education as a direct response to fears of waning attachment (Horowitz, 2012). The teachers' claim that "Israel should be regarded as a special place for Jews" and that individual students "should feel a strong positive and personal connection to Israel" informs the teaching strategies they develop during the Qushiyot Fellowship. These teaching strategies are in turn a case study not only of Israel education, but education for Jewish collective identification. The teachers are in practice promoting a "Jewish sensibility" (Moore & Woocher, 2019) in which students come to view the world—and Israel as an authentic part of it—as Jews. We argue that particular institutional conditions—paramount among them a collective focus on shared Jewish values—are needed for teachers to successfully promote Jewish collective identification, which includes the nurturing of a positive sense of connection to Israel among their students.

The Qushiyot Fellowship

This article draws on four years of evaluation research for the Qushiyot Israel Education Fellowship (Kopelowitz, 2020). Participants included 78 educators at 56 Conservative, Reconstructionist, and Reform congregations in the Greater New York area, including 24 teachers and 54 synagogue school directors, in six annual cohorts from 2016 through 2020 (see Appendix for participating synagogues). The fellowship was run by The Jewish Education Project and Makom: The Jewish Agency Education Lab and sponsored by the UJA (United Jewish Appeal) Federation of New York.[3]

The goal of the Qushiyot Fellowship was to grow the number of synagogue educators in the Greater New York region who have both the confidence and skills to nurture their students' connection to Israel alongside the willingness and ability to tackle social and political complexity that is increasingly a contentious topic in many synagogues. Each annual cohort participated in two local seminars or workshops and an eight-day seminar in Israel. Each participant also facilitated at least two teaching modules for their schools and received mentoring support. Many fellows continue to participate in ongoing meetings organized through an alumni network.

This chapter does not provide an evaluation of the Qushiyot Fellowship. Rather, we draw on survey data and interview notes from the evaluation, as well as additional interviews, to explore how the Qushiyot educators frame and teach Israel at their schools.

Methodology

Our investigation of the Qushiyot Fellowship included online surveys conducted at the start, mid-point, and end of each cohort, as well as an alumni survey conducted with all Qushiyot graduates in July 2020. The surveys included a mix of closed (quantitative) and open (qualitative) questions. Alongside the surveys, three rounds of semi-structured in-depth interviews were conducted with a total of 31 participants in 2018, 2019, and 2020. In addition, a focus group consisting of four of the educators interviewed in 2020 was conducted in May 2021 for this article. When taken together, these multiple data points provide a robust picture of the types of pedagogical strategies, as well as the educational philosophies that undergird those strategies, employed by synagogue supplementary-school educators committed to fostering their students' connections to Israel.

Synagogue Supplementary Schools

Synagogue schools are the educational institution that reaches the greatest number of American Jewish children and teens in the United States. American Jews ask their synagogues to fulfill more vital functions than any other communal agency, serving ritual, social, and educational needs. The local synagogue provides Jewish education to everyone from early childhood to adults, providing classrooms, teachers, and curriculum for school-age children in the community who come to learn Hebrew and Judaica in the years before, and sometimes after, their Bar or Bat Mitzvah (Reimer, 1997, p. 1; Wertheimer, 2009a).

A 2008 census estimated that there were at that time between 2000 and 2100 supplementary synagogue schools in the United States, reaching 230,000 students in Grades 1 through 12 (Wertheimer, 2008, p. 3). A normative practice at these schools, alongside providing positive Jewish experiences and teaching a modicum of Hebrew and other Judaic skills, is to foster attachment to Israel and the Jewish people (Wertheimer, 2009b, p. 347). Yet despite the prevalence of nurturing a connection to Israel at the level of the vision and mission, few American synagogues have a well-defined educational strategy of what to teach, how to teach, and, most importantly, why to teach Israel to American Jews (Ackerman, 1996; Chazan, 1979; Grant, 2007, p. 3)

In these synagogues, the connection to Israel is present in multiple ways, including displays that can be found in the physical environment (such as art, maps, flags, and the presence of modern Hebrew on art, posters, advertisements, newspapers, and as labels for items in the classroom). They also hold ceremonies that take place over the course of the year for Israel's Independence Day, Israel's Memorial Day, and other Israel-focused events. These schools also welcome Israeli emissaries who teach the students, participate in twinning programs in which students have direct connection with their counterparts in Israel, and even go on educational trips to Israel. The synagogues also provide parents opportunities to learn about Israel by organizing adult educational programming and rabbinic sermons about Israel (Grant & Kopelowitz, 2012, pp. 29–36). And while many of the synagogues in the Qushiyot Fellowship also offer these robust

Israel-related programs, our chapter focuses exclusively on the formal teaching of Israel within a synagogue school's curriculum.

Teaching for a Personal Connection

The synagogue educators who participated in the Qushiyot Fellowship provide a case study for how synagogue schools seek to teach Israel. Of note is that none of the synagogue educators in this study predicated their success on their students learning a given body of knowledge, replete with tests and grades. While acquisition of knowledge may be an ancillary goal, their primary purpose is to foster a personal connection between the learner and Israel. The teachers want their students to view Israel as a special country for Jews, a Jewish homeland, a place that they want to learn about, visit, and even seek out by forming personal connections to Israelis.

In the survey taken at the start of the program, 81% of the fellows answered that being better able to help their students develop a positive relationship to Israel was a goal of their participation "to a great extent," with an additional 9% answering "to an extent" (see Figure 12.1). The following three responses provide representative examples of how, in the start of the program survey, the majority of teachers presented their goals for teaching Israel at their synagogue schools.

> I want my students to develop some sense of connection to Israel. I want them to understand how and why modern Israel came into being, to understand the complexity of the Palestinian–Israeli conflict, and the importance of Israel's existence.

> I would like for our 6th-grade students, in particular, to feel that they have had a meaningful experience learning about Israel and want to know more. I would also like to see Israel infused in other grade levels as well.

> I would like to have all classes at all levels feel a connection with Israel, through class material covered and/or connecting with Israeli students of similar ages.

In laying out their goals, the teachers were in fact grouping diverse pedagogical strategies and educational goals that can include different ideological understandings of the relationship of Jews to Israel (Isaacs, 2011; Winer, 2019). Yet, underlying their differences is a common interest for classroom learning to "make Israel relevant to their students' lives," establishing the importance of Israel for Jews.

From this perspective, teaching Israel in synagogue schools is similar to teaching Israel in experiential educational institutions, such as summer camps and youth movements (Aharon & Pomson, 2018; Benor et al., 2020; Sales & Saxe, 2003). Synagogue schools do include classroom teaching and also often teach a particular curriculum. However, the focus is not on

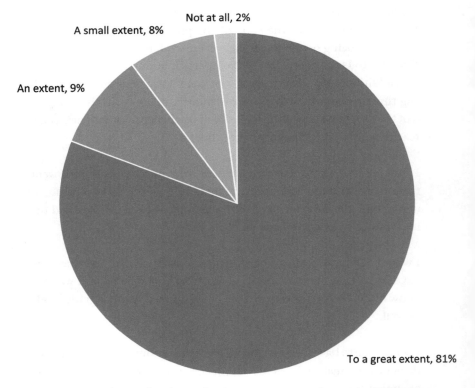

FIGURE 12.1. Qushiyot Fellowship teachers' survey responses to the question "To what extent is helping your students develop a positive relationship to Israel a goal of your participation?"

acquiring knowledge on which students are then tested. What students know is situated as secondary to how they feel. The primary goal is to nurture the feeling of connection to Israel (Grant & Kopelowitz, 2012, pp. 14–21).

The commitment to fostering young Jews' connection to Israel extends far beyond the synagogue-school context. Pomson et al. (2009) show that Jewish day schools also have a similar emphasis on experiential education with the goal that their students develop a strong positive connection to Israel. However, at the day school there is also a normative expectation of formal in-class instruction for the purpose of knowledge acquisition, which in practice is often neglected. Pomson et al. (2009) view the resulting situation as problematic.

> The materials that schools use in the classroom also tend to be heavily skewed towards what we call an "experiential" rather than a "cognitive" perspective.... Of course, in and of itself, a preference for informal/experiential education is not necessarily problematic. Our concern is with the skewing of practice towards informal education in a setting whose raison d'être was, historically at least, the provision of formal education. It leads us to wonder whether in the field of Israel education we are witnessing what Isa Aron (following Christian educator, John Westerhoff) once called a paradigm of "enculturation" rather than one of "instruction." (pp. 11–12)

From the perspective of the synagogue educator in the Qushiyot Fellowship, the tension between "instruction" vs. "enculturation" pointed out by Pomson et al., while present, is decided clearly in favor of enculturation, as there is no expectation or desire to test and grade students based on knowledge learned.

The Common Denominator: The Self in the Context of the Group

Synagogue educators' unmitigated commitment to enculturation offers a challenge to existing paradigms in Israel education. In discussing the goals of contemporary Israel education, Laura Novak Winer (2019, see also this volume) shows two developing, and often overlapping, schools of thought.

The "relational approach" focuses in on the Jewish self and the formation of individuals' Jewish identity as they develop their personal relationship to Israel. The "complexify approach" focuses on the Jewish collective and on the formation of bonds between Jews in America and Israel, with the individual developing their understanding of the breadth and depth of Israeli society and the implications for the connection to Israel.

Winer sees a tension between the "relational" and "complexify" approaches, with the former focused on the individual and the latter on collective educational goals. Other researchers also point to a tension between personal and collective. On one hand, the individual student should be free to craft his or her personal relationship with Israel; on the other hand, educators perceive the relationship demanding positive adherence to core collective values, referred to colloquially as "a love of Israel." The result is to introduce conflicting educational messages which can lead to ambivalence on the part of the students (Pomson et al., 2009; Zakai, 2011).

Our understanding of the educational strategy pursued by the synagogue educators offers an alternative understanding of the relationship between individual and collective, one in which individuality develops *within* a collective context. The latter is necessary for the former. Individual identification with Israel and the ability of the student to grapple with nuance and the complexity of the Jewish relationship to Israel are both outcomes of a broader Jewish collective experience that the teachers are promoting. In this approach to Jewish education, individuals develop their personal sense of Jewish consciousness in a relationship with other Jews while grappling with shared issues and dilemmas. Students are challenged to think, view, and act within a social context in which Israel is integral. They make sense of the environment they find themselves in, react to one another and their teachers, and in the process develop their personal sense of Jewish self, their opinion about Israel-informed issues and dilemmas, and their overall relationship to Israel.

Focusing on Core Values

The educational strategy the fellowship encouraged was for the educators to focus on core concepts that evoke the values they want their students to consider and grapple with as they develop their personal connection to Israel as part of a collective connection to the Jewish people. Some of the educators came into the fellowship with a developed understanding of the values-informed concepts that inform their strategy for teaching Israel. They used the fellowship to further refine their approach. Other fellows developed their values-focused strategy during the fellowship.

Two concepts rose to the fore in their reflections on the values that undergird their work: 1) Israel as a Jewish "home"/"homeland" and 2) Israel as an expression of "Jewish peoplehood." These two concepts are each developed as a distinct pedagogical goal by the teachers and are often brought into a complementary relationship in which one supports the other.

Israel: Our Jewish Home

In the teachers' framing, Israel as a "Jewish home" is a personally meaningful place that students can share with others because they are Jewish. Yael, a senior administrator and teacher at a Conservative supplemental school, describes how she changed her approach to teaching Israel as a result of participating in the Qushiyot Fellowship in order to focus on the value of Israel as a Jewish home.

> What I taught about Israel this year was completely different than in past years. I previously focused on wars, this time I barely touched on them. I started with the idea of "homeland" and "land." The significance of these ideas as an emotional and cognitive anchor. For me it was a given that Israel is our homeland, but for my students it was not a given. My question is "Why should they care?" If they don't get the concept of "Why the land?" If they don't get that, nothing else we teach means anything. I felt they did get it. They all remembered from week to week our discussions from the previous week. Miracles of miracles. In a few sentences they would be able to recap the key point like "What is a home?"

The teachers emphasized three distinct elements of "Jewish home"

» 1. Home Is Familiar

The teachers want their students to feel a sense of familiarity with Israel. Jane, a synagogue assistant education director at a Reform supplemental school explained, "[I hope] my students will feel more connected to Israel when they feel it is more familiar to them." She had her fourth-grade teacher develop lessons that make aspects of Israel more familiar and concrete, highlighting the common ground between the United States and Israel. Based on Jane's mentoring, the teacher ultimately decided to have her students work with a partner class in Israel, in which they developed family trees and examined the similarities and differences between them. The students compared Israel's national anthem, "HaTikvah," to the American anthem, the "Star-Spangled Banner," discussing the common and disparate values. She also had students do projects on popular culture and high-tech innovation in Israel with the goal that they see Israel as a place to which they can connect through music, arts, and technology.

Michelle, the director of education at a Reform supplemental school, shared with us that her goal is to create "authentic connections" between her students and Israelis. She feels that if her students can connect with "real humans," they will see that Israel is a place that is not so distant, and this will result in a strengthening of their feelings of connection to Israel. To achieve that goal, Michelle's seventh graders are connected with a group of seventh graders at the Leo Baeck Education Center in Haifa, an affiliate of the Reform movement. They have a WhatsApp group and meet virtually in real time about once a month to explore the similarities between their Reform communities. As Jane, Michelle, and other educators strove to enculturate students into communal norms that situated Israel as a core aspect of Jewish life, they worked to frame Israel as a place both familiar and accessible.

» 2. Home Is About Relationships

In order to establish Israel as familiar and personally meaningful, the teachers situated relationships with Israelis as one core practice. They did so by setting up interactive experiences with Israelis through one of two methods: 1) educationally informed interactions with Israelis living in their own local community and 2) planned educational encounters with Israeli peers in Israel.

Donna, a director of education at a Reform supplemental school, has her third-grade students conduct interviews with synagogue members from a variety of personal backgrounds, including those who emigrated from Israel. The students then take their stories and write and perform plays for the parents and second graders. Donna reported that the process of interviewing, writing, and performing broadened the students' consciousness of what it means to be part of a people, including the exposure to and familiarity with Israel through the life stories of the congregants.

Jason, from his similar perch at a Conservative supplemental school, developed a series of virtual encounters between his synagogue's teens and Israeli teens. He aimed to foster personal connections through person-to-person conversations as teens explored shared and differing experiences, such as stress regarding upcoming army service and college acceptances. In May 2021 during the Gaza conflict (*Shomer HaHomot*), the teens compared attacks respectively on Israelis (airstrikes) and American Jews (by way of social media).

In many of the synagogues, the educators are also working alongside young adult Israelis (called *shinshinim*) who fulfill a national-service year after high school by working in Diaspora communities. Among their responsibilities is to create social relationships with children and teens at the synagogues. The educators situate the relationships that the *shinshinim* cultivate with their students as an integral part of their teaching Israel.

» 3. Home Is Safe

In addition to establishing familiarity and connections with Israel and Israelis, the teachers also want to convey that "home is a place where you feel safe." Jane reports that an overriding message in her teaching on Israel is that "Israel is a place where you *feel safe*, and you'll always come back." Jason designed an educational program for students and their families at his synagogue to learn about Israel, including a focus on how Israel protects its citizens from physical and existential threats. Families explored how Israel addresses several major challenges, including the existential military threat to Israel and the country's approach to nuclear arms. By explicitly conveying the message that Israel is a safe haven for Jews, educators like Jane and Jason attempt to foster a sense of connection to Israel.

Peoplehood Equals Jewish Diversity

While establishing familiarity with Israel, many of the teachers also seek to enable their students to grapple with the complexity of Israeli society. For example, Anne, the director of education at a Conservative supplemental school, wants her students to see that Israel belongs to them because they are Jewish, and she *also* wants them to understand that their relationship to Israel is complicated, meaning that simple explanations regarding Israel are not accurate. In her words,

> We live in a world where Israel is glorified and criticized. I want my students to be able to articulate their thoughts and feelings. They should be able to defend Israel when it needs to be defended and critique when it needs to be critiqued. I realize some of the unconditional love is sacrificed when complexity is introduced because some things are not attractive. My goal is to curate the complexity.

Many of the teachers reference the value of "Jewish peoplehood" in order to emphasize that the relationships among Jews are complex. The Jewish people are connected to one another but are also diverse, and this can lead to conflict. Anne and Jason teach their students, third and fifth grade respectively, a range of perspectives among different Zionist thinkers and their visions for the modern state of Israel. The goal is for their students to appreciate that despite Zionist thinkers' differences and diverse opinions, they all recognized the centrality of creating a modern state. Anne's fifth graders also learn about diverse Jewish communities in Israel, mark Mizrahi Expulsion Day,[4] celebrate the Ethiopian-Jewish holiday of Sigd, and commemorate those who died coming to Israel from Ethiopia.

Donna's fifth graders learn about diverse Jewish cultural and political groups in Israel, with an emphasis on locating themselves within Israel's diversity. They do so by learning about a variety of Israeli personalities and their opinions, actions, and beliefs. Students share their reflections at a special fifth-grade Shabbat service for their families and the congregation. Later that same year, they continue the exploration of the Israeli Jewish social and political spectrum and locate themselves on it through a 10-session weekly unit about the Israeli government.

Not everything is political, and not all diversity is complex. The teens at Jason's school are charged with implementing learning experiences for younger grades (second and third grades). The teens' teaching explores both the commonalities and diversity of the Jewish experience in Israel. One educational experience the teens developed focused on the diversity of Israel through the metaphor of the array of food at an Israeli *shuk* (market). Teens prepared matzah balls and *jachnun* (a Yemenite baked good) to represent the wide range of ethnic backgrounds found in Israel.

From early primary grades, Michelle aims to cultivate a mindset that Israel is a complex country. She introduces the third and fourth grade to the diverse population groups: Jews, Arabs, Bedouins, Druze, and so on. To provide insight into Israeli diversity, she draws on an educational experience developed by Makom, an Israel education organization. The students view pictures of actual graffiti with the phrase *"Am Yisrael Chai,"* or "the people of Israel lives," painted on numerous walls around Tel Aviv. First, they explore and discuss what "the people of Israel" means. Does the phrase refer to all the Jews in the world, all Israeli citizens, or all Jews in Israel? Second, they view the rejoinders that have been added to the graffiti phrase, such as "…barely," "…with the money of America," "…in India," and "…by the sword." The students explore these additions or "graffiti conversations," consider the context and mindset of the graffiti artists, and are invited to share what they might add to the phrase *"Am Yisrael Chai."* In framing the learning this way, the educators emphasize *both* collective commitments *and* personal interpretation and meaning making.

Connecting the Personal to the Collective Through Values-Infused Education

The synagogue educators' emphasis on teaching for "a personal connection" to Israel is consistent with overall trends towards increasing personalization of Jewish identity in America (Cohen & Eisen, 2000; Wertheimer, 2018), which is in turn expressed in the relationship of Jews to

Israel (Sasson, 2014; Winer, 2019). Researchers and educators stress that considering the reasons a young person should regard Israel as personally relevant to them is more central to effective Israel education than a singular focus on modern Israeli history or knowledge about Israeli society (Grant & Kopelowitz, 2012). Translating this research to practice, a major national Israel education initiative, the iCenter for Israel Education, was founded in Chicago in 2008 for the express purpose of creating a relation-focused approach to teaching Israel in which the personal connection of American Jews to Israel is the focus.[5]

Integral to this shift is a desire on the part of the teachers for their students to grapple with the complexity of Israeli society. "Rather than teaching only myths about a beleaguered Jewish state surrounded by hostile enemies, educators and scholars have begun to suggest a more nuanced approach to Israel education that engages American Jewish students in conversations about the complex political and social realities of the Jewish state" (Zakai, 2011, p. 240; also see Grant, 2008; Grant & Kopelowitz, 2012; Sinclair, 2013). By introducing a curriculum of this nature, the educators hope to further inculcate a sense that Israel should be personally important to the learners.

The examples of teaching provided here evidence a pedagogical strategy that aspires for students to create a personal connection to Israel while simultaneously featuring Israel as a complex site. The strategy makes intentional use of values and concepts, including "home" and "peoplehood," which in turn rest on other values and concepts, such as centrality of "the biblical land of Israel" in Jewish tradition, the need Jews had and have for "security," the "diversity" of world Jewry, and the consequent need for "pluralism" as integral to the experience of Jews as an extended "family."

In each of the examples, teachers present students with a values-informed narrative that anchors the idea of Israel as "home" and an expression of "Jewish peoplehood." To participate in the educational experience, students need to think, view, and act within a social context in which Israel is integral to make sense of what is happening. The educational experience is infused with collectivity, and students are ideally encouraged to reflect on the experience and offer their personal interpretation and reaction in the context of the educational activity.

For example, when Donna's students interviewed synagogue members about their life stories and then wrote and performed a play based on the interviews, they were at once thinking, viewing, and acting out the value of "Jewish diversity," of which Israel is an authentic part. Donna explained:

> We begin with the assumption that our students don't have a "love for Israel" that comes naturally from their home experience. We need to nurture their connection through lived experiences. The best way is to step into the shoes of others—see the world through an Israeli's eye.

"The diversity of the Jewish people" provides a values-informed framework that runs throughout Donna's educational program. Donna calls her synagogue school's pedagogical approach "learning through doing." Students research, write, create, and tell stories with a focus on Jewish diversity. As they advance from grade to grade, students repeat the experience of exploring diversity in different ways. In the earlier grades, the focus is on Jewish diversity in their own community. In later grades, the focus shifts to Israel and to the students developing their personal story within the context of the broader Jewish people, including Israel. Hence, we saw Donna's fifth graders learning about diverse Jewish cultural and political groups in Israel, with an emphasis on locating themselves on Israel's sociopolitical spectrum. Here too they process the learning, sharing their reflections at a special fifth-grade Shabbat service for their families and the congregation.

A Condition for Success: A Broader Approach to Values Education

For the Qushiyot Fellows' emphasis on teaching for a personal connection to Israel to succeed, the act of teaching needs to occur in an educational environment that supports the goal. Some of the Qushiyot teachers describe their work taking place in sophisticated synagogue schools whose teaching of Israel plays out as part of a broader approach to values education in which values-informed concepts and themes infuse the educational experience. An example is given by Anne:

We have value themes that pull our curriculum together from early childhood through 12th grade. With a focus on Israel, the themes include areas such as "shared society," "moving from powerlessness to powerfulness," "what is it to be a Jewish nation," "creating a Jewish national and civic culture," and "claim to the land." Some of the Israel themes crosscut the rest of the program or are similar. So, for example, American Jewish history has similar themes: How do you create an American Jewish culture within a civic culture—to be separate, but a part at the same time. Throughout the whole curriculum there is an exploration of particularism vs. universalism. We want our students to grapple with the particular ways of being Jewish, but also that we are part of a larger society.

Anne, like Donna, is describing an educational environment in which her students grapple with a set of values-informed issues and dilemmas that connect their educational experience from grade to grade. Through repeated contact with the same values over time, she hopes that her students come to see themselves as part of the broader society through a Jewish lens.

We have found that a clear articulation of values-informed concepts is a crucial component of creating rich Israel educational experiences, a finding that is supported by prior research in Jewish education. In *Learning and Community: Jewish Supplementary Schools in the Twenty-First Century*, Jack Wertheimer (2009b) and his colleagues produced portraits of best practice at 10 innovative supplementary schools. All of the schools had a strong values vision and implementation plan for their core educational values.

To the extent that synagogue educators like Anne intentionally utilize a core set of values, they create a "consciousness" among students of collective belonging that transcends any one point in time (Ravid, 2014, p. 34). Jeff Kress (2012) describes the creation of holistic educational environments in which students develop Jewish cognitive schemas to understand their worlds. These Jewish cognitive schemas are anchored in a core set of educational values that a school utilizes for creating Jewish reference points in the lived environment of the school. The benefits of doing so, writes

Keren E. Fraiman and Dean P. Bell (2021), are that, over time, students are exposed to diverse narratives and understandings of common values and associated memories within which they can develop their personal understanding of their place in the world.

In his seminal work on synagogue education, Joseph Reimer (1997) advocates for a values-infused approach to education that stresses "collective self-definition." Tali Zelkowicz (2019) refers to the educational process of the type that Reimer describes as "identification formation process" or "identity work" (p. 158). Reimer explains:

> By working hard at defining a collective identity for this congregation, the rabbis have built upon the long history of this congregation and fashioned a Jewish message that is both clear and controversial.... Perhaps this clear sense of collective identity helps explain why I rarely encountered bored children or adults in the many educational contexts of this congregation that I observed. When there is a clear message that gives shape to the educational agenda, children and adults sense that message and respond to it. They are challenged. One can accept or reject it, but it is not so amorphous that it leaves one swimming in confusion and boredom. (Reimer, 1997, p. 185)

Developing Jewish Sensibility: Beyond Individual Versus the Group

The values-infused environments described by Kress (2012), Reimer (1997), and Wertheimer (2009b) are vital to students gaining a sense of collective Jewish consciousness, of which Israel is a part. In the ideal, synagogue educators enable their students to adopt what Moore and Woocher (2019) call a "Jewish sensibility." This is a Jewishly informed way of seeing and interacting with the world in which Israel is an authentic reference point within an educational environment in which students spends much of their childhood and teen years. The goal is to create an environment that is infused with values, such as "Israel as home" and an "expression of peoplehood," that inform their experience over time. The result is intended to create a sense of citizenship, or consciousness, in which Jewish reference points, including Israel, are simply part of the way students think, view, and act in social interactions with others. If successful, the student might arrive at any point of the political spectrum, take on a left- or right-wing opinion, but not be apathetic, as Israel is a meaningful place to them.

Israel education, as with Jewish education, succeeds when "being Jewish" informs individuals' consciousness of who they are as human beings. Jewish education is one part of a broader complex of experience, learning, and growth that informs individuals' understanding of themselves in the world (Chazan et al., 2017, p. 116; Horowitz, 2008, p. 77; Ravid, 2021). As such, individuality does not need to sit in conflict with collective identification, but rather is nurtured when individuals develop their personal sense of consciousness in a relationship with other Jews while grappling with collective values. From this educational perspective, individuality and collective Jewish life do not sit in tension with one another.

Creating a Values-Informed Educational Environment

Developing Jewish sensibility at an educational institution requires three elements:

1. Intentionality: An intentional approach to selecting value themes that serve as reference points for the students through their educational career.
2. Professional Awareness: The educators at the school are aware of those values.
3. Application: Educators give thought to their application through collaborative discussions and planning for the development of pedagogical strategies of the type described in the examples in this chapter.

The challenge is twofold: To bring individual teachers to adopt an intentional approach to utilizing values in their teaching, and to enable that teaching to integrate into a broader institution-wide strategy that utilizes the same Jewish values. The Qushiyot Fellowship focused on the individual teachers, and indeed, in the alumni survey, all reported intentionally integrating Jewish values related to Israel into their teaching, a practice which most had not previously pursued.

However, at the Qushiyot schools where there is not a school-wide strategy for values education, the teachers end up working alone. They might seek to infuse their teaching with Jewish values and nurture their students' personal connection to Israel and the Jewish people in a systematic way, but they do so without reference to a broader set of agreed-upon values that the students should encounter elsewhere in the synagogue school. Such a synagogue school is likely representative of the norm when teaching Israel in synagogue supplementary schools in the United States.

The challenge is evident when we look at the strategic planning that was conducted by fellows who were directors or associate directors. We learn that prior to the fellowship, just 10% of the schools had an organized strategy for teaching Israel (see Table 12.1). Since their participation, 30% report an organized strategy in place, and an additional 47% are conducting planning discussions in that direction, with an additional 17% planning on doing so.

Hence, we learn that the normative situation in these New York–area schools prior to the fellowship was that 90% of the schools had no organized strategy in place and no staff discussion for that purpose. Even after the end of the fellowship, the majority do not have a school-wide strategy in place. The takeaway is that a professional-development program for teaching Israel should not only encourage the intentional use of values for teaching Israel by individual teachers, but it must also work to ensure that those values, as selected by the school, are developed at a school-wide level.

TABLE 12.1. Developing an Organized Strategy

Response	%
No	5%
No, but we are intending to launch such a discussion.	17%
Yes, we have had such discussions but have not yet developed an organized strategy.	47%
Yes, there was a discussion and we have developed an organized strategy.	20%
We were already engaged in such a discussion and have an organized strategy.	10%

Survey response to the question: "Since your participation in Qushiyot has there been a discussion at your school with the goal of developing an organized strategy to further develop Israel education?" $N = 59$

Conclusion

In this chapter we provided examples of how teachers in synagogue supplementary schools, who completed a professional-development program for Israel education, teach Israel. We highlighted the fact that these educators do not emphasize knowledge acquisition and success as measured through testing and grades. Rather, they desire that their students acquire a "Jewish sensibility" in which they come to view the world as Jews, of which Israel is an authentic part. The values they evoked almost always included the concept of Israel as "home," meaning a familiar place to which one has personal connections and which provides a feeling of safety and security. Complementing the value of home is the value of "peoplehood" with an emphasis on Jewish diversity and the sociopolitical diversity that results.

Sophistication for teaching Israel occurs when an institution intentionally infuses its educational environment with values-informed themes that invite students to grapple with Jewish ways of seeing the world around them. The goal is for the student to develop their individual sense of self within the context of the collective and as a result to create a Jewish sensibility in which Israel is an authentic part.

Many institutions of Jewish education—perhaps the large majority—do not have an intentional approach to bringing their educators to adopt a common set of Jewish values in general, or for teaching Israel in particular. They essentially leave it in the hands of individual educators to nurture a positive relationship to the Jewish people and Israel however they see fit.

By exploring the different ways that some of the synagogue schools of the Qushiyot Fellowship alumni approach values education for the purpose of teaching Israel, we gain insight into an educational strategy that focuses on nurturing Jewish collective consciousness. The goal is for a synagogue school to integrate Israel into the broader Jewish educational environment by infusing the educational experience with a core set of values and concepts like "home" and "peoplehood." Over time, the teachers at these schools come to expect that their students will develop a worldview in which these concepts and values, and hence Israel, are a meaningful part.

APPENDIX

TABLE 12.2. Participating Synagogues

Bet Torah	Park Slope Jewish Center
92nd Street Y	Pelham Jewish Center
Bet Am Shalom Synagogue	Plainview Jewish Center
Bnai Jeshurun	Recon Syn of the North Shore
Brooklyn Heights Synagogue	Romemu
B'ShERT	SAJ
Central Synagogue	SSTTE
Cong Emanu-El of Westchester	Stephen Wise Free Syn
Congregation Beth Elohim	Temple Beth Abraham
Congregation B'nai Yisrael Armonk	Temple Beth El of N. Westchester
Congregation HaBonim	Temple Beth El of Great Neck
Congregation Kol Ami	Temple Beth Emeth of Mt. Sinai
Congregation Rodeph Sholom	Temple Beth Sholom
Congregation Shir Shalom	Temple Chaverim
Congregation Tifereth Israel	Temple Isaiah of Stony Brook
Congregation HaBonim	Temple Israel Center of White Plains
CSAIR	Temple Israel of New Rochelle
Dix Hills Jewish Center	Temple Israel of Northern Westchester
East Midwood Jewish Center	Temple Israel of the City of New York
Forest Hills Jewish Center	Temple Israel of Great Neck
Jewish Comm Ctr of Harrison	Temple Judea of Manhasset
Kane Street Synagogue	Temple Shaaray Tefila (Westchester)
Kehillath Shalom Synagogue	Temple Shaarei Tefila (NYC)
MakomNY	Temple Sinai of Roslyn
Merrick Jewish Center	Town and Village Synagogue
Midway Jewish Center	Village Temple
North Shore Jewish Center	Westchester Reform Temple
Park Avenue Synagogue	Woodlands Community Temple

ACKNOWLEDGMENTS

The authors thank the Jewish Education Project and UJA Federation of New York for their permission to draw on the evaluation research commissioned for the Qushiyot Israel Education Fellowship.

NOTES

1. There is a larger body of literature on American Jewish relationships to Israel that situates the idea of young Jews' weakening sense of attachment to Israel as the subject of a robust scholarly debate. Some scholars (e.g., Cohen & Kelman, 2007, 2010) have suggested that attachment has waned over time, while others suggest that young American Jews are still attached to Israel even if in different ways from previous generations (e.g., Sasson, 2014). Regardless of this larger debate in the *academy*, the synagogue educators we studied clearly situated their *practice* on an assumption of weakening attachment.

2. These scholars argue that there is a need to pay attention to changing modes of connection and the influence of increased Israel educational travel and the diverse ways different Jewish populations connect to Israel in practice (Sasson, 2014; Sasson et al., 2010; Tabory, 2010).

3. Abby Pitkowsky was, at the time this research was conducted, the director of the Qushiyot Fellowship. Ezra Kopelowitz conducted the evaluation.

4. Formally known as the Day to Mark the Departure and Expulsion of Jews from the Arab Countries and Iran, the commemoration day was inaugurated in 2014 at the behest of Mizrahi—Judeo-Arab—Israelis who were forced to flee their countries of origin due to persecution following Israel's birth in 1948.

5. See https://theicenter.org/resources/

REFERENCES

Ackerman, W. (1996). Israel in American Jewish Education. In G. Alon (Ed.), *Envisioning Israel: The changing ideals and images of North American Jews* (pp. 173–190). The Magnes Press and Wayne State University Press.

Aharon, N., & Pomson, A. (2018). What's happening at the flagpole? Studying camps as institutions for Israel education. *Journal of Jewish Education*, 84(4), 337–358. https://doi.org/10.1080/15244113.2019.1522564

Benor, S. B., Krasner, J., & Avni, S. (2020). *Hebrew at North American Jewish overnight summer camps*. Rutgers University Press.

Chazan, B. (1979). Israel in American Jewish schools revisited. *Jewish Education*, 42(2), 7–17. https://doi.org/10.1080/0021642790470203

Chazan, B., Chazan, R., & Jacobs, B. M. (2017). *Cultures and contexts of Jewish education*. Palgrave MacMillan.

Cohen, S. M., & Eisen, A. M. (2000). *The Jew within: Self, family, and community in America*. Indiana University Press.

Cohen, S. M., & Kelman, A. Y. (2007). *Beyond distancing: Young adult American Jews and their alienation from Israel*. The Jewish Identity Project of Reboot Andrea and Charles Bronfman Philanthropies.

Cohen, S. M., & Kelman, A. (2010). Thinking about distancing from Israel. *Contemporary Jewry*, 30(2-3), 287-296. https://doi.org/10.1007/s12397-010-9053-4

Fraiman, K. E., & Bell, D. P. (2021). A new approach to education and peoplehood: Diversity as a key to a sustainable model of peoplehood. *The Peoplehood Papers*, 30, 42-50.

Grant, L. D. (2007). Israel education in Reform congregational schools. *CCAR Journal: A Reform Jewish Quarterly*, 27, 2-24.

Grant, L. D. (2008). Sacred vision, complex reality: Navigating the tensions in Israel education. *Journal of Jewish Educational Leadership*, Fall Edition.

Grant, L. D., & Kopelowitz, E. (2012). *Israel education matters: A 21st century paradigm for Jewish education*. Center for Jewish Peoplehood Education.

Horowitz, B. (2008). New frontiers: "Milieu" and the sociology of American Jewish education. *Journal of Jewish Education*, 74(1), 68-81. https://doi.org/10.1080/15244110802493370

Horowitz, B. (2012). *Defining Israel education* [Report]. The iCenter for Israel Education.

Isaacs, A. (2011). Israel education: Purposes and practices. In H. Miller, L. Grant, & A. Pomson (Eds.), *International handbook of Jewish education* (pp. 479-496). Springer International Publishing.

Kopelowitz, E. (2020). *Sophisticated and sustainable Israel education: Four year perspective from the Qushiyot Israel Education Fellowship for synagogue educators*. The Jewish Education Project.

Kress, J. (2012). *Development, learning, and community: Educating for identity in pluralistic Jewish high schools by Jeffrey Kress*. Academic Studies Press.

Moore, L., & Woocher, J. (2019). Jewish sensibilities: Towards a new language for Jewish educational goal-setting. In J. A. Levinsohn & A. Y. Kelman (Eds.), *Beyond Jewish identity* (pp. 241-265). Academic Studies Press.

Pew Research Center. (2021). *Jewish Americans in 2020*. https://www.pewresearch.org/religion/2021/05/11/jewish-americans-in-2020/

Pomson, A., Deitcher, H., & Muszkat-Barkan, M. (2009). *Israel education in North American day schools: A systems analysis and some strategies for change*. Melton Centre for Jewish Education, The Hebrew University of Jerusalem.

Ravid, S. (2014). Between defining peoplehood and exploring its meaning. *Peoplehood Papers*, 13, 34-35.

Ravid, S. (2021). Peoplehood education – A work in progress. *Peoplehood Papers*, 30, 95-102.

Reimer, J. (1997). *Succeeding at Jewish education: How one synagogue made it work*. The Jewish Publication Society.

Sales, A. L., & Saxe, L. (2003). *"How goodly are thy tents": Summer camps as Jewish socializing experiences*. Brandeis University Press.

Sasson, T. (2014). *The New American Zionism*. New York University Press.

Sasson, T., Kadushin, C., & Saxe, L. (2010). *Trends in American Jewish attachment to Israel: An assessment of the "distancing" hypothesis*. Brandeis University, Cohen Center for Modern Jewish Studies.

Sinclair, A. (2013). *Loving the real Israel: An educational agenda for liberal Zionism*. Ben Yehuda Press.

Tabory, E. (2010). Attachment to Israel and Jewish identity: An assessment of an assessment. *Contemporary Jewry, 30*(2–3), 191–197. https://doi.org/10.1007/s12397-010-9052-5

Wertheimer, J. (2008). *A census of Jewish supplementary schools in the United States.* The Avichai Foundation.

Wertheimer, J. (2009a). Introduction. In J. Wertheimer (Ed.), *Learning and community: Jewish supplementary schools in the twenty-first century* (pp. xi–xvii). Brandeis University Press.

Wertheimer, J. (2009b). *Learning and community: Jewish Supplementary schools in the twenty-first century.* Brandeis University Press.

Wertheimer, J. (2018). *The new American Judaism: How Jews practice their religion today.* Princeton University Press.

Wertheimer, J. (2022, March 3). Which American Jews are most distant from Israel? *EJewish Philanthropy*.

Winer, L. N. (2019). *Teaching who they are: American-born supplementary school teachers connections with Israel* [Doctoral dissertation, The Jewish Theological Seminary of America]. ProQuest Dissertations Publishing. https://www.proquest.com/openview/4f7df7d2d80492079b57d2d0133852d4/1?pq-origsite=gscholar&cbl=18750&diss=y

Zakai, S. (2011). Values in tension: Israel education at a U.S. Jewish day school. *Journal of Jewish Education, 77*(3), 239–265. https://doi.org/10.1080/15244113.2011.603070

Zakai, S., & Cohen, H. T. (2016). American Jewish children's thoughts and feelings about the Jewish state: Laying the groundwork for a developmental approach to Israel education. *Contemporary Jewry, 36*(1), 31–54. https://doi.org/10.1007/s12397-016-9160-y

Zelkowicz, T. (2019). Jewish educators don't make Jews: A sociological reality check about Jewish identity work. In J. A. Levinsohn & A. Y. Kelman (Eds.), *Beyond Jewish identity* (pp. 144–166). Academic Studies Press.

13
A Kite on a String and a Box That Opens
The Challenges of Transformative Professional Learning for Israel Educators

LAUREN APPLEBAUM

In an era fraught with controversy about the teaching of Israel, Israel educators face significant pressure to succeed at their work. Communal concern about the role of advocacy in the classroom (Horowitz, 2012) and educational questions about developmental appropriateness (Zakai & Cohen, 2016) have led to a proliferation of professional-development initiatives to help them succeed, from seminars and workshops to in-depth learning opportunities (Pomson & Grant, 2003; Sinclair et al., 2013). Yet despite significant investment in a range of programs, little is known about the learning experiences of Israel educators who participate in professional development. This chapter focuses on the learning of two experienced teachers as a window into the challenges faced by Israel educators working to improve their own practice. Their stories demonstrate that even with high-quality program design by facilitators (Darling-Hammond et al., 2017) and whole-hearted effort by the teachers themselves, growth and change for Israel educators is slow, inconsistent, and deeply personal.

To develop their teaching practice, Israel educators need more than infusions of increased content knowledge or pedagogical technique (Shulman, 1986). As in any subject area, high-quality professional learning for Israel educators should be collaborative and content-focused; include active learning, reflection, coaching, and feedback; and take place over a sustained period of time (Darling-Hammond et al., 2017). As part of a process of collaborative and individual reflection, educators first need to define "success" for themselves and their communities and then to align their own teaching to move towards those goals. The goals of Israel education can be deceptively simple, such as "Be connected to Israel" (e.g., Chazan, 2016), or extremely sophisticated, such as "Love Israel while developing a critical perspective" (Alexander, 2015). Those who teach about Israel have complicated and often unexamined beliefs about how Israel should be taught and about Israel itself (Winer, 2019). Articulating those beliefs can lead to a reexamination of their approach to their work and give shape to their professional growth. To do this, Israel educators need not only high-quality professional training but the opportunity for transformative professional learning.

Transformative learning is a type of adult learning that involves surfacing, examining, and (sometimes) changing the assumptions that lie beneath our beliefs and actions (Mezirow, 1990, 1991, 2000). Transformative professional learning is crucial for Israel educators because beneath their goals and their teaching practice lie core beliefs about religion, peoplehood, culture, and identity. The depth and complexity of these beliefs can lead to a learning process that can be uncomfortable or even painful (Cranton, 1996, 2006). Scholars and practitioners of transformative learning particularly note the central role of disorientation, when a learner confronts an assumption she previously hadn't articulated for herself and which, upon reflection, she might find inadequate (Mezirow, 1991, 2000). To help make sense of that disorientation and move through it, facilitators need to create what the adult-development scholar Robert Kegan (1994) calls a "holding environment," which provides a carefully balanced mix of support and challenge for teachers as they stretch and grow.

The two educators portrayed in this chapter, whom I'll refer to by the pseudonyms Yaffa and Ronit, were participants in a yearlong initiative for Israel educators designed to help them learn more about the field of Israel education, deepen their teaching practice, and examine their own beliefs about teaching Israel.[1] Based in a large metropolitan city, a group of 10 educators met in person monthly for three-hour sessions that I co-facilitated with a colleague. Yaffa and Ronit were enthusiastic, eager participants throughout the year. Middle-aged Israeli women who became Jewish day school teachers after moving to the United States, they share many demographic characteristics. Yet their experiences of the possibilities of transformative professional learning were significantly different. Yaffa responded to challenges to her assumptions about teaching Israel by strongly reaffirming them, while Ronit proclaimed that her beliefs had been "exploded." Both described their own learning as deeply meaningful, but during the year neither of them exhibited substantive changes in her teaching practice. Their classroom pedagogy remained largely unchanged. In this chapter, I offer their stories as an illustration of the challenges faced by Israel educators looking to grow, and I unpack their experiences to offer perspective for facilitators and researchers who wish to understand the complexity and unevenness of transformative professional learning.

Context and Methods

The data for this chapter were drawn from a larger study of a yearlong professional learning initiative, during which a group of 10 Israel educators grappled with contemporary research in their field, considered questions designed to challenge their thinking about their own work, and reflected on a wide variety of educational activities. I co-facilitated the group and recorded the meetings, collected artifacts, and conducted three semi-structured individual interviews with each participant at the beginning, middle, and end of the year.

After transcribing, I coded the data from sessions, interviews, and observations using Atlas.ti and created memos based on emerging themes (Patton, 2002). Data were coded for indications of potential transformative learning, such as assumptions, disorientation, and critical reflection, as well as other salient categories, such as relationships between participants and goals for learning. In analyzing the data, I looked for evidence of learning: When did teachers struggle? What did it look and sound like when they engaged with uncomfortable ideas? How did they speak about what they were doing back in their classrooms?

In this chapter, I focus closely on the learning experiences of two teachers to allow a rich view into the complexity of the transformative professional-learning process (Dorph et al., 2002; Merriam & Kim, 2012).

While this approach, associated with both case studies (Savin-Baden & Major, 2013) and portraiture (Lawrence-Lightfoot & Davis, 1997), does not allow for generalization to all teachers, it provides opportunities for theory generation and deep exploration of the learning process, which I hope can offer new perspective for Israel educators and those who are invested in their growth and success.

"A Kite With a Long String": The Case of Yaffa

Yaffa is an Israeli-American woman in her early 50s with a warm smile and a quiet, understated presence. She described herself as someone who "loves to learn" and names continuing education as a significant side benefit of her career in teaching, which has taken her from a synagogue to the day school where she teaches middle school Judaic studies and helps lead an Israel trip. Yaffa believes that if her students learn a lot about Israel, they will commit to it. She named students who have made *aliyah* (immigrated to Israel) as measures of success for her teaching about Israel. With determination and focus, Yaffa joined the group "to collaborate with other [local] educators who have a passion for... learning effective pedagogic techniques." For Yaffa, the work of improving Israel education is a challenge of organization and clarity. "It is all good and fine to talk about these paradigms and theories," she noted once, "but how can we bring topics to the classroom and use [them]?"

In her own classroom, Yaffa designed activities that promoted "Israel literacy" (Troen & Fish, 2017), such as virtual geography walks and skits about ethnic groups in Israel. She also favored activities that helped students become advocates for Israel. As a teacher who felt strongly about including these approaches in her practice, Yaffa was delighted when the professional-learning group learned language for describing the differences between education and advocacy (Horowitz, 2012), and she later identified the terms signifying this distinction as one of the most valuable pieces of learning for her. While others found the distinction intriguing because it highlighted their uncertainty about what they should be doing in their schools, Yaffa loved the new language, saying, "[It] give[s] me clear ideas of... how to create the units." Instead of an opportunity to reconsider her assumptions about her role, the session offered a way of describing that role with precision. Yaffa wanted to feel more competent and confident about her teaching practice, and she used her new learning to describe her approach more accurately.

Seeking Alignment

In addition to feeling passionately about her goals, Yaffa felt deeply aligned with her own school's stance on teaching Israel. She assumed that all other Israel educators shared the same goals. This desire for alignment with her own school and her colleagues in the larger field was a source of strength, but also a potential roadblock to her ability to learn. Early in the year, participants were asked to articulate why they each believed students should learn about Israel. Yaffa answered:

> The philosophy at [my school] is teaching about Israel, creating that connection between students and families and Israel...we want students to find that connection, to know about it, and to develop that love to the State of Israel.

She did not respond to the prompt with *her* ideas about why students should learn about Israel. Her reason for doing so may have been revealed in her answer to a later question: "How should Israel be taught and why?" She answered "First, I think if you work in a school you need to figure out the philosophy of your school, what they say about Israel education." She added, "I think I found my place where my values and the school's values are similar, so it's a happy, win-win situation." Yaffa wanted to be tightly aligned with her institution and with her colleagues.

This strong sense of being united for a common purpose caused disorientation for Yaffa when she ventured outside of her school environment to the cross-institutional professional-learning initiative and encountered competing assumptions and beliefs. During a deeply personal dialogue exercise, participants shared their hopes and fears about the Israeli–Palestinian conflict. Jon, a teacher from another school with whom Yaffa usually felt strongly aligned as a fellow Jewishly observant, self-identified Zionist, commented angrily that sometimes Israel seemed like "one hell of a booby prize." His public anger shook Yaffa badly. While she made no response in the moment, she said in an interview afterwards, "Just the thought of doubting Israel's existence, made me feel really hard. It was painful." When she and I spoke about it later, she acknowledged that while she had obviously heard such sentiments before, it was particularly hard coming "from another Jew, from a teacher, an Israel educator, and a person who is observant." It was jarring for Yaffa to recognize that her beliefs were not shared by colleagues whom she thought would agree. How could she be unified with those who didn't share her core beliefs?

Yaffa struggled throughout the year to come to terms with her desire for unity among Israel educators and her belief in her own vision for Zionism. This disorientation could have produced a variety of responses (Helsing et al., 2008; Kegan, 2000). For example, she might have responded by engaging in dialogue with Jon. Such a conversation might have let her "try on" Jon's perspective even if she ultimately rejected it, or might have resulted in a shift of perspective. It may have led to her reconsidering and perhaps even changing her own belief that Zionist educators should not publicly express anger towards Israel, or it might have expanded her understanding of her need to have complete agreement with those whom she considered allies. Instead, Yaffa quietly backed away from a reconsideration of either of her assumptions about the unity within the field of Israel education and from her own assumptions about what a Zionist "says."

Values in Tension

Yaffa found it intolerable to focus on disagreement with colleagues. She also found it difficult to reflect on any internal disagreement or tension within her own beliefs. For example, like many Israel educators, she grappled with her commitments to teaching both critical thinking and *Ahavat Zion* (love for Israel).[2] In thoughtful private discussions, Yaffa revealed a complex relationship to Israel. She spoke movingly about her qualms about wars and her own experiences learning about dark parts of Israel's history. But in the very same interview where she articulated that complexity, she used as examples of success in her own educational practice a project where students learned about different ethnic groups in Israel and got to "dress up and do skits about each one" and a geography activity with riddles about Israeli cities. She told me in interviews that students should have a safe space to raise questions about Israel but blanched with discomfort when she recounted how a student once "took the Palestinian point of view" when she did encourage questions. When Yaffa spoke privately about her own feelings about contemporary Israel, the conversation was very nuanced. When she talked about Israel education, it was very straightforward. Yaffa was guiding her students to have a less complex relationship with Israel than she herself possessed.

In another session, I asked Yaffa to name an example of where her own beliefs about Israel or teaching Israel might be in tension or conflict. But instead of lining up possible conflicts, she divided them neatly into traditional curricular categories—affective, behavioral, and cognitive. I pointed out that the goals she listed for herself were wide ranging but not actually in tension with each other. She hesitated and responded by offering a story about how some teachers in her school had objected to a political cartoon shown in a school assembly and that this was an example of tension. She could talk about external disagreements, but the very idea of internal tension or conflict was nearly impossible for her to identify within herself.

Yaffa worked diligently and seriously. But after a year of intensive learning, she didn't change her beliefs or practice. The disorientation produced by unexpected ideas from colleagues or facilitators did not lead Yaffa to overturn her original beliefs. Instead, it helped her find her "bright lines": It is okay to ask questions *if* the questioners maintain a positive attitude towards Israel. Critical thinking is acceptable and welcomed—*but only* in specific situations. When she taught other topics in Jewish studies, Yaffa told me that she felt confident that students could be critical of ideas or even theology and still love Judaism. But when the topic was Israel, contradiction and complexity could not be part of her classroom environment.

A Kite With a Long String

In the final session of the year, the group discussed two archetypal metaphors of Israel educators: explorers and exemplars (Pomson et al., 2014). Israel educators who try to inculcate love of Israel through modeling their own personal experiences are referred to as "exemplars," while those who try to guide students through their own inquiries are "explorers." Yaffa offered her own metaphor in response. "For me," she said, "the explorer is like a kite with no strings and the exemplar is the person that has a kite with a very short string because it has to be in control... and has to pull it." Later she extended the metaphor to reflect on her learning for the year:

> You know, I think that this [year] helped me move to have this longer string.... A very long string... I still don't think that we need to just let the students fly their kites with no strings, but not with a short leash also.

Even when the conditions are set for transformative learning, "sometimes people question, reflect, and discuss, but do not experience any fundamental changes" (Cranton, 1996, p. 96). While this may be frustrating to those invested in transformative professional learning for Israel educators, or in designing professional learning that leads to the adoption of specific pedagogical approaches, the adult-educational theorist Carolin Kreber (2012) reminds us that "for some the costs of growth are too dear. It is therefore up to the learner to decide when or whether to move forward" (pp. 331–332). With her full-hearted effort to learn and steadfast commitment to maintaining her personal convictions, Yaffa demonstrated how—regardless of what a facilitator or theorist might want—a teacher might want to feel like she can soar without letting go of the string.

"Once You Open a Little Box in Your Head, You Cannot Close It Again": Ronit's Story

Ronit is an energetic teacher who once ruefully described herself as a "stereotypical older, white, Jewish woman who comes from Israel"—though she did not fit into stereotypes very easily. The same can be said of her learning process, which she frequently described as "profoundly transformative," even while it didn't always match descriptions of a transformative learning process (Mezirow, 1990, 1991, 2000).

Frustrated by Misalignment

Unlike Yaffa, Ronit was frequently frustrated by the general approach towards Israel education at her school, even while she expressed deep affection for the institution and the community. In an early session, she responded with a loud sigh to the prompt "If you could wave a magic wand and make the world over in the way you would like it, how would American Jews today be talking about Israel?" Exasperated, she exclaimed, "At [my school], I would like much more information, correct information, nuanced interaction." She was constantly fretting about the disengagement—or even hostility—towards Israel that she perceived to be part of the school culture. Her disappointment created a sense of urgency to improve her own practice in the hopes of making an impact. As she mentioned to Yaffa,

> When I said in an open meeting that...going to Israel and meeting Israelis will prepare [students] eventually to face possible criticism on campus and they could advocate, a couple of the parents almost ate my head.

In contrast to Yaffa's school, where advocacy was prized, Ronit felt that the parents at her school did not want their children to be trained as Israel advocates. She was also dissatisfied at what she saw as the school's failure to give Israel compelling space in the curriculum and with her colleagues' lack of enthusiasm for experimentation. Her frustration led her to join the professional-learning initiative in the hopes of figuring out how to "to really have [the parents and school community] on board wholeheartedly" with both the curriculum and a class trip to Israel. The idea of being "onboard" was multilayered for Ronit. She wanted greater connection to *Am Yisrael* (the global Jewish community) and to Jewish identity in general. For her, Israel education represented Jewish education and overall Jewish commitment. As she said when describing her philosophy of Israel, she wanted students to love Israel so that they would be "proud as Jews, proud of what our people contributed to civilization, proud of our history and heritage, really fostering pride, fostering identity and a backbone and a set of values that will guide them and be with them."

Her disconnect with her school and belief in the high stakes of the enterprise led Ronit to experience a sense of being beleaguered. With her customary flair for the dramatic, she spoke vividly about how she "got in trouble with using the word 'advocacy'" or said that she was constantly "walking the tightrope." Ronit was able to exist within a space that did not reflect her own ideas by focusing on her own values and by looking for support and a better articulation of her beliefs from a larger sphere of colleagues and scholars.

Tension Between Old and Emerging Beliefs

Ronit devoured readings and was a particularly active member of group discussions. After months of considering issues of complexity and nuance (Grant & Kopelowitz, 2012), the differences between advocacy and education (Horowitz, 2012), and the possibility that committed Zionists could engage in critical thinking about Israel (Sinclair, 2013), she felt disoriented and drained. She explained, "The first two months and the first couple of readings in just the exposition was huge for me. I was...not confused, but...there was a lot of emotion attached to it." Reading what she understood to be critiques of her approach and perspectives that destabilized her own assumptions about the role of an Israel educator was upsetting, and she mentioned in later interviews that she "started feeling very depressed, really upset." "The more I read [for each seminar]," she commented, "the more frustrated I am and the more I second-guess myself."

Scholars of transformative learning argue that this disorientation is an essential part of the transformative process because it begins to surface the inadequacy of the assumptions that were once difficult to "see" (Mezirow, 2000). For Ronit—unlike Yaffa—the jarring early months of reading and thinking led her to want to try on a new approach towards her role as an Israel educator. With her characteristic sharp wit, she mused that she wanted to be a "hybrid," who tries to balance teaching love and facilitating critical thinking about Israel, rather than an "enabler," coining her own sarcastic term for "exemplars" (Pomson et al., 2014). As she exclaimed in an interview, "[Joining this group] was the revolution that I absolutely needed and that I was ready for. I started transitioning [away] from being the staunch advocate, Israel no matter what." Ronit's perspective on her work changed dramatically. But it was extraordinarily difficult to make this transition in her teaching practice, despite her strongly articulated desire.

While Ronit was genuinely committed to embracing a new approach to Israel education, she, like Yaffa, continued to champion pedagogic choices that were not aligned with her description of her new vision. While her enthusiasm for complexity was genuine, her lesson plans remained straightforward. She eagerly described a plan to encourage math teachers in the school to use Israeli cities in word problems and told me with great excitement about what she called a "profound" rethinking of her curriculum, which turned out to entail only a switch from organizing the curriculum around geography to organizing it around "an achievement, either a technical achievement or medical achievement" from various locations in Israel. She was not planning her curriculum in a way that reflected her "revolution" and was not yet making "productive use" of her new insights (Kegan, 1994).

Ronit enthusiastically participated in sessions designed to help her find ways to enact that revolution. She worked in a small group trying to figure out what it would look like to have a dialogue between her students and Israeli students about the thorny issues of religious pluralism and gender egalitarianism in Israel (see also Sinclair, 2013). Her partner in the exercise offered many suggestions about approaches and strategies to design such a conversation. Ronit struggled hard to respond to her partner's brainstorming. She raised objections again and again of why it would not work: because of time constraints, because of what Israeli parents would say, because of her specific role, because of student interest or ability. She wrote in her reflection sheet afterwards that she aspired to "to be able to insert varied voices and perspectives into [her] content, to create more space for dialogue," but she was unable to plan to put this into concrete practice yet.

A Box That Opens

While Yaffa articulated at the end of the year, in what felt like a hard-won realization, that she had not lost any clarity about her vision, Ronit spent much of the year marveling at the fact that the fellowship had, as she colorfully described, "dropped a bomb" on her world. When she reflected aloud at the end of the year, she laughed that her previous stance had been extremely simplistic: "Rah, rah, rah, this is the most fabulous place, nothing is wrong, it's great, it's a wonderful experience for the children, they will only gain." As passionately as she first spoke about her beliefs, she now dismissively rejected them in conversations within the group and with the facilitators. Ronit was appreciative when other participants presented examples from their own classrooms that were designed from a perspective that valued complexity and challenge, calling them "terrific" and "very courageous." She "tried on" her new commitment by rehearsing what she might say when a challenging moment came up in her class. She mused, "I will allow, now, myself to listen in more openly. If a child says, 'I don't really care [about Israel]' [I will] not be upset and instead say, 'Well, tell me more about it.'" She cringed at her past assumptions, but she wasn't yet prepared to take on educational practices that would support her nascent new stance.

We might imagine that given the opportunity to pause, reflect, and discuss, teachers can change their deeply held assumptions and then act upon them. But scholars and facilitators alike know that "new ways of thinking do not necessarily lead to altered practice in a facile manner" (Dorph et al., 2002, p. 60). As inconsistent as it might seem, Ronit's "trying on" of her new perspectives is consistent with the "messiness in practice" (Servage, 2008, p. 70) of transformative learning and of all professional learning, especially when the stakes are high and the content is deeply personal.

At the end of the year together, another participant shared a story about a time where she tried to be an "explorer" (Pomson et al., 2014) and allow her middle school students to delve into complex questions about Israel's approach to immigration. After hearing the story of angry parent phone calls and uncomfortable class discussions, Ronit borrowed Yaffa's kite metaphor and reflected:

> This is pretty scary. Especially with children who are that young, who are just starting to form feelings and perspectives...how much can I let go of the string and not pull to safe parameters. That's the question. It's very delicate.

Whereas Yaffa ultimately rejected the idea of incorporating critical thinking in her teaching about Israel, Ronit tried to simultaneously hold both her strong commitment to Israel and her strong commitment to critical thinking. She vacillated, producing a gap between her ideas and her actions. She herself identified the challenge of this liminal space, laughing in an interview about why she continued to pursue further learning through public lectures and reading, exclaiming,

It's almost like I want to saturate myself to possibly inoculate myself so I don't fall back to my old ways. [Laughing] Definitely, I'm not going back. Once you open a little box in your head, you cannot close it again.

While Ronit never reported any background in developmental psychology, her metaphor references a key concept in stage theory: Once a phase of development has been completed and a new stage reached, an individual cannot "go back" or return to a prior stage (Kegan, 1982, 1994; Piaget, 1954; Tennant & Pogson, 1995). While Ronit is still on the "growing edge" (Berger, 2004) of a shift in thinking, she is vehement that she is "not going back," even if she will require further practice and support to enact her new beliefs in her classroom.

Similar Learners, Different Stories

Ronit and Yaffa have much in common. They are both Israeli-American women who turned to teaching to preserve Judaism and share their love of their home country. Both came to the year with the desire to grow as educators, and both would describe their learning experiences as deep and impactful. They both experienced intense emotional and intellectual challenge during a year of diving deep into their beliefs and practice as Israel educators. Yet their learning experiences were immensely different. Yaffa came out of the year of learning with a resolution to maintain her cherished assumptions and beliefs. Ronit leaped at the chance to embrace a new stance. But for the most part, neither of them changed their teaching practice. The complexity of their stories can highlight some of the factors that make transformative professional learning for Israel educators so challenging: the educator's own goals for their learning, their school contexts, and the heightened sense of urgency in the field of Israel education.

Goals for Professional Learning: What Does "Getting Better" Mean?

Both Ronit and Yaffa wanted to "get better" at teaching Israel. While "getting better" seems like an obvious goal of professional learning, defining what it means to "get better" turns out to be quite complex. Yaffa, along with many other Israel educators, craved more skills and more certainty about her work. She frequently expressed the belief that there were surefire ways to teach Israel "better," and she wanted to discover them. She was genuinely open to and strongly motivated by the idea of getting better at teaching Israel, which she understood to be a process of reflecting on her current practice:

> It might be I will realize, "Wow, this is great what we're doing, and just let's stick with that, we can just change a little bit," or I'll learn, it's like, "Wow, we probably need to change a few things." This is what I was hoping.

Even while she committed to a year of learning, Yaffa longed for a kind of professional growth that could be described as "growth as getting bigger" (Daloz, 1986) rather than a "form that transforms" (Kegan, 2000). She wanted to be more effective in her teaching practice, not transform the practice altogether.

While Yaffa wanted it all to be clearer, Ronit reveled in the complexity of teaching Israel, and wanted to "dig deeper" into that complexity. She was interested in being "critically reflective" (Brookfield, 2017) about the messy and uncertain business of teaching Israel and was intent on diving into this complexity in order to develop her craft. Ronit came hoping that the group would be "dealing with the struggle that we have within ourselves and our dilemmas...to get into the meat of, 'What does it really mean to be an Israel educator and how do you approach it?'"

While they wouldn't have articulated this before the year began, Ronit and Yaffa displayed varying degrees of affinity for different traditions in teacher reflection, and different levels of interest in the possibilities that might result from that reflection. When Ronit welcomed the uncomfortable experience of questioning what she was doing when she taught about Israel and why she was doing it, she was looking to engage in critical reflection, to "correct distortions in [her] beliefs" (Mezirow, 1990, p. 1). In contrast, Yaffa's desire for better teaching through better research-based technique is rooted in the "social efficiency tradition" of teacher reflection (Zeichner & Liston, 1996), which focuses on the study of research literature and personal experiences of teachers (Feiman-Nemser, 1990). The adult-learning theorist Stephen Brookfield (2017) is dismissive of reflection in this "technical realm" (p. 9). But the teacher-learning expert Sharon Feiman-Nemser (2001) argues that this kind of repertoire building is a crucial component of teacher development, particularly in the early years of practice. In the small field of Israel education, where most Israel educators lack subject-specific training (Sinclair et al., 2013), it may be that Yaffa (and many others) feel themselves to be in this "early career" category regardless of the number of years in the classroom. While facilitators may have their own strong beliefs (perhaps unexamined!) about the need for professional development to be rooted in one or the other of these categories, professional learning for Israel educators needs to honor the desires of both kinds of learners. Articulating assumptions about what "success" looks like—and examining those assumptions—is a responsibility for those who teach Israel educators just as it is for the educators themselves.

Contexts, Not Holding Environments

Though they shared the context of the professional-learning initiative all year, Ronit and Yaffa had strikingly different environments back at their schools. Yaffa worked in a team of educators with highly aligned philosophies, under the direction of a department head and within a school that shared those philosophies. Ronit did not feel aligned with her school in the same way. In addition to her repeated concern about parents' skepticism about Israel, she did not feel surrounded by colleagues who thought about Israel education like she did. This significant difference in alignment in their school contexts may be another factor in their divergent professional-learning experiences.

For Yaffa, "trying on" new ideas would have put her at odds with her school. When she found ideas and assumptions destabilizing or uncomfortable, she returned after each session to a school environment which was supportive of her own original assumptions. She could settle back into them. Ronit already felt at odds with her school, and therefore may have come into the year with more openness to consider new ideas and the shifting allegiances they might represent. When she found herself unsettled or uneasy at the end of a session, her school environment did not allay her disorientation, perhaps allowing her to dwell in it and reflect upon it for longer. However, the lack of interest in exploring Israel education did not give her a supportive space to experiment with new strategies in practice.

Neither Yaffa nor Ronit had a "holding environment" that provided the right balance of challenge and support back at their own schools to allow for productive experimentation (Kegan, 1994). Yaffa's school was overly supportive of her original assumptions and therefore didn't offer opportunities for her to stay uncomfortable, while Ronit's environment felt overly challenging of her work and lacked space to support her experimentation. A holding environment is neither a refuge nor a gladiatorial arena. It cannot be solely affirming or constantly combative but must contain *both* support and challenge to create the conditions to make transformative learning possible.

"Like Somebody's Mother":
The High Stakes of Teaching Israel

While they did not articulate the need for a holding environment that would provide both support and challenge, both Ronit and Yaffa had yearned for a place where they could, as Yaffa said, "know [they were] not the only person out there [teaching Israel]." The education researchers Lisa Grant, Daniel Marom, and Yehudit Werchow (2013) note that Israel educators are "compartmentalized," perhaps even more than most classroom teachers.[3] Ronit, Yaffa, and the other participants particularly craved collegial community because their role as Israel educators—sometimes as the only one in their school—frequently left them feeling even more isolated than other teachers (see also Zakai, 2012). Another participant noted during the final session of the year, "[Israel education is] the furthest thing from simple, and we don't necessarily have the opportunity to talk that through with anyone. And [this group] was ... something that I definitely looked forward to. Almost like therapy." The participants in the study group, all of whom also taught other subject areas, often repeated the idea that teaching about Israel was profoundly unique and fraught. One called teaching Israel "a full-contact sport." Another commented, "This isn't teaching Renaissance history. This is talking about somebody's *mother*." Ronit once declared that she saw Israel education as the cornerstone of Jewish education:

I think that's probably still the driving thing behind me [as an Israel educator]. I cannot stop the wheel from turning, but I can contribute in my way to help those children to be educated Jews. Jews is the operative word. I don't want them not to be Jews....Woe is us if they are not going to stay connected to Jewish people.

With a similar worried tone, Yaffa told me that she was willing to experiment and push and risk things in her Tanakh (Bible) classroom—even that it was okay if in the end some students have "doubts" about the Bible—but that the possibility of doubt had no place in the Israel classroom. She explained, "[In] Tanakh, I push them...to doubt the Tanakh and to find gaps, but am I willing to do that with Israel? To the extent that they will start doubting the existence of Israel? No." It may have been too hard for Yaffa to complicate her assumptions or for Ronit to fully enact her newer beliefs because of the high stakes they themselves felt for the enterprise (Isaacs, 2011) and their worries about the consequences of a misstep.

Challenging content, ferocious communal dialogue, and a subject perceived by its practitioners to have profound implications for personal and religious identity make for fraught territory. Lessons learned—or mislearned—might shape a roomful of students' Jewish identities and commitments to Israel. The experience of this extreme level of challenge can make it difficult for teachers to fully explore disorientation, consider assumptions, and experiment with practice. School leaders and community stakeholders need to provide support by moderating the tone of conversations about Israel and by incorporating Israel education into multiple contexts within the school year so that teachers feel like they have a little more breathing room to experiment and explore in their own classrooms without as much fear and trepidation.

Conclusion

Yaffa described herself with satisfaction as a kite with a string, while Ronit took pride in her mind as a box that had opened. While Ronit was gratified to be in the midst of the transformation of her beliefs, Yaffa was equally pleased by her lack of transformation. They were both confident in their choice of metaphors and secure in the success of their learning experiences, even while neither of them changed much about the ways they teach Israel.

The intricacies of adult learning and the complexities of teaching and learning mean that the distance from ideas to classroom practice is always challenging to navigate. In the case of Israel education, this is exacerbated by the complex beliefs and heightened sense of urgency that make up the contested landscape—both within schools and in the larger community—in which the educators teach. It is difficult to design professional-learning initiatives to respond to the challenges of this complex context, both within schools and surrounding them.

While this initiative brought teachers together out of their school environments, professional learning that is embedded within the school community where inquiry, challenge, and support are blended into the everyday life of educators is often thought of as the "gold standard" (Darling-Hammond et al., 2017). When Israel educators need to seek a professional community outside of their own schools, the challenge of experimenting with ideas and implementing new practices back at school can be exceptionally difficult. School-based learning might have provided clear opportunities for Ronit to experiment with her pedagogy and might have created space for Yaffa to unpack the internal resistance she experienced in considering her assumptions. At the same time, stepping outside of the school environment can offer a new perspective on the assumptions embedded within the school culture and offers a new vantage point for considering daily classroom practice.

Any transformative professional-learning opportunity for Israel educators should be designed with touchpoints both in and outside of school in order to combine support and challenge. Programs external to schools need to build in significant time spent observing and debriefing with teachers when they are "back home." While internal school-based programs are less common in Israel education, their design would need to include ample opportunity to encounter and grapple with the disorientation of new ideas and perspectives. A hybrid approach of assembling small teams from schools to come together with teams from other schools for professional learning would allow for support and collegial challenge for new ideas while at school, while preserving the opportunity to learn in a setting outside the norms and prevailing assumptions of the school environment.[4] Regardless of the specific structure, it is crucial for facilitators of professional development to be aware of the challenges inherent in maintaining and deepening the insights gained in professional development during regular daily work (see also Feiman-Nemser, 2008a; Stieha & Raider-Roth, 2012).

In order to fully support Israel educators as they learn, the larger field of Israel education needs to see their professional development as adult learning, with the long time horizon and careful attention to the needs of individual learners that is a hallmark of all thoughtful education. When we understand professional development as an ongoing learning experience rather than the memorization of a how-to manual, we can shift our expectations and our time horizon. The one-year fellowship program in which Yaffa and Ronit participated would have been significantly strengthened with an additional year of coaching to supplement and extend the cohort-based learning and allow them time to fully engage in a cycle of exploration, disorientation, experimentation, and reflection. We do not expect children to fully and deeply learn about complex subjects—including Israel!—after a handful of classes. We should not assume that teachers can deeply learn about, shift, and transform the complex habits of mind and sophisticated pedagogic practice required for teaching Israel in a short time frame either.

Just as the field of Israel education has begun to listen carefully to the voices of the students studying Israel (e.g., Reingold, 2017; Zakai & Cohen, 2016), we need continued research that looks carefully at Israel educators as they learn. Most crucially, we need thoughtful facilitation and design of the holding environments in which they can do that learning. Making collegial space and sufficient time for Israel educators to experience learning that balances challenge and support for them as individuals will allow them to offer those gifts of challenge and support to their own students.

NOTES

1. I collaborated on the design, facilitation, and research of the initiative under the auspices of Project ORLIE (Research and Leadership in Israel Education).

2. Horowitz (2012) notes that this is a contemporary challenge for scholars and practitioners, commenting that "figuring out ways these approaches can most effectively be intertwined remains a subject for further investigation" (p. 16).

3. Lortie (1975) refers to teaching as "cellular," and McDonald (1992) describes all teachers as "severely isolated."

4. This is the design of some professional-development initiatives in Jewish education, such as the Boston and Bay area cohorts of the Mandel Teacher Educator Institute (Stodolsky et al., 2004) and in general education, such as the Challenge Success project (Pope et al., 2015). However, because Israel educators are often the only ones in a setting or department, they often lack a group of internal colleagues with whom to form such teams.

REFERENCES

Alexander, H. A. (2015). Mature Zionism: Education and the scholarly study of Israel. *Journal of Jewish Education*, 81(2), 136–161. https://doi.org/10.1080/15244113.2015.1035979

Berger, J. G. (2004). Dancing on the threshold of meaning: Recognizing and understanding the growing edge. *Journal of Transformative Education*, 2(36), 336–351. https://doi.org/10.1177/1541344604267697

Brookfield, S. (2017). *Becoming a critically reflective teacher* (2nd ed.). Jossey-Bass.

Chazan, B. (2016). *A philosophy of Israel education: A relational approach*. Palgrave Macmillan.

Cranton, P. (1996). *Professional development as transformative learning*. Jossey-Bass.

Cranton, P. (2006). *Understanding and promoting transformative learning*. Jossey-Bass.

Daloz, L. (1986). *Effective teaching and mentoring: Recognizing the transformational power of adult learning experiences*. Wiley.

Darling-Hammond, L., Hyler, M. E., & Gardner, M. (2017). *Effective teacher professional development*. Learning Policy Institute. https://learningpolicyinstitute.org/product/teacher-prof-dev

Dorph, G. Z., Stodolsky, S. S., & Wohl, R. (2002). Growing as teacher educators: Learning new professional development practices. *Journal of Jewish Education*, 68(1), 58–72. https://doi.org/10.1080/0021624020680108

Feiman-Nemser, S. (1990). Teacher preparation: Structural and conceptual alternatives. In W. R. Houston (Ed.), *Handbook of research on teacher education* (pp. 212–233). Macmillan.

Feiman-Nemser, S. (2001). From preparation to practice: Designing a continuum to strengthen and sustain teaching. *Teachers College Record*, 103(6), 1013–1055. https://doi.org/10.1111/0161-4681.00141

Feiman-Nemser, S. (2008a). Learning to teach. In R. L. Goodman, P. A. Flexner, & L. D. Bloomberg (Eds.), *What we now know about Jewish education: Perspectives on research for practice* (pp. 213–222). Torah Aura Productions.

Feiman-Nemser, S. (2008b). Teacher learning: How do teachers learn to teach? In M. Cochran-Smith, S. Feiman-Nemser, & D. J. McIntyre (Eds.), *Handbook of research on teacher education: Enduring questions in changing contexts* (pp. 697–705). Routledge.

Grant, L. D., & Kopelowitz, E. M. (2012). *Israel education matters: A 21st century paradigm for Jewish education*. Center for Jewish Peoplehood Education.

Grant, L. D., Marom, D., & Werchow, Y. (2013). *Israel education for what? An investigation of the purposes and possible outcomes of Israel education*. Israel Education Research Briefs for the Consortium for Applied Studies in Jewish Education. https://www.bjpa.org/search-results/publication/20971

Guskey, T. R. (2000). *Evaluating professional development*. Corwin Press.

Helsing, D., Howell, A., Kegan, R., & Lahey, L. (2008). Putting the "development" in professional development: Understanding and overturning educational leaders' immunities to change. *Harvard Educational Review, 78*(3), 437–465. http://dx.doi.org/10.17763/haer.78.3.888l759g1qm54660

Horowitz, B. (2012). *Defining Israel education*. The iCenter for Israel Education. www.theicenter.org

Isaacs, A. (2011). Israel education: Purposes and practices. In H. Miller, L. D. Grant, & A. Pomson (Eds.), *International Handbook of Jewish Education* (pp. 479–496). Springer.

Kegan, R. (1982). *The evolving self: Problem and process in human development*. Harvard University Press.

Kegan, R. (1994). *In over our heads: The mental demands of modern life*. Harvard University Press.

Kegan, R. (2000). What "form" transforms? A constructive-developmental approach to transformative learning. In Mezirow & Associates (Eds.), *Learning and transformation: Critical perspectives on a theory in progress* (pp. 35–70). Jossey-Bass.

Kegan, R., & Lahey, L. L. (2009). *Immunity to change: How to overcome it and unlock potential in yourself and your organization*. Harvard Business Press.

Kreber, C. (2012). Critical reflection and transformative learning. In E. W. Taylor & P. Cranton (Eds.), *Handbook of transformative learning* (pp. 323–341). Jossey-Bass.

Lawrence-Lightfoot, S., & Davis, J. H. (1997). *The art and science of portraiture*. Jossey-Bass.

Lortie, D. C. (1975). *Schoolteacher: A sociological study*. University of Chicago Press.

McDonald, J. (1992). *Teaching: Making sense of an uncertain craft*. Teachers College Press.

Merriam, S. B., & Kim, S. (2012). Studying transformative learning: What methodology. In E. W. Taylor & P. Cranton (Eds.), *The handbook of transformative learning: Theory, research, and practice* (pp. 56–72). Jossey-Bass.

Mezirow, J. (1990). How critical reflection triggers transformative learning. In Mezirow & Associates (Eds.), *Fostering critical reflection in adulthood: A guide to transformative and emancipatory learning* (pp. 1–20). Jossey-Bass.

Mezirow, J. (1991). *Transformative dimensions of adult learning*. Jossey-Bass.

Mezirow, J. (2000). Learning to think like an adult: Core concepts of transformation theory. In Mezirow & Associates (Eds.), *Learning as transformation: Critical perspectives on a theory in progress* (pp. 3–33). Jossey-Bass.

Patton, M. (2002). *Qualitative research and evaluation methods*. Sage.

Piaget, J. (1954). *The construction of reality in the child*. Basic Books.

Pomson, A., & Grant, L. (2003). *From in-service training to professional development: Alternative paradigms in Israel for diaspora educators*. Jewish Agency for Israel. https://www.bjpa.org/search-results/publication/787

Pomson, A., Wertheimer, J., & Hacohen-Wolf, H. (2014). *Hearts and minds: Israel in North American Jewish day schools*. Avi Chai Foundation.

Pope, D., Brown, M., & Miles, S. (2015). *Overloaded and underprepared: Strategies for stronger schools and healthy, successful kids*. Jossey-Bass.

Raider-Roth, M. (2017). *Professional development in relationship learning communities.* Teachers College Press.

Reingold, M. (2017). Not the Israel of my elementary school: An exploration of Jewish-Canadian secondary students' attempts to process morally complex Israeli narratives. *The Social Studies, 108*(3), 87–98. https://doi.org/10.1080/00377996.2017.1324392

Savin-Baden, M., & Major, C. H. (2013). *Qualitative research: The essential guide to theory and practice.* Routledge.

Servage, L. (2008). Critical and transformative practices in professional learning communities. *Teacher Education Quarterly, 35*(1), 63–77.

Shulman, L. (1986). Those who understand: Knowledge growth in teaching. *Educational Researcher, 15*(2), 4–14. https://doi.org/10.3102/0013189X015002004

Sinclair, A. (2013). *Loving the real Israel: An educational agenda for liberal Zionism.* Ben Yehuda Press.

Sinclair, A., Solmsen, B., & Goldwater, C. (2013). *The Israel educator: An inquiry into the preparation and capacities of effective Israel educators.* The Consortium for Applied Studies in Jewish Education.

Stieha, V., & Raider-Roth, M. (2012). Presence in context: Teachers' negotiations with the relational environment of school. *Journal of Educational Change, 13*(3), 511–534. http://dx.doi.org/10.1007/s10833-012-9188-z

Stodolsky, S., Dorph, G. Z., Feiman-Nemser, S., & Hecht, S. (2004). *Boston MTEI: Leading the way to a new vision for teachers and schools.* Mandel Foundation, Mandel Center for Jewish Education at Brandeis University, Bureau of Jewish Education of Greater Boston.

Stodolsky, S., Dorph, G. Z., & Rosov, W. (2008). Teacher professional development in congregational settings. *Religious Education, 103*(2), 240–260. https://doi.org/10.1080/00344080801910073

Tennant, M., & Pogson, P. (1995). *Learning and change in the adult years: A developmental perspective.* Jossey-Bass.

Troen, S. I., & Fish, R. (2017). *Essential Israel: Essays for the 21st century.* Indiana University Press.

Winer, L. N. (2019). *Teaching who they are: American-born supplementary school teachers connections with Israel* [Doctoral dissertation, The Jewish Theological Seminary of America]. ProQuest Dissertations Publishing. https://www.proquest.com/openview/4f7df7d2d80492079b57d2d0133852d4/1?pq-origsite=gscholar&cbl=18750&diss=y

Zakai, S. (2011). Values in tension: Israel education at U.S. day school. *Journal of Jewish Education, 77*(3), 239–265. https://doi.org/10.1080/15244113.2011.603070

Zakai, S. (2012, November 27). Jewish education caught in the crossfire of a most uncivil war. *The Times of Israel.* http://blogs.timesofisrael.com/

Zakai, S., & Cohen, H. T. (2016). American Jewish children's thoughts and feelings about the Jewish state: Laying the groundwork for a developmental approach to Israel education. *Contemporary Jewry, 36*(1), 31–54. https://doi.org/10.1007/s12397-016-9160-y

Zeichner, K., & Liston, D. (1996). *Reflective teaching: An introduction.* Lawrence Erlbaum Associates.

Conclusion

MATT REINGOLD

On a snowy Friday afternoon in March 2023, Shawn stops me in the hallways of the Jewish secondary school where we both teach. He asks if I have a moment to talk about something that happened that morning in his 11th grade course on the Arab–Israeli conflict. Shawn is a new teacher at the school, and as one of the heads of the Jewish History Department, I frequently meet with him to discuss how his courses are going and whether I might be able to offer any feedback or suggestions. On this day, he shares with me his surprise that he was branded a right-wing Zionist in class by his students for what his learners perceived as his failure to adequately account for the ways that Jews mistreated Arabs in British Mandate Palestine in the 1920s.

Shawn's surprise at the accusation was threefold. First, Shawn personally identifies as a left-wing Israeli. Second, despite being a new teacher at our high school, he had been teaching Israeli history in elementary Jewish day schools in North America for almost a decade and had never once been called right-wing by any of his students. Third, having completed his teacher training in Israel, where he was born and raised, he had always prided himself on developing balanced lessons that presented multiple sides to an issue.

The confluence of factors—Shawn's Israeli nationality, his personal politics, his pedagogical orientation, his newness to teaching Israel in a North American high school—yielded a pedagogical conundrum for him. As Shawn and I debriefed the experience, what first stood out to me was his deep desire to understand this moment in his teaching. This was not just a desire to catalogue a curious incident; rather, it was an attempt to understand better what he had done that led his students to steer the lesson in a direction away from the history of Israel and towards Shawn's own politics. Analyzing the incident by discussing what had happened in his lesson design and implementation would, he hoped, not only help him understand that morning's lesson but be able to better plan his future lessons.

As I reflected on our conversation that weekend, I kept thinking about Shawn's classroom experience and his reflections upon it. First was Shawn's concern not just that students felt that the lesson was politicized, but rather that it was politicized in a way that ran counter to his own identity. I wondered whether, in his attempt to *depoliticize* the learning and avoid teaching to his own politics, he had veered too hard in the opposite direction and presented unintentionally a lesson that was misconstrued as single-sided and biased in favor of right-wing ideology. Second, I wondered whether despite having taught high school students in Israel and taught about Israel in Canada, Shawn's newness at teaching about Israel to high school students was a factor. Students' sensitivity to his language, his greater awareness of the geopolitics involving Israel, and his being more attuned to the pedagogical moves he was making made teaching Israel in high school very different from teaching Israel in elementary school. What also stood out to me was the fact that Shawn's classroom moment lasted for far less time than the amount of time he and I spent reflecting on what it could mean for his pedagogy.

Each of the preceding chapters in this volume offer educators like Shawn cases to learn from and ways to conceptualize and think about how to teach Israel. In this conclusion, I offer cross-cutting conclusions that emerge from considering how individual chapters speak to or work in concert with other chapters. These conclusions are intended to draw the readers' attention to broader pedagogical considerations in the teaching of Israel and to identify lines of inquiry that can shape future research agendas. Perhaps most importantly, reading about the practices of others can provide an impetus to revisit our own pedagogy and to interrogate how we teach learners about Israel.

Learning About Teaching From Diverse Learning Sites

For better or worse, many educators spend the entirety of their teaching careers in one type of educational setting. As a result, they rarely have the opportunity to engage with educators who teach learners at different

CONCLUSION · 357

stages of life or in different educational environments. Teacher research has demonstrated that teachers work better when they have the opportunity to collaborate and learn from others (Dorph, 2011; Duckworth, 1997; Dufour & Eaker, 1998; Raider-Roth, 2017), and this volume provides such opportunities for teachers to learn not only from settings that are similar to their own but also from settings that differ from the contexts in which they teach. This is because, as the authors of this volume have shown, different educational sites require different pedagogical approaches. Thoughtful educators will recognize that foreign sites can be viewed as fertile learning grounds and not be dismissed out of hand. As Lauren Applebaum mentions in Chapter 13, "stepping outside of the school environment can offer a new perspective on the assumptions embedded within the school culture and offers a new vantage point for considering daily classroom practice."

An example of where cross-site learning may prove beneficial can be seen when day-school Israel education and experiential gap-year programs are analyzed in relation to each other. In my chapter coauthored with Alexa Jacoby and Benjamin Day, we identified that a unique feature of my contemporary Israeli society class is that it introduces students to perspectives and voices of authors from Israeli communities that most students have never before encountered. These include Arab citizens of Israel, like Sayed Kashua in his *Haaretz* newspaper columns and his television program *Arab Labor*, the poetry of the Mizrahi (Judeo-Arab) author Adi Keissar, and the political cartoons of the religious-nationalist artist Shay Charka. I prided myself on creating a course that disrupted students' assumptions of Israel by introducing them to Israelis who are different from the ones they knew in the hope that these meetings would lead to new understandings of Israel.

Reading Bethamie Horowitz's analysis of the gap-year program Kivunim highlighted for me how, despite my best intentions, my own curricular approaches remain incomplete. She writes: "By situating the teaching of Israel within a broader frame that allows for different positionings of Israel and Jewish peoplehood, the program design in effect *decenters* Israel... and thereby serves to expand the understanding and placement of Israel in the Jewish imagination." Kivunim's robust travel itinerary calls attention to the unidirectionality of the meeting point that I am able to provide in my own classroom. Reading poetry, watching television programs, and parsing cartoons introduces students to new texts, but they do not provide opportunities for actual engagement. When students have questions about the text or the authorial intention or questions that extend beyond the text, the best that I can offer is the author's voice mediated through my own understanding of the author's work.

The problem that I am identifying is not so easily solvable; what Kivunim can do exceeds both the financial and logistical realities of most day schools. Furthermore, I like the course that I teach. I maintain that there is value in reading texts of this nature, and I believe that I play an important role in the classroom as the educator in the room. Kivunim reminds me to be more consciously aware of my role as a facilitator of dialogue and not as the owner of the content. I select and share texts but do not speak on behalf of texts. This awareness also raises important questions about the place of guest speakers in the classroom. The Kivunim model suggests that guest speakers do not need to be famous in order to be valuable. Instead, the opportunity to meet and converse in a purposeful dialogue can result in a meaningful engagement. Finding Mizrahi or Arab citizens of Israel who are willing to do less formal presenting and more discussing ideas and answering students' questions about their experiences may create an entirely new type of educational model in the classroom.

The opportunity to learn new practices from sites that differ from our own can operate in multiple directions. Just as my own classroom can benefit from methods employed by Kivunim and other gap-year programs where learners can interact with Israelis on a regular basis, Day's reflection on what he experienced in my classroom offers a model that may prove useful for Kivunim. Based solely on Horowitz's observations of the program in action, Kivunim's educators seem to prize oral forms of communication. She writes about the participants purposefully arranging themselves in a shared space in order to be receptive to each other and to reflecting out loud, often immediately following an experience. In my coauthored piece with Day and Jacoby, Day's inclusion of the assignment that he submitted weeks later speaks to the value of providing adequate time for learners to process deeply meaningful experiences and also to the importance of alternative modes of communication. Sometimes, thoughts need time to percolate before they are able to germinate; at other times, they need to be written down in order to capture the author's thoughts and feelings. Allocating time for these types of educational opportunities in experiential programming may prove beneficial for participants who are less comfortable speaking at short notice. Perhaps more importantly, doing so will also reinforce the notion that some ideas do take time to develop and that it is worthwhile to engage in a deeper and lengthier reflective process.

Diverse sites of learning can provide thoughtful teachers the opportunity to consider their own best practices and what works in their own classrooms in light of the practices of teachers who work in different educational settings. They can also help introduce educators to novel approaches that can be transposed across sites by adaptation to suit individual needs.

Educator Identities and Pedagogical Practice

One of the consistent themes running through this volume is the intersection of questions surrounding educators' personal politics and the ways that these politics impact how they approach their classrooms. To what extent should the educator's own politics—irrespective of what they are—be present in the classroom? Should there be a space where students come to learn what the educator believes or thinks about a given topic? Does not doing so demonstrate a personal engagement with Israel that teachers want their students to have? Or, alternatively, is the teacher's personal politics a type of privileged information that does not belong in the classroom because it may influence learners' beliefs or because it could overshadow the curriculum and inhibit students' abilities to think critically?

Three authors provide insights into these types of questions. In her examination of her evolving relationship with the boycott, divestment, and sanctions (BDS) movement, Mira Sucharov presents a compelling argument for why educators should be more transparent with their students about their own stances. She writes that by "incorporating an educator's own political thinking" in the classroom, "they are modeling what it looks like to be a scholar-activist." As opposed to worrying that she will coopt students' agency to arrive at their own political orientations towards Israel, Sucharov highlights the value of sharing her personal narrative. Doing so opens the lid on the process of arriving at political stances, modeling for students the complex navigating that thoughtful individuals do when thinking about Israel.

In a very different context, Diane Tickton Schuster's examination of the Israeli educator Rachel Korazim offers a beautiful portrait of how Korazim creates space in her classroom for what she calls "intimate dialogue." Schuster explains that "implicit in her reflections is Korazim's deep resolve to speak her truth while making it safe for others to voice what may be alternative perspectives." In Schuster's telling, the educator's truth or story is not tangential to the learning but central to it. Hearing the educator's own Israel story models for students how to craft their own Israel story and helps learners carve out a space where their truths can be heard, seen, and considered. This is a classroom space that is safe, where simultaneous truths are told and where learners can even disagree with each other all the while remaining civil and respectful. It is also a space that embraces Israel Scheffler's (1965) claim that teaching should be "practiced in such manner as to respect the student's intellectual integrity and capacity for independent judgment" (p. 131).

Lastly, Laura Novak Winer's study of how educators approach curriculum and teaching shows the folly of believing that personal politics and beliefs can ever be truly separated from the classroom. Instead, she advises that given this reality, "Israel educators who can consider their personal beliefs about Israel as a precursor to their interpretation and implementation of curricular materials will be more successful in their teaching." Her educators were more successful in the classroom once they came to accept that they always bring themselves into the classroom.

These three authors offer a compelling statement about why educators should be more willing to bring themselves into the classroom. I know, however, that this is something I have always been hesitant to do. Partly it has to do with my own discomfort sharing myself and being vulnerable amongst a group of people, but it also has to do with my own desire not to make the curriculum about me. I am also aware that some educators may not be comfortable telling their Israel stories because their personal politics do not align with their institution's political affiliations. Sivan Zakai (2011) has documented how ideological conflict between teachers, learners, administration, and even parents can lead to tension in both the institution and the classroom. Educators' reticence—for either personal or political reasons—in bringing themselves into the classroom is therefore understandable given these considerations.

Despite my own reservations, and inspired by these three scholars, I decided to try a pedagogical experiment by sharing with my students my own Israel journey in my fall 2021 section of a 12th-grade elective on contemporary Israeli society. On the concluding day of the course, I traced my history from an apathetic and uninterested Zionist to a right-wing anti-disengagement protestor to distancing myself from right-wing Israeli politics and shifting leftward. I revealed that the impetus for this shift was my own frustrations with Israeli policies, like the state's refusal to legitimize LGBTQ marriages or to recognize the contributions and merits of non-Orthodox streams of Judaism. I also invited students into the ways that I have become engaged in academic writing about Israel, showing them my published books about Israeli graphic novels and comics and explaining how engaging in academic pursuits has also contributed to my understanding of and relationship with Israel.

Admittedly, I was nervous to reveal so much of myself. I felt it was a calculated risk. I intentionally planned it for the last day of the course. I did not want my politics to be known in a way that might come to more explicitly shape the way my students read and thought about texts or to unduly influence their study of the established curriculum. I therefore simultaneously recognized the potential dangers of revealing personal politics while also accepting that it is disingenuous if not impossible to entirely omit my own biases. I hoped that by openly revealing them at a purposefully timed juncture that mitigates their impact, they can be more comfortably addressed. Much like Sucharov, I believed that by sharing in this way, I could model for the students how they too can evolve in their relationships with Israel in the directions that work best for them, especially since the students explicitly asked for this type of lesson and wanted to hear my story. Guided by Sucharov, Schuster, and Winer, I felt empowered by the experience, and it subsequently opened up dialogue with a number of students who asked follow-up questions and wanted to discuss their own evolving relationships with Israel and how our course of study has impacted their thinking.

Whether to bring one's own story into the classroom is dependent on a number of factors, including institutional policy, educator comfort, and student receptiveness. Nevertheless, the chapters authored by Sucharov, Schuster, and Winer offer a compelling case for the pedagogical benefits of linking together teachers' stories with the study of Israel. Effectively done, the classroom becomes a more personal space where individuals can explore their own connections and disconnections with Israel.

Creating Space for the Learner to Construct and Share Ideas

Intimately tied to educators' willingness to bring themselves into the classroom is their willingness or ability to draw their students into the learning experience. Four chapters addressed the fact that when teachers make the learning personal and relevant, students learn better as a result. Alongside my own essay with my students, Robin A. Harper, Joshua Ladon, and Jonathan Golden and Yoni Kadden also wrote about the pedagogical imperative of carving out space for learner voices.

In Ladon's philosophical inquiry into the nature of source sheets, he positions the authors on the page as participants in dialogue with the learners in the room. Notably, he highlights that it is not a unidirectional conversation; instead, the educator helps to curate the voices on the page and facilitate a dialogue on their behalf with the learners in the room, whose voices are just as important in the exchange. He writes: "these textual voices should be held as contributions to a conversation that also takes students' voices seriously... it is the role of the educator to draw participants into the ever-evolving tradition and invite them to prod, pushback, listen, and ponder." The clarity of Ladon's description of good pedagogy is that it gives a framework to explain the observations of many seasoned educators that the classroom experience can vary depending on the learners in the room even if the educator and the texts remain the same. By viewing the students in this way, Ladon not only elevates the students to a place of great importance within the classroom, but he suggests that the educational experience *should* be different with each pedagogical iteration because the variables have changed through the introduction of new learners in the space.

Much like Ladon's observation about the place of the learner, what both Jacoby's and Day's reflections demonstrate is that the dynamic they experienced in my classroom went beyond perfunctory respect towards the learners; instead, it was "a pedagogical orientation to the place of the learner as a partner in the educative process in which each meaningfully contributes to the learning and teaching processes." According to Jacoby, the atmosphere created—and my willingness to both cede space to the learners and to discuss sensitive topics—allayed her own anxieties and made her more comfortable to share her ideas with the classroom. Thus, the more opportunities that students have to share ideas coupled with demonstrations of validation by the educator, the more likely students will come to see their classroom as a community in which they are willing to bring themselves into the learning space and share.

Jacoby's openness towards acknowledging that she is both critical and connected to Israel offers a model for the type of connection that Golden and Kaden sought to inculcate in their learners. They write: "Connectedness is complicated, and teachers need to help students understand that sometimes connection takes the form of feelings we might code as warm or affectionate. And connection sometimes can take the form of struggle or feelings we might code as disappointment or anger." Jacoby's reflections of how I helped her navigate her disappointments with Israel resulted in her taking a stronger stance towards what she hopes Israel will become, rather than deciding to abandon the country altogether because of her frustrations. Thus, what both chapters highlight is the role of the educator in facilitating dialogues that lead students to gain more nuanced perspectives on how to be connected to Israel and how to more clearly name their own experiences as learners without abandoning their critical faculties.

Lastly, Harper's exploration of teaching about Israel at a multiethnic and multireligious urban college offers an alternative reason for the importance of granting students space to raise their voices. Unlike many of my own students who have been steeped in Israel-related discourse for almost their entire lives, for Harper's ethnically, culturally, and religiously diverse students, Israel is not a place they call home or even one that they spend much (if any) time thinking about. Instead, it is a country just like any other, and getting her students to buy in to the learning can take considerable work, just as it would require effort to get my students to buy in to learning about a country they have no connection to. And yet, as Harper writes, it is also *not* a country just like any other. It is one where many of the students *do* often have connections through their religious traditions. She writes that even though:

Israeli current affairs [may be] unknown... students may be intimate with Jerusalem from religious practice. Jerusalem is not foreign to them; it is the site where Jesus walked or Mohammad ascended. "Knowing" Jerusalem facilitates a conversation. It's a beginning. They can tell me about these places and then move from the ancient and religious/mythic to the contemporary, or from their religious practice to religious conflicts in contemporary Israel.

Giving space for learners to talk, reflect, and co-construct their own educational experiences transforms Israel from being an abstract, unknown place into a site of inquiry where learners do have connection, familiarity, and even interest.

What emerges from examining how learners reflected on their teachers' choices is a keen appreciation of how educators were able to draw the learner into the educational experience. When this was effectively done, the classroom became a space where learners felt that they, too, could become part of the educative process, where their ideas about Israel could be refined and honed, and where they could see that their thoughts and opinions actually mattered.

The Importance of Professional Learning Communities

Reading Harper's worries from the night before her first lesson of the semester about Israel reminded me of the staff-room conversations that I hear in my own school. She writes: "I couldn't sleep the night before the lesson about Israel. With so much antisemitism and anti-Israel sentiment in colleges across the nation, what will my class be like? Will there be backlash? Will my class end up on social media?" Harper's questions and concerns are different from the ones that I overhear in my Jewish day school; this is to be expected given the differences in our schools (high school vs. college) and learners (Jewish teenagers vs. religiously, culturally, and ethnically diverse adults). But despite these differences, educators who teach in Jewish day schools also espouse anxieties about teaching Israel.

Worries about the educator's role in negatively shaping student connections to Israel were evident in the responses of many of the Jewish educators in Keren E. Fraiman's study. The early childhood educators in

Sivan Zakai and Lauren Applebaum's study also voiced concerns about the role that they played in predetermining Israel's importance for students who have not made that decision on their own. Thus a common link runs through Harper's, Fraiman's, and Zakai and Applebaum's chapters, showing how teachers' orientations towards subject matter impact their perceived abilities to be effective in the classroom. While this is perhaps not surprising, neither is it surprising that their institutions continued to assign the educators courses about Israel because their schools believed they were effective Israel educators. It would behoove schools to find ways to address these anxieties in order to increase teacher self-confidence and performance as educators.

Beyond uncovering or exposing the anxieties that teachers demonstrate regarding the teaching of Israel, the chapters written by Fraiman, Applebaum, and Zakai and Applebaum testify to the role that professional learning communities can play in helping alleviate some of educators' concerns—and help them raise new and deeper questions about their own practice. All three of these chapters include rich descriptions of professional development amongst educators from different institutions. Fraiman contends that this professional development must provide educators "with a toolbox for creating a productive space for navigating... difficult conversations." This professional development directly acknowledges teachers' fears and confronts concerns head-on by trying to provide both practical solutions and strategies and also a space where teachers can discuss together in a group the pedagogical problems that cannot always be easily solved.

A further strategy that would help alleviate the worries raised in both Fraiman's and Harper's chapters can be found in Applebaum's chapter. As noted previously, Applebaum writes that for the educators she studied, the opportunity to learn about alternate sites provided new perspectives on what they experience in their own schools. Applebaum's emphasis on leaving the familiar milieu is important because it requires educators to hear about contexts and circumstances that are very different from their own. This can allow educators to hear perspectives that are both similar and different from their own. Sharing and brainstorming together with educators from different contexts can—hopefully—yield new insights into the concerns and worries surrounding the teaching of Israel.

Lastly, while not explicitly about teacher worries, the primary factor motivating Zakai and Applebaum's educators to form a community of practice was a desire to teach Israel more effectively to their young students. While the educators all wanted to offer meaningful Israel education, their own professional and academic backgrounds did not provide them with an understanding of best practices or even what the larger goals of Israel education are or should be. Through the dialogues that the early childhood educators had with their own teachers, both early child educators and their teacher educators came to a better understanding of the nature of the dilemmas and, even more importantly, to add layers of nuance to them. Zakai and Applebaum specifically identify, note, and emphasize that these new insights were only able to emerge "in the presence of external thought partners who help revisit, refine, and sharpen these questions." Thus, the opportunity to talk through pedagogical and professional challenges provided an impetus for professional growth. Zakai and Applebaum conclude that educators should not shy away from their uncertainties, but instead should lean into them in order to become even stronger educators. Were Fraiman's educators able to form a similar type of learning community and embrace their concerns as Zakai and Applebaum's early childhood educators have done, they might come to feel more comfortable in their professional practice and be more willing to teach about the Israeli–Palestinian conflict.

Teaching about Israel can be a fraught and lonely experience. It can make even the most seasoned and skilled educators anxious because of the complexities of the subject matter and the stakes involved because of the importance of the subject to teachers, administrators, parents, and even students. Professional learning communities (PLCs) can offer one possible solution to teachers' anxieties by providing educators a safe-enough space to voice these concerns and, more importantly, allow for collaboration to problem-solve and arrive at novel solutions to teach Israel more effectively.

New Models for Facilitating Personal Connections

In her literature review, Horowitz helpfully orients the reader to some of the models that have been designed to help students develop personal connections to Israel. She cites Robbie Gringras's (2004) "hugging and wrestling" model of simultaneously loving and being challenged by Israel, along with Lisa Grant and Ezra Kopelowitz's (2012) interest in moving students towards a place of mature love and critical engagement with Israel through an acceptance of Israel's faults alongside its merits (see also Alexander, 2015; Waxman, 2016). Horowitz writes that these models encouraged teachers to teach in ways that let students "move from black-and-white thinking to greater 'complexity,' to be able to see Israel in higher resolution and finer detail, instead of continuing to rely on simplistic ideas and images" while still ensuring that students have strong personal connections to Israel. Forming a personal connection between learners and Israel has long been a goal of Israel educators (Zakai, 2014), and a number of chapters in *Teaching Israel* offer novel strategies for helping build this type of emotional connection.

Golden and Kadden's qualitative study of Gann Academy's new model for teaching Israel to high school students shows how their school's approach calls for students to explicitly form relationships with Israel. Their curriculum is built on three pillars: connection, knowledge, and stance. In their chapter, they explain that the three pillars are interwoven, with each one leading to the next. For example, they write, "The acquisition of knowledge is action oriented and deeply connected to...stance." In their model, knowledge is a means to an end and not an end in itself. Being able to take a stance will allow students to form an even more intimate connection with Israel. Golden and Kadden's evaluation of learners' experiences demonstrates that being expected to take stances effectively helped students develop connections and gain knowledge. Moreover, their respondents concluded that "stance-taking [was] the linchpin to developing high rates of connection and knowledge on Israel." The novelty of Gann's approach is in how it structures connection as an academic requirement that students are assessed on as a component of their learning. An obvious concern is that students learn to parrot back what they think their teachers want of them. To this, Golden and Kadden highlight the importance of modeling a diverse set of acceptable stances.

In their study with a cohort of synagogue educators, Ezra Kopelowitz and Abby Pitkowsky determined that a common pedagogical goal running through the schools' pedagogy was a desire for students to "view the world as Jews." This approach emphasizes prioritizing student attachment to

Israel as a Jewish homeland as opposed to expecting students to memorize historical details about Israel. The educators' anecdotal observations was that their pedagogical approach was successful, with students seeing Israel as part their of Jewish identities.

Lastly, Horowitz's examination of a gap-year program that brings Diaspora Jewish youth to Israel to study together for a year reveals that participants' relationships with Israel were enhanced by positioning Israel as one among many sites of contemporary Jewish habitation. This is accomplished by having students spend the year based in Israel but engaged in extensive travel around the Jewish Diaspora, where they live amongst local Jewish communities. Horowitz contends that this experience enhances participants' relationships with Israel. "This approach of decentering and expansion situates Israel in a comparative mode, rather than bracketing it off as a mythic exemplar." The resulting relationships with Israel may seem counterintuitive since the program introduces students to a rich array of Jewish communities, but Horowitz shows how the experience of seeing other viable Jewish spaces leads students to refine their own thinking about the salience of Israel in their lives.

On the surface, Horowitz's, Golden and Kadden's, and Kopelowitz and Pitkowsky's chapters have very little in common. The studies are set in different educational spaces and even the roles of the interviewees in the educational experience differ. Yet what links them together is a common interest in highlighting pedagogical choices aimed at strengthening the relationships between students and Israel. What works in one setting may very well not work in another, and this is to be expected, but therein lies the beauty of considering these three chapters together. I will not be taking my high school students to India or Croatia, nor will I be teaching Israel as a part of a broader Jewish curriculum like Kivunim does. Furthermore, my own pedagogical orientation towards teaching Israel differs from the approach of Golden and Kadden at Gann, so I am less inclined to frame my curriculum around stance taking. And yet from each of these chapters I am able to extract nuggets of wisdom alongside practical strategies in order to help my students continue to develop their own connections and relationships with Israel. This can at times even include temporarily embracing these strategies for the purpose of selective lessons; for instance, I have arranged for structured debates in my classroom around specific Israeli policies in which students must take and defend a stance. Is this model the cornerstone of my teaching Israel philosophy? No, it isn't. But Golden and Kadden's chapter—much like the other two considered thus far in this section—should encourage educators to reconsider what they do in the classroom and to be willing to embrace alternative teaching choices in order to more effectively help students sharpen their connections with Israel.

Even as many Israel educators value cultivating their students' connections to Israel, the desire to form connections between learners and Israel also seems to be a source of angst for the Jewish educators featured in the chapters by Fraiman and Winer. The teachers they studied were concerned about the extent to which their own teaching of Israel's history may negatively impact existing connections between students and Israel and, in Fraiman's case, whether they could effectively teach the subject given uncertainties about their own connection to the country. Writing about very different settings, Amin Tarzi and Robin Harper employ orientations and tactics in teaching about Israel that might prove useful in allaying the kinds of worries expressed by Fraiman and Winer's respondents.

Tarzi is a professional military educator "not intimately involved in Israel studies" or personally connected with the story of Israel. In his chapter, he shares that he embraces his outsider standing and prizes the position that being one affords. In particular, he identifies his dispassionate stance towards Israel as a strength because it allows him to listen and learn—and therefore teach—more carefully and critically. As he explains, his stance allows him to arrive at Israel education goals that run counter to the ones espoused by many other Israel educators. He writes: "my goal is not to alter their perspectives or convictions about that country or what to think about it. Rather I seek to grow their abilities in perspective taking, listening, and analyzing objectively complex, layered situations, places, and people. Through the lens of Israel, I hope they learn these skills to apply in their future military endeavors."

In a similar vein, Harper's experiences teaching about Israel at York College elicited curiosity from her colleagues about why non-Jewish students would enroll in a course about Israel. Harper responds by asking why *not* study about Israel given that "Israel provides a fascinating case of settlement and return, refugees/asylum seekers, absorption and exclusion, border policies and citizenship, temporary labor migration, and ethnonational citizenship." While it is true that the types of classrooms where Tarzi and Harper teach differ from the classrooms where Fraiman's and Winer's study participants teach, their claim that Israel is intrinsically interesting has no relationship to the age of the learners. Tarzi and Harper both view the modern nation-state of Israel as a fascinating site of inquiry irrespective of a student's personal connection, suggesting that Israel educators do not need to sell Israel to their students in order to be effective teachers. While few Jewish day and supplementary schools would likely be willing to embrace the distanced position of these university educators, Israel education may at times be better served by adopting a teaching stance that gives students greater latitude to find Israel without the teacher serving as both educator and promoter. Trusting that students who learn about the complexity of Israel and the richness of its society without being told that "this place is amazing!" will require a recalibration for many educators, especially for those who teach in Jewish institutions. But I see this as a vital step in allowing students to form their own connections independent of their teachers' connections. Similarly, it may be liberating for some teachers—including the ones Fraiman identifies who shied away from teaching about Israel—to not have to take upon themselves the responsibility of teaching emotional connections. Instead, they can do what they do best, which is teach content and critical thinking without having to be an Israeli ambassador in the process.

What I am proposing here does not negate the reality that most Israel educators in Jewish educational settings do have stances towards Israel and are personally invested in the classroom. Furthermore, as I identified earlier when I documented my own experience of sharing my Israel story, there can be merit to bringing these perspectives into the classroom. Rather, I am suggesting that a move away from connection and relationship as explicit and primary curricular goals may prove liberating for students and teachers and allow for more authentic engagement in meaningful teaching and learning about Israel.

Admittedly, this new orientation will require a paradigm shift amongst many educators along with the institutions that teach about Israel. This is because an emphasis on students' connections to or love of Israel have long played a prominent role in the educational agenda of many North American Jewish schools and organizations (Zakai, 2014). Even in more recent years, where love has been tempered with content knowledge or with acceptance of Israel's imperfections, the educational enterprise in Jewish elementary schools, high schools, and supplementary schools has remained deeply and actively invested in building an emotional relationship between learners and Israel. This stems from a concern that absent connection-based learning, a personal relationship will not develop. What I am suggesting here, and this has been shown in small studies (e.g., Reingold, 2017, 2018), is that even absent an explicit pedagogical agenda to promote connection, relationships are still cultivated and nurtured through deliberate teaching.

Next-Step Questions for Research and Practice

In Chapter 10, Zakai and Applebaum introduce the idea of next-step questions, a tool that helps raise important issues which can guide both research agendas and classroom instruction. In identifying both research-based and practice-based next-step questions, a new conceptualization of the field of Israel education can begin.

Next-Step Questions for Research

» Teaching–Learning Nexus

This volume has sought to serve as a counterweight to what I see as an imbalance in the scholarly literature—of which I am also guilty—that has often prioritized outcomes over inputs, and the perspectives of learners over educators. This volume emphasizes the importance of teaching, shifting the focus away from learners and learner outcomes that have been so prominent in the discourse around Israel education. By bringing to the fore scholarship that primarily considers the choices and rationales of educators, this volume begins a scholarly shift towards a more complete understanding of what happens in the classroom and beyond. This move is crucial because in order to gain a fuller understanding of Israel education and the teaching of Israel, the role of the educator is no less important than that of the student.

At the same time, I would be remiss not to recognize that the teaching–learning nexus is not so easily divided and that the two are inexorably linked. While it is certainly cliché, it is also true that good teaching and good learning operate in tandem. And yet, scholars do not know very much about how this actually functions in the Israel education or Israel studies classroom. I believe that a future evolution for the research agenda of Israel education is to develop a stronger understanding of how the relationship between teachers and learners operates and how each plays a crucial role in the educational process.

A further research need emerges in relation to educators' identities. While students' relationships to Israel evolve over time (Zakai, 2021, 2022) and teachers learn and develop over time (Cochran-Smith, 2012), how this change process is manifested with regards to Israel educators or Israel studies professors has not yet been studied. It is safe to assume that educators' orientations towards Israel *do* shift over time and that these shifts lead to changes in their pedagogy, but there is a need for longitudinal studies of Israel educators in order to understand how teachers' identities evolve, what contributes to the impetuses for pedagogical change, how these changes are expressed in the classroom, and what professional supports might help teachers as they develop and refine their practice

In order to effectively implement such studies to better our understanding of Israel education over time so that even richer education can be offered to learners, the field needs to expand in two different ways. First, we need scholars who are capable—both in terms of skill set and institutional support—of developing robust long-term research agendas and of collaborating with colleagues on joint ventures like this. Additionally, studies like those proposed here require access to significant funds, and therefore grants—from both within and without the Jewish community—need to be secured alongside new fundraising initiatives that explicitly target these types of long-term study.

» Studying Alternative Teaching Sites

One of the broad claims of this volume is that the teaching of Israel takes place in a variety of settings and that while there are transferable lessons between them, each milieu poses its own unique set of challenges and opportunities. This book includes chapters where Israel is taught in early childhood classrooms, Jewish day schools, synagogue congregations, gap-year study-abroad programs, adult-education classes, college and university lecture halls, and professional military institutions. Despite this breadth, this list is not exhaustive. Missing are other sites where the teaching of Israel occurs, some of which—like summer camps, online education, heritage tours—have received scholarly attention elsewhere (Reingold, 2021; Sasson et al., 2014; Saxe & Chazzan, 2008; Sinclair, 2009), while others—like museums, guided tours, rabbinic-studies programs for clergy from a range of religious communities, sessions led by Israeli emissaries teaching about Israel in Diaspora communities, the halls of congress, and elsewhere—have not yet received sufficient scholarly attention. Studying how Israel is taught in these sites needs to be conducted not just so that as a field we can say that research was conducted there too. Rather, studying these types of sites requires a recognition of the unique ways that different educational sites present both pedagogical challenges and opportunities. To understand better the ways that teachers of Israel teach and learners of Israel learn, we need to expand to under-studied sites of Israel education while asking new questions about the places where we already have begun to gain an understanding of how Israel is taught and learned.

Next-Step Questions for Practice

In considering the types of next-step questions that can inform practice, I use the four sections that constitute *Teaching Israel* to structure this part of the conclusion. Doing this recognizes the unique merits of each section's focus and the ways that each can lead to transformations in pedagogy.

» The Reflective Teacher

In the first section of *Teaching Israel*, Harper, Tarzi, and Ladon reflect on their own practice as Israel educators and teachers of Israel in different settings. In their own way, each makes a powerful case for the importance of reflection in improving their pedagogy and for helping them develop a sharper understanding of the choices that they make in the classroom. While I would like to believe that all teachers engage in reflective practice—at least implicitly and subconsciously—my own experiences tell me that this is not the case. The three chapters in this section therefore raise questions about how to help coach and guide teachers to become reflective in their practice and to see the benefits associated with regularly engaging in this type of exercise.

Over the previous three decades, considerable scholarly attention has been given towards understanding how reflective practices can be taught (Richert, 1990) and used to improve teachers' professional competencies (Brookfield, 2017; Larrivee, 2000; Valli, 1992), and there is also evidence of its practice in Jewish education (Hassenfeld & Levisohn, 2019; Stodolsky et al., 2006). Despite this, the role of reflective practice in Israel education or Israel studies has not been explored, nor has how to best support teachers of Israel in becoming reflective practitioners. Gaining this knowledge of reflective practice in a field-specific context has practical benefits in that it will help educators evolve in their practice, refine their pedagogy, and make more informed choices about what they want to have happen in their classrooms. What is therefore needed are studies that examine how teachers alter—or do not alter—their own teaching as they engage in reflective practice. By way of example, much of my own research in Israel education involves practitioner research studies, but I have never formally returned to any of these studies to trace the ways that my own study results have actually impacted what I do in the classroom and to share these reflections in a public and scholarly forum. A further line of inquiry that would be worthwhile when thinking about educators and reflective practice is to what extent educators are aware of their own biases in teaching and how these biases impact their ability to teach a diverse student body and to hear the voices of different learners.

» Using Student Voices to Examine Teacher Choices

Three chapters introduced student voices to reflect on the pedagogical choices made by their classroom teachers. With the exception of a few instances of dissent from the surveyed alumni in Golden and Kadden's study, all three of Reingold, Jacoby, and Day's; Golden and Kadden's; and Schuster's chapters introduced student voices reflecting on the pedagogical choices made by their classroom teachers. With few exceptions, students offer positive reflections on their experiences in class. This is not merely lip service paid to educators with whom they enjoyed learning. The first-person narrated portraits provided by Day, Jacoby, and Schuster highlight how, from their perspective, their educators effectively balanced complex texts, topics, and interpersonal dynamics.

At the same time, the voices of other learners, ones who perhaps felt alienated or who did not benefit from the instruction, could prove even more useful because they could help facilitate transformation in practice through an increased awareness of how diverse learners received the instruction. The question, and this is certainly evident in Golden and Kadden's low response rate to their alumni survey, is how to engage with and elicit responses from students who are either not forthcoming in their classroom reflections or who actually had negative experiences in the Israel classroom.

Hearing difficult feedback from students—even if presented in a respectful way—is hard for many people. How can teachers of Israel be coached to listen with an open mind to the feedback without becoming defensive? Directly related to listening to feedback is determining whether the feedback has merit; therefore, it is important to ask how teachers can be helped to make informed choices about which feedback should be integrated into their teaching and which should not.

» Navigating the Teaching of Politics and the Politics of Teaching

Section 3 introduced readers to questions about how politics shape teaching. I valued learning from educators who grappled with the dynamic between their own political stances and how they were able (or unable) to bring those perspectives into the classroom. The three chapters approached the question from different vantage points, with Sucharov speaking from the classroom, Horowitz's facilitators representing a single private educational organization, and Fraiman's respondents representing educators from diverse settings from across North America. Additionally, these authors and educators had different attitudes towards what types of politics can be given space in the classroom. Their perspectives reveal that beyond their different political orientations, they also have different orientations towards politics in relation to teaching. For me their work raises questions about the place of institutional red lines—what is considered acceptable and unacceptable Israel discourse and how individual Israel educators should maintain their institutional commitment while retaining their personal integrity. When they experience conflict between the two, how are they navigating it?

The question that links the three chapters together is "How does politics shape teaching?" An equally important next-step question is "How does teaching shape politics?" This question is not so highbrow as to assume that what an individual teacher does in a classroom has the potential to reshape our geopolitical landscape and affect the decisions made by world leaders. Instead, it raises questions about how and to what extent the teaching of Israel can lead students to experience shifts in their own political stances. The assumption underlying this question is that students and learners of all ages are impressionable and that therefore what teachers do in the classroom can lead to new attitudes. Therefore, a related next-step question could ask teachers to consider to what extent they should be actively aware of their ability to affect learners and how or if they should manage this in the classroom when teaching complex topics.

A further question that links together pedagogy and politics is what the place is for contemporary events in Israel to be brought into the classroom. In theory, integrating current events into learning makes sense because it shows students what is happening in Israel in the present. In practice, however, doing so is not so simple. First, any change to classroom practice moves slowly (Tyack & Cuban, 1997). Reading the news to inform students of current events is not teaching; educators need time to not only prepare thoughtful lessons but to also study how to teach current events if they do not have the pedagogical content knowledge to do so. A second concern is the uncertainty of what is newsworthy enough to interrupt the curriculum in order to add in new material. A third concern is the uncertainty of when a news story is finished; teaching partial stories or incomplete narratives could lead to confusion amongst students and educators given the rapid pace that news changes. Teaching current events also requires educators to be very informed on the news, sometimes even during the middle of the day, and this, too, can be a challenge. None of these concerns should negate the value of teaching current events, especially if students are already talking about them. Rather, institutions need to find ways to grant educators the time and space to make these important and necessary changes to curriculum so that the current events can be taught in an effective and meaningful way.

» When Teachers Learn

Section 4, titled "When Teachers Learn," turns the scholarly gaze towards how teachers' ongoing professional development creates enrichment and paradigm-shifting opportunities for teaching Israel. As a next-step question, teachers may want to consider how they can hold themselves accountable to actually implementing the new pedagogies they learned into their practice. On an institutional level, next-step questions can be raised about how administrators and senior staff can affect cultural shifts such that gleanings from professional development are actually integrated within the organization and its members' practice. Additionally, given the rich data about professional development operating best when focused on problems of practice and where dissenting voices and perspectives are encouraged (Raider-Roth et al., 2014), it bears asking how institutions are supporting the creation of purposeful professional learning communities (PLCs) to enhance teacher professional development. Given the widely differing political stances on Israel and pedagogical orientations towards the teaching of it, PLCs addressing the challenges in Israel education can be rich sites for professional development in which open-minded educators can share ideas, learn from colleagues, and refine their own practices.

Conclusion

In the introduction, Zakai identified this volume's goal of shifting the gaze of Israel education and Israel studies away from the outcomes of teaching in order to focus on the pedagogical choices made by the educators who help bring about those outcomes. By placing the spotlight on teaching, this volume has sought to expand the field's understanding of the crucial role that teachers and the choices they make play in the teaching of Israel.

Teaching Israel is designed to spark a conversation and fill a gap in the existing literature about the ways that educators teach about Israel, but it is not designed to be the final chapter on teaching Israel. Many educators are doing fascinating work in their own as-yet-unstudied classrooms, lecture halls, camps, and synagogue discussion groups. Chapters about these spaces and the teachers who staff them remain to be written, and I look forward to reading about them so that our field can continue to expand through increased opportunities to learn from one another. Only then will we truly have a robust understanding of the complexities of teaching Israel and how teaching shapes (or hinders) meaningful student learning about Israel across context, setting, and age group. What I have seen throughout this volume is the transformative power of good teaching; it can change the learner, the teacher, the subject matter, and even how pedagogy is understood. Yet the full potential of teaching in general and teaching Israel in particular can only be realized if we continue to explore what good teaching is and what it can offer the fields of education and Israel studies.

REFERENCES

Alexander, H. (2015). Mature Zionism: Education and the scholarly study of Israel. *Journal of Jewish Education, 81*(2), 136–161. https://doi.org/10.1080/15244113.2015.1035979

Brookfield, S. D. (2017). *Becoming a critically reflective teacher*. Jossey-Bass.

Cochran-Smith, M. (2012). A tale of two teachers: Learning to teach over time. *Kappa Delta Pi Record, 48*(3), 108–122. https://doi.org/10.1080/00228958.2012.707501

Dorph, G. Z. (2011). Professional development of teachers in Jewish education. In H. Miller, L. D. Grant, & A. Pomson (Eds.), *International handbook of Jewish education* (Vol. 2, pp. 959–980). Springer.

Duckworth, E. (1997). *Teacher to teacher: Learning from each other*. Teachers College Press.

Dufour, R., & Eaker, R. (1998). *Professional learning communities at work: Best practices for student achievement*. Solution Tree.

Hassenfeld, Z. R., & Levisohn, J. A. (2019). The challenge of professional development in Jewish studies: Why the conventional wisdom may not be enough. *Journal of Jewish Education, 85*(1), 53–75. https://doi.org/10.1080/15244113.2018.1558386

Larrivee, B. (2000). Transforming teacher practice: Becoming the critically reflective teacher. *Reflective Practice, 1*(3), 293–307. https://doi.org/10.1080/713693162

Lortie, D. C. (1975). *Schoolteacher: A sociological study*. University of Chicago Press.

McDonald, J. (1992). *Teaching: Making sense of an uncertain craft*. Teachers College Press.

Raider-Roth, M. (2017). *Professional development in relational learning communities: Teachers in connection*. Teachers College Press.

Raider-Roth, M., Stieha, V., Kohan, M., & Turpin, C. (2014). "The false promise of group harmony": The centrality of challenging practices in teachers' professional development. *Journal of Jewish Education, 80*(1), 53–77. https://doi.org/10.1080/15244113.2014.875348

Reingold, M. (2017). Not the Israel of my elementary school: An exploration of Jewish-

Canadian secondary students' attempts to process morally complex Israeli narratives. *The Social Studies, 108*(3), 87–98. https://doi.org/10.1080/00377996.2017.1324392

Reingold, M. (2018). Broadening perspectives on immigrant experiences: Secondary students study the absorption difficulties faced by Mizrachi immigrants in Israel. *Journal of Jewish Education, 84*(3), 312–329. https://doi.org/10.1080/15244113.2018.1478531

Reingold, M. (2021). Meaningful Zoom education?: A 2020 coronavirus case study on emotionally engaging Israel learning. *Journal of Jewish Education, 87*(4), 417–443. https://doi.org/10.1080/15244113.2021.1928571

Richert, A. E. (1990). Teaching teachers to reflect: A consideration of programme structure. *Journal of Curriculum Studies, 22*(6), 509–527. https://doi.org/10.1080/0022027900220601

Sasson, T., Shain, M., Hecht, S., Wright, G., & Saxe, L. (2014). Does Taglit-Birthright Israel foster long-distance nationalism? *Nationalism and Ethnic Politics, 20*(4), 438–454. https://doi.org/10.1080/13537113.2014.969149

Saxe, L., & Chazzan, B. (2008). *Ten days of Birthright Israel: A journey in young adult identity*. Brandeis University Press.

Scheffler, I. (1965). Philosophical models of teaching. *Harvard Educational Review, 35*(2), 131–143. https://doi.org/10.17763/haer.35.2.l662lq6433oml253

Sinclair, A. (2009). A new heuristic device for the analysis of Israel education: Observations from a Jewish summer camp. *Journal of Jewish Education, 75*(1), 79–106. https://doi.org/10.1080/15244110802654575

Stodolsky, S. S., Dorph, G. Z., & Feiman-Nemser, S. (2006). Professional culture and professional development in Jewish schools: Teachers' perceptions and experiences. *Journal of Jewish Education, 72*(2), 91–108. https://doi.org/10.1080/00216240600561866

Tyack, D., & Cuban, L. (1997). *Tinkering toward utopia: A century of public school reform*. Harvard University Press.

Valli, L. (Ed.) (1992). *Reflective teacher education: Cases and critiques*. State University of New York Press.

Waxman, D. (2016). *Trouble in the tribe: The American Jewish conflict over Israel*. Princeton University Press.

Zakai, S. (2011). Values in tension: Israel education at a U.S. Jewish day school. *Journal of Jewish Education, 77*(3), 239–265. https://doi.org/10.1080/15244113.2011.603070

Zakai, S. (2014). "My heart is in the East and I am in the West": Enduring questions of Israel education in North America. *Journal of Jewish Education, 80*(3), 287–318. https://doi.org/10.1080/15244113.2014.937192

Zakai, S. (2021). "It makes me feel many different things": A child's relationships to Israel over time. *Journal of Jewish Education, 87*(2), 120–143. https://doi.org/10.1080/15244113.2021.1926375

Zakai, S. (2022). *My second-favorite country: How American Jewish children think about Israel*. New York University Press.

Contributors

SIVAN ZAKAI is the Sara S. Lee Associate Professor of Jewish Education at the Hebrew Union College-Jewish Institute of Religion and an affiliated scholar at the Jack, Joseph and Morton Mandel Center for Studies in Jewish Education at Brandeis University. She directs the Children's Learning About Israel Project, a longitudinal study of American Jewish children, and codirects Project ORLIE: Research and Leadership in Israel Education, a professional-development and research program for Jewish educators who teach about Israel. She is the author of *My Second Favorite Country: How American Jewish Children Think About Israel* (winner of the 2022 National Jewish Book Award in Education and Jewish Identity) and over a dozen academic articles about teaching and learning about Israel in the United States.

MATT REINGOLD is a practitioner-researcher of Israel education. He teaches at TanenbaumCHAT in Toronto, Canada, where he also serves as the cohead of the Jewish History Department. He has published many journal articles about arts-based learning, Israel Education, and Jewish graphic novels. His book, *Gender and Sexuality in Israeli Graphic Novels: Contested Masculinity and Independent Femininity*, was published by Routledge in 2021 and is the first to explore the unique contributions of graphic novels for understanding Israeli society. He is also the author of *Reenvisioning Israel Through Political Cartoons: Visual Discourses During the 2018–2021 Electoral Crisis* (Lexington), *Jewish Comics and Graphic Narratives* (Bloomsbury), and *The Comics of Asaf Hanuka: Telling Particular and Universal Stories* (Academic Studies). He earned his PhD from York University while serving as a Wexner Fellow and Davidson Scholar.

LAUREN APPLEBAUM is the director of DeLeT: Day School Leadership Through Teaching at Hebrew Union College-Jewish Institute of Religion and the codirector of Project ORLIE: Research and Leadership in Israel Education.

BENJAMIN DAY is an engineering physics student at Queen's University in Canada. He is an alumnus of Toronto's Jewish day school system and graduated TanenbaumCHAT in 2019.

KEREN E. FRAIMAN is the dean and chief academic officer at Spertus Institute for Jewish Learning and Leadership and professor of Israel studies. She holds a PhD in political science from the Massachusetts Institute of Technology.

382 · CONTRIBUTORS

JONATHAN GOLDEN is the Director of Wellspring Leadership Initiatives at the Shalom Hartman Institute of North America. Prior to his role at Hartman, he served as the Israel Curriculum Coordinator at Gann Academy in Waltham, Massachusetts.

ROBIN A. HARPER is professor of political science at York College (City University of New York), where her research and teaching centers on policies of comparative citizenship, immigrant incorporation, borders, inclusion/exclusion, and temporary labor migration policies in Germany, Israel, and the United States.

BETHAMIE HOROWITZ is director of professional learning communities for CASJE (Collaborative for Applied Studies in Jewish Education) at George Washington University. A sociopsychologist, she has published widely on the sociology of American Jews in terms of population, identity, community, and education. From 2007–2020 she was a faculty member and eventually codirector of the PhD program in education and Jewish studies at New York University.

ALEXA JACOBY is an undergraduate student at Queen's University pursuing a bachelor of arts. She graduated from TanenbaumCHAT in 2021, where she served as copresident of the Student Council.

YONI KADDEN is a history teacher at Gann Academy in Waltham, Massachusetts. He recently served as department chair and leads a number of project-based learning initiatives, including "Ma'avar," Gann Academy's senior capstone experience.

EZRA KOPELOWITZ is the CEO of Research Success Technologies, a company that specializes in research and evaluation for Jewish organizations. He is on the faculty of the Spertus Institute for Jewish Learning and Leadership.

JOSHUA LADON is the director of education for the Shalom Hartman Institute of North America.

ABBY PITKOWSKY, the former director of Israel education and Westchester Region of New York at The Jewish Education Project, is currently the program director of The Covenant Foundation.

DIANE TICKTON SCHUSTER directs the Portraits of Adult Jewish Learning Project for the Jack, Joseph and Morton Mandel Center for Studies in Jewish Education at Brandeis University. She is the author of *Jewish Lives, Jewish Learning: Adult Jewish Learning in Theory and Practice* (URJ Press, 2003).

MIRA SUCHAROV is professor of political science and former university chair of Teaching Innovation at Carleton University in Ottawa, Canada. She is the author or editor of five books, including *Social Justice and Israel/Palestine: Foundational and Contemporary Debates* (University of Toronto Press, 2019), coedited with Aaron J. Hahn Tapper.

AMIN TARZI is the director of Middle East Studies, Krulak Center for Innovation and Future Warfare, and professor at the Marine Corps University in Quantico, Virginia (USA), and a senior fellow for the Program on the Middle East at the Foreign Policy Research Institute. He is also an adjunct professor of international relations at George Mason University.

LAURA NOVAK WINER is the director of the Master of Educational Leadership Program for the Rhea Hirsch School of Education at Hebrew Union College-Jewish Institute of Religion (HUC-JIR) in Los Angeles. She holds an EdD from the William Davidson Graduate School of Jewish Education at the Jewish Theological Seminary of America and rabbinic ordination from HUC-JIR.

Index

Page numbers in *italic* refer to tables.

academic boycotts, 206, 207–210, 217–218, 219, 220–221
academic freedom, 208–210, 218–220, 224
acceptance of Israel's faults, 367, 371
acquisition of knowledge, 6, 7, 155, 156, 161, 240, 313–315, 328
acquisition of skills, 6, 69, 76, 223, 236–237, 369
adult learning, 130, 272, 334, 350–351. *See also* professional development and learning
advocacy, 157, 333, 336, 341, 342
AfD (*Alternative für Deutschland*), 195, 202n13
aggadah (folklore), 89
Ahad Ha'am, 88–90, 92, 94, 97, 100
Ahavat Zion (love of Israel), 338, 339
Alexander, Hanan A., 111
alignment, 337–338, 340–342, 347–348
aliyah (immigration to Israel), 50, 86, 114, 293, 295, 296, 300, 336
Alma (house of study), 87
Altalena (film), 77
Alterman, Natan, 138, 141–142
alternative teaching sites to classrooms, 372–373
Ambrose, Susan, 37, 42
American-born teachers, 283–304
American Jews, 3, 14–16, 86, 179–200, 229, 275, 284, 288, 289, 309–310, 312, 316, 322, 330n1, 341
American public opinion about Israel, 14
Amichai, Yehuda, 41
Am Yisrael (global Jewish community), 341

Anderson, Benedict, 43, 92
anger, 241–243
anthologies, 89–91
anti-oppression pedagogy, 210–224
antisemitism, 48–50, 208, 217
Applebaum, Lauren, 357, 365–366, 371
Arab citizens of Israel, 191, 357–358
Arabic, 190–192, 199
Arab–Israeli conflict, 7–8, 63–64, 69, 112, 141, 212, 355
Arab-Israeli-Palestinian Conflict course, MCWAR, 67–68
Arab Labor (television program), 357
Arab states, 67, 69, 81n12, 169, 212, 213, 215
Arian, Asher, 39
arms-manufacturing companies, 210
Aron, Isa, 11, 315
Ashkenazi, 57n3
asking questions, 192–193, 195, 272, 339. *See also* stances
assessment, 41–45, 50, 107, 120, 198, 202n12, 215, 358–359
Association of Israel Studies, 68–69
assumptions and beliefs, 111, 122, 334–335, 337–339, 342, 343–344, 345, 347–348, 349, 350
asymmetrical conflicts, 213
attachment to Israel, 309–312, 330n1. *See also* connections to Israel

Bain, Ken, 37, 41, 47–48
banking model of education, 124–125. *See also* Freire, Paulo
Barghouti, Omar, 209, 224
Baron, Ilan Zvi, 14

barriers to engagement. *See* conflict education
Bartal, Israel, 90–91
Barton, Keith C., 234, 251n5
BDS (boycott, divestment, and sanctions against Israel), 205–224; academic and cultural boycott, 207–210; anti-oppression pedagogy, 210–224; both sides conundrum in the classroom, 221–224; educator identities, 359; outcomes and tactics, 215–220; personal reflection, 220–221; social justice, 210–216
Beghetto, Ronald, 109–110
Beit El, 136–138, 141, 143
Beit Shmuel, 187
beliefs. *See* assumptions and beliefs
Bell, Dean P., 325
Ben-Gurion, David, 199–200
Ben-Peretz, Miriam, 93–94
Berger, David H., 62–63
Berila, Beth, 212
best practices in early childhood Israel education, 274–275
Bialik, Hayim Nachman, 88–90, 92, 100–101
Biesta, Gert, 97–99
Birthright Israel, 184–185
bonds between Jews in America and Israel, 287, 316
Borg, Walter R., 160
Bortolin, Kathleen, 211
both sides conundrum in the classroom, 221–224
boycott, divestment, and sanctions against Israel (BDS). *See* BDS (boycott, divestment, and sanctions against Israel)
bridge building, 189–190, 192, 197
British Mandate, 17, 57n1, 355
Brookfield, Stephen, 140, 347
Brooks, Laurie, 241
Brother Daniel, 111, 113, 115, 116, 117, 119, 122
Brown, Matthew W., 95
Buber, Martin, 289

Calderon, Ruth, 86–88, 90
campuses, 217–219
Center for Nonproliferation Studies (CNS), 65, 81n8
Centre for Innovation and Excellence in Learning, 211
charged learning experiences, 240–241
Charka, Shay, 357
Chazan, Barry, 12, 17, 130, 140–144, 146, 288, 304n4
child-centered learning environments, 266–267. *See also* early childhood education and educators
children's relationships with Israel, 288–289
Christian Evangelicals, 93
Christianity, 67, 111
church and state, 54, 113–115
citizenship, 98, 111–112, 113–114, 117, 295, 325–326
classroom learning/practice, 107–126; adult learning, 350; connections to Israel, 298–301; creating space, 362–364; educator identities, 359–362; next-step questions, 268–276, 371–376; synagogue supplementary schools, 312–315
coalition system, 119–120
coexistence, 191–192
cognition, 92, 93–94, 96
Cohen, David K., 221
collaboration, 258–259, 274–275, 333–334, 357, 366
collective trauma, 223–224
collective values, 325–326
commonplaces, 11
communal leaders, 184
communal norms, 318
communal pressures, 230, 233, 245, 247–249
communal support, 246–247
Community of Practice (CoP), 258–259, 265
compendiums of Jewish texts, 89, 92
complexify approach, 286–287, 289–290, 292–293, 300, 302, 316

INDEX · 387

complexities, 185–187, 366; assumptions and beliefs, 343–344; connections to Israel, 154; critical thinking, 124, 344; getting better, 345–346; Israeli-Palestinian conflict, 10, 36–37, 39, 57n12, 207, 212–215, 218, 242; and Korazim, 146–147; prior knowledge, 51–53; in teaching practices, 73–75, 107–126, 283, 376; values in tension, 241, 338–339
complexity of Israel, 126n2, 134, 140, 146–147, 195–197, 235, 289–290, 311, 320, 321, 322, 370
confidence in knowledge, 78, 237–240
conflict education, 229–250, 250n4; community reactions and institutional support, 243–247; conclusions and recommendations, 247–250; emotions, role of, 241–243; Israeli-Palestinian conflict, 234–247; knowledge barrier, 237–240; methodology and participants, 232–234; pedagogy of navigating difficult conversations, 240–241
conflict label, 212–213
congregational supplementary schools. *See* synagogue supplementary schools
congregations, 287
connectedness, 363–364
connections to Israel, 283–304, 309–328; classroom learning/practice, 298–301; complexify approach, 289–290, 316; continuums, understanding of, 297–298; core values, 317; early childhood education, 273; educational goals at Gann, 153–154, 170, 173; goals of Israel education, 286–287; Insider-Outsider Continuum, 295–297; Israel education's aims and goals, 302; Jewish Collective-Jewish Self Continuum, 292–295; Jewish self, 315–316; new models for facilitating, 366–371; pedagogic imperatives, 171–172; professional development for Israel educators, 303; relational approach, 287–289; safe haven for Jews, Israel as, 319–320; stance, 156–157, 161–163, 165–169; synagogue supplementary schools, 312–315; typology for understanding, 291–292; values-infused education, 321–322, 327
Conservative communities, 115
constructive conversations, 240–241, 248
constructivist approaches, 259, 266
consumer boycotts, 217
contemplative practices, 214–215
contemporary Israel, 107–108, 141, 182, 195, 235, 241, 315–316
contemporary students, 47, 51
content knowledge, 2–3, 234, 239–240, 290, 333, 376
CoP (Community of Practice), 258–259, 265
co-resistance, 224
critical thinking, 40–41, 43, 44, 63, 66–67, 78–79, 113, 124, 134–135, 141, 147, 156, 162, 180, 182, 186, 207, 222, 236–237, 338–339, 342, 344, 359, 363, 367, 370
cross-site learning, 356–359
CSC (School of Advanced Warfighting, and Command and Staff College), 63, 69, 70, 78, 79
Cuban, Larry, 221
cultural boycotts, 207–210, 217
cultural literacy, 155
cultural offerings, 216–218
cultural Zionism, 86–88, 91, 97, 100
culture building, 140, 142–143
current events, 54, 167, 296, 364, 376–377
curriculum and teaching, 93–95, 360; curricular choices, 95, 195, 270, 272; curricular materials, 88–91, 93, 94–95, 302, 303, 360; curricular revisions, 162

Darling-Hammond, Linda, 6, 6
Day, Benjamin, 107–126, 126n1, 126n3, 357–358, 362, 374–375
Day to Mark the Departure and Expulsion of Jews from the Arab Countries and Iran, 330n4
debate, 97, 155–156, 221–222

388 · INDEX

decision-making processes, 3–4, 6, 8, 264
Delight in the Sabbath (*Oneg Shabbat*), 101
democracy, 222
design of education programs, 302
destigmatizing the study of Israel, 72
developmentally appropriate practices, 265–268, 275–276, 333
Diaspora Jewish visitors, 270–271
Diaspora Jews, 8, 100, 129–147, 181, 186, 224, 259, 275, 319, 368, 373
difficult conversations, 123–125, 186, 240–241, 248
Diplomacy and Statecraft curriculum, MCWAR, 66–67
disciplinary knowledge, 7, 207. *See also* subject matter knowledge
disengagement, 240–241, 341
disorientation, 334, 339, 342, 349, 350–351
dissonance, 54, 124, 185
diverse learning sites, 356–359
diverse narratives, 36, 124, 235–236, 325
diversity, 35–56, 189
divesting from Israel, 165. *See also* BDS (boycott, divestment, and sanctions against Israel)
Dorph, Gail, 284
Dotan, Shimon, 217–218
double helix analogy, 67
dramatic play, 262–263
dual commitments, 266, 268

early childhood education and educators, 257–277, 364–366; context, 258–259; pretend Israel trip, 260–276; questions about pedagogy and practice, 259–260
economic boycotts, 207
educational constraints, 304
educational encounters, 95–96, 185, 319. *See also* trips to Israel
educational environments, 37, 64, 110, 113, 115–116, 118–119, 243, 266, 273, 312, 323–328, 339, 357
educational experiences, 94, 99, 108, 110, 234–237, 249, 273, 321–324, 328, 362, 364, 368

educational goals and outcomes, 9, 18, 41, 91, 94, 97–99, 100, 156, 159, 161, 169, 170, 242, 265, 269, 272–273, 276, 284, 287–288, 297, 302, 314, 371, 377
educational opportunities, 232, 238, 249, 358–359
educational simulations, 262–263
education directors, 233, 239
Elon, Emuna, 130–144
Elon, Rabbi Benny, 136
emotions, 68, 74, 107–126, 161, 166, 185, 230, 241–243, 247–248, 370–371
enculturation, 315, 318
engagement with Israel, 39, 126, 174, 183–184, 289, 359, 367
engaging prior knowledge, 51–55
equality and non-Jewish citizens of Israel, 118, 191, 216, 219
Eretz Yisrael, 17
Eurovision, 161, 167
exemplars, 339–340, 342
experiential education, 314–315
explorers, 339–340, 344

facilitating conversation and discussion, 2, 54, 68, 71, 73, 96, 97, 98, 101, 123–126, 140, 142, 155, 234, 240–241, 248, 351, 358, 362–364
familiarity, 39, 42, 54, 90, 295–296, 318, 319–320
Feiman-Nemser, Sharon, 347
film, 52, 217–218
Fish, Rachel, 219
Fishman, Ann Arnof, 51
Fishman, Shira, 7
Fogel, Shimon Koffler, 216
formal education, 195, 230, 249, 313, 315
Fraiman, Keren E., 325, 364–366, 369–370, 375
Freire, Paulo, 124–125
Fritzsche, Lauren, 214

Gall, Meredith D., 160
Gann Academy, 151–172, 367
gap-year programs, 180–182, 188, 192, 357–358, 368. *See also* Kivunim

Gaza, 73, 148n9, 186, 213, 218, 220, 319
Geffen, Peter, 180, 188–189, 191, 199, 201n4
gender egalitarianism, 343
Gen Z students, 51, 57n11, 57n13
gilyonot (mimeographed worksheets), 90
Giroux, Henry A., 13
global citizenship, 111, 207, 211, 237
Global Language Dictionary, 51
Golden, Jonathan, 362–363, 367–369, 374–375
The Good Teacher Mentor (Trubowitz and Picard Robins), 108
government sanctions, 217
Grant, Lisa, 348, 367
Greenberg, Uri Zvi, 84
Gringas, Robbie, 231, 366–367
Gross, Magdalena H., 124
grounded theory, 131, 265
group discussions, 2, 40, 46, 48, 68, 70–75, 79, 100–101, 113, 116, 119, 123, 130, 136, 140–142, 145–146, 156, 158, 166–167, 224, 241, 248, 342, 344
group reflection, 181, 192, 195
guest speakers, 76–77, 240, 358
guided meditation, 214

Haaretz (newspaper), 357
halachic and non-halachic Jews, 118
halakha (Jewish law), 89, 216
"Halakhah and *Aggadah*" (Bialik), 89
Halevi, Yossi Klein, 163
Hamas, 215
hands-on learning experiences, 271. *See also* mapmaking; trips to Israel
hard truths, 53, 126n2
Haredim (ultra-Orthodox Jews), 74, 81n13, 115
Harper, Robin A., 362–365, 369–370, 373–374
Hassenfeld, Jonah, 155
havruta (leaning partners), 99
Hebrew, 39, 45, 92, 101–102, 151, 167, 181, 191, 199, 216, 275, 291, 295–296, 301, 312
Hebrew culture, 85–89, 216
Hebron, 158–159
Hess, Diana, 244

Hezbollah, 215
hidden curriculum, 92–94
higher education, 3–4, 7, 15, 16, 207
Hirst, Paul H., 6
holding environments, 334, 347–348, 351
holistic educational environments, 324
Holocaust, 48–51, 57n11, 124, 132–133, 193–195
Holzer, Elie, 99
home/homeland, Israel as, 310, 317, 322, 325, 368
Horowitz, Bethamie, 351n2, 357–358, 366–368, 375
House on Endless Waters (Elon), 135
How Learning Works (Ambrose), 37
hugging and wrestling model, 154, 180, 290, 366–367

iCenter, 233, 289, 304n4, 322
identification formation process, 325
identity in the Israeli-Palestinian conflict, 67
iEngage curriculum, 83, 101n1
iFellows program, 232–234
imageability, 44
Imagined Communities (Anderson), 92
immigration, 53–54, 86, 107–109, 111–112, 117–118, 213, 216–217, 344. *See also* right of return
inaccurate prior knowledge, 42, 48–49
individual and collective, relationship between, 316
individuality, 316, 326
informal educational programming, 65, 153, 315
information overload, 238
inquiry-oriented approach, 187, 192–193, 200
Insider-Outsider Continuum, 292, 295–296, 297
institutional boycotts, 208–209
institutional support, 230, 243–245, 247–249, 251n6, 372
instructional materials, 94–95. *See also* source sheets

instrumentalization, 96–100, 101
intellectual work, 157–158
intentionality, 77, 234, 326
interactive experiences, 318–319. *See also* pretend trips to Israel; trips to Israel
internal school-based programs, 350
international relations, 64–65, 211–212, 214
international travel to Diaspora Jewish communities, 181, 201n5. *See also* trips to Israel
interpretive dialogic encounter, 98
intimate dialogue, 360
intimate Israeli discourse, 130–145
inventory model of knowledge, 155
invisible knapsack exercise, 222–223
inward-seeking exercises, 215
Ironi Hey, Haifa, 154
Islam, 67
Israel education and educators, 4, 16–19; adult learning, 350–351; aims and goals of, 302; alignment, 337–338, 340–342, 347–348; alternative teaching sites, 372–373; BDS (boycott, divestment, and sanctions against Israel), 205–224; classroom learning/practice, 107–126; comparison of approaches to, *291*; complexify approach, 286–287, 289–290, 292–293, 300, 302, 304n3, 316; conflict education, 229–250, 250n4; connection, 16–17, 84, 109, 310, 366–371; diverse learning sites, 356–359; early childhood education, 257–277, 364–366; Gann Academy, 151–172; high stakes, 348–349; history, good and bad sides, 116–121; individuals' consciousness, 326; institutional commitment, 375–376; Israeli-Palestinian conflict, 67–68, 151–172, 185, 212–215, 218–220, 229–250, 250n3, 337–338, 366; Kivunim, 180–200, 201n5, 201n7, 202n17, 357–358; and Korazim, 129–147; mapmaking, 42–45; metaphors of, 339–340; next-step questions, 268–276, 371–376; organized strategy, 327; parents, 246–247; pedagogic interventions, 171–172, 248–250; PME (professional military education) institutions, 61–80; as a political endeavor, 13–16; professional development and learning, 303, 340, 345–348, 364–366; Quishiyot Fellowship, 309–328; relational approach, 287–289, 290, 292–293, 302, 304n3, 315–316; subject matter as commonplace of education, 11–12; survey of knowledge about Israel, 56; synagogue supplementary schools, 283–304, 309–328, 370–371; teacher identity and beliefs, 73, 291–292, 298–301, 303, 359–362, 372; teaching, 4–9, 283–304; teaching-learning nexus, 371–372; text study, 83–101; transformative professional learning, 333–351; in the United States, 284; values-informed, 309–328; values in tension, 241, 338–339
"Israel Experience" programs, 179–200, 357–358, 368–369
Israeli academic institutions, 208–209, 219
Israeli academy, 207–208
Israeli–Arab conflict, 7–8, 63–64, 69, 112, 141, 212, 355
Israeli cinema, 166–167
Israeli culture, 87, 169, 172, 275, 295–296
Israeli Declaration of Independence, 118
Israeli diversity, 231, 299–300, 321–323
Israeli emissaries, 312
Israeli history, 237
Israeli Jews, 55, 202n16, 289
Israeli life, 143, 185, 198, 297
Israeli literature, 131, 142–143
Israeliness, 39, 87
Israeli–Palestinian conflict, 67–68, 151–172, 185, 212–215, 218–220, 229–250, 250n3, 337–338, 366
Israeli policies and practices, 107–126, 205–206, 361, 368–369
Israeli products, 207, 217, 224. *See also* BDS (boycott, divestment, and sanctions against Israel)

Israeli religious policies, 112–116
Israeli society, 13–16, 72, 107–126, 130, 153, 183, 195, 289, 295–296, 316, 320, 322, 361
Israel literacy, 79, 336
Israel Literacy Measurement Project, 42
Israel Project's Global Language Dictionary, 51
Israel's identity as a Jewish state, 9, 36, 100, 111, 216, 310, 322
Israel studies, 4, 7–9, 16, 18, 39–40, 61–80, 369, 372, 374, 377
Israel's War of Independence, 137
I-Thou relationship with Israel, 289

Jacoby, Alexa, 107–126, 126n1, 126n2, 357–358, 362–363, 374–375
James' Journey to Jerusalem (film), 52–53
Jerusalem, 54, 187–189, 262, 296, 299
Jewish cognitive schemas, 324–325
Jewish collective, 285, 286–287, 299–301, 310, 316
Jewish Collective–Jewish Self Continuum, 292–295, 297–298
Jewish communal politics, 15–16
Jewish community, 117, 133, 182, 189–190, 293–294, 341, 372
Jewish continuity, 86, 155
Jewish day schools, 160, 188, 302, 315, 358, 364, 370
Jewish diversity, 111, 299–300, 320–323, 328
Jewish education, 4, 8, 14, 17–18, 39, 83–85, 86, 101, 154, 168, 184–185, 231–233, 260–264, 267–271, 274–275, 276, 312–313, 316, 324, 326, 328, 341, 348–349, 352n4, 374. *See also* Israel education and educators
Jewish educational institutions and settings, 4, 14, 16, 94, 153, 231–232, 235–236, 258, 275, 302, 356–359, 370, 372–373
The Jewish Education Project, 311
Jewish holidays, 84, 269
Jewish identities, 39, 107–126, 132, 286, 288, 300–301, 316, 321–322, 341, 349, 368
Jewish learners, 8–9, 17, 130, 232, 236–237, 268
Jewish literature, 87

Jewish Lives, Jewish Learning (Schuster), 130
Jewishness, 76, 101, 111, 117, 184, 199, 297, 310
Jewish peoplehood, 100, 132, 181, 288–290, 304n9, 317, 320–321, 322, 325
Jewish self, 285–300, 315–316
Jewish sensibility, 310, 325–326, 328
Jewish state, 100, 111, 216, 322
Jewish status, 122, 125, 126n3, 295
Jewish texts, 83–101
Jewish values, 89, 157, 289, 309–328

Kadden, Yoni, 362, 367–369, 374–375
Kashua, Sayed, 357
Kegan, Robert, 334
Keissar, Adi, 357
Keller-Cohen, D., 92
Kelman, Ari Y., 14
Kent, Orit, 99
kibbutzim, 45, 137
Kivunim, 180–200, 201n5, 201n7, 202n17, 357–358
knowledge, 7, 12, 36–37, 230, 247–248, 367; acquisition, 155, 313–315; assessment, 41–45; barriers to engagement with conflict education, 237–240; confidence in, 78, 237–240; Gann Academy, 151–172; of the Holocaust, 49–50, 57n11; of Israel, 124, 155, 266, 322; Israeli-Palestinian conflict, 238–239; knowledge gaps, 39, 42, 237; prior knowledge, 36, 40, 42, 48–50, 51–56, 124, 196; source sheets, 93–96; survey of knowledge about Israel, 56; transmission of, 91–93
Kohlbergian approach to moral questions, 155
Kopelowitz, Ezra, 367–368
Korazim, Rachel, 129–147, 360
Koren, Annette, 7
Kreber, Carolin, 340
Kress, Jeff, 324–325

labels, 72, 212–213
Ladon, Joshua, 362, 373–374

Lampert, Magdalene, 221, 273
land rights, 137–138, 141
Law of Return, 111, 116, 117, 121–122
Lawrence-Lightfoot, Sara, 131
lay and professional educational leadership, 249
learning, 5–9, 10, 11–12, 18, 37, 47–48, 94, 107–126, 356–359, 362–363, 364–366, 371–372, 377; about the Other, 189, 190–192; child-centered learning and teaching about Israel, 266–268; hands-on learning experiences, 271; inventory approach to, 174n2; language of, 98; opposing viewpoints, 70; personal journeys, 70–71; perspective taking, 76–77; teacher identity and beliefs, 298–300; transformative, 333–351. *See also* reflection
Learning and Community (Wertheimer), 324
Leibowitz, Nehama, 90, 94–95
Leuenberger, Christine, 43
Levinger, Moshe, 158
Levstik, Linda S., 234, 251n5
liberal Zionists, 219–220
listening across differences, 241, 248
literacy, 42, 79, 92–94, 155, 207, 336
Lortie, Dan C., 292, 352n3
love of Israel, 284, 299, 338, 339, 367, 370–371
Luntz, Frank, 51
Lynch, K., 44

Magnus, Robert, 76
"The Maidservant's Son" (Elon), 135, 137, 139, 142, 143, 147–148n4
Makom Matrix, 297, 304n12
Makom: The Jewish Agency Education Lab, 311
Mandel Teacher Educator Institute, 352n4
mapmaking, 40, 42–45. *See also* pedagogical dilemmas; reflection
March of the Living, 112
Marine Corps War College (MCWAR), 63, 66–68, 71, 79

Marom, Daniel, 46, 54, 348
marriage, 114
masking, 98
McAvoy, Paula, 244
McIntosh, Peggy, 222
MCU (U.S. Marine Corps University), 62–80, 81n10
MCWAR (Marine Corps War College), 63, 66–68, 71, 79
Meltzer, Brad, 147
Mendelsohn, David, 190, 192–193, 196, 202n11
mentoring, 260
micromoments, 109–110, 116, 123, 125–126
Middle East, 57n3, 64–69
mifgash (face-to-face encounters), 275, 290
migration, 35–55, 86
migration to Israel (*aliyah*), 50, 86, 114, 293, 295, 296, 300, 336
military education, 61–80
millennial students, 51, 57n11, 57n13
Mizrahi, 57n3, 330n4, 357–358
mock-elections, 163
modern Israel, 54, 114–115, 320, 322, 370
Moore, L., 325
morally complex narratives, 39, 126n2, 242
moral questions, Kohlbergian approach to, 155
multiple Israels, 9–10, 12, 46, 54

Nagammy, Amal, 190–191
Nakba, 213
Naksa, 213
nationalism, 48, 88–92, 100, 198
National Security Strategy Research and Practicum and Applications in National Security Strategy, 64
national-service year, 319
Nelson, Rabbi David, 130
neutrality, 219–220
new Jews, 87, 90–91, 101
next-step questions, 268–276, 371–376
Nieto, Sonia, 13

Noddings, Nel, 241
non-instrumentalist pedagogy, 101
non-Orthodox American Jews, 184
nontraditional students, 35–56
normalization projects, 208
norms, 92, 248, 318
North America, 3–4, 14–16, 17, 101n1, 355, 375
North American Jewish young adults, 179–200

occupation, 100, 138, 210, 213, 216, 218–219, 221
Oneg Shabbat (Delight in the Sabbath), 101
O/other, 144, 147, 189, 190–192
opposing viewpoints, 46, 61, 70, 71, 76
oppression, 210–224
Orthodox, yeshiva-based programs, 182
Orthodox communities, 118
Orthodox Jewish law, 114
Oslo peace negotiations, 184
Otsar Hayahadut Belashon Ivrit (A Treasury of Judaism in the Hebrew Language), 89
outcomes. *See* educational goals and outcomes

PACBI (Palestinian Campaign for the Academic and Cultural Boycott of Israel) guidelines, 207–209, 225n1
Palestine/Palestinians, 57n1, 90, 132, 136, 141, 169, 185, 202n16, 205, 207–210, 213, 215, 218–220, 223–224. *See also* Israeli-Palestinian conflict
Palestinian Authority, 215
Palestinian Campaign for the Academic and Cultural Boycott of Israel (PACBI) guidelines, 207–209, 225n1
Paley, Rabbi Michael, 179–180, 201n1, 201n3
Palmer, Parker, 141, 143–144, 283, 303–304
parents, 243–244, 246–247, 249
partnership model, 249
Passmore, Ashley, 75

peace education, 231
pedagogical choices, 9, 13–15, 16, 36, 43–45, 84, 95, 130, 242, 263, 270, 272–273, 298, 368, 373, 374–375, 377
pedagogical dilemmas, 3, 5, 7, 14, 84, 156, 174, 242, 260, 268, 272–273, 373
pedagogical questions, 2–4, 7–9, 15–16, 257–277; context, 258–259; as a core educational practice, 259–260; of Jewish early childhood educators, 265–272; pretend Israel trips, 260–276; of teacher educators, 272–276
pedagogical strategies, 314, 322
pedagogical technique, 333
pedagogic interventions, 171–172, 248–250
pedagogy of difference, Alexander, 111
personal conceptualizations, 301
personal identities, 349
personal interpretation, 321
personal journeys, 70–71
personal meaning, 116, 134, 154, 155, 173
personal subjectivity, 214, 215
perspective taking, 76–77
philosophical stances toward Israel education, 8–9, 97, 126, 157, 210–212, 286–290, 311. *See also* complexify approach; relational approach
Picard Robins, Maureen, 108
Pitkowsky, Abby, 367–368
play, 262–263
PLCS (professional learning communities), 364–366, 377
pluralism, 272, 322, 343
PME (professional military education) institutions, 61–80
political endeavor, teaching Israel as, 13–16
politics, 205–224
Pomson, Alex, 231, 315
portraiture, 131, 336
positive relationship to Israel, 313–314
Power, B. M., 259
power relations, 222
Precious Legacy docent program, 133
preschools, 259

pretend trips to Israel, 260–276
primary and secondary sources, 75, 76, 111, 165
prior knowledge, 36, 40, 42, 48–50, 51–56, 124, 196
problem-solving, 73
professional development and learning, 234, 238, 239, 247–249, 260, 271–273, 302, 303, 327, 333–351, 364–367, 377. *See also* iCenter
professional learning communities (PLCs), 364–366, 377
professional military education (PME) institutions, 61–80
professional status of students, 77–78
progressive pedagogies, 93, 259
purpose, 234–237

questions. *See* pedagogical questions
"Questions for Reflection Prior and During Our Visit to Germany," 193–194
Qushiyot Fellowship, 309–328

Rabbinate, 113–118
rabbinic sermons about Israel, 312
Rabin, Yitzhak, 65, 137, 231
race and racism, 123, 236
Rawnitzki, Y. H., 89
reading, 92–94
red lines, 244–245, 375–376
reflection, 48, 75–76, 79, 169, 181, 192–195, 215, 264, 334, 346–347, 373–374
Reform communities, 115, 188, 318–319
Reform or Conservative conversions, 111–115
refugee return, 216–219
Reggio-Emilia, 266
Reimer, Joseph, 325
Reingold, Matt, 39, 107–126, 126n1, 126n2, 126n3, 374
relational approach, 287–289, 290, 292–293, 302, 304n3, 315–316
relationship building, 140, 141–142, 154, 289
relationship of Jews to Israel. *See* connections to Israel

relationships among Jews, 320. *See also* Jewish peoplehood
relationships and education, 98
relationships with Israelis, 318–319
relationship with Israel. *See* connections to Israel
religious courts, 111–112
religious identification, 114–115
religious identities, 349
religious knowledge, 53–54
repertoire building, 347
research agendas, 40, 130–131, 356, 371, 372
reticence to teach, 234–235, 237, 247
right of return, 113
risk-taking, 244
Rossman-Benjamin, Tammi, 219
Rotberg, Robert I., 67

safe haven for Jews, Israel as, 319–320
Sall, D., 53
sanctions, 210, 217
Scheffler, Israel, 5–6, 360
Schnell, Izhak, 43
scholarly exchange, 208
scholarly investigation, 3, 6–9, 10, 16, 18
school environment, 347–348, 350
School of Advanced Warfighting, and Command and Staff College (CSC), 63, 69, 70, 78, 79
Schuster, Diane, 360–362, 374–375
Second Intifada, 86, 184
second language development, 275
Sefer ha-Aggadah, 89
self-directed study, 6, 8–9, 45, 275. *See also* source sheets
self-understanding, 75–76, 184, 190, 288, 295, 299
seminar records, 263–264
semi-structured interviews, 233, 263–264, 271, 311
settler movement in the West Bank, 136–143, 158–159
The Settlers (film), 217–218
Shagoury, R., 259
Shen, D., 155–156

shinshinim (young adult Israeli emissaries to Diaspora Jewish communities), 319
Shtif, Nokhum, 97
shuk (open-air market), 262, 270, 321
signature pedagogies, 262
Simon, Kathy, 110
Simon, R. I., 99
simulations, 262–263
Sinclair, Alex, 289, 296, 297
Six Day War, 138, 158, 213
skill sets, 140–145, 148n8, 372
social justice, 210–216
social studies education, 263
Socratic method of teaching, 71
solitary reader, 92
source sheets, 83–101, 130, 362
stage theory, 345
stances, 151–172, 359, 367–370
State of Israel, 71, 73, 86, 91, 100, 113, 117–118, 132, 138, 151–152, 153, 156, 269, 292, 295
state Zionism, 90, 97, 100
storytelling, 133, 154
strategy for values-informed educational environment, 326–327
student-centered learning, 41–45, 47
subject matter knowledge, 1–3, 4, 9–10, 11–12, 13, 15, 16, 110, 155–156, 237, 238, 251n6, 290–292, 365, 366
subject-specific training, 347
Sucharov, Mira, 359, 361–362, 375
Sue, Derald Wing, 123
synagogue educators, 309–310, 313, 315–316, 321–322, 324–325, 330n1, 367–368
synagogue supplementary schools, 283–304, 309–328, 370–371

tactics of the academic boycott, 208, 224
Talmud study, 88, 182
Tanakh (Bible) classroom, 349
TanenbaumCHAT, 110–126
Tarzi, Amin, 369–370, 373–374
teacher educators, 257–277, 284
teachers: connections to Israel, 283–304; courage, 50, 141, 143–145; identity and beliefs, 73, 291–292, 298–301, 303, 359–362, 372; Insider-Outsider Continuum, 295–296, 297; and intimacy, 145–147; Jewish Collective-Jewish Self Continuum, 292–295, 297; learning process, 94; systematic documentation, 131; teacher development, 277, 347; teacher-directed approaches, 259, 266; teacher-tool relationship, 95; trust, teacher-student, 42, 157–159; typology for understanding connections to Israel, 291–292
teaching, 1–19, 107–126; anxieties about teaching Israel, 364–366; and curriculum, 93–95, 360; early childhood education, 257–277; linked with learning, 3, 5–6, 9–10, 12, 15, 18, 37–38, 45–46, 107, 211, 231, 258, 350, 370–372; pedagogical dilemmas, 3, 5, 7, 156, 174, 260, 268, 272–273; philosophies, 210–212; as political work, 13–16; scholarly investigation, 6–9; teaching-learning nexus, 371–372
Teaching Controversial Issues (Noddings and Brooks), 241
teaching diary, 48
Teaching History for the Common Good (Barton and Levstik), 234
teaching strategies, Quishiyot Fellowship, 310
Teaching the Arab-Israeli Conflict (Weiss), 64
Tel Aviv, 135, 137–138, 143, 262, 321
texts that talk, 142
"time-on-task" problem, 182
tourists, 270–271
"Tourists" (Amichai), 41
transformative professional learning, 333–351
transmission of knowledge, 17, 91–93
trauma, 223–224
trips to Israel, 154, 168, 184–185, 260–264, 267–271, 274–275, 276, 312
Troen, S. Ilan, 68–69, 81n11

Trubowitz, Sidney, 108
trust, teacher-student, 42, 157–159
Tsur, Ilana, 77
twinning programs, 312
typology for understanding connections with Israel, 291–292

United States, 67, 71, 166, 188, 199
university campuses and BDS, 219
U.S. Marine Corps University (MCU), 62–80, 81n10
U.S. National Defense Strategy, 62

value of teaching about the Israeli-Palestinian conflict, 234–237
values-informed education, 309–328, 338–339
values in tension, 241, 338–339
Vasquez, James, 46–47
virtual encounters, 319

Wallach, Yair, 43
Walzer, Michael, 67
Weiss, Robert, 264
Weiss, Shayna, 64
Werchow, Yehudit, 348
Wertheimer, Jack, 324–325

West Bank, 72, 73, 136–143, 158–159, 185, 186, 202n16, 210, 213, 218
What the Best College Teachers Do (Bain), 37, 47
Winer, Laura Novak, 315–316, 360–362, 369–370
Wisse, Ruth, 132–133
Wogan, P., 92
Woocher, Jonathan, 325
workforce management, 51
workshops, 232–233
world consciousness, 189–191

Yom Ha'atzma'ut (Israeli Independence Day), 153
Yom Hazikaron (Memorial Day), 153, 166
York College, 36–57
You Never Told Me, 202n15

Zakai, Sivan, 126n1, 130, 134, 146, 148n10, 154, 235, 289, 290, 360, 365–366, 371, 377
Zelkowicz, Tali, 325
Zionism, 48, 86–91, 97, 100, 181, 187, 188, 195–200, 213, 217, 338
Zionist settlement, 157
Zionist thinkers, 86, 320
Zionist youth programs, 184, 202n15